BUSINESS IMPROVEMENT DISTRICTS AND THE CONTRADICTIONS OF PLACEMAKING

BUSINESS IMPROVEMENT DISTRICTS AND THE CONTRADICTIONS OF PLACEMAKING

BID Urbanism in Washington, D.C.

SUSANNA F. SCHALLER

The University of Georgia Press
Athens

Paperback edition, 2021
© 2019 by the University of Georgia Press
Athens, Georgia 30602
www.ugapress.org
All rights reserved
Designed by Kaelin Chappell Broaddus
Set in 10/13.5 Utopia Std Regular
by Kaelin Chappell Broaddus

Most University of Georgia Press titles are
available from popular e-book vendors.

Printed digitally

The Library of Congress has cataloged the
hardcover edition of this book as follows:
Names: Schaller, Susanna F., author.
TITLE: Business improvement districts and the contradictions of placemaking :
BID urbanism in Washington, D.C. / Susanna F. Schaller.
DESCRIPTION: Athens, Georgia : University of Georgia Press, [2019] |
Includes bibliographical references and index.
IDENTIFIERS: LCCN 2018057928 | ISBN 9780820355160 (hardcover : alk. paper) |
ISBN 9780820355177 (ebook)
SUBJECTS: LCSH: Central business districts—Washington (D.C—Planning. |
Gentrification—Washington (D.C.) | Washington (D.C—Social conditions.
CLASSIFICATION: LCC HT177.W3 S33 2019 | DDC 307.3/4209753—dc23
LC record available at https://lccn.loc.gov/2018057928

Paperback ISBN 978-0-8203-6168-0

For . . .

My mother Sue, ever the scholar . . .

My daughter Alessia, my creative joy . . .

D.C., my first home in the U.S.

CONTENTS

ACKNOWLEDGMENTS

A book, I have come to learn, is an immense undertaking that requires support from many people and places. Mentors, friends, and family have provided intellectual accompaniment and personal encouragement, offered pointed criticism and gentle suggestions, enabled financial stability, or just made me laugh when I might rather have cried.

This book is dedicated to D.C., my first home in the United States and perhaps now a city largely of memories. Until age fourteen, I lived in Köln, Germany. I am the daughter of an architect who spent years excavating for me the histories of buildings and places, deciphering the social meanings, political perspectives, and economic forces embodied in the built environment. But it was in D.C. that I really began to recognize neighborhoods as social products, created not only by public polices and plans but also by our perceptions and actions (Lefebvre 2011). The city awakened my desire to decode the storytelling that translates plans into the realities conditioning people's lives, advantaging some and harming others (Throgmorton 2003; Lefebvre 2011). How we participate in shaping our neighborhoods and cities matters, I learned.

Even as official crime figures soared in the late 1980s and early 1990s, a mosaic of third places distinguished D.C. from the federal city (Oldenburg 1999). My teenage self recalls hearing Sweet Honey in the Rock at All Souls Church, listening to jazz at Café Lautrec in Adams Morgan, attending poetry readings at d.c.space and later dancing to "Go Go"—a homegrown rhythm—at the 9:30 Club and a kaleidoscope of beats at Tracks in Southwest. As my brother notes, at that time the 9:30 Club was also a hub for punk musicians connected to other inner cities. Whether it was drummers on Dupont Circle, renowned African musicians at the Kilimanjaro, or punk at Madams Organ and la nueva canción in Mount Pleasant, the music scene reflected the imprint of the multifaceted communities producing D.C.'s urban space.

In 1992, one year after the "riots" in Adams Morgan and Mount Pleasant, I began teaching bilingual education in a local public school. From my students, many of whom had fled civil wars in Central America, I learned about the dangers of living in the shadows of the law and about the incredible perseverance young people can summon against all odds. By 1999 I began working as a newly minted planner for the Latino Economic Development Corporation (LEDC), born out of the riots. Gentrification as lived experiences suffused our everyday conversations. These were the fiscal control board years (1995–2001). City planners carried a clear message to our neighborhoods: D.C. needed to shift direction, to use its considerable assets to attract investment and above all new, preferably high-income, residents. Thus, my work involved me in the complex and conflict-ridden politics around "economic development" and "revitalization," which became the catalyzing material shaping this book's storyline.

This project would not have been possible without the amazing people at LEDC. I thank Marla Bilonick, Ayari de la Rosa, Vikki Frank, Josh Gibson, Larisa Gryzco-Avellaneda, Leda Hernandez, Christine Hurley, Judy Little, Galey Modan, Jose Rodriguez, and Celina Treviño. In 2006, the acting executive director welcomed me back, offering staff time and space. Galey Modan has been a continual intellectual partner, and her insights, understanding, and analysis form an integral part of this work. Vikki Frank has generously provided not just continued friendship and conversation but a second home.

I am indebted to ANC commissioners, residents, community-development professionals, and merchants who shared their experiences and knowledge and gratefully acknowledge government officials and planners in the deputy mayor's Office of Economic Development and Planning, the Office of Planning, and the Department of Transportation, who communicated their views and expertise. Many BID executives and professionals graciously sat down for informative, constructive, and rich conversations: I am deeply appreciative.

The actual written words first emerged at the Department of City and Regional Planning (CRP) at Cornell University under the supervision of Mildred Warner, Lourdes Beneria, and Susan Christopherson, three women who helped me develop my arguments while allowing me the space to integrate scholarship, practice, and, yes, family. Mildred Warner's pathbreaking work on governance turned my attention toward examining BIDs through the public-choice frame. Lourdes Beneria's expertise as a feminist economist directed me to eschew simple categorizations to examine everyday experiences through the structures shaping them. Susan Christopherson, a pioneer in the field of economic geography, pressed me to sharpen my analysis of the spatial dynamics transforming D.C. I was surrounded by brilliant planning scholars: Bill Goldsmith, Pierre Clavel, and John Forester. Their work resounds through this book. Thank you also, Anouk Patel-Campillo and Rhodante Ahlers, fellow PhD travelers. Finally, I thank CRP for its generous financial support in the form of tuition and research grants and fellowships. Columbia University's Urban Planning Department provided a home in New York City. I thank Susan Fainstein, Peter Marcuse, and Johannes Novy, in particular, for their intellectual sustenance.

I am extraordinarily privileged to work in the Division of Interdisciplinary Studies at the City College of New York (CCNY). Dean Juan Carlos Mercado's unwavering support at a crucial crossroads in my career and his continuing encouragement of my scholarly pursuits have changed my life's direction: thank you. As department chair, Kathy McDonald has fostered an incredibly reassuring and emboldening environment. Susanna Rosenbaum's beautiful sarcasm, sharp mind, and constancy kept me real every day. Alessandra Benedicty-Kokken offered friendship and crucial insights. And John Calagione accompanied me on a crucial journey into Lefebvre's writings. Thank you to Carlos Aguasaco, Marlene Clark, David Eastzer, Debbie Edwards-Anderson, Vicki Garavuso, Mary Lutz, Elizabeth Matthews, Justin Williams, and Martin Woessner for their camaraderie. Luisa Perez's intellectual acumen and friendship infused the first revision with renewed creative (mapping) energy: the conversations continue.

The Faculty Fellowship at the Center for Politics Place and Culture at CUNY's Graduate Center under the guidance of Ruth Wilson Gilmore, David Harvey, and Peter Hitchcock, nourished the revision of my doctoral dissertation. I also want to thank my colleagues in the City University of New York's Faculty Fellowship Publication Program: Sarah Bishop, Eduardo Contreras, Christian Gonzalez, Sophia Maríñez, Trevor Milton, and Elizabeth Nisbet. Particular gratitude goes to Stephen Steinberg for his extraordinary mentorship. Thank you to Elizabeth Nisbet at John Jay College and Sandra Guinand, a cofellow at the Graduate Center, for pulling my scholarship in new directions. I received crucial support through PSC-CUNY Awards jointly funded by the Professional Staff Congress and the City University of New York.

I am fortunate to have sent the manuscript to Mick Gusinde-Duffy, executive editor at the University of Georgia Press, who believed in the project and shepherded it across the finish line to production. The final revisions benefited immensely from Peter Wissoker's editorial eye and Andrea Johnson's GIS mapping and layout expertise. Thank you to Jon Davies, assistant director for EDP, for managing a smooth production process, and to Jane Curran for her meticulous editor's eye. Thank you to the press's team: Kaelin Broaddus, production coordinator; Rebecca Norton, ebook production coordinator; and Beatrice Burton, indexer. Moreover, this book benefited immensely from the incredible insights of two anonymous reviewers, who pressed me to hone my analysis.

Previous work reappears throughout, including a 2005 coauthored article with Gabriella (Galey) Modan titled "Contesting Public Space and Citizenship: Implications for Neighborhood Business Improvement Districts," published in the *Journal of Planning Education and Research* 24 (4): 394–407, https://doi.org/10.1177/0739456X04270124, copyright © 2005 Association of Collegiate Schools of Planning, reprinted by permission of SAGE publications, and reprinted as chapter 16 in Goktug Morcol, Lorene Hoy, Jack Meek Ulf Zimmerman's *Business Improvement Districts: Research, Theories, and Controversies* published by CRC Press (Taylor and Francis) in 2008 (copyright © 2008 by Taylor and Francis Group, LLC, reprinted by permission of Taylor and Francis Group, LLC, a division of Informa plc), and an unpublished presentation, "'Safe and Clean': Community Reactions to Neighborhood Business Improvement District (NBID) Marketing in a Multi-ethnic Neighborhood," also with Galey. The storyline in chapter 7 draws on "Situating Entrepreneurial Place Making in Washington, D.C.: Business Improvement Districts and Urban (Re)Development in Washington, D.C.," a chapter in the edited book *Capital Dilemma: Growth and Inequality in Washington, D.C.* published by Routledge Press. Derek Hyra and Sabiyha Prince generously included my work in the project.

Inwood, in New York City, my second home in the United States, appears in the conclusion. I have met incredible people actively working to achieve a "more just city" in the Northern Manhattan Not for Sale Coalition, especially Eleazar Bueno, Graham Ciraulo, Ava Farkas, Karla Fisk, Paloma Lara, Nova Lucero, Chris Nickell, Cheryl Pahaham, Mike Saab, and Phil Simpson to name only a few. This includes also my colleagues John Krinsky and

Shawn Rickenbacker at CCNY. I want to thank Vincent Boudreau, our college's president, for his vision that urban universities should lead the way in socially engaged scholarship.

I would not have reached the finish line without my extended family's resoluteness. I draw inspiration from my father Christian Schaller's commitment to equity planning. My lifetime friend Bilgehan Köhler keeps me real and laughing. Shari Evans has been there since D.C., providing brilliant insights. Trena Klohe's incisive mind forced me to become a better writer (I hope) years back. My deep appreciation goes to Agustin Cortes for providing our family with the stability to see this through and to his mother, Fulivia de Cortes, for her vast kindness.

My daughter, Alessia Cortes-Schaller, is an enigma. This project and D.C., a city in her mother's imagination, has suffused the everyday of her whole life. Yet, from age two and a half, I have been able to count on her beautiful gaze, quizzical scrutiny, a hug, and an exclamation: "Go work, Mom!" Finally, I thank my mother, Sue Schaller, who taught me to extend beyond myself, to develop my awareness of others, and to reach for solidarity. Whether I succeed in this remains to be seen. Her countless hours of dedication, reading just one more chapter, once again, helped this book see the light of day.

BUSINESS IMPROVEMENT DISTRICTS AND THE CONTRADICTIONS OF PLACEMAKING

BID Urbanism in Washington, D.C.

In September 2016 *Crain's New York Business* published an article about New York City's business improvement districts (BIDs): "Shaping a Neighborhood's Destiny from the Shadows." In vivid language, its author recounted how the visionary and some would say legendary place entrepreneur Dan Biederman organized local property owners and business owners around Bryant Park into a BID to provide the "blue print" for this now much-hailed urban revitalization strategy. This blueprint has been widely credited with enabling the renaissance of urban America, including in Washington, D.C. (Hoffman and Houstoun 2010; Houstoun 2010; Levy 2010; J. Mitchell 2008). The article opened with the oft-repeated explanation of why business improvement districts became imperative in New York City: the "dystopian" conditions of the late 1970s and early 1980s—rampant crime, homelessness, and drug use—were undermining the viability of the city's public realm and required a new management paradigm (Elstein 2016).

The basic elements of this storyline have been retold from city to city: visionary urban entrepreneurs and effective urban leaders roused the civic engagement of the business community and convinced "businesses" to tax themselves to enhance the public's urban experience. Ultimately, we are told, BIDs saved the city at a time when federal neglect, retrenchment, and poor policy choices had systematically drawn the life out of central cities. The creation of downtown BIDs, their advocates argue, proved to be auspicious for city life. Astonishingly, the subtitle of the *Crain's New York* article continued: "Business Improvement Districts Were Created to Rescue a Dirty, Crime-Ridden City. *With Order Restored, Some Say It's Time to Bid Them Goodbye* (emphasis added)." Today, the existence of BIDs in New York City is no longer undisputedly accepted, and for good reasons. In fact, the "growth of BIDs" has led to "fierce power struggles across the city," and not just in New York City (Elstein 2016).

New York City has been the epicenter of the BID policy movement. By 2015, the city boasted seventy-two BIDs (SBS 2015). Washington, D.C., a city that embraced BIDs later, had ten, with several more in the works. BIDs continue to proliferate rapidly as the International Downtown Association (IDA) and individual BID policy entrepreneurs, such as New York City's Biederman and Philadelphia's Paul Levy, market and sell them to cities across the country and indeed throughout the world.[1] The model, developed in the North American context, has transferred to cities in Africa, Europe, and Latin America (Didier, Morange, and Peyroux 2013; Hoyt 2008; Peyroux, Pütz, and Glasze 2012; Ward 2006).

This book centers on the business improvement district: known colloquially by its acronym BID. In particular, it focuses on Washington, D.C. —also called the District of Columbia or simply D.C.—and examines how business improvement districts, large and small, collectively transformed this city's urban landscape. As part of sophisticated public-private partnership (PPP) regimes, BIDs have redesigned and taken ownership of large areas of the public realm in cities across the country, including parks and main streets. Public-private partnerships are "working arrangements based on a mutual commitment (over and above that implied in any contract) between a public sector organization with any other organization outside the public sector"; they act strategically and endure over time (Bovaird 2004, 199). The aim of PPP regimes is to collaborate and gain the capacity to respond in a coordinated way to changing economic conditions to create new growth potential in and through the urban landscape (Harvey 2005; Stone 1993; Zukin 1995). Because cities, most notably New York City, have focused on extending the coverage of BIDs to neighborhoods, this book also scrutinizes the implications of incorporating neighborhood-based BIDs (NBIDs) into this governance regime (Martin 2004). From this perspective, BIDs form part of broader BID-public-private partnership (BID-PPP) regimes (Stone 1993) that have worked to reset policy priorities to reignite the downtown "growth machine" (Molotch 1976) as a centrifugally expanding force to create value in and capture profits from urban neighborhoods as well (Thomas 1989).[2] Accordingly, the book examines the establishment of the Adams Morgan Partnership, the result of an NBID demonstration project proposed for one of the most ethnically and economically diverse neighborhood areas in D.C. at the time.

By now, business improvement districts have become ubiquitous. Walk through any major city's downtown districts or central city neighborhoods, down main streets in smaller towns and even in the suburbs, and you are likely traversing a business improvement district. You may recognize the telltale banners and standardized trash receptacles, notice the decals on the uniforms of street-cleaning personnel, or encounter the local visitor "ambassadors" who are there to add a sense of "friendliness," as the founder of the DowntownDC BID executive in Washington, D.C., has emphasized. Each encounter calls out the district's name to reinforce the perception that you have entered a unique place: this is its purpose. BIDs refashion, manage, brand, market, and even redevelop downtown districts and neighborhoods (Sorkin 1992; Zukin 1995; Mele 2000). But BIDs do not do this alone. BIDs do this in partnership with elected officials, public and nonprofit agencies, and philanthropic organizations. I call the combined "placemaking" activities of these kinds of BID-public-private partnership regimes "BID urbanism." This book tells the story of how a new BID-PPP urban regime, working through the various BIDs, including neighborhood BIDs, collectively redeveloped and refashioned Washington, D.C.

But what are BIDs, and what do they do? The short, one-dimensional answer to these questions is that business improvement districts are geographically bounded areas where local property owners can assess themselves a fee to solve problems that are negatively impacting the local business environment. A BID is typically formed through state and local enabling legislation. In most cities BIDs are incorporated as nonprofit organizations designated for a specific geographic area of the city (Morçöl et al. 2008).[3] The district's property owners are supposed to pay the fees, but generally landlords can pass them on to their tenants. This is the case, for example, in cities like Washington, D.C., and New York.

The legal language in the United States as well as other places has set out the requirement that these fees, which are not to be confused with general property taxes, be used for "supplemental" services, such as cleanliness, seasonal atmospheric decorations and programming, security, and marketing (Briffault 1999; Houstoun 1997; J. Mitchell 2001). Yet, what is viewed as "supplemental" is a matter of debate and practice. BIDs not only run programs to keep the streets clean and safe; they also take on a sense of ownership of and redesign large areas of the public realm in our cities, including the main streets of our neighborhoods. More important, collectively they have become a powerful voice shaping land use, zoning, transportation, and urban redevelopment planning. But despite the expanding influence of BIDs in shaping urban life, citizen representation and participation is limited because BIDs legally reserve majority-voting power on their board of directors for property owners (Briffault 1999; Mallett 1994).

Beginning in the late 1970s, as part of their response to real and perceived urban crises, urban regimes relied more and more on new forms of public-private partnerships (Pierre 1998). BIDs emerged in New York in the late 1970s and early 1980s, in Philadelphia around 1990, and in D.C. in the late 1990s. In each of these cities BIDs were legally enabled and organized after the installation of some variation of a fiscal control board. Generally, these "neoliberal" new regimes worked to cut back the local welfare state and to streamline, shrink, and reorganize public bureaucracies (Brenner 2004; Hackworth 2007; Harvey 2005). They advocated for policies to enhance the business climate, which also meant countering the omnipresent narratives of urban crime and filth through rebranding campaigns. This required marketing the historical heritage of a neighborhood or downtown and the convenience of a built and social environment where work, play, and day-to-day necessities, such as shopping, could be fulfilled within a small, easily accessible radius. Selling this competitive advantage (Porter 1995), which distinguished traditional downtowns and urban neighborhoods from their suburban neighbors, required "cleaning up" neighborhood commercial spaces and creating place-based images free of danger and deterioration (Briffault 1999). The early work of BIDs was to secure this feeling of safety and familiarity (as well as novelty) and to pull businesses, visitors, and new residents, especially from the suburbs, back into the central cities they had abandoned. As they have worked to attract these shoppers and, more important, residents back into the city, BIDs and the specific form of urbanism they promote have been decisive in oiling the gentrification machine (N. Smith 1996, 2002; Zukin 1995, 2011). To be clear, I do not argue that single BIDs are responsible for gentrification, but I do advance the case that BID urbanism is.

BID urbanism is especially about urban placemaking to revalorize the dense, walkable city. This kind of placemaking as a form of urbanism gained salience through the dissemination of key ideas about urban life captured in Jane Jacob's *Death and Life of Great American Cities* and Holly Whyte's study *The Social Life of Small Urban Places*. These works propagated insights about the everyday life of urban places that helped to refocus the profession of urban planning on the relationship between the built environment and how people actually use, move through, and interact in urban space. Placemaking scholarship, consequently, focuses on understanding how mere locations in space become identified as particular places (Relph [1976] 2008; Gehl 2010). Thus, placemaking is about asserting or facilitating a sense of belonging in space to create a sense of place. Placemaking activities range from clean and safe initiatives and design interventions to activation through events and cultural performances as well as mobile or seasonal street vendors.

The visions and placemaking tactics to which BIDs subscribe—the "livable city," the "creative city," and more recently the "pop-up city"—have become pervasive monikers, marking these also as globally diffusing approaches to urban growth and planning (Beekmans and Boer 2014; Florida 2003; Landry 2008; Lydon and Garcia 2015).[4] The Project for Public Places defines this placemaking on its website as "more than just promoting better urban design" but as "facilitate[ing] creative patterns of use, paying particular attention to the physical, cultural, and social identities that define a place and support its ongoing evolution." These, often temporary, activation strategies create "eventscapes" that bring people together to assert their presence in a specific location (Furman 2007). This production of eventscapes, as Jeffrey Hou argues, perhaps can empower local communities, which have been invisibilized or marginalized, such as recent immigrant groups, for example, to affirm a collective right to the city (Hou 2010). Eventscapes, however, are also increasingly mobilized as "value creation platforms" (Richards, Marques, and Mein 2015, 2–6; Suntikul and Jachna 2016). From this perspective, which is prevalent in tourism scholarship, eventscapes are seen as purposively drawing people and places together, producing experiences through which visitors "undergo emotional sensations," which generate a sense of attachment to a site or place. BID urbanism has increasingly focused on this latter kind of placemaking to mold downtown and neighborhood districts into eventscapes. As the D.C. case illustrates, BIDs seek to be at the forefront of strategies to activate the public realm of their districts, such as streets, plazas, sidewalks, and vacant lots, to attract visitors, placemaking entrepreneurs, and ultimately higher-income residents, often at the cost of destabilizing existing residents and small businesses in place (Friedmann 2010; Furman 2007; Hou 2010).

BIDs take placemaking a step further to ensure the "competitive advantage" (Porter 1995) of their districts in the marketplace of places. BIDs are an integral arm of postindustrial redevelopment regimes that mobilize the "symbolic economy," the technology, media, entertainment, and cultural industries, to produce urban eventscapes (Zukin 1995). BID urbanism, then, represents the concerted placemaking work that BIDs perform in partnership with public officials, public agencies, and other private organization to forge new place-identities and in some cases new neighborhoods. However, the visible and seemingly local displays of urban placemaking divert attention from the governance strategy that has propelled the expansion of this BID urbanism.

BID Urbanism Comes to D.C.

The BID lore repeats itself. In 2006 during a conversation with BID executives, I heard an almost identical story to the description recounted in the above cited *Crain's New York* article: BIDs in Washington, D.C., had played a significant role in the efforts to finally halt the city's precipitous downward spiral in the 1990s. BIDs, as such, came relatively late to D.C., although local officials, aware of New York City's experiment, had already floated the idea for a BID-like entity in the late 1970s. But the idea seemed to go nowhere for a decade. By the early 1990s, however, government leaders were deeply concerned about the city's fiscal health and its tourism industry (Walsh and Burgess 1989; Wyman 1989), and BID-enabling legislation was seriously discussed, studied, and proposed.

It is true that in the early 1990s, D.C. seemed to have reached its nadir in the mainstream media and public perception. In January 1990, the *Washington Post* had broken the following incredible and surreal news story: "[D.C.'s Mayor Marion] Barry Arrested on Cocaine Charges" (LaFraniere 1990). D.C. had also recently been "dubbed" the "murder capital" of the nation, and in 1991, a civil uprising—known as the "Mount Pleasant riots"—in the Adams Morgan and Mount Pleasant neighborhoods shook the city to its core (Pratt 2011). In retrospect, former mayor Sharon Pratt Dixon, who had only recently been inaugurated when the "riots" exploded, observed in 2011: "Whatever my personal disappointment 20 years ago, I now appreciate that the disturbances presaged a city on the cusp of growth." This growth was propelled through the restructuring of the city's governance regime in the mid-1990s only about twenty years after D.C. had attained home rule and D.C.'s "mayor for life" lost control over the city's governance to the Fiscal Control Board.

Marion Barry, a civil rights activist, had defined D.C.'s political landscape since the advent of home rule in 1973, and his mayoral administration had initially embodied the aspirations for "Chocolate City"—the first majority black city in the nation (Asch and Musgrove 2017). The nickname "Choco-late City" or simply "CC" immortalized in George Clinton's song released by Parliament in 1975, communicated a particular message about D.C. as the space of "neighborhoods, playgrounds, stores, churches and relatives": "Chocolate City [had risen] from the ashes of 1968 along with black people's hopes for self-determination" (Carroll 1998). Throughout his sometimes brilliant but also flawed political career, Mayor Barry had tried to recon-cile growth with racial equity (A. Williams 2017). But the constricting con-ditions of home rule, the decline of federal support for major urban centers, the continuing suburbanization of the middle class, and to no small mea-sure his increasingly erratic and even corrupt management style led the city into a fiscal straight jacket. By the 1990s, although Barry had won reelection, middle-class residents, black and white, and especially the city's congres-sional powerbrokers, were tired of his regime and the city's mounting insta-bility. They were clamoring for change.

The initial removal and subsequent chastening of Mayor Barry by Con-gress—with the consent of the Clinton administration—after his 1994 sur-prising reelection paved the way for new leadership. The Fiscal Control Board, installed in 1995, and a political shift on the City Council marked the transition to a post–civil rights urban regime and laid the groundwork for a new public-private alliance to govern the city. It finally enabled BID urbanism to become firmly rooted in D.C., and the new regime effectively unbridled the "city as a growth machine" (Molotch 1976). This book exam-ines the "nested interest groups with common stakes in development" that organized the BID-PPP regime in D.C. in order to create the "institutional fabric, including the political and cultural apparatus, to intensify land use and make money" (Molotch 1976, 31). In contrast to Mayor Barry's explicit racial understanding of the city's urban landscape, which was reflected in many of his administration's early policy initiatives, the new urban regime consciously adopted a color-blind or post-racial stance, promoting abstract liberal values (Bonilla Silva 2010), including strengthening private property markets, the liberalization of consumer choice, civic engagement, and en-trepreneurial community self-reliance. Upon the election of a new genera-tion of black "technocratic" mayors in the postcontrol period, the BID-PPP regime continued to pursue a governance and redevelopment approach unmoored from a historical analysis of D.C.'s development patterns (Har-ris 2010; Spence 2015). It strengthened real estate interests and turned to market-based tools to solve D.C.'s fiscal crisis without adequate policy safeguards and public investments to prevent the rising inequities that ultimately have produced racially disparate patterns of dislocation and displacement (Lauber 2012).

The BID-PPP regime released a strategic plan, "The Economic Resurgence of Washington, D.C.: Citizens Plan for Prosperity in the 21st Century," in 1998 to guide this change (Monteilh and Weiss 1998). The national planning consultants and public officials who assembled this plan both revived old urban renewal plans from the 1940s–1960s and articulated action steps to adapt and diversify D.C.'s economic foundation and to build "a city well suited for the 'New Economy' of the 21st century" (4).[5] The plan's main elements focused on rebuilding the center city area, recovering the Anacostia waterfront, and facilitating the targeted investment in and the remaking of existing neighborhoods. To achieve these initiatives, the "Citizens Plan" (the name I use throughout the book) emphasized the role that BIDs both large and small needed to play. Since then three types of BIDs have been at work in D.C.: (1) the two downtown BIDs to refashion the downtown core; (2) the redevelopment BIDs to manage the production of new, fairly high-density, mixed-use neighborhoods, also referred to as Central Employment Areas; and (3) the smaller neighborhood-based BIDs (NBIDs) to "restore" or "revitalize" the city's existing historical neighborhoods.

The plan makers also sought to symbolically reclaim the city (Zukin 1995). Since the late 1990s, BID urbanism has refurbished and restructured downtown, produced new urban districts, and redefined urban living to market new lifestyles (Zukin 1995). The vision entailed a "successful residential strategy" that called for "a substantial increase in the District population" (O'Cleireacain and Rivlin 2001, 3). To the uninitiated, this goal seemed out of touch and out of reach at a time when D.C. was still hemorrhaging middle-class households and seemed to stand at the precipice of collapse. While policy briefs called for a balanced residential strategy that would bring young professionals into D.C. as well as keep families there, the BID urbanism that finally achieved this residential strategy homed in on the needs of "young professionals in their 20s and 30s" (O'Cleireacain and Rivlin 2001, 3). The 2001 policy brief cited here noted that this demographic was "enthusiastic about city life, attracted by the city's cultural amenities, restaurants, nightlife, and racial, ethnic and income diversity," but they also would demand a sense of "safety, attractive surroundings, and a well-managed government" (3). Furthermore, these young professionals would "have an extremely positive impact on the city's tax base and revenue" (3).

This insight was not new. Already in 1979, a critical real estate commentator noted that the "recruitment specifications for the urban populace" were to be "white collar and computer-oriented" and that "blacks, browns and poor whites" were to be "recycled off the prime land in the central city areas of many of our oldest cities," including Washington, D.C. (Travis 1979, 1). Tellingly, still at the dawn of home rule, the powerful Washington Board of Trade, an organization that has historically been and to this day continues to be intimately involved in the planning and governance of Washington, D.C., proclaimed this future: "In the next decade the District will be solidly middle class and upper class, racially balanced, with the poor pushed into the suburbs" (9). At the time, the city was 70 percent black with a black mayor at its helm. Yet, wrote Travis (1979), "their economic impotence [was still] all present" (12). These forecasts have come to pass, although they took a little longer to take hold. In the decades following the crisis of the 1990s, Washington, D.C. indeed rewrapped itself in the cloak of a successful twenty-first-century city, the nation's capital, and became the poster child of the widely acclaimed urban renaissance (Hyra and Prince 2015). And as predicted, the regime shift that enabled BID urbanism rekindled the property markets. So, by 2011, the city had undeniably been growing, but so had displacement. The trend has continued. Today D.C. is no longer a majority-black city, and redevelopment and gentrification have inescapably changed the physical, political, symbolic, and social landscape of the downtown core and of many of its neighborhoods.

The Book's Central Questions and Arguments

As recently as 2010 in the context of a symposium on Philadelphia BIDs, legal scholar Gerald Frug perspicaciously and pointedly probed "why there seems to be an almost automatic answer when one seeks to create an organization to improve neighborhood life: 'Let's create a BID.' The problem with this automatic instinct is that such a model might empower the wrong people" (Frug 2010, 17). Yet, the precept that BIDs represent local democracy at work continues to proliferate in policy circles as the BID idea spreads across the globe.

This book draws on more than fifteen years of research to present a direct, focused engagement with both the planning history that shaped D.C.'s landscape and the intricacies of everyday life, politics, and planning practice as they relate to BIDs. I dissect and evaluate the theoretical tenets that undergird the BID ethos, which draw on the language of economic liberalism (individual choice, civic engagement, localism, and grassroots development) to portray this governance approach as color-blind, democratic, and equitable. The purpose of this book is to examine and reveal the contradictions embedded in the BID policy paradigm and governance model. For the last thirty years, BID advocates have engaged in effective and persuasive storytelling (Throgmorton 2003); as a result, many policy makers and planners perpetuate the BID narrative without analytically examining the institution and the inequities it has wrought. The *Crain's New York* article, cited previously, is but one indication, however, that many urban residents and small business owners have seriously questioned and resisted BIDs and BID urbanism. Thus, to foster this ongoing critical discussion (Christopherson 1994; Frig 2010; Gross 2013; Mallet 1994; Ward 2006), the following questions guide this book:

(1) What are the theoretical principles, values, and historical antecedents that underlie BID urbanism and its governance model and inform the policy language used to legitimize it among direct stakeholders and the public more broadly?

(2) Whose and what interests have aligned to constitute these BID-PPP regimes? Whose vision of urbanity and sensibilities of place do they reproduce in the urban landscape? Whose visions and memories of place are likely left out?

(3) And, finally, what are the broader implications of BID urbanism for equity and the ability of different populations to assert a "right to the city" (Lefebvre, Kofman, and Lebas 1996)?

Many of these questions are particularly fraught in the context of D.C., given the contradictory histories of marginalization and incorporation that have created this starkly segregated and now increasingly hip yet exclusionary city (Asch and Musgrove 2015; Modan 2007; Summers 2015; Hyra and Prince 2015; Hyra 2017). This line of questioning purposefully targets the inherent conflict in how this public-private partnership (PPP) governance strategy has been presented (as a progressive and grassroots economic development strategy) and the way it structures interests and voice (Christopherson 1994; Mallett 1994). Several cities, most notably New York City and Washington, D.C., have focused on increasing the coverage of BIDs in neighborhoods. Thus, the book is organized as a nested case study. It both analyzes the citywide impact of BID urbanism and takes a look inside a neighborhood BID establishment process to illuminate how the outcomes of this process fall short of the democratic promises advocates seek to associate with the BID model. Central to the book are three core arguments, which also align with the research approach embedded in its structure:

First, BIDs as part of a public-private governance coalition both concentrate and amplify the voice of real estate interests as decision makers in postindustrial urban growth regimes (the people in the public, private, and nonprofit sector who shape local growth policy), thereby producing new development trends and reinforcing historical patterns of exclusion and displacement. Consequently, a historicized understanding of their work that includes a deliberate focus on race—especially in the U.S. context—ethnicity, culture, and class is crucial to keep at the forefront of policy discussions the inequities that BID urbanism tends to reinforce.

Second, because neighborhoods are characterized by complex and often contentious spatial politics, the entrepreneurial placemaking that BIDs pursue often further marginalizes less powerful actors on the local level. Thus this book examines the micropolitics of place to highlight the multiple memories, experiences, and norms of behavior that coexist in these types of urban areas and to illustrate how BIDs are likely to valorize place aesthetics and norms of behavior that reproduce historical paths to privilege.

Third, neighborhood-based BIDs subsume neighborhood social spaces into market rationality, creating an artificial boundary between a neighborhood's residential space and its value as a commercial district. Within the latter, they privilege the rights of commercial property owners and the interests of those entrepreneurial tenants positioned to pay higher lease rates and produce revenues for the city's tax base (Ocejo 2014). In so doing, this book argues, they turn the public realm into a "club" (Hoyt 2005; Warner 2011) that is apt to suppress the interests of neighborhood constituents, whose interests do not readily align with what a locally elected neighborhood official called an "outwardly focused" development strategy.

To pursue my arguments, the rest of this book is divided into three parts. Part 1, the first chapter, frames the book's arguments. It provides an expanded analysis of BIDs and offers a look at the ideas and values that underpin them. It discusses how BID proponents have constructed a policy advocacy narrative that draws both on an idealized repertoire of nineteenth-century progressivism and on public choice theory to sell these institutions as quintessentially American and as local democracy at work. I argue that BIDs and BID urbanism are best viewed through the lens of local regime formation in the context of the broader political economy in which "economic forces both shape and are shaped by political arrangements" (Stone 1993, 2). I close the chapter with a discussion that critiques BID urbanism by drawing on Lefebvre's notion of "the right to the city" (Lefebvre,

Kofman, and Lebas 1996). Part 2, chapters 2 through 4, focuses on Washington, D.C., as a whole. I begin by historically locating BIDs in the city's planning trajectory to situate their work firmly in the local political, social, and spatial context. Then I examine how their work as part of a new BID-PPP regime remade D.C.'s geography of neighborhoods. Part 3, chapters 5 through 8, examines the micropolitics of BID formation, looking at how different interests on the neighborhood-level fared during an attempt to create and run a BID, in this case in the Adams Morgan and Mount Pleasant neighborhoods. The work closes with some reflections on BID urbanism in other cities to situate D.C.'s experience in the broader BID movement.

In order to maintain the confidentiality, to the best of my ability, of the many people, such as business owners, residents, BID professionals, public officials, and organizational staff, who were willing to be interviewed for this book or who participated in mapping workshops and the subsequent group discussions, I have anonymized their contributions and used names only when the person has been identified in a media accessible by the public, such as reports, hearing statements, newspaper articles, presentations, or radio broadcasts.

CHAPTER 1

Framing BID Urbanism
and Placemaking

Business improvement districts have played a significant institutional and leadership role in D.C.'s transformation into a "world class city" (Monteilh and Weiss 1998). This book shows that this urban "regeneration" linked to the BID governance strategy had been discussed among business and political elites since the 1950s. While BID urbanism did not make inroads until the late 1970s and 1980s, by the late 1990s, BID urbanism had metamorphosed into best practice. This book aims to pierce through the "seduction" of the BID form (Frug 2010) to demonstrate how BIDs have been used not to further democracy but rather to reconsolidate "the city as a growth machine" (Molotch 1976), fueling the iniquitous trio of dislocation, displacement, and replacement (Fullilove and Wallace 2011; Davidson 2008). In the process, many of D.C.'s longtime residents and businesses, especially low-income residents and small, neighborhood-based businesses, lost their sense of belonging—that is, their sense of place—as "revitalization" efforts marginalized and even questioned their contribution to the city's life and sought to create new or recuperate "historical" place identities (Howell 2013; Hyra 2017; Modan 2007; Schaller and Modan 2005; Summers 2015).

In cities like Washington, D.C., New York, and Philadelphia, the BID institution is formed through state and local enabling legislation. As noted in the introduction, the distinguishing feature of BIDs is their special power to levy a mandatory, district-wide property-based assessment (colloquially these are referred to as "taxes"), which was initially only placed on commercial properties but has now been expanded in some cities to include residential properties. The mandatory fee is potentially enforceable through the placement of a lien on the property of a BID member who becomes delinquent in these payments. The BID tool is increasingly being used to revitalize downtowns and existing inner-city neighborhoods, in some cases replacing grant-supported "Main Street" commercial corridor revitalization initiatives (Isenberg 2004). New York City and Washington, D.C., are cases in point. The Bloomberg administration in New York City, for example, supported the rapid expansion of neighborhood-based BIDs, at times in conjunction with rezoning proposals, and this policy has been continued by the so-called progressive de Blasio administration in his rezoning proposals. D.C. seems to be going down a similar path after the expansion of smaller BIDs had slowed between 2005 and 2016 (Regan 2016).

BIDs do not work alone, however; they are part of placemaking urban regimes focused on restoring order, branding new urban lifestyles, and marketing and managing urban districts that gained ascendance, especially after the urban fiscal crises of the 1970s. Business elites, public officials, and philanthropic thought leaders collaborated "to blend their capacity to govern" (Stone 1993, 6) and harnessed their resources in order to create urban spaces responsive to the consumer preferences of higher-income residents and visitors (Zukin 1995); these "back to the city" consumers, moreover, were often bringing suburban sensibilities to urban experiences (Hyra 2015; Modan 2007; Schaller and Modan 2005; Sorkin 1992; Zukin 1995). Therefore, the emergent urban regimes had to mobilize a sufficiently persuasive policy narrative about urban life(styles) and democratic urban governance that would both enhance the capacity of private sector actors to shape policy and resonate with and be accepted by the broader population (Throgmorton 2003; Healey 2013).

BIDs in fact are integral to contemporary progressive yet neoliberal urban regimes (Brenner 2004; Leitner, Peck, and Sheppard 2007; Spence 2015; Ward 2006). Neoliberalism, according to David Harvey, "in the first instance is a theory of political economic practices that proposes that well-being can best be advanced by liberating individual entrepreneurial freedoms and skills within an institutional framework characterized by strong property rights [and] free markets" (Harvey 2005, 2). BID-PPP regimes may support progressive social, environmental, and urban design policies (Stone 1993), but they endorse a marketized policy rationale, which both individualizes responsibility for personal progress (to create economic opportunities, find adequate housing, good schooling, and so forth) and promotes public-private partnership models to fund and produce public goods, such as parks, schools, and sanitation, by turning them into "common" or "club" goods (Krinsky and Simonet 2017; Nisbet 2018; Warner 2011).[1] When necessary, they have also resorted to class-based and "cultural" arguments to support their clean and safe campaigns and placemaking policies (Spence 2015). Through the story of BID urbanism in D.C., this book explicitly illustrates how this governance strategy, rooted in a color-blind neoliberal policy approach, including tenets of public choice theory, has propelled gentrification processes that have, however, reinforced not only class privilege but in cities like D.C. also racial privilege (Bonilla Silva 2010).

This chapter grounds the examination of the Washington, D.C., case theoretically. I briefly situate BIDs and BID urbanism historically to provide an overall context. Then I proceed to discuss and critique the public choice principles and the nineteenth-century ideals that underpin this BID public-private governance model. These ideas and values provide the foundational elements for the persuasive storytelling propelling BID urbanism (Throgmorton 2003). Finally, I offer an alternative framing for placemaking, drawing on equity-planning frameworks as linked to "the right to the city" (Fainstein 2009; Harvey 2008; Krumholz 2011; Lefebvre, Kofman, and Lebas 1996; Purcell 2014).

Situating BIDs

BIDs have their own policy mythology or origination story. Their proponents engage "in planning as persuasive storytelling in a global scale web of relationships" (Throgmorton 2003). Search for the term on Wikipedia, and it will tell you that BIDs apparently came from Canada. Lore has it that the Bloor West Village Business Improvement Area, the "first BID," established in Toronto in 1970, was hatched in a local coffee shop as the brainchild of a local official, a lawyer, and a business owner on this neighborhood's retail corridor (Charenko 2015, 5). While this origination tale is disseminated in international BID-focused literature, this property-based urban regeneration strategy is actually deeply rooted in (and grew out of) U.S. political culture and history of urban governance (Monti 1999).

The urban crises, precipitated in no small measure by the global financial crisis of the 1970s, might be viewed as presenting the conjuncture that created the "political opportunity structure" (Tarrow 2011) for downtown advocates to bring to fruition their vision to reclaim the city. By the 1970s, the suburbanization of people and jobs had taken its toll on central city tax bases. It was time to experiment. Federal retrenchment during the Reagan era followed by Clinton's neoliberal restructuring of welfare and the commitment to "reinvent" government only pushed municipalities ever more forcefully to focus on entrepreneurial economic development to compensate for the continuing disinvestment from the urban core (Spence 2015). These trends also undermined the viability of urban regimes trying both to redistribute the fruits of economic progress and to provide welfare services to those not reaping the benefits of economic prosperity (Harvey 2005). But the roots of BID urbanism, the intellectual foundations, and organizing efforts of this movement reach further back.

Since the 1930s "white flight" had been subsidized by the same Federal Housing Authority (FHA) that had "redlined" inner-city neighborhoods but provided mortgage guarantees to enable the suburbanization of white residents (Jackson 1987). Redlining categorized central city neighborhoods as high-risk investments, paralyzing the flow of loans and capital into central city neighborhoods, trapping communities of color in "declining" urban spaces. After the 1948 decision to declare racially restrictive covenants unenforceable and after the 1954 *Brown v. Board of Education of Topeka*, 347 U.S. 483 (D.C. case: *Bolling v. Sharpe*, 347 U.S. 497) decision mandated the desegregation of schools, white flight only accelerated. Retail and other firms followed this trend. Downtown elites began to organize in the 1950s to stem the declining value of central city properties.

During this period, visionary developers, such as James Rouse, both shaped the creation of suburbia and a suburban lifestyle and advocated for urban renewal policies to revive faltering central city economies and real estate markets (Gillette 2012). For the sprawling suburbs, Rouse drew on the design breakthroughs of architect Victor Gruen to create tightly managed suburban malls where people could shop, eat, socialize, play, and even enjoy cultural programs all in one place (Bloom 2004; Gillette 2012). Moreover, suburban consumers could enjoy these without having to enter the "noisy and dirty and chaotic" environments of central city downtowns (Gillette 2012, 43).

To revive the ailing central cities, Rouse, through persistent policy advocacy, helped design downtown-focused urban renewal policies that included an expansive use of eminent domain, first to improve housing conditions in the inner cities and then to encourage economic development (Bloom 2004). In addition, Cold War politics during the 1940s and 1950s created an ideological environment that hindered a policy commitment to public housing by branding it "socialistic," thereby limiting the scope of this type of government-owned housing as part of urban renewal (Bloom 2004,

13). Instead, the real estate industry and ideologically aligned policy makers saw in urban renewal the opportunity "to reinvent the capitalist city" in alliance with the private sector in order to reconstitute a central city consumer base as well as a retail and office market (27).

In urban renewal, public authority, which held the power to condemn "blighted" areas, would fuse with the private sector's ability to raise capital to modernize the city's built environment. As a result, local authorities sanctioned the razing of whole communities and disproportionally displaced communities of color, particularly African Americans (Fullilove 2005). This was happening in a context when the civil rights movement was challenging the foundations of the "U.S. urban racial state," which had actively worked to uphold the "racial status quo" (Cazenave 2011, 1) by not just maintaining but exacerbating prevailing economic, educational, and political inequalities through segregation in housing, the workplace, and education as well as commercial and social institutions. Widespread opposition finally halted urban renewal's overtly destructive approach to urban redevelopment, but swaths of land had already been cleared, awaiting redevelopment. Additionally, after Dr. Martin Luther King's assassination in 1968, rebellions or "riots" shook U.S. cities, and central city buildings lay smoldering. Redevelopment in many cities took decades to materialize.

At this time, the civil rights movement introduced an advocacy, community-based, and participatory planning ethos into the planning profession, which was initially embraced by the federal government in President Johnson's Model Cities programs. Already in the early post-1968 period, however, federal policy makers, in conversations with private sector interest groups, began to actively transform these participatory community development and planning models, and community empowerment gave way to local control and neighborhood entrepreneurialism (Cummings 2001; DeFilippis 2004).

The BID urbanism that finally emerged in the post–civil rights era in the late 1970s and early 1980s incorporated an amalgam of James Rouse's ideas and coopted the language of grassroots empowerment while increasingly shifting the discourse toward entrepreneurial self-help and civic engagement. Instead of razing entire neighborhoods, as was the case during the urban renewal of the 1950s and 1960s, the nascent BID urbanism focused on privately led urban management, preservation, and redevelopment to rescue the city for the middle class. BIDs combined Rouse's concept for the American mall, a highly choreographed, managed, but fun and social place and his concern with downtown renewal and urban festival markets

(Gillette 1999, 2012). Urban BID districts, to be successful then, not only had to control urban "noise, dirt and chaos" but also had to engage in proactive placemaking to create and support new forms of urban sociability and consumption behaviors. A generation of professionals, many of whom lead BIDs today, including some in D.C., trained in the Rouse company and were ready to adapt both these management and placemaking ideas to city environments. To anchor their work, BID entrepreneurs have also drawn on the keen observations of urban life and human behavior developed by luminary urbanists, such as William Holly Whyte (1988), Jane Jacobs ([1961] 1992), and Jan Gehl (2010). Added to this mix of ideas was an attraction to New Urbanist principles—progressive planning principles rooted in a renewed commitment to urbanity, but an idealized nineteenth-century urbanity—by which living, working, strolling, and shopping are designed to coexist in one district (Hirt and Zahm 2012).

The adoption of these planning and governance concepts has indeed remade many downtowns into 24/7 mixed-use, pedestrian-friendly neighborhoods. In 2016, a BID executive in Washington, D.C., succinctly captured this development: "The very first BID was a response to declining conditions, trash, crime . . . [this] morphed over time to enhancement, placemaking and growth . . . we needed to create a brand, an identity, a sense of place so that we would be recognized in the market place" (Stevens, Suls, and Avery 2016; my transcription). More recently, BIDs have also been adept at absorbing other, newer planning tools, such as "pop-up" urbanism and "tactical urbanism," to create temporary interventions that help market their particular district's identity (Beekmans and Boer 2014; Lydon and Garcia 2015). Thus, BID initiatives and BID urbanism more broadly have focused on reclaiming an image of urban America that evokes a cosmopolitan urban world (Bookman 2013; Zukin 2009): exciting, convenient, culturally textured, historically rooted, and above all safe and familiar for a "diverse" urban population. And to be sure, some of the ambitions that BID professionals and advocates have articulated—to improve the cleanliness, safety, and aesthetics of the public realm as well as to update the various infrastructures of central cities in order to fashion, in their words, "inclusive" downtown districts—were and continue to be laudable.

Richard Florida's (2003) exaltation of the "creative class" as the key to urban and regional growth and Michael E. Porter's (1995) analysis of the "competitive advantage of the inner city" buttressed the BID movement's rebranding of urban areas as desirable and profitable markets. Not unlike Rouse, they saw, albeit through distinct lenses, that place-based economic development policies promised a way out of reinvestment bottlenecks to unlock the potential of inner-city markets (Porter 1995; Florida 2003). While Florida focused on the lifestyles and values of the creative class, which informed the rebranding of urban areas as mosaics of "diverse" and "inclusive" places, Porter also articulated the persuasive entreaty to business interests, including retailers, that they had underestimated the market potential of urban neighborhoods. Consequently, place-based urban development strategies were to be designed not just to foster municipal entrepreneurialism but to invigorate and stimulate "community" entrepreneurialism to enhance an area's competitive market position (Cummings 2001).

BIDs as Club Politics

The theoretical foundation of BIDs weaves together defining tenets of neoliberal urban policy (localism, choice, and fiscal responsibility as well as U.S. privatism), which were developed in the post–World War II era and became fully entrenched by the 1990s (Harvey 2005, 51). In particular, BIDs are rationalized through public choice theory, a theory that grounds their form of privatism in abstract economic arguments. According to legal scholar Louise A. Halpern, these arguments are used to endorse governance changes "to strengthen the bonds of property" that "will not harm current interests" and will preserve the "existing distribution" of benefits (Halper 1993, 270–72). In the late 1950s, this theory's abstract argumentation lent itself to ahistorical analyses of urban conditions and subsequently to decontextualized governance and planning solutions (Bonilla Silva 2010; Halpern 1993; MacLean 2017). By turning over planning for urban areas to BIDs, municipal governments realigned the ability of different actors to influence and shape urban redevelopment and placemaking, sidelining political citizenship while empowering economic or consumer citizenship (Christopherson 1994; Zukin 1995). The impetus is to come from local, civically engaged businesspeople, particularly property owners, willing to organize themselves into BIDs. To show how this occurs, I unpack the theoretical principles underlying this apparent shift from political to economic citizenship and club politics, which sidesteps the messiness of decision making by elected representative bodies. My intention is to create signposts that flag the use of these framing devices in the discussions of the BID-enabling legislation in D.C. and the subsequent planning strategies of the BID-PPP regime.

In 1956, Charles Tiebout built an economic model that provided supportive arguments to decentralize the governance of rapidly suburbanizing areas. The idea was to create a marketplace of localities that would vie with each other for residents. In this model, local governments try to induce potential residents and by extension taxpayers to "vote with their feet" and to choose their locality as a place of residence (Tiebout 1956). To attract the kind of taxpayers they desire, local governments provide tailored bundles of goods, services, and amenities, which in turn are financed through local taxes (Tiebout 1956; Oates 2006). This "competition among local authorities," in the words of Friedrich Hayek, provides "opportunity for experimentation with alternative methods" for developing localizing governance strategies (Hamowy and Hayek 2011, 380).[2]

Entrepreneurial approaches to urban governance at a very local level, according to public choice theorists, could also stimulate the "shared" provision of goods and services not adequately delivered by higher levels of government. This is where the Tiebout model and "the economic theory of clubs" pioneered by James M. Buchanan in 1965 meet (Tiebout 1956; Buchanan 1965). The idea is that local stakeholders in an issue (e.g., education or economic development) and in a specific place (e.g., neighborhoods or commercial districts) are reframed as members in a club (Warner 2011; Nisbet 2018). These "members" organize into a collectivity and pay dues to fund services and amenities they need or see as beneficial to their interests (Buchanan 1965); these might include additional safety services, well-maintained parks, stellar educational facilities, and an attractive common space, for example. In the concept of the bounded community, Tiebout (1956) and Buchanan (1965) converge to create a practicable solution for urban theorists and practitioners who seek to simultaneously devolve and partially privatize the governance of urbanizing areas (McKenzie 2011). Most important, public choice theory holds that this method for selecting a place to live is democratic precisely because it allows those people who have worked hard to use their purchasing power to move to as well as to create and contribute to a community of their choosing.

This public choice theory has provided a rationale for the global production of "gated" communities or private neighborhoods (McKenzie 2011; Glasze 2003). For example, in subdivisions known as common interest communities (CIDs), private homeowners associations (HOAs) are funded through maintenance fees paid by community (club) members. These HOAs become the stewards of the public realm or, in this case, the commonly shared areas. They also contractually regulate and enforce acceptable conduct and design standards, including in the common areas, such as sidewalks, streets, and plazas. Club members, namely the residents who buy into these communities, have to abide by these rules. While many of these communities are physically gated, physical walls are not necessary to signal and enforce exclusivity; rather, even without resorting to material barriers, internal community regulations in conjunction with land-use, zoning, and design controls; as well as home prices and rents, serve as boundaries that can effectively lock out less desirable residents or those with weaker purchasing power (Scotchmer 2002, 2019–22; Webster and Lai 2003).[3] In this manner, communities can create economic as well as intangible cultural and social boundaries that nevertheless signal either belonging or exclusion.[4]

The model exhibits a suburban bias where neighborhoods or subdivisions can easily be built as distinctly marketable places and administrative jurisdictions, which can be sold to specific segments of the residential market (Oates 2006; McKenzie 2011; Webster and Lai 2003). In line with New Urbanist trends in urban analysis and design, many such communities are no longer designed as purely residential enclaves but replicate mixed-use neighborhoods, offering walkable access to traditional urban amenities, such as civic centers, shops, entertainment venues, and parks (Grant 2007; Manzi and Smith-Bowers 2005). But suburban New Urbanist projects that have additionally tried to create greater social diversity through affordable housing mandates have apparently been less successful (Trudeau 2018).

BIDs represent a submunicipal application of this governance trend, even if BIDs are physically accessible and more open than suburban "gated" communities or "clubs" (Warner 2011). The Tiebout hypothesis and Buchanan's theory have been further developed to incorporate, for example, the idea that governing entities act "as territorial enterprises for residents and other jurisdiction-users" (Vanberg 2005, 10–18; 2016). This more open notion recognizes the particularity of BIDs, for instance, that cannot physically gate their districts. Thus, the amenities and services they provide are accessible to outside visitors. Nevertheless, BIDs take seriously the tenets that inhere in public choice theory. The elegance and legally enshrined precept in the BID model requires that those property owners who must legally pay the assessments (although these are usually passed on to commercial tenants through their leases) must also be the direct beneficiaries of the positive spillover effects, such as increased real estate values and lease rates, that BID activities produce (Briffault 1999; Davies 1997). Those who are mandated to pay then become members of the club. This emphasis on linking the BID payments to BID planning emerges as a recurring theme in discussions with BID stakeholders in the United States because it is how BID advocates persuade key business interests, especially real estate interests, to participate.

By influencing and even taking over the planning for these neighborhoods, BIDs obfuscate the distinction between the interests of their "members" and a broader set of urban constituents, including both residents and business owners. In this way, public choice theory strips urban governance of its mooring in political voice and purposefully depoliticizes and dehistoricizes not only the provision of local amenities, public goods, and services (Oates 2006) but also the formation of neighborhood character and identity. In this governance model, as the further discussion of D.C. illustrates, consumer citizens who "choose" to live or do business in BID districts have also been reframed as club members who buy a stake in or lay claim to urban territory in the city, including the public realm. But this model of fragmented governance promotes a marketplace of distinct BID districts and treats neighborhoods as "discrete economic units in need of rebuilding" (Cummings 2001, 442). It also naturalizes inequality (Christopherson 1994) because it discursively "shift[s] the basis of exclusion from group (racialized categories) to individual (affordability)," thus masking or normalizing historical patterns of group exclusion (Miraftab 2005, 25).

BID-PPP Regimes and Selective Amnesia

Integral actors in what Clarence Stone and others might refer to as sophisticated public-private partnership (PPP) regimes (Molotch 1993, 32; Stone 1993), BIDs constitute part of the "consensus-seeking para-apparati," which Mickey Lauria identifies as "forging [a] new type of corporate-led governing coalition" (Lauria 1999, 137).[5] As these new urban regimes engage in placemaking primarily to compete for those consumer and residential segments with the economic purchasing power to fuel their economic development agendas and shore up their local tax bases, BID urbanism is consolidating a class-based revitalization strategy (Zukin 1995).

Besides public choice theory, which uses the abstract language of economics, BID proponents draw on nineteenth-century privatism and associational life to remind their stakeholders that BIDs represent "nothing new" in the U.S. context (Monti 1999). In fact, they argue, BIDs represent a quintessentially American and progressive governance philosophy rooted in civically engaged localism. In 2010, Paul Levy, an internationally recognized BID consultant, proposed that "BIDs tap into a deep strain in American culture that Alexis de Tocqueville first noted in the early nineteenth century—the tendency to form local associations to address community problems, rather than look to state or national government" (77). Grounding BIDs in nineteenth-century imaginaries and hailing the civic involvement of businessmen is common. Urban scholar Daniel Monti has similarly noted that "business men dunning each other so that they can improve the area where their shops are located . . . has been going on for over 200 years in the United States . . . [and] latter day 'business improvement districts' reassert the legitimacy of bourgeois values in parts of cities which seem to have forgotten them" (Monti 1999, 13–14). Business improvement districts from this perspective signify a renewed "progressive" response to the consequences of urban conflict, crisis, and disinvestment.

This narrative enacts what scholars Casey R. Kelly and Kristen Hoerl have called "selective amnesia," which functions as a "rhetoric of absence, or what goes unstated within public discourse" (Kelly and Hoerl 2012, 4). The lore of civic, "bourgeois," or business engagement is problematic because it selectively draws out progressive discursive strategies, using abstracted language about efficiency and effectiveness in governance, which were used in the nineteenth and early twentieth centuries to deflect racist as well as status and wealth-preserving intentions (Yellin 2016; Asch and Musgrove 2017). The contemporary praise of nineteenth-century civic business culture has decoupled these historical "associational" precursors from their racially discriminatory intentionality and outcomes.

Numerous studies confirm that intergenerational "opportunity hoarding," which is clearly associated with segregated urbanization patterns, persists today (Reeves 2017). This is because whites have historically ensured that they as a group accrue and are able to pass down through inheritances not just housing but also income and educational advantages in relation to African Americans and other historically "non-white" populations (Freund 2007; Rothstein 2017).[6] The contemporary use of public choice theory to legitimize property-based governance eschews the fact that choice of neighborhood or the ability to vote with one's feet has been historically circumscribed and curtailed by public policy and private practices in urban property markets, including racially restrictive covenants on property deeds, redlining through federally sanctioned discriminatory underwriting criteria, and racial steering of potential homebuyers, for example.

By 1956, when Tiebout wrote his article, one of these practices, namely restrictive covenants, had only recently been declared unenforceable by the courts (*Shelley v. Kramer* 1948). And it was not until the Fair Housing Act of

1968 that discriminatory practices in the housing market, such as redlining and racial steering, became illegal. Both redlining and racial steering practices, however, persisted and have continued into the twenty-first century even after the passing of the Fair Housing Act (Glantz and Martinez 2018; Lauber 2012). Public choice theory, by retheorizing the provision of public goods and local property markets as reflective of the aggregation of choices made by individuals as consumer citizens through their purchasing power, performed the theoretical work to neutralize and mask these historical antecedents and their overtly discriminatory intents. This theoretical basis now also provides an apparently apolitical rationale for the BID model. But the history and the deployment of "selective amnesia" are political.

This market-based rationale appeared in full force in the post–World War II period. In *Colored Property*, David M. P. Freund painstakingly examines how policy makers and private industry actors transmogrified the explicitly racial language that had guided regional development into economic terminology and a free market mythology that served to naturalize the highly racialized property markets in many U.S. metropolitan areas. It also permitted suburban residents to remain "invested in the assumptions about property, neighborhood, and the nature of the free market" that allowed them to organize unquestioningly "in defense of their privileges as homeowners, as citizens and as white people," synthesizing a market rationality with ideas about middle-class values and aesthetics (Freund 2007, 241). This legacy, as Gabriella Modan's 2007 study *Turf Wars* illustrates, translates into powerful and persuasive "ideologies of place."[7] Thus, the back-to-the-city movement, which BID urbanism anchored and helped to expand, legitimizes the seemingly unselfconscious assertion of "economic" prowess by members of historically privileged consumer citizen groups, primarily whites, because their lifestyle tastes dovetail with profit-making strategies in today's marketplace of places (McFarlane 2009). Today, African Americans and other racialized groups, including Latinx, are incorporated through a broader placemaking discourse around "diversity" that has been mobilized to depoliticize ongoing gentrification strategies (Modan 2008) if "they have the money and know-how to follow middle-class norms and culture" (McFarlane 2009, 165) or their presence adds to the "coolness" of a place (Summers 2015).[8]

In the public choice worldview richer and more entrepreneurial district-based associations, especially of property owners, are entitled to unreservedly demand and fund local amenities and services, including safety and sanitation. Often, as the neighborhood case study shows, they also seek to enforce rules of acceptable conduct and aesthetics in the public realm and the commercial environment (Schaller and Modan 2005; D. Mitchell 2003). But public choice theory denies foregoing historically unjust structuring of choice and posits that urban marketplaces are meritocratic because they recognize an objective measure of value, namely purchasing power. In this fictional account of the free U.S. (property) market, hard work and intergenerational success are rewarded. This framing lies at the heart of color-blind racism because it perpetuates the mythology that if only hard-working families had passed on their work ethic and secured educational achievements for their children, then they would have built economic success (Bonilla Silva 2010). It suggests that government policy has played no role in shaping these opportunities (Freund 2007). The BID policy discourse then leaves unstated how the history of nineteenth-century as well as twentieth-century urban governance and planning policies intersected with the construction of racial hierarchies that led to widespread disinvestment and the creation of the discriminatory and iniquitous property and neighborhood markets; yet precisely these markets have been the targets of coordinated public and private investment to catalyze profit making and wealth creation (Mitchell and Franco 2018). The BID urbanism policy narratives because they are built on public choice values and presumptions fail to fully interrogate who benefits and at whose expense from this investment.

Placemaking and the Right to the City

Today, the District of Columbia or Washington, D.C., which has frequently served as a laboratory for national urban policies, is considered a "21st century post-industrial power house" (Hyra and Prince 2015). D.C.'s path from deep crisis in the early 1990s to its recent "resurgence" through targeted reinvestment and placemaking may be emblematic of global urban trends that have reactivated urban centers. Yet, the advent of BID urbanism in D.C. in the mid-1990s, I argue, marked the transition to a new kind of post–civil rights urban regime that has become implicated in the "patterned serial forced displacement" of low-income communities of color, especially of African Americans (Fullilove and Wallace 2011).[9] Thus, the displacement that BID urbanism both accelerated and catalyzed has produced distinct racially disparate outcomes in D.C. as well as in other cities, such as New York City, for example (Angotti and Morse 2016). In *Root Shock*, Fullilove lucidly crystallizes how the effects of these kinds of urban policies reverberate through the urban built environment and the personal and collective life spaces of the people who are displaced. They induce "root shock," she insists, by severing social networks and, as a consequence, people's ability to maintain a sense of place and belonging (Fullilove 2005). BID urbanism must be contextualized within this history. BIDs also need to be understood as placemakers that can and did perpetuate not only physical displacement but also a sense of dislocation in place as lower-income people begin to lose access to the businesses, parks, and plazas through which they defined their sense of territorial belonging (Davidson 2008).

"Place matters," asserted the 1998 strategic plan: "The Economic Resurgence of Washington, D.C.: Citizens Plan for Prosperity in the 21st Century" (Monteilh and Weiss 1998, 40). But how place matters also matters (Dreier, Mollenkopf, and Swanstrom 2004). In this "Citizens Plan," place and placemaking were deliberately tied to economic growth. The vision was that the creation of "vibrant" and "real" places would attract investment and new residents back into the city. But place is a multidimensional concept, and as Edward Relph outlines in his seminal book *Place and Placelessness*, place is intimately related to the emotions, fantasies, and the everyday life experiences people associate with a particular location in space and moment in time (Relph [1976] 2008). Thus, urban environments represent a palimpsest of placemaking histories (Huyssen 2003).

While BID placemaking is about a restrictive, bounded production of place, Doreen Massey, grappling with what a "progressive" sense of place would entail, observes that "places can be conceptualized in terms of the social interactions which they tie together"; in this way places might be thought of as "processes" (Massey 1994, 141). Thus, she argues for an open conception of place because places are also products of what Clara Irazábal calls "transbordering" activities; these define an alternative sense of place through economic, social, and political networks and practices that defy official jurisdictional boundaries or borders (Irazábal 2014a). They include, as in the case of D.C., the social, economic, and institutional relationships immigrants might forge across historical neighborhood boundaries that they do not recognize in their adopted cities to create an entirely different sense of place, one that is often invisible to planners or other authoritative actors in neighborhood development politics (Schaller and Modan 2005). Transbordering activities are thus "transgressive" because they are not officially sanctioned and often contradict the needs of those invested in the revalorization of property (Irazábal 2014a). This dynamic can create the paradox of placemaking, especially in social contexts where power resides in the ownership of territory or land because the drawing of fixed boundaries has historically been and continues to be an integral part of defining different property markets (Stuart 2003).

BIDs specifically deny the openness of place Massey envisions. BIDs create assessment or taxing districts, which means they are legally obligated to draw very clear boundaries. At times, as in the case of D.C., the resulting formal jurisdictional boundaries ignore or suppress the alternative and informal boundary or rather transbordering work that various groups of residents perform as they go about their daily routines, such as shopping, socializing, visiting places of worship or healing, congregating in play, or vending their wares (Schaller and Modan 2005). Thus, depending on who is asked, what different people consider their notion of the spatiality of a "neighborhood" can be fairly narrowly defined or expansive. This indicates that the meanings that different people and groups of people attach to a particular place often conflict with one another. Yet, historical value suppositions, rooted in race, class, and culture, as described above, valorize particular place identities. Accordingly, certain aesthetic norms and behaviors in the public realm as well as in relation to the use and look of private properties are imbued with more value than others; these value suppositions simultaneously devalue those who fall outside the privileged norm. This is how power and privilege become congealed in place. In the United States, writes Audrey McFarlane, "privileged places" are the ones in which "normalcy, wealth, advantage and presumptions of innocence are still implicitly predicated on whiteness." Therefore, the "economic structure of white privilege and advantage" continues to be "inscribed into the geography of the physical landscape," especially of cities, such as D.C. (McFarlane 2009, 165).

This historical mechanism of deeming some aesthetics and norms of behavior more desirable than others produces a class- and race-inflected politics that extends to downtown districts and to neighborhood commercial corridors or main streets, including to the products and services that are sold there (Zukin 2009). The politics of attaching intangible values to place identities, which can then be monetized, supports a politics of selective amnesia (Kelly and Hoerl 2012; Farrar 2011). Margaret Farrar in her critique of heritage and preservation urbanism, for example, writes: "Not just how the places we make are shaped through the exercise of power and privilege but how they assist or inhibit the potentially transformative work of memory" matters (Farrar 2011, 730). More insidiously, writes Hoerl (2012), "silence may be the most effective rhetoric in the maintenance of existing power relations, as those who would seek to challenge prevailing hierarchies may face recriminations for doing so" (182). Often planners, residents, and place entrepreneurs pursuing "revitalization" or "improvement" strategies activate aspects of an area's history and seek to impose a specific aesthetic of place to create a recognizable identity (Fernandes 2004). But, simultaneously, they may suppress aspects of these histories that require having to reckon with injustices both past and present (Farrar 2011).

Placemaking practices and emergent trends in urbanism have drawn on elements of Henri Lefebvre's work, especially his essay on "the right to the city" in which he recognizes that the city is not solely a domain for production and consumption but a space "for formation, symbolism, the imaginary and play" in which people develop their unique capabilities as humans (Lefebvre, Kofman, and Lebas 1996, 147; Nussbaum 2003). The call for ephemeral, short-lived, temporary design ideas and planning tactics that have grown out of this philosophical stance to catalyze change and effect "long-term transformations" are exciting developments because they seek to inspire people to actively cocreate urban life and space (Lydon and Garcia 2015). They are rooted in the experimental ethos Lefebvre stresses in his work. But these placemaking interventions are also increasingly guided by placemakers who sell their expertise to cities, including D.C., and codify their versions of do-it-yourself (DIY) urbanism, such as tactical urbanism, pop-up urbanism, or the latest iterations, "love your city" urbanism, and creative placemaking (Beekmans and Boer 2014; Lydon and Garcia 2015; Kageyama 2011).

With their focus on today's young, creative placemakers or cocreators, the authors and practitioners of this planning genre in the U.S. context draw on but fail to give full recognition to those communities and activists who actively "loved" their cities and neighborhoods against all odds through the urban crises and in the face of active disinvestment: creating community gardens out of neglected sites, shutting down streets to cars, setting up businesses on their sidewalks, organizing dance parties and music festivals on urban streets and vacant lots, and creating spontaneous splash parks (Mukhija and Loukaitou-Sideris 2014). Local officials in cities such as D.C., however, often shut down these informal activities in which street entrepreneurs and community activists engaged at the time, effectively denying them the right to the city that tactical urbanists are urging young new urbanists to seize. Breaking the rules in the 1980s and 1990s, unlike today, was not acceptable practice in urban neighborhoods; young people of color, who informally congregated to socialize or make music, were and continue to be criminalized (Hopkinson 2012b). Therefore, the praise of contemporary informal and temporary placemaking interventions and the call to encourage rule breaking by young urban innovators today also represent a case of selective amnesia and even dog whistle politics that signals who continues to be privileged in their ability to exercise a right to the city.

Eric Shaw, Washington D.C.'s director of planning, highlighted this disconnect in a 2016 *Washington Post* article. Apparently supportive of tactical urbanism, he nevertheless cautioned, "[a] lot of the approaches inherently sometimes assume a privilege in using public space and existing in public space. . . . I've told my staff that PARK(ing) Day is really nice. . . . But if five black males took over a parking spot and had a barbecue and listened to music . . . would they last 10 minutes?" (Hurley 2016). Thus, placemaking urbanism even in its most recent flexible, DIY, and creative form raises thorny questions about who is able to assume the risk of participating in this entrepreneurial production of place. Director Shaw's commentary also points to the ironies embedded in BID placemaking tactics that seek to activate the public realm through these kinds of programming activities after having "restored order" in inner cities (Elstein 2016; MacDonald 1996a).

In 2016, the American Planning Association in Washington, D.C., presented a panel of D.C. BID professionals to talk about the role BIDs were playing in the city's redevelopment. "Business improvement districts are playing a transformative role in economic and placemaking efforts throughout Washington, D.C.," the event's announcement read, and the executive of the Capitol Riverfront BID explained to the audience of planners how the "city has invested heavily in each of them, so this is where our city is going to grow." The imperative is to "to keep capturing our fair share of the regional economy," he declared (Stevens, Suls, and Avery 2016; my transcription). John R. Logan and Harvey Luskin Molotch observe that "the city is a growth machine, one that can increase aggregate rents and trap related wealth for those in the right position to benefit" (1987, 50). "For those who count," local BID-PPP regimes, like the one in D.C., create highly controlled and programmed environments, which harness an idealized or sanitized informality (Mukhija and Loukaitou-Sideris 2014) and produce "eventscapes" in the name of inclusivity and diversity (Brown et al. 2015; Furman 2007). D.C.'s resultant growth, however, has to date not been distributed equitably. In fact, BID urbanism has intensified inequalities since its installation in the late 1990s.

Urban planning scholar Susan S. Fainstein asserts: "planners, policy makers, and political activists, cannot wipe out history and act as if they start from scratch." To the contrary, "they have to be contextualists" (Fainstein 2011, 28). A historically contextual understanding of equity should place special emphasis on ensuring planning actions benefit populations that have been historically forced to sacrifice well-being. This position contradicts how public choice theorists, who decontextualize urban policy making, imagine change because any change "is prospective" while "uncompensated redistribution is wrong" (Halper 1993, 275, 272); thus, public choice theory can be used to normalize governance arrangements and policies that may exacerbate existing inequalities. An affirmative policy stance toward equity, however, would "favor the less well off more than the well-to-do" (Fainstein 2010, 36). Equity planning also tolerates inequality only in so far as it serves to build the economic dynamism necessary to improve the quality of life for all inhabitants without increasing insecurity and precarity. Equity planning thus establishes the notion that all inhabitants of a city have a right to access the capability-supporting facets of urban life (education, housing, art, open space) and the freedom to stay (Nussbaum 2003; Young 2011). This right also entails the recognition and ability to participate in the decision-making processes that are likely to shape and impact one's daily life (Holston 2009).

Fainstein (2010) analytically separates out democracy, equity, and diversity as criteria to assess urban policies as well as to serve as guidance for planning practice. Her tripartite lens—democracy, diversity, and equity—offers a way to critically examine BID urbanism in relation to both the decision-making processes shaping their urban redevelopment activities and the substantive outcomes these have produced (Fainstein 2010). This book shows how business improvement districts as part of placemaking urban regimes have compromised all three of these criteria. To illustrate this, I develop three themes as leitmotifs throughout the chapters of the book: voice, belonging, and the iniquitous trio of dislocation, displacement, and replacement.

The next chapter anchors the origins of the BID-PPP regime in relation to the foregoing public policies and private practices that produced D.C.'s racialized urban space. Pro-growth coalitions and cooperation with the private sector, particularly with the land-based business community, represent a thread in the history of Washington, D.C. Moreover, D.C.'s geography tells the stories of restrictive covenants, urban renewal, participatory planning and coalition building, the struggle for home rule, the 1968 riots, international immigration in response to U.S. policies, and the 1991 Latinx uprisings in Mount Pleasant. The consolidation of the BID-PPP regime under the auspices of an undemocratic Fiscal Control Board, which replaced the preceding "black nationalist regime" (Reed 1999) that had sought to conjoin growth and affirmative action (Huron 2014; A. Williams 2017) with a "technocratic" urban regime (Harris 2010), removed the friction between D.C.'s urban regime and the national (racial) state. The BID structure, by officially sanctioning the ability of commercial property owners and local business elites to tax themselves and in many cases even to float public bonds that impact and constrict the general borrowing capacity of local governments, has given public officials little choice but to fully realign their economic development strategies with the interests of property owners and developers and their placemaking partners. Moreover, this regime actively courted historically privileged consumer citizen groups. In doing so, the BID-PPP regime (re)produced an iniquitous, unfair urban landscape.

CHAPTER 2

Urban Governance and Planning before BIDs

D.C. was and is a "wounded" city, injured by successive urban policies and systematic racism, which reproduced "structures of violence" through serial "displacement, material devastation and root shock" (Till 2012, 6; Fullilove 2005; Fullilove and Wallace 2011). Washington, D.C., is also a city of "missed opportunities" (Gillette 1995). From the outset, different actors, not only local residents and businesses but also members of Congress and outside interest groups, have sought to impose their own vision on the city and its neighborhoods. In D.C., as in so many U.S. cities, these abstract and often idealistic plans, which French philosopher Henri Lefebvre has called grand "representations of space," ended up being refracted through a prism of racial fears and prejudice (Lefebvre 2011). The purpose of this chapter is to contextualize BID urbanism, which I view as the set of public policies and private practices that contemporary urban regimes deploy to restructure their economies. It takes a closer a look at what came before the city's 1998 "Citizens Plan" (Monteilh and Weiss 1998) and before the positive "inclusive city" slogan was embossed on its 2004 Comprehensive Planning Framework (Office of Planning 2004). I also examine how different regime constellations worked to produce the inequitable political, economic, and social urban landscape onto which the BID-PPP regime grafted its "Citizens Plan," the 2004 "Inclusive City," and subsequent planning frameworks, such as the "Creative Capital Agenda" in 2010 (Office of Planning 2010).

This places BIDs within a history of urban governance regimes in D.C. that developed in tension with the U.S. racial state (Cazenave 2011). In his discussion of this state formation, political scientist Noel A. Cazenave (2011) observes that the interlocking actions of public and private institutions over time integrated goals that reinforced white privilege at all levels of government and translated these into official urban policies (Lipsitz 1995). BIDs and BID urbanism grew out of successive urban regime configurations that sought simultaneously to steer economic growth and to actively manage race relations through the production of particular urban spaces (Lefebvre 2011) from defensible urban residential enclaves to suburban landscapes and postindustrial urban entertainment districts. This dynamic has created perniciously persisting inequalities across our urbanizing landscapes.

BIDs also operationalize rationales that find their origins in nineteenth-century progressivism, and advocates have embedded these in a color-blind, economistic approach to urban governance, one that idealizes self-reliance, competition, freedom of choice, and civic engagement by business elites (Bonilla Silva 2010). Much like city boosters of that era, contemporary BID-PPP regimes have uncritically promoted their placemaking activities to unlock the potential of the territorial assets within their districts' boundaries, including the built environment, transportation networks, and potential neighborhood brands, to leverage real estate-driven economic growth. In doing so, they not only ignored the needs and demands of lower-income populations more broadly, but they have also displaced different working-class cultures from urban neighborhoods (Paton 2016). Moreover, in many U.S. cities, BID urbanism has extended the "racially disparate outcomes" (Angotti and Morse 2016), wrought by preceding urban regimes, into the future.[1]

In D.C., specifically, regime formations and planning strategies in the post–Civil War era and up until the 1970s were largely suffused with racial and class ideologies overtly designed to restrict African Americans and other "minority" groups from gaining access to economic, social, and political power and in so doing to diminish competition for employment, property, and business opportunities (Asch and Musgrove 2017; Gillette 1995). The way to accomplish this has been to access power. With brief interludes over the last century, key urban policies and the private practices they sanctioned were used to secure the property values and wealth creation opportunities for whites more broadly.[2] Successive and overlapping "ideologies of place" justified these mechanisms and helped lay the foundation for the structural inequalities underlying contemporary place-based initiatives (Avila 2004; Modan 2007). Historical ideologies of place continue to echo through contemporary plans and discourses, normalizing specific aesthetics of place and appropriate uses of, and behaviors in, the public realm. Ideologies of place thus both reflect and reproduce the class, ethnic, gender, and cultural privileges that shaped these experiences. They influence how we conceive of as well as perceive and experience urban life (Lefebvre 2011; Modan 2007; Schaller and Modan 2005).

These ideologies of place produced stark contradictions in wealth and poverty across D.C.'s landscape. Not surprisingly, they spawned resistance to build neighborhood-based economic, social, and political power both in the form of collective protest and oppositional practices. Representations of space (Lefebvre 2011) such as maps, plans, and policies that by design reinforce inequalities tend to generate conflict and, in extreme cases, events such as the 1968 uprisings in response to Dr. Martin Luther King Jr.'s assassination and the 1991 Latinx "riots" in Mount Pleasant and Adams Morgan. This history of inclusion, exclusion, and resistance is fundamentally a political and spatial story. It is also a governance story.

Inclusion Foreclosed

During the post–Civil War era, Washington, D.C., experienced the ascendance of a progressive "biracial" urban regime (Asch and Musgrove 2017). This radical Republican regime, which lasted until the end of Reconstruction (1863–1871), included black elected officials and embraced principles of economic opportunity and the expansion of citizenship and civil rights (Gillette 1995). Its initiatives overlapped with priorities at the federal level to counter the twin legacies of slavery and racial oppression. Supporting the reorganization of racial relations, President Grant, for example, "signed bills vetoed by his predecessor that struck the word 'white' from the charters and laws of Washington and Georgetown" and supported black male suffrage (Asch and Musgrove 2017, 151).[3]

Washington, D.C., had long been a magnet for African Americans migrating from the rural South and its adjacent states in search of economic opportunities. This trend accelerated during the 1860s, and by 1870 blacks constituted one-third of the population.[4] Historian Lois Horton notes that the extension of civil rights persuaded African Americans to seek a better life in the city: "None [of these rights] was more important than the right to vote" because this right, in particular, "was seen as the safeguard of black freedom" (Horton 2003, 70).[5] But this "freedom" proved short-lived. After only a decade, an alliance of property owners, bankers, and public officials reasserted their "monopoly over political power" (Asch and Musgrove 2017, 239). The local, biracial regime had overextended itself trying to simultaneously manage race relations and take on ambitious infrastructure improvements to "modernize" the capital city (Gillette 1995). Discontent with the regime and charges of corruption levied against radical Republican mayor Sayles J. Bowen precipitated a reorganization of local governance institutions to install an undemocratically run public-private growth coalition (Asch and Musgrove 2017; Gillette 1995).

For those who sought to curtail black power in D.C. and to limit voting to property-owning men, the city's debt burden presented an auspicious opportunity to wrest control from the elected municipal government. Congress intervened directly, first by establishing an interim territorial government in the early 1870s. A new government purpose also emerged to pursue a bricks and mortar economic development vision (Asch and Musgrove 2017; Gillette 1995). Developers and planners during this period engendered visions of "Greater Washington" (Gillette 1995). Alexander "Boss" Shepherd, who ran the Board of Public Works during the territorial government, oversaw Washington, D.C.'s first urban renewal period, the large-scale infrastructure improvements of the early 1870s. Foreshadowing the place-based planning discourses that reemerged in 1998 in the "Citizens Plan," these early improvements emphasized urban design, national heritage, and the need for an amenity- and hospitality-focused economic development strategy (Gillette 1995). The regime sought to represent Washington, D.C., as a "city built for visitors and residents" and invested in physical upgrades to "attract and hold prosperous residents in the city" (Gillette 1995, 71–72). As historian Kathryn Allamong Jacob reports, during this period—drawn in by the parks, avenues, and infrastructure improvements—the "nouveaux riches were flocking to D.C.," and they began to leave their stamp on the architectural heritage of the city, a heritage recognized recurrently by planners and civic advocates as one of its main assets (Jacob 2003, 81). But as "shrewd realtors for the wealthy" bought up tracts of land to develop new neighborhoods, these nineteenth-century city improvement strategies also displaced low-income, especially black, residents from desirable areas (Gillette 1995, 71–72). Linking Shepherd's D.C. to the city's late twentieth-century spatial organizations, Chris Myers Asch and George Derek Musgrove (2017) write: "In the decades after disfranchisement, developers cashed in on the real estate frenzy by building suburban residential areas for white homebuyers along what would later become the Red Line of the Metro," that is, the contemporary metropolitan commuter train system (190).

Not unlike Mayor Bowen, Shepherd ran the District's fiscal health into the ground. With local fiscal insolvency hastened by the 1873 financial collapse (Horton 2003, 75), Congress took the opportunity to revert control over the city's governance to members of the federal government. Congressional interference definitively revoked municipal self-determination in 1878. For the next century, presidentially appointed city commissioners and the House Committee on the District of Columbia acted as gatekeepers and managed access to decision makers and resources (Harris 2010). The rhetoric that had been used to discredit the elected regime had focused on the dangers inherent to black suffrage, and discourses to restrict suffrage, especially by property ownership, persisted over time, creating a linkage between efficient governance and the development of an orderly city. In 1895, the *Evening Star*, a leading local newspaper, hailed "the city's freedom from noisy local politics, and its rapid improvement under the present system" and the "purity of administration of municipal affairs" (Noyes 1895). In this vein, the *Evening Star* additionally observed that the aforementioned "rapid improvement" spoke against undermining these gains "for a sham in the form of suffrage" unless perhaps suffrage at the municipal level were "restricted by property" (Noyes 1895). Moreover, the media and other power-brokers apparently tied this "progressive" governance regime to the notion that municipal democracy could only be "restored" if D.C. could be established as a white space (Asch and Musgrove 2017, 176).

By 1897, D.C. was "a representative aristocracy" in which business elites and white property owners through local citizens associations gained access to the power structure (Asch and Musgrove 2017, 419). C. Meriwether, an analyst writing in this period, deemed this appropriate, given that the city was "a resort for the idle and shiftless, a paradise for negroes, Mecca for tourists [and] at the same time a growing center of fashion and culture" (Meriwether 1897, 415). He characterized D.C. as "really a big government reservation" and as a place where a multitude of inhabitants, visitors, and political men, who had no clear roots or stake in ensuring the city's prosperity, converged.[6] Thus, it would only be fitting that those with a well-defined and focused interest, whether in local commercial ventures or in the enhancement of properties, should have a voice in securing the city's fortunes. It is not difficult to see the parallels between this late nineteenth-century rendition of public-private collaboration and Logan and Molotch's analysis of the city as a growth machine, which recognizes that urban space is an "interest-driven social construct" (1987, 4).

In the post-Reconstruction era, D.C.'s racially conservative urban regime simultaneously implemented and supported policies that advanced the interests of those groups trying to preserve the U.S. racial state (Cazenave 2011).[7] With municipal self-determination blocked, the Board of Trade in alliance with local all-white citizens associations, whose membership was generally restricted to property owners, filled the political vacuum created by federal control. The Board of Trade itself was a club funded through membership dues. Commissioners were generally selected from the board, and the club in turn used its economic and political power to facilitate access to resources and to guide D.C.'s spatial development. This undemocratic governance regime, Meriwether noted, was an apt vehicle for representation: "as many of its members are actively connected with the smaller associations, it is fairly representative of the whole District," he argued. Moreover, this governance structure, he added, created "an atmosphere of hard facts and cogent reasoning" (Meriwether 1897, 418–19). The reliance on citizens associations from this perspective had banished the political "appeal to emotions" and the "soul-stirring eloquence" that undermined rational decision making and instead had delegated power to "some of the foremost men in every vocation in the city," who addressed the city's development issues "with a fullness of detail and of technical precision that would never be dared before the usual political audience" (Meriwether 1897, 418–19). Yet, this progressive, "rational" approach to governance also masked elite intentions to disempower not only the District's African American citizens but also its non-property-owning citizens.

Planning Defensible White Space

Shepherd's urban renewal efforts had laid the physical groundwork for comprehensive planning and the aesthetically oriented City Beautiful movement (Gillette 1995; Asch and Musgrove 2017). This wing of the Progressive Era movement included luminaries such as Daniel Burnham, chief architect of the 1893 "White City" at the World's Columbia Exposition in Chicago, and the immensely influential landscape architect Frederick Olmstead. But the linkages between progressive planning and the continued production of a racialized space can also be gleaned from the two visions of America presented at the Chicago World's Fair.[8] The City Beautiful, represented in the "White City" (Asch and Musgrove 2017), had its counterpart in the Midway Plaisance, a spatially segregated entertainment area where "non-white" cultures were on exhibit. This bifurcated spatial organization, as Robert Rydell (1987) illustrates, legitimized nineteenth-century racial hierarchies in the American imagination and overtly linked whiteness and "ruling class authority" (41). Moreover, the World's Fair symbolized the spatialized racism that operated both within and outside of the fair's gates, producing what Mindy Thompson Fullilove has called "the sorted-out city" (Fullilove 2013; Brooks and Rose 2013).

The story of how property markets and neighborhood spaces in D.C. were explicitly racialized is a story in which the planning profession is entangled (Gillette 1995; Freund 2007). A budding public-private alliance among planners and private interest groups, which by the 1910s included most notably the National Conference on City Planning (NCCP) and the National Association of Real Estate Boards (NAREB), manipulated the property markets of many U.S. cities and their regions beginning in the late nineteenth century and early twentieth century (Freund 2007, 51). By the 1910s, federal approval of segregation dovetailed both with late nineteenth-century progressive governance ideals and the urban "improvement" strategies spearheaded by all-white citizens associations. These strategies comprised the insertion of racially restrictive covenants on property deeds and subsequently the neighborhood-wide enforcement of these deeds (Shoenfeld and Cherkasky 2017). To actively "amplify" the effectiveness of these strategies NAREB, for example, "published numerous textbooks, pamphlets, and periodicals, warning real estate firms that racial minorities threatened property values and that neighborhoods should be racially homogenous to maintain their desirability" (Gotham 2000, 621).[9] So, while the District's planning-minded city commissioners facilitated the subdivision of outlying tracts of land according to a city grid, developers and citizens associations, politically aided by a national public-private consensus, conceived these new streetcar suburbs as defendable, homogenous enclaves.

"Progressive reformers," observes Eric Steven Yellin (2016), "demanded segregation" in multiple spheres of life, including employment in the federal government, "to make the federal government more efficient and the capital a happier, more attractive city" (Yellin 2016, 6). Enforced segregation, also in the labor market, intensified under the Wilson administration (1913–1921). Segregation was seen as a precondition "if the city was to be a model city" for the rest of the nation (Yellin 2016, 6). The confluence of these policies, economic exclusion and housing segregation, resulted in the spatial concentration of African Americans. Because their mobility was constrained, African Americans moved into sections of the city where developers in turn created a speculative profit-making market for a captive audience in desperate search for housing (Asch and Musgrove 2017). By 1948 when racially restrictive covenants finally became unenforceable (*Shelley v. Kramer*; the D.C. companion cases were *Hurd v. Hodge* and *Urciolo v. Hodge*), two-thirds of the African American population lived within a two-and-a-quarter-mile radius surrounding the city's monumental core (Manning 1998, 333).[10]

D.C.'s black communities nevertheless produced flourishing economic and social spaces in spite of formidable barriers. By the early twentieth century, D.C. had the "largest [African American] middle class in the country," and black-owned businesses proliferated in neighborhoods near the urban core (Perl 1999). The most prominent of these neighborhoods were Shaw and LeDroit Park, near Howard University. Another area, Southwest, became an infamous example of the urban renewal project of the 1950s (Hyra 2017).[11] Segregation, however, forced local businesses and local leaders to harness resources from within the community and to develop protective strategies to prevent exploitation by outside investment interests (Crew 2003). Economic boycotts, pickets, and intentional public gatherings were necessary to create what Lefebvre (2011) calls "spaces of representation," generating also alternative urban "lifeworlds," including economic, cultural, social, and political organizations (Forester 1993, 4), in defiance of the dominant white power structure. The menace of displacement, however, continually threatened these lifeworlds.[12] Consequently, values of self-reliance, as Sigmund C. Shipp (1996) notes, resonated with diverse African American intellectual traditions: they can be found in Booker T. Washington's model of individual advancement and business entrepreneurship, Marcus Garvey's "cooperative or collective" economic development paradigm "to bring self-sufficiency to black communities" (88), and in W. E. B. Dubois's conceptualization of "black self-determination" and "group solidarity" (89).[13]

Producing Middle-Class Space

As the country sank into economic depression in 1929, D.C. was still governed through the congressional committee structure, and the city served as a laboratory for the increasingly direct federal incursion into central city redevelopment planning. Beginning in the 1930s, federal policies, tailored to pull the country out of the Great Depression, not only helped revive the real estate and building industries but also expanded wealth-creation possibilities for working-class whites (Jackson 1987). Thus, even in the environment of the New Deal, which promised to lift millions out of poverty and into the middle class, prevailing racial regimes continued to block paths to upward mobility for the majority of black residents in D.C. (Asch and Musgrove 2017; Gillette 1995). New Deal (1933–1940) and post–World War II policies shaped the fate of D.C. and its metropolitan region. With the creation of the Home Owners' Loan Corporation (HOLC) in 1933 and the 1934 Federal Housing Act, which authorized the Federal Housing Administration (FHA), the federal government simultaneously backed homeownership in suburban areas and made reinvestment in most central city neighborhoods difficult, if not impossible (Jackson 1987).

The *Underwriting Manual* created by the FHA in the 1930s classified neighborhoods to systematize and standardize their mortgage guarantee programs and private lending practices. Underwriters, using this manual, deployed racial variables, including the existence of restrictive covenants on properties, to assess the risk of loans. Suburban areas were generally outlined in blue or green on property appraisal maps and designated as great investment areas to produce new capital assets for an outward expanding "white" population. Conversely, many central city areas, particularly African American and other poor, ethnic, working-class neighborhoods were colored red—that is, they were "redlined" and deemed "hazardous," high-risk investment areas; hardly any loans flowed to people in these neighborhoods, commencing a cycle of terrible disinvestment and decline.[14]

The FHA, through its underwriting standards, initially socialized potential white homebuyers to use a racial lens when choosing a home and neighborhood and eventually normalized this process as an economic transaction and investment decision (Freund 2007). The pseudoscientific appraisal methods exploited the emotional attachments individuals develop to their homes and the location of their homes and molded this desire (Freund 2007). By 1962, a federal report by the United States Commission on Civil Rights, which compiled testimony on housing patterns in the District, made clear that these public policies, practices, and buyer perceptions all played a part in the maintenance of a segregated spatial organization in Washington, D.C., and the broader region. "Many Washington area builders," it noted, "appear to believe their reputations and profits depend upon their ability to bring about cultural and racial similarity in new developments" (U.S. Commission on Civil Rights 1962, 10). It cited a witness who declared that the "wall of prejudice is hardest to break down [in housing]. Here the defenses of custom are most difficult to breach" (9).

At this time, real estate professionals, planners, and policy makers as well as the media increasingly mobilized ideas, such as individual freedom of choice and expression of consumer preferences, to explain the self-segregation of residents as a natural economic "sorting" process (Downs 1977). Resulting urban policies and real estate industry practices, as the testimony recorded by the U.S. Civil Rights Commission in 1962 illustrated, successfully reinforced the belief in the link between first white and then middle-class homeownership, place aesthetics, and responsible citizenship (Freund 2007; McCabe 2016). While this narrative binding together property ownership and citizenship began to eschew overtly racial language, by now the "suburbanite's most personal family situation," as one witness observed, was "affected"; at the same time, it had "not been brought home to the privileged white suburbanite that this [the resulting discrimination] should concern him [sic] as a moral issue" (U.S. Commission on Civil Rights 1962, 9). A statement by Riggs Bank, a family bank and a prominent powerbroker in Washington, D.C., also cited in the 1962 report, encapsulated a shifting rationale from overt racial discrimination to a question of consumer choice: "People have moved to the suburbs so that they could live with the people that they want to live with, and if we're going to have integrated housing out there, they'll move farther out. Is there no end to it? I mean, don't we have the freedom of living where we want to and whom we want to live with?" (5). Whites, he implied, should simply be able to exercise the freedom to choose according to their residential preferences by "voting with their feet," even if this meant choosing all-white, homogenous suburban districts (Oates 2006).

A majority of white Americans had by this time secluded themselves in suburban jurisdictions beyond city boundaries and sought consumption, entertainment and socializing opportunities in a new urban formation, the suburban mall. To help engender a new lifestyle, developers, such as James Rouse, invented "special features," such as "soft music, nurseries, fireworks, band concerts and square dances, [and] fashion shows" (Gillette 2012, 79), which aimed to transform the retail center into what Ray Oldenburg might call a "third place" for the suburbs, in this case a stage-managed social place between home and work (Oldenburg 1999). The "color-blind" storyline to explain the possibility of this lifestyle produced a new sense of middle-class privilege. At the same time, discomfort with place-based racial and class-based diversity persisted (Bonilla Silva 2010).[15]

Federal Urban Policy and Urban Renewal

While New Deal policies through newly flexible mortgage products along with federal loan guarantees had made accessible a new nonurban or anti-urban lifestyle in the suburbs, underwriting criteria developed to guide "prudent" investment methodically devalued large swaths of the older urban built environment in central cities (Jackson 1987, 94). In this context, urban renewal in the District, which was the result of both local and national forces, sought both to stem decline and to revalorize the central city. The 1934 Federal Housing Act, the 1949 Housing Act, and later the 1954 Omnibus Housing Act, in particular, authorized "slum clearing" and "urban renewal" inside its boundaries, while the 1956 Highway Act subsidized highway construction, facilitating the ever outward migration of people and jobs. The enactment of the 1934 Alley Dwelling Act and the creation of the first local housing authority in 1937 served as precursors to the enactment of the Housing Act of 1949 and the creation of the D.C. Redevelopment Land Agency (RLA), a quasi-public entity to oversee redevelopment projects.

By this time, the 1948 court decision to render restrictive covenants unenforceable had generated anxiety among D.C.'s white homeowners. Many white residents were fleeing city neighborhoods. They crossed into the new real estate frontier, D.C.'s suburbs. The 1954 Supreme Court decision to desegregate public schools intensified this out-migration. Additionally, deliberate actions by real estate brokers to scare white homeowners continued to hasten white flight (Shoenfeld and Cherkasky 2017). Population figures demonstrate the exodus of white residents from D.C. In 1950, D.C.'s population as a whole peaked at 802,178. At the time, African Americans constituted 35 percent (280,803) of the residents, and whites 65 percent (517,865). D.C. became the first "Chocolate City" (majority black city) in 1957. Although the 1960 census confirmed that D.C.'s population had dropped to 763,956, blacks now numbered 411,737 (54 percent), while whites accounted for only 345,263 (45 percent). The map of the 1960 census in figure 1 also quite clearly illustrates D.C.'s segregated landscape at the time and indicates that majority black neighborhoods disprorportionally became targets of urban renewal efforts.

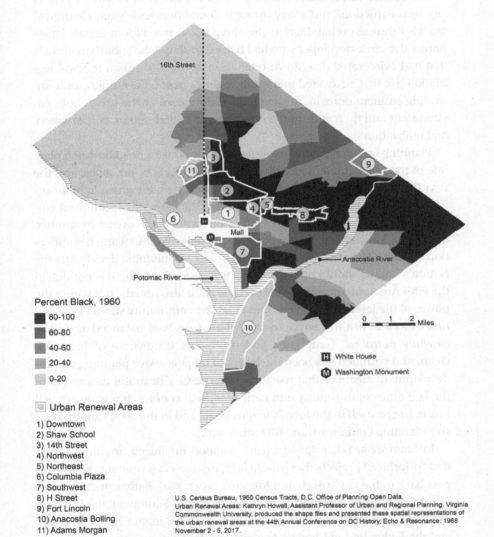

Percent Black, 1960

- 80-100
- 60-80
- 40-60
- 20-40
- 0-20

Urban Renewal Areas

1) Downtown
2) Shaw School
3) 14th Street
4) Northwest
5) Northeast
6) Columbia Plaza
7) Southwest
8) H Street
9) Fort Lincoln
10) Anacostia Bolling
11) Adams Morgan

16th Street

Mall

Anacostia River

Potomac River

0 1 2 Miles

H White House
M Washington Monument

U.S. Census Bureau, 1960 Census Tracts, D.C. Office of Planning Open Data.
Urban Renewal Areas: Kathryn Howell, Assistant Professor of Urban and Regional Planning, Virginia
Commonwealth University, produced the shape files and presented these spatial representations of
the urban renewal areas at the 44th Annual Conference on DC History, Echo & Resonance: 1968
November 2 - 5, 2017.

FIGURE 1. Percent Black Population 1960 with Urban Renewal Areas

Meanwhile "business-mayoral coalitions" with direct investment interests in central cities "maneuvered the 1954 Housing Act to further central city reconstruction," not solely through demolition and "slum clearance" but also through rehabilitation (Isenberg 2004, 170; Bloom 2004). James Rouse, the same developer who had helped to shape the suburban lifestyle that had eviscerated downtown retail, also influenced urban renewal legislation. He first advocated that municipalities needed to employ tools, including eminent domain, to clear land and modernize the urban built environment and then endorsed a combination of demolition, conservation, and renovation.

Planning was already underway for D.C.'s Southwest neighborhood plan, one of the most emblematic urban renewal projects of the 1950s, and the 1954 *Berman v. Parker* Supreme Court decision gave the green light for urban renewal to move forward. Significantly, the case fully legitimized eminent domain and the transfer of land from one private owner to another, not just for housing but also for commercial redevelopment and beautification. It read: "If those who govern the District of Columbia decide that the Nation's Capital should be beautiful as well as sanitary, there is nothing in the Fifth Amendment that stands in the way." It also noted: "It is within the power of the legislature to determine that the community should be *beautiful* as well as healthy, spacious as well as *clean*, well-balanced as well as *carefully patrolled*" (emphases added)."[16] This triumvirate of beautiful, clean, and patrolled has been the leitmotif for successive planning and redevelopment alliances that reach back to the City Beautiful movement of the late nineteenth century and early twentieth century. It also, as we will see, reasserts itself in the 1998 "Citizens Plan" and in the 2004 Comprehensive Planning Framework and BID urbanism.

In Southwest, D.C.'s "pro-growth" coalition organized around a vision that "prioritized projects that [would lure] middle-class residents and shoppers back to the city" (Asch and Musgrove 2017, 320). Rather than focus on housing for those residents living in the "blighted" Southwest, the RLA and its allies, including the Committee of 100, the Washington Board of Trade, and the Federation of Citizens Associations, lent active support to the idea that the project should create the "opportunity for persons . . . who prefer the amenities of . . . a highly convenient and attractive location to a long commuter's journey to a larger suburb" to move back to the city (Gillette 1995, 163). The RLA, indeed, expressed hopes of wedding suburban sensibilities to urban amenities. "Southwest offered a particularly attractive site for this type of urban renewal as its location—right next to the Capitol and the central business district on the north and the waterfront on the south—could be highly desirable to would-be suburban commuters" (Rusello Ammon 2004, 18). To support their vision, urban renewal proponents demanded stipulations that would allow the use of FHA guarantees to facilitate the provision of the kind of landscaping and "amenities" middle-class residents might demand (Russello Ammon 2004, 3). The urban renewal regime of the 1950s, which took the form of a federal-local and public-private growth coalition, sought to draw a tax base back into the city by clearly appealing to suburbanites. The existing residents and businesses mattered little: place mattered, as would again be the case in 1998 (Monteilh and Weiss 1998).

At the time, the Southwest neighborhood was 76 percent black. Even the RLA described it as having a "high level of residential stability" despite the prevailing discourse of blight (Gillette 1995, 161). Rather than use rehabilitation as a tool to prevent widespread displacement, however, the local regime still authorized the leveling of existing residences. While local officials initially argued for the inclusion of low-income housing and mitigation of displacement, threats that the project would lose national funding foreclosed rehabilitation of the existing housing stock (Russello Ammon 2004). The discourse of blight removal and urban rebirth triumphed, and despite opposition from African American civic associations, the vast majority (99 percent) of the Southwest renewal area was razed, making room for largely upper-income housing; apparently only very few, namely 310, of the 5,900 units were affordable units (Pritchett 2003). And so the neighborhood's "voice was lost," writes Zachary Schrag, and "by 1965 the renewal area was 88 percent white" (Schrag 2014, 23).

The 1954 Housing Act had also opened up new opportunities, not just for downtown commercial redevelopment, but also for a more extensive and ostensibly more finely tuned urban renewal (Gillette 1999). The city's 1950 Comprehensive Plan and required "workable plan," *No Slums in Ten Years*, which James Rouse coauthored with Nathaniel Keith in 1955, presented a scheme for the transformation of Washington, D.C., not just for "blighted" areas in the neighborhoods surrounding the monumental core but also beyond (Gillette 1999). These plans, which were obligatory for federal urban renewal funding, envisioned extensive highway construction within District lines, principally through predominately black neighborhoods in the Southwest and Southeast of the city but also through the majority-white neighborhoods in the city's Northwest quadrant. When urban renewal and highway construction threatened to touch their own residential districts, the Committee of 100, along with other preservation-minded prominent white residents, began to organize to oppose urban renewal (McGovern 1998). The unanimous outcry and condemnation helped stem the tide and finally halted large-scale demolition.

A dual dynamic leading to displacement had already been underway. Demolition, as noted, had razed Southwest, and restoration was transforming Georgetown, a neighborhood in the city's Northwest quadrant. By the 1940s, early historic preservation and reinvestment efforts in Georgetown were beginning to catalyze a first wave of gentrification (Asch and Musgrove 2015, 2017; Gale 1987). According to Michael deHaven Newsom, real estate brokers had "recognized that the historically significant origins of Georgetown could, upon rehabilitation of the area, attract new white residents willing to pay handsomely for an association with history" (Newsom 1971, 23). The Georgetown experience illustrated the efficacy of less invasive private reinvestment when supported through public policy, such as the "Old Georgetown Act" of 1950, which provided historic preservation designation to the area. The record shows that citizens associations and private developers played a key role in this revival and consequently the displacement of the black population from Georgetown (Asch and Musgrove 2015; Lesko, Babb, and Gibbs 2016). The gentrification of Georgetown demonstrated that deteriorating inner-city neighborhoods could become zones of reinvestment. Depending on who evoked Georgetown, this paradigm entered the city's placemaking narratives, signifying either an aspiration or an unwanted transformation.

From Urban Renewal to Advocacy Planning

By the 1960s, opposition to urban renewal precipitated a foundational crisis for rational comprehensive planning, a model that held that experts, such as government officials, planners, and architects (or, for that matter, business elites), were most equipped to envision urban futures and lead urban redevelopment. The brewing urban crisis necessitated new responses on the national, state, municipal, and local levels. The Ford Foundation's Gray Areas program, initiated in 1961 under the leadership of national business elites, funded urban demonstration projects in several cities; these also informed the urban policies of President Johnson's administration (1963–1969) and "helped to mediate an intellectual and policy shift away from the bricks and mortar concern of early urban renewal and toward a human face of the urban crisis, partly in response to growing community-based opposition" (O'Connor 1996, 588). In D.C., as in other cities, organizing by civil rights leaders and neighborhood activists began to compel a shift in planning paradigms, finally ushering in an era of advocacy planning (Davidoff 1965), founded on the principles of participation and empowerment (Arnstein 1969).

Two neighborhoods designated as urban renewal planning areas, Adams Morgan (1958–1962) and Shaw (1959–1969), became examples where residents rejected top-down proposals, such as those used in Southwest D.C. In both neighborhoods, indeed across the country, the new, insurgent planning ethos was gaining a foothold even among planners (Davidoff 1965). Moreover, activists in both neighborhoods insisted that renewal plans in contrast to the Georgetown private reinvestment and Southwest urban renewal models should focus on people first, then on place.[17] In an effort to diffuse neighborhood tensions, Johnson's programs introduced the concept of institutionalized local-level participation into national urban policy, an innovation Shaw activists used to their advantage (Halpern 1995, 117). The Equal Economic Opportunities Act of 1964 officially incorporated the acknowledgment that poverty was in part the result of "a community's lack of political effectiveness" and required community participation in local planning and social service provisions (Goldfield 2011, 398). And the Model Cities projects, funded through the newly created Department of Housing and Urban Development (1965), channeled resources to local organizations, including territorially based community development corporations (CDCs), paving the way for their subsequent political incorporation into local regimes (Halpern 1995, 118).

In Shaw, with Southwest as the cautionary tale, Reverend Walter Fauntroy, a well-known civil rights leader active in the Southern Christian Leadership Conference (SCLC), studied the area carefully to develop a neighborhood plan and built a coalition of 150 local organizations to "unite" Shaw (Gillette 1995, 175). The "umbrella organization," the Model Inner City Community Development Organization (MICCO), incorporated in 1965, led the efforts to coordinate a different kind of urban renewal planning under the Model Cities program. According to Reginald Wilbert Griffith, "MICCO's principal technical staff person" at the time, the organization wanted to integrate as many voices as possible in the planning and execution process whereby "Shaw was to be renewed in a fashion, which would allow the people living there a choice of new and rehabilitated housing" (1969, 26). But history tragically interceded in bringing the plan to full fruition.

On April 4, 1968, the day of the assassination of Dr. Martin Luther King Jr., D.C. burned. The 1968 "rebellion" or "riot" followed on the heels of Watts (1965) in Los Angeles and insurrections in other major cities, including Detroit, Michigan, and Newark, New Jersey. To some extent, Johnson administration officials were surprised by the riots in Washington, D.C. (Gillette 1995). Johnson, recognizing the changing demographics of the city, had appointed Walter Washington, a former official of the Alley Dwelling Authority and New York City Housing Authority, as the first black mayor in 1967 (Gillette 1995). At the federal level, policies were also being enacted to expand both political rights and economic opportunities, and federal officials had attempted to avert violence through the funding of targeted programs.

During the months leading up to the riots, Marion Barry, a civil rights activist who had come to Washington to lead the Student Nonviolent Coordinating Committee (SNCC), launched himself onto D.C.'s political stage (Jaffe and Sherwood 2014). Barry had "a sharp mind" and excelled at "populist political organizing" (Gillette 1995, 191). And in 1967 with the help of federal officials, particularly Labor Secretary Willard Wirtz, Barry and associates organized Pride, Inc., a program designed to incorporate young African American men in neighborhood-building programs. In line with the Johnson administration's approach, the organization served the purpose of neighborhood action and empowerment, educating residents about building regulations and tenant rights, for example.

But fury in response to a legacy of injustices wrought by the U.S. national racial state (Cazenave 2011) in alliance with an undemocratic urban regime boiled over in 1968 (Asch and Musgrove 2017, 334). By the evening following King's assassination large tracts of downtown and the formerly vibrant African American commercial and residential areas lay smoldering, the fires "consuming 14th Street NW, U Street NW, H Street NE, 7th Street NW, downtown areas, and parts of what is now Historic Anacostia" (J. Muller 2011). The long history of economic, social, and political policies, ostensibly to produce a capital worthy of admiration and reflective of the country's democratic ideals, had fallen victim to the concept of a City Beautiful built on an exclusionary social order. The conservative racial regime (Fauntroy 2003) had instead produced a "city [and region] divided" (Pratt 2011). The city's scarred physical landscape served as a persistent reminder of the failures of this regime until the turn of the twenty-first century: BID urbanism has since sutured many of the physical injuries, but it has exacted new rounds of dislocation and displacement.

"Chocolate City," an Elusive Dreamscape

In 1973, five years after the riots, D.C. achieved home rule, albeit limited. The attainment of this home rule was bittersweet. Its terms hobbled the municipal government's revenue-raising ability. The most damaging regulations became the prohibition on collecting income tax from commuters earning salaries in D.C. and the inability to tax approximately 42 percent of the properties within its boundaries allocated to the federal government, nonprofits, and international ambassadorial properties (O'Cleireacain and Rivlin 2001; O'Cleireacain 1997).[18] Additionally, Congress maintained oversight over the budget as well as the review of local legislation, thereby symbolically placing it under congressional tutelage and strategically limiting the city's political independence. At the same time, D.C. residents could elect their municipal government. Activists continued to advocate for more local control, including for "elected neighborhood legislative councils and neighborhood executives" (S. Smith [2006] 2016). D.C. journalist and activist Sam Smith explained the mood. "Back then," he wrote, "you proposed all sorts of new ideas and just talking about them made you feel hopeful . . . We tend to forget this now, but back then, decentralization and community power were important progressive ideas" ([2006] 2016). Home rule did create locally elected Advisory Neighborhood Commissions (ANCs) in 1974 to decentralize power to the neighborhood level, but these organizations' capacity to provide a venue through which to effectively participate in the day-to-day neighborhood planning lacked substance.

Nationally, conservative policy advocates were already supporting the development of strategies that would inhibit broad-based, neighborhood power in urban governance. The Nixon administration (1969–1974) transformed the community development empowerment focus, characteristic of some of the War on Poverty programs, into a new local development paradigm. The Housing and Community Development Act of 1974, which devolved responsibility for many federal urban programs to the state and local levels, funded these through new Community Development Block Grants (CDBGs). This mechanism integrated community-based organizations, such as community development corporations (CDCs), into a complex funding hierarchy and incentivized or compelled organizations, many of which had activist roots, to align their work with federal, state, and municipal policy priorities (Vidal 1996). These organizations increasingly faced the reality that they also had to leverage funding from philanthropic sources, creating an entrepreneurial imperative and redirecting CDCs to work as "promoters of capitalism [rather than] community developers" (Halpern 1995, 138). In fact, the pursuit of self-reliance under the CDC model created long-term dependencies both on the patronage of local political regimes and philanthropic largesse (Cummings 2001).

Still, for many, D.C.—dubbed "Chocolate City" (CC) in the 1975 song —became, in the words of Kenneth Carroll, "a metaphorical utopia where black folk's majority status was translated into an assertion of self-consciousness, self-determination and self-confidence" (Carroll 1998). And indeed, Mayor Marion Barry's election in 1978 marked a dramatic shift in the political regime of the city. Historian Frederick F. Siegel has described the riots and the electoral victory of Barry as a turning point in the city's history: the installation of an urban regime characterized by a "mix of black nationalism and economic leftism" that became riddled by divisive racial politics and corruption (Siegel 1997, 76–77). Siegel's is perhaps a reasonable reaction given the patronage networks that indeed developed during the successive Barry administrations. But this view forgets the political patronage partnerships that ruled D.C. prior to 1973 and blames the decline of D.C. largely on the misguided governance of Barry and his political machine (Hyra 2017). It also sidelines the recognition that D.C. and its neighborhoods had already been shaped by the palimpsest of racialized property markets as well as national urban policies and their local expressions in its urban landscape (Freund 2007; Rothstein 2017): residential segregation, suburbanization, disinvestment, and a limited form of home rule.

Political scientist Adolph L. Reed explains Barry's ascent and challenges differently: "The regime forms and legitimizes itself (that is, establishes its credibility as a contender for power, builds the allegiance required for winning office and governing, and articulates its policy agenda) in a local political culture and system dominated hegemonically by the imperatives of the very 'growth machine' that is the engine of black marginalization" (Reed 1999, 99). This view recognizes that Mayor Barry inherited a city crippled by its particular history and by the national political culture and the urban policies it had spawned. Fauntroy (2003) in his assessment of D.C. governance history adds: "Corruption, inefficiency and crime were among the watchwords of the day used by members [of Congress] to support their contention that the District was not ready for home rule" (51). Thus, white powerbrokers, including business interests, who were still operating in largely segregated spheres, kept alive old storylines that reached back to the usurpation of democracy in the nineteenth century (Fauntroy 2003).[19] Most crucially, Fauntroy agrees that the "deficiencies" of the home rule act "severely undercut the ability of the city to protect itself against poor fiscal times" (57).

The Barry regime, accordingly, moved to create a "pro-growth" downtown coalition of its own, but also one that sought to carve out an alternative path, even within the dominant U.S. racial state that had set the terms in which D.C.'s nascent urban regime could operate (Cazenave 2011). Like most mayors, he sought linkages with the white power structure, courting downtown commercial interests and developers (Jaffe and Sherwood 2014; McGovern 1998). Mayor Barry's particular style in managing the "growth machine" nonetheless was marked by the individual, tight control he sought to exert over the process of downtown development to exact benefits for his electoral constituents as well (Jaffe and Sherwood 2014; Barras 1998). His administration's "linkage" policies "granted zoning variances worth millions of dollars to downtown developers, who according to a *Washington Post* article in 1991, agreed in return to pump money into low-cost housing and social services in other parts of town" (Abramowitz 1991). Additionally, *Washington Post* columnist Courtland Milloy reminded readers in 2014, "Barry's hand in growing the black middle class" represents "a monumental achievement, but one that is rarely acknowledged because of the controversial way that he did it" (Milloy 2014).

Barry also strengthened minority business contracting requirements through a 1984 "First Source" hiring law to support local entrepreneurs through government largesse and opened up the D.C. bureaucracy to make it "possible for more black people to get jobs in D.C. government—and win promotions for jobs well done" (Milloy 2014). By 1989, when the Supreme Court curtailed these kinds of affirmative action programs in *City of Richmond v. J. A. Croson Co.*, "the amount of D.C. government business awarded [to] minority firms [had] increased from five percent to about 40 percent" (C. H. Davis and Jackson 1990, 74). In this manner, Barry sought to wed, albeit imperfectly, downtown development to equity goals. Thus, an alternative reading of his mayoralty might be that Barry's policies, not just his increasingly erratic, brash, and flawed behavior, led to his political demise. Through these and other policies, he tried to reconcile increasingly contradictory goals in times of federal austerity and animosity (Fauntroy 2003).

Mayor Barry's policies were anathematic to the Republican establishment. A conservative backlash had been brewing since the Johnson administration's War on Poverty programs, and even dating back to the earlier days of urban renewal. In 1954, business elites, resenting the diversion of resources to inner-city neighborhoods, had organized to found the International Downtown Executives Association (IDEA) in Chicago (in 1985 it became the International Downtown Association or IDA). In a retrospective of the organization's history, both suburbanization and the "social movements" of the 1960s were cited as detrimental factors threatening urban downtown business districts (Feehan, Gomez, and Andreski 2005). In response, the IDEA's mission was to work out "a long-term strategy for downtown revitalization." This had included lobbying the federal government, and during the Nixon administration it worked "to start a dialogue on inner cities" and, specifically, "a relationship with the Department of Housing and Urban Development (HUD) and Members of Congress" (Feehan, Gomez, and Andreski 2005).

At the time, economists such as Anthony Downs, who viewed patterns of decline and abandonment in the central cities—that is, the regional core—as an inefficient outcome of suburbanization, influenced the administration's urban policy development (Metzger 2000, 13). Downs, however, also developed a "law of dominance," which held "that middle-class whites would support integration only if they remained in the numerical majority and maintained 'cultural dominance'" in urban neighborhoods (14). This notion, incorporated in the Housing and Community Development Act of 1974, "called for the spatial deconcentration of housing opportunities for persons of lower income and the revitalization of deteriorating or deteriorated neighborhoods to attract persons of higher income" (Metzger 2000, 19).[20] This call for class-based integration of neighborhoods, in which middle-class or "bourgeois" (Monti 1999) norms would predominate, set the stage, not only for the IDA's work with BIDs to carve out safe and clean districts in an otherwise struggling, "dangerous" inner city, but also for the HOPE VI razing of public housing to make room for mixed-income developments (Steinberg 2010).

By the 1980s, Mayor Barry's regime had to contend with a sea change in urban policy framed by national discourses, wherein (once again) racialized stereotypes were also prominently used to legitimize cutbacks in public sector spending on welfare and housing (Spence 2015). During this time, Congress and the Reagan administration enacted sharp cuts in aid to urban areas while the courts redefined affirmative action programs, such as D.C.'s successful minority contracting program. Legal scholar Scott Cummings argues, moreover, that "in addition to curtailed social programs

and heightened economic insecurity for the poor, one of the main legacies of the Bush/Reagan years was the increasing importance of market-
oriented . . . local revitalization efforts" (Cummings 2001, 425). Community development corporations—such as Manna (1982), the Columbia
Heights CDC (1984), and the Congress Heights Community Training and
Development Corporation (1988), which worked East of the River, Anacostia, Congress Heights, and Southeast D.C.—became incorporated into the
paradigm, first as affordable housing developers and then providing commercial development and revitalization. This evolution also paved the way
for BIDs, which represented the culmination of this shift toward local incorporation and entrepreneurialism. The BID institutional formation, especially the ability to levy assessments, was to sever dependence on outside
funding while empowering property-based interests in decision making regarding local revitalization.

By the late 1980s, it was clear that D.C. was heading toward fiscal insolvency, all but guaranteed by its limited fiscal capacity, which had been created in large part by home rule regulations, the federal retreat from cities,
and finally the 1987 economic crash. In the two decades from 1950 to 1970
the population as well as the geographic area of the metropolitan statistical
area (MSA) had tripled (Manning 1998, 336), but the position of the central
city vis-à-vis the suburbs had declined significantly, both in terms of population numbers and in terms of the changing landscape of jobs (O'Cleireacain 1997). By 1990 the majority of jobs were located in the suburban area;
64 percent of jobs within the MSA were located outside of the District of Columbia (Manning 1998, 343). Adding insult to injury, over two-thirds of the
jobs within the District were held by non-District residents (Shapiro and
Bowers 2003, Manning 1998). Additionally, the entire city had been ideologically branded as black, urban, and dangerous (Modan 2007). At the same
time, Barry's administration and regime had become increasingly discred-
ited as a corrupt political machine, and incredibly in January 1990, he was
arrested on drug charges (Hyra 2017, 37; Siegel 1997).

The "Other" (Immigrant) City

As the seat of the federal government, Washington, D.C., has always also
been the host of foreign embassies and international institutions, including
post–World War II institutions, such as the World Bank, the International
Monetary Fund (IMF), and Inter-American Development Bank, which occupied buildings in the city's "old" and "new" downtown districts. The in-

flux of international professionals also supported the incipient revitalization and gentrification of selective central city neighborhoods, particularly
the Dupont Circle area and the surrounding neighborhoods situated not far
from Georgetown (Gale 1987). But as Cold War policies wreaked havoc in
countries across the globe, Central American refugees and other immigrant
groups also increasingly sought refuge and a better future in lower-cost,
centrally located neighborhoods, especially in Adams Morgan and Mount
Pleasant beginning in the late 1970s and early 1980s (Asch and Musgrove
2017).

In D.C., these Latinx immigrants, which were the most visible and numerous in Adams Morgan and Mount Pleasant, found little political space
to insert themselves into the municipal power structures (Asch and Musgrove 2017). Many refugees from Central American countries, moreover,
were undocumented. Thus, their economic situation as a group was defined
by precariousness, intensified by the 1990 recession. The failure of the D.C.
government to respond to the specific needs of this population exaggerated
intra-neighborhood and interracial competition and conflicts (Asch and
Musgrove 2017).

By 1990, D.C. was notoriously labeled the murder capital of the United
States, many of its African American neighborhoods were ravaged by the
crack epidemic and violence, and the downtown boom of the 1980s had
collapsed. In 1991, D.C. inaugurated Sharon Pratt Dixon, its first new mayor
since Barry's election in the 1970s. Where D.C. for many exemplified the
stark segregation between black and white populations associated with
many U.S. cities, 1991 shone a spotlight on the difficult living and livelihood
conditions experienced by immigrants, particularly recent Central American refugees, in the shadows of the White House. During the 1980s the demographic composition of D.C. had begun to alter more significantly as
international immigrants, many fleeing war, increasingly moved into neighborhoods only a walk up 16th Street NW from the seat of national power.

In May 1991, the Mount Pleasant "riot" erupted after the shooting of Daniel Enrique Gomez, who had only recently come to D.C. Images of burn-
ing storefronts and helicopters hovering over the commercial corridors
in Mount Pleasant, less so in Adams Morgan, flickered across television
screens in the U.S. and abroad. It seemed D.C. had reached a point of no
return. But as Mayor Pratt Dixon later noted, D.C. was "a city on the cusp
of growth," a city ready to take off (Pratt 2011). It would require a new governance regime, however, to guide this growth.

CHAPTER 3

The Push for BIDs

Today BIDs are a global phenomenon. But, in the early 1990s, business improvement districts and the placemaking urbanism they have come to epitomize were still "a trend to watch" (Hood 1996). Those years marked a period of deep crisis for the District of Columbia. Recognizing the looming catastrophe, Mayor Barry had commissioned a study to examine the roots of the city's financial woes. Published in 1990, the resulting "Rivlin Commission" report concluded, as did later studies, that this crisis and its symptomatic fiscal difficulties were due in large part to structural constraints having to do with D.C.'s position as the nation's capital (D.C. Commission on Budget and Financial Priorities 1990). But it would take rescinding the city's home rule, already characterized by limited municipal self-determination, to finally implement some of this report's suggestions and to usher in a new period of strategic planning to guide Washington, D.C.'s economic resurgence.

Until the takeover of the city by a Financial Control Board in April 1995 created the conditions to install a new urban regime in the nation's capital (Congress 1995), it was not clear that the City Council would sanction BIDs. In retrospect, however, it comes as no surprise that BID urbanism took hold. Local BID supporters promised to restore the city to its rightful place as the nation's capital and promoted the idea that it could become a "world class" city (Monteilh and Weiss 1998). Nationally, business elites had been developing the governance tools for decades. In D.C., these efforts first seemed to gain momentum in 1993. This chapter traces the political process that eventually led to the establishment of BIDs in D.C. in 1997. I first discuss the vision of the "living" downtown that initially surfaced during the mayoralty of Marion Barry. It preceded and eventually informed the work of D.C. BIDs in the central city. I then trace the evolution of the BID-enabling legislative proposals through a close reading of the various bills and hearing reports between 1991 and 1997 and flesh out three interrelated themes from the discourse stakeholders employed during these deliberations: the politics of voice, the assertion of a self-help ethos, and the discourse of entrepreneurial municipal governance to reinvigorate D.C. downtown and neighborhood markets. These themes highlight how BID advocates used the tenets of public choice theory to persuade potential stakeholders, including residents, business owners, property owners, and local officials, of the model's democratic roots and of its efficacy in providing local services and addressing redevelopment challenges.

The Vision of a "Living Downtown"

In 1981, James Rouse shared a meal with reporters from *Time* magazine (Demarest, Stoler, and Grieves 1981; Graham 2016). Their reportage yielded the magazine's iconic cover of Rouse proclaiming: "Cities are fun!" (Gillette 1999). Over lunch, before the publication of the article, Rouse had apparently voiced his exasperation with the prevailing malaise pervading American cities and their suburban neighbors. "We have lived so long with grim, congested, worn-out inner cities and sprawling, cluttered outer cities that we have subconsciously come to accept them as inevitable and unavoidable. Deep down in our national heart is a lack of conviction that cities can be beautiful, humane, and truly responsive to the needs and yearnings of our people." But, he continued: "The old dream of suburbia—the house with a fence and the backyard barbecue—is fading. Young people increasingly tend to look at the suburbs as sterile and uninteresting" (Demarest, Stoler, and Grieves 1981).

This 1981 interview presaged the urban resurgence that began to seriously take hold in major U.S. cities in the mid-1990s, including New York, Philadelphia, and, eventually, Washington, D.C. Howard Gillette notes, "Rouse recognized that the features of his early shopping centers—the creation of spaces 'in which people can drift, relax, smile, contemplate, and enjoy the living, working, shopping for which they are there'—could be applied to cities" (Gillette 2012, 90–91). A "reorganization" of the central city could be achieved through coordinated public and private cooperation (Bloom

2004; Kowinski 1981). The late 1970s and early 1980s marked the (re)birth of public-private partnerships (Beauregard 1998; Lyall 1986) and the urban growth machine, in which private sector business elites would once again play a leading role in shaping and implementing policy (Molotch 1993).[1] D.C. was no exception. BIDs and BID urbanism evolved out of these trends.

The International Downtown Executive Association (IDEA), founded in 1954, worked tirelessly to redefine the position of central cities in the face of rapid suburbanization. It both focused attention on the troubles downtown retailers and property owners faced in the aftermath of the 1960s urban up- heavals and framed the "energy crisis" of the early 1970s as an opportunity to promote the advantages of downtown living (Seigel 1974). In an open letter to President Nixon, IDEA expressed its belief that urban renewal had been derailed "around 1968–1969" by "urban warfare," which "suddenly caused Washington to get all excited about the poor, the non-white, and all sorts of social and political problems" (Seigel 1974).[2] Thus, "the hearts and guts were chopped out of urban renewal and especially downtown renewal," it con- tinued. IDEA, the letter illustrates, was keenly interested in policy solutions to make possible "the preservation of a way of life in the cores for those who want to and must live in the center" (Seigel 1974). Since the 1950s, Down- town Progress (DP), an association of local business people and developers and the forerunner of what would become the D.C. Downtown Partnership in 1984, had been working with the Redevelopment Land Authority on ur- ban renewal plans (1961–1977), including a Downtown Action Plan. Down- town Progress specifically advocated for development around mass transit, establishing the essential linkage between Metro (mass transit) develop- ment and the health of retail and commercial development in downtown D.C. (Schrag 2014).

In 1978, when Marion Barry became mayor, urban renewal in its previous form was dead, however, so downtown stakeholders turned their collective advocacy activities toward the creation of new kinds of public-private part- nerships, specifically "to define the emerging concept of 'downtown man- agement'" and to find mechanisms to control downtown environments and leverage redevelopment (Feehan, Gomez, and Andreski 2005);[3] this would include BIDs and the increasing use of financing tools, such as tax incre- ment financing (TIF) (Briffault 1997, 2010).

Over the ensuing decade, D.C. interest groups, including the IDEA (which later became the IDA), allied developers, and by 1984 the newly formed Downtown Partnership, tied their policy activism to the idea of a "living downtown." In his first term (1979–1982), Mayor Barry put together a task force of experts, charged with developing strategies to "make down-town a people place" (Hilzenrath 1988).[4] This would require a two-pronged approach, a technical planning and rezoning strategy and a management or coordinating body to guide the actual development and rebrand down-town. Not surprisingly, the concept for a BID-type organization surfaced. The Greater Washington Board of Trade proposed such a public-private partnership and taxing district in 1980 (Hilzenrath 1988), and a 1982 arti-cle proclaimed: "District of Columbia officials and Washington business leaders want to create what accounts to a mini-government for downtown Washington, a public-private partnership to oversee the 660 acres between the Capitol and White House" (Knight 1982).[5] This new organization, the article continued, would be "more than a cheerleader; it would have both money and clout . . . to take action on its own."

The campaign to officially enshrine the "living downtown" in D.C.'s com-prehensive plan gained momentum in the early 1980s "with the issuance of the "Downtown D.C.: Recommendations for the Downtown Plan" by the mayor's Downtown Committee (McCarthy 2008).[6] Echoing the language of Jane Jacobs ([1961] 1992), who had described the lifeless canyons of New York City's financial district, Mayor Barry recognized the potentially deadening effects of a monotonous forest of office buildings on downtown. They "open up . . . at 9 o'clock" and "at 6:30 they close and everything is shut up and bar-ren," he warned (Lardner 1978). While downtown office development had been moving westward to the "new downtown" to what has become iden-tified as the Golden Triangle area, now the frontier was moving eastward to the languishing "old downtown," where speculative activities threatened to rapidly displace local retail (McGovern 1998; Pyatt 1985). Some developers in tune with emergent trends, such as the ones identified by Rouse and the IDEA, counseled that this momentum needed to be redirected toward im-proving the "livability" of downtown districts (McCarthy 2008).[7]

Key both to D.C.'s BID movement and the "living downtown" were the IDEA's 1978 move to the city and the leadership Richard Bradley brought to the organization in 1984; furthermore, Ellen McCarthy, his wife, took an ex-ecutive position at the D.C. Downtown Partnership.[8] According to the orga-nization's history brief, the IDEA, now renamed International Downtown Association or IDA, with the support of the Department of Housing and Ur-ban Development (HUD), had been able "to study the concept of central-ized retail management" for urban districts (Feehan, Gomez, and Andreski 2005).[9] Under Bradley's direction, the IDA subsequently became a highly effective advocacy organization to promote BIDs, not just nationally but also internationally. Now in D.C., IDA could locally promote a downtown D.C. BID, and the newly minted Downtown Partnership provided a local forum for discussion and a platform for collective advocacy focused on transforming the "old" downtown in line with the "Downtown Plan."[10]

The Barry administration's "livable city" approach proved "fairly forward looking," from the perspective of a former staff member of the Downtown Progress interviewed in 2015. The plan's recommendations focused on creating uniquely identifiable areas accessible by mass transit and characterized by a diversity of uses within each district. "They recognized one of the strengths of downtown: it had distinctive sub areas, like Chinatown and the convention center area and the retail core and the arts district," the former Downtown Partnership staff person emphasized. The D.C. Downtown Partnership in collaboration with public officials and other civic groups also sought to parlay downtown placemaking into a new growth orientation. In 1984, as the *Washington Post* noted, the Rouse Company "gambled" on this strategy, investing in the National Place development, a "100-store four-floor mall off Pennsylvania Avenue NW between 13th and 14th streets," anchored by "national chains" but predominately made up of "eateries" (Mayer 1984).

But such "forward-looking" urban design ideas did not yet sit well with some of the major developers in the office market. Consequently, the Downtown Partnership's support for zoning and management changes created internal fault lines. While some members, foreseeing the end of the office boom, sought to prepare for this eventuality, others, hoping to continue to ride the wave, were loathe to ratify changes that might impact the short-term profitability of downtown development. Among the latter, a powerful group of property owners, some of whom had built a parking (lot) empire (Bell 2015, 54, 62), which allowed them to hold on to undeveloped properties for long periods without taking losses, were adamantly opposed to zoning changes that would require housing as well as retail. The powerful Board of Trade also actively opposed the rezoning plan, especially its housing requirement, at that time. Together, these stakeholders effectively stymied early efforts by Mayor Barry's regime, including the D.C. Downtown Partnership, to redirect development or to create a corresponding downtown management structure.[11]

Additional battle lines initially obstructed the "living downtown" plans (McGovern 1998). Affordable housing advocates decried the administration's focus on downtown, arguing that many D.C. neighborhoods outside of downtown were in distress and needed resources. They also warned about a brewing affordable housing crisis as gentrification pressures were beginning to spread to neighborhoods around the city's core. These included Capitol Hill, Hill East, Logan Circle, Dupont Circle, and, to a lesser degree, Mount Pleasant, Adams Morgan, and LeDroit Park, all of which lay in close proximity to Center City, potentially forming a larger contiguous area with the already gentrified Georgetown and Foggy Bottom (Asch and Musgrove 2015; Gale 1987). Historic preservationists, in turn, wanted to secure greater restrictions to safeguard existing nineteenth-century buildings (McCarthy 2008; McGovern 1998). And although some small business owners hoped to benefit from projects, such as National Place on Pennsylvania Avenue, others organized, forming the Downtown Retail Merchants Association (McGovern 1998, 203). A *Washington Post* reporter had already identified small retailers as "an endangered species" in peril of being swallowed up by the "rising tide of downtown development" (Knight 1981), but their interests and voice seem to have gotten diluted in the struggle among the various interest groups seeking to shape downtown's future.

According to McCarthy, who served on the Downtown Partnership, it took several years of negotiations to finally develop a workable land use and zoning framework to advance the "living downtown" goals. Crucially, preservationists achieved a victory in 1984, which marked the authorization of two downtown historic districts and the passage of the Comprehensive Plan (Slacum 1984a, 1984b). Any new zoning regulations to incentivize housing would still have to be worked out, albeit within these constraints. Compromises struck to get developers on board included an agreement to allow the transfer of development rights (TDR) from historic structures to new projects to increase their development potential and a residential use requirement for any additional square footage allowable under the new zoning; the latter did not impinge on the commercial space property owners could have developed without the new zoning (McCarthy 2008). In late 1991, new zoning regulations passed, but barely.[12] And BIDs were on the horizon.

Enabling BIDs

In the early 1990s, two attempts to enact BID-enabling legislation prior to the law's passage in 1996 failed (Wolf 2006). These years were also unpropitious times for the city. The recession virtually halted development, and the idea of a "living downtown" remained an aspiration: by the time the rezoning plan passed in December 1991, "the bottom had fallen out of the commercial real estate market" (McCarthy 2008, 78). During the ensuing years of flagging investment, however, the D.C. Downtown Partnership and its allies persisted and continued to promote the idea that BIDs offered the key to restructuring both downtown and neighborhood commercial corridors. But the political winds were still not blowing favorably despite the sponsorship of two councilmembers, Jack Evans and Charlene Drew Jarvis, allied with the D.C. Downtown Partnership (Wolf 2006). Crucially, the collaboration between the two councilmembers suggested a biracial (middle-class) coalition in support of this public-private partnership. Jarvis, a veteran of the City Council, represented Ward 4 in the Northern quadrant of the city, known for its black middle- and upper-middle-class neighborhoods, and Evans, recently elected in Ward 2, represented the majority white areas of Georgetown, Foggy Bottom, and Dupont Circle as well as the new and old downtown areas. Their BID-enabling legislation bill, however, was blocked.

In December 1992, *Washington Post* business columnist Rudolph Pyatt, a proponent of BIDs, pointedly remarked: "This is not a town that likes new ideas, a Washington executive complained" (Pyatt 1992). BID legislation, "which the [Downtown] partnership drafted a year ago," Pyatt explained, "was seen as creating a stronger bond that would unite the interests of retailers, developers, bankers and others in the downtown area." After highlighting the Center City District in Philadelphia, he declared: "The D.C. Council has slept long enough on the BID legislation. It's time to wake up and smell the coffee and join progressive thinkers in other communities around the country." A follow-up article on January 11, 1993, also in the *Washington Post*, lamented the dissolution of the D.C. Downtown Partnership. "Downtown Coalition Mourned: Partnership's Demise Seen as Lost Opportunity," read the headline. In 1993 the partnership, it seems, was literally being picked apart piece by piece as various nonprofit organizations hauled off its office furniture and fax machine (Swisher 1993). Some, the article reported, "said that [the partnership] lost when it staked too much on an important gamble—the willingness of the District government to pass legislation for the BID" (Swisher 1993). In an ironic twist, opposition by "a group of Georgetown merchants" to a proposed neighborhood BID in Councilmember Evans's home turf had helped scuttle the BID legislation he had sponsored (Pyatt 1992). The reporting in 1993 indicates that the D.C. Downtown Partnership and its BID idea seemed a lost cause, but with continued strong support from the two councilmembers, its time was to come.

The Politics of Voice

How the legislation eventually came to pass is partially recorded in a series
of public hearing transcripts, which shed light on the doubts and demands
different interest groups brought to the discussion of the BID-enabling bills
and explain the various adaptations made over time. In a 2006 interview, a
D.C. government official, looking back, articulated some of the questions
roiling BID policy formation: how many property owners, business tenants, or even residents should have to agree to form the BID, after which the
rest are required to comply, was a particularly vexing issue, as was the role
these stakeholders would eventually be able to play in the district-based
governance organization.[13] Critical urban scholars, including legal scholars, at the time had homed in on these questions and elucidated the democratic deficit BIDs signified (Christopherson 1994; Davies 1997; Mallett
1994). Hearing records also illustrate that representation and voice, both in
the establishment process and in the governance of potential BID areas, remained a central concern among potential BID stakeholders.

The legislation introduced on December 17, 1991, whose failure had
spelled the temporary demise of the Downtown Partnership, provided
multiple pathways to establish a BID. It permitted property owners, a local councilmember, or the mayor to initiate a BID process. But to request a
BID, a positive petition had to be submitted to the Council by owners representing at least 51 percent of the assessed value within the BID boundaries.
Conversely, if property owners who together represented 33 percent of the
assessed value in a proposed BID district filed an objection, they could prevent its establishment.[14] In this bill, commercial tenants were to be incorporated into the BID-planning process, but it did not delineate how this was to
happen. On March 17, 1993, after the first bill had been blocked, Chairman
Wilson and Councilmembers Jarvis and Evans introduced a new bill ("Business Improvement Districts Act of 1993, B10–0186").

While the 1991 legislation had focused on the criteria of assessed value
only, potentially giving large property owners monopoly power over the decision to create (or not) a BID, the 1993 adaptation created space for small
property owners and tenant-businesses to initiate a BID process. It allowed
BID organizing to move forward if the mayor certified that at least one of
the following stakeholder groups had agreed in writing to a proposed BID's
assessment formula and its planned activities: (1) "at least a majority" of all
property owners; (2) property owners representing "at least a majority" of
the assessed value in the district; or (3) tenants "occupying at least a ma-

jority of the square footage of retail space" (Wilson, Jarvis, and Evans 1993). This iteration of the bill more fully acknowledged different groups as direct stakeholders in the creation of BIDs. Responding to some of the most strident critiques that had been levied against BIDs by small business owners and residents, especially in Georgetown and Adams Morgan (Wolf 2006), the 1993 bill also seemed to better recognize the difference between areas, such as downtown, with concentrated property ownership and existing neighborhoods with fragmented ownership patterns—that is, with multiple, smaller landlords and small business tenants.

BID critics also disputed the actual governance structure the various bills described. They questioned who would get to make decisions about a district's priorities, budget, and BID activities once it was established. The changes in the legislative proposals between 1991 and 1997 regarding the composition of BID boards of directors did not, however, expand representation and voice, which is what critics were demanding. Instead, the successive bills increasingly tilted decision-making power toward property owners and sidelined public officials, commercial tenants, and residents. A staff person with historical knowledge of the discussions told me in 2006 that some D.C. government officials in the early 1990s remained uneasy about relinquishing too much power to BIDs. The 1991 bill seems to reflect this apprehension: the mayor was to retain the power to appoint two public sector ex officio voting members to allow the public sector to maintain a stronger foothold in the BID decision-making structure. It also set aside seats for one local councilmember and one Advisory Neighborhood Commission (ANC) representative, respectively, and both were to be ex officio voting members (Jarvis and Evans 1991, 10).[15] This bill then assured residents representation and a decision-making voice through their locally elected officials; however, the 1993 bill, unlike the 1991 bill, maintained public sector representatives, but as *nonvoting* members, making their presence an advisory one and reframing it as providing expertise, in matters of public safety or transportation, for example.

In an apparent attempt to limit the influence of large property owners, both the 1991 and 1993 bills specified that no single entity or person could hold more than 20 percent of the votes on a BID board. This measure, it seems, was to serve as a safeguard against large property owners gaining an outsized voice in the district's affairs if, for example, the bylaws allowed votes to be weighted by assessed value, not numbers of owners. The legislation that finally passed in 1996 created flexibility in the allocation of votes on BID boards, but two prescriptive caveats written into the bill answered specifically to the interests of property owners. It still required the majority of board members to be owners of property, and it increased the threshold of votes that a single member could hold from 20 percent to 33⅓ percent (Council of the District of Columbia 1996). Thus, the final BID-enabling legislation weakened earlier provisions to create a more broadly representative institution wherein various stakeholder interests might have had a voting voice in the BID.

Some stakeholders, representing both small business interests and residents, adamantly opposed BIDs in the early 1990s, fearing the reprivatization of D.C.'s governance regime by insulating it from democratic processes (Wolf 2006). In a 1993 written statement to the Council, Goldie Cornelius Johnson, a self-identified small business owner of thirty years, warned against diluting democratic governance and home rule. She observed, "elected officials are the only group citizens can hold accountable" and argued that this "power should not be given or delegated to anyone who would not be accountable to anyone or anything." Furthermore, she found the legislation to be "naive, misguided and misdirected at this time in the life of our city" because "nothing should be done to harm and impede our progress in getting 'Home Rule'" (Johnson 1993). Given D.C.'s history with congressional interference, it is not surprising that for some of these District residents and small business owners, attempts to weaken democratic representation and home rule tapped into deeply held suspicions about the motivation behind these proposals (Fauntroy 2003).

By 1995 with the installation of the Fiscal Control Board, intrusion into home rule was no longer a suspicion but a fact. That year, Harvard University economist Michael Porter's seminal (and controversial) article, "The Competitive Advantage of the Inner City," had just proclaimed the "economic distress of America's inner cities . . . [to be] the most pressing issue facing the nation" (Porter 1995, 55). For some, including powerful members of Congress, Washington, D.C., in fact represented the most galling and embarrassing example of a failing city. With D.C. confronting bankruptcy, Congress stripped it of its limited home rule powers, and city councilmembers, among them a new cohort apparently more favorably inclined toward BIDs, considered enabling legislation once again.

Even then, not everyone, especially representatives of tenant small businesses and residents, was sanguine about BIDs, especially about neighborhood BIDs. They questioned the linking of decision-making voices to property ownership in matters of neighborhood development. In his testimony, the chairman of the Dupont Circle Merchant and Professional Association (DCMPA) noted the organization had previously "supported the BID concept [but] opposed the 1993 bill as drafted." He also acknowledged that "several of the concerns [had] been resolved" in the 1995 draft, yet "critical elements of the legislation had not been modified" (Dupont Circle Merchants and Professionals Association 1995). He specifically cautioned against transferring a downtown model to neighborhood corridors. "While the proposed BID board structure perhaps would be viable in a downtown business district or an area with a large volume of commercial space that is currently managed by a few property owners or commercial space management companies, it will not foster landlord / tenant harmony in most of the city's small neighborhood retail business areas," he posited. Finally, he asked for an "inclusive" neighborhood BID model. A representative of the Adams Morgan Business and Professional Association further warned that BIDs as a "new layer of bureaucracy with the D.C. government's involvement is exactly what we don't need: it will pit landlord against tenant, tenant against landlord, and tenant against tenant" (Adams Morgan Business and Professional Association 1995). This position, perceived as "contrarian" by one BID advocate I interviewed in 2006, proved prescient in the case of Adams Morgan.

The Citizens Association of Georgetown (CAG) similarly demanded a more tailored approach to neighborhood BIDs. Its representative expressed displeasure with the vague BID board structure under consideration, stating that CAG expected "at least two voting members" to be allocated to "recognized citizens associations," especially since this reflected an agreement CAG and the Georgetown Business and Professional Association had made in 1993. Instead, he noted, the legislation under consideration "in effect" treated ANC members and other community organizations as "second-class citizens, with no real voice" (Citizens Association of Georgetown 1995).

The 1995 hearing and contemporaneous newspaper articles indicated a coordinated effort to push through the legislation despite these concerns. IDA president Richard Bradley, who would come to lead the DowntownDC BID for two decades after its establishment in 1997, called for flexibility in the BID governance structure. He advised "against making the bill so specific that we end up micromanaging the BID organization" (International Downtown Association 1995). His appeal could in theory have accommodated the demands advanced by residents and commercial tenants that they be allocated voting representation on neighborhood BID boards. This focus on flexibility, however, never questioned the need to reserve a majority voice for property owners, and the final legislation did not proactively reserve voting seats for other stakeholders, such as local public officials or neighborhood residential representatives on BID boards.

The Politics of Competitive Advantage and Self-Help

Despite lingering misgivings about BIDs and calls for further revisions, by 1995 the times for BID advocates in D.C. were finally propitious. D.C.'s entrepreneurial turn, which included this shift toward a PPP district-based governance, was not an isolated one (Weaver 2016). The changing political climate and the reform of D.C.'s government under the Control Board was what political scientist Sidney Tarrow described as a "political opportunity structure" (Tarrow 2011), a confluence of events that made it ideal for BID advocates to seize the moment. Confidence in the public sector had reached rock bottom. Given the national discourse around municipal entrepreneurial governance with its emphasis on public-private partnerships and local self-reliance, business improvement districts were now framed as an imperative, not an option. Looking back, a DowntownDC BID executive involved in the political process at that time observed, "we were in such bad shape . . . things were so bad that there was a lot of pressure to try anything." The 1995 hearings reflected both an utter lack of faith in the public sector and an uncritical confidence in the ability of the private sector to pull the city out of the crisis.

The testimony indicates a consensus among business stakeholders: they needed to harness local acumen and resources to help themselves and, by extension, the city. One Georgetown advocate called BIDs "self-help at its best" (Georgetown Business and Professional Association 1995). A restaurant owner observed that the "bill will be a very important self-help initiative action, and model for community businesses" (Hunan Chinatown Restaurant 1995). BIDs, in keeping with predominant economic governance theories, were to exhibit and teach community entrepreneurialism at the neighborhood level (Cummings 2001; Brenner 2004). The BID-enabling legislation, however, proposed to introduce "club-like" power structures wherein property ownership and political influence were overtly linked. However, the self-help focus missed two shortcomings of the model: BIDs were likely to have different resource capacities, initially creating what Warner (2011) called the "Swiss Cheese effect," rich islands surrounded by poorer districts, and the preexisting resource gaps, rooted in local property markets determining BID budgets, were likely to translate into political inequality.

The IDA president hinted at these problems, in his testimony: "The Downtowns and commercial areas compete against managed environments," and "the legislation allows for a large variety of management services to be implemented—security, maintenance streetscaping, marketing and promotions, business development, transportation management, etc.—creating an opportunity for local areas to determine what services best meet the needs within their financial capabilities in order to compete more effectively" (International Downtown Association 1995). This statement tellingly underscored the inevitable resource and, by extension, power differential among BIDs.

In 1995, Porter's "competitive advantage" thesis suffused BID discussions. Additionally, the principle that government needed to redirect its energies to "assume a more effective role by supporting the private sector in new economic initiatives" (Porter 1995, 65) infused the New Public Management (NPM) movement to "reinvent government" (Osborne and Gaebler 1992) the Clinton administration (1993–2001) was spearheading (Spence 2015), and the administration was by now involved in structuring D.C.'s governance regime. Inner-city governments, such as the District of Columbia, could no longer afford to allow their potential and their fortunes to be thwarted by the unproductive "social perspective" guiding their welfare policies; rather, they had to work to create "a favorable environment for business" (Porter 1995, 67).

In D.C., as in other cities, this philosophy resonated among D.C.'s powerbrokers, including influential African American leaders (Prince 2014), thus forging an effective middle-class and business-friendly political alliance (Spence 2015). Councilmember Jarvis's policy language, for example, closely aligned with these ideas, which were circulating widely, not just nationally but also internationally (Porter 1995; Kantola and Seeck 2011).[16] Jarvis, speaking in support of BIDs, wholeheartedly endorsed these tenets: "Government is a less effective business networker, recruiter, or developer than business itself." Instead, she proffered, "when the private sector is empowered to organize itself to market and develop specific areas and receives sufficient funds to run a program, the results are remarkable" (Jarvis 1995, 3).

BID proponents additionally argued that multiple BIDs would have a much broader development impact. Sheldon Repp of the Greater Washington Chamber of Commerce, for example, argued that enabling BIDs "will cost the city government next to nothing and has the potential for benefiting the areas involved and the city as a whole" (D.C. Chamber of Commerce 1995). Not only would BIDs increase the competitive edge of individual areas, but they also would strengthen the city in the region, vis-à-vis the suburbs, to vie for and attract economic activity. A local economic development professional reasoned that in "enacting this self-help legislation, the Council will allow for the possibility that the city's commercial areas can become more competitive . . . at a time when businesses are leaving the city, consumers are shopping in suburban malls, sales are slumping and sales tax revenue is declining" (Marshall Heights Economic Development Corporation 1995). BIDs, all of this advocacy implied, would be crucial players in guiding the resurgence of Washington, D.C., through concrete services and rebranding efforts (Monteilh and Weiss 1998).

In this, D.C. could not afford to fall behind its peers but should learn from other cities. One supporter of the legislation pointedly asked: "When the District of Columbia was dubbed the 'Murder Capitol [sic] of the World' . . . New York City and New Orleans had more homicides, but you didn't hear the media nicknaming them the 'Murder Capitol [sic] of the World.' Is it because New York City and New Orleans both have BIDs, and they were able to mask the reality of life in their city through well-developed marketing campaigns that were funded by the BIDs?" (Neighborhood Development Assistance Program 1995).[17] BIDs from this perspective were necessary to construct a counternarrative to D.C.'s prevailing image even if this might obscure "reality." A number of local advocates in fact mentioned they had either visited Philadelphia and New York or had met with their representatives, and other stakeholders simply attached news stories from other cities to their statements (Council of the District of Columbia 1995; D.C. Chamber of Commerce 1995; Federal City Council 1995; Georgetown Business and Professional Association 1995; Giant Food Corporation 1995).[18] In her 1995 report to the full Council, Jarvis wrote: "Business Improvement Districts ('BIDs') exist in every major American city except the District of Columbia and Chicago. . . . D.C. has far too many documented problems in its commercial areas to ignore the successes that other cities have had with BIDs." Perhaps the Urban Land Institute's 1994 report, "Betting on BIDs," penned by BID consultant Lawrence O. Houstoun, had circulated among reporters and some of the stakeholders who testified at the hearing, because, like Jarvis, they repeatedly cited the "over 1000 BIDs" that were successfully working in locations across the country (Houstoun 1994).[19]

In December 1995, shortly after the hearings and before the Council's vote, Pyatt, whose *Washington Post* stories had long supported if not championed the creation of a downtown BID, warned: "Shelving that [1992] bill was a mistake, and any attempt to defeat the current version would be highly irresponsible. Simply put, attempts to block passage could sabotage a sincere effort to improve economic development" (Pyatt 1995). The testimony before the Council and the stories in the *Washington Post* and the *Washington Business Journal* framed the creation of BIDs as perchance the last opportunity to rescue the city (Judith Evans 1996; T. C. Hall and Lombardo 1996; Lundegaard 1996; Pyatt 1996).

On December 30, 1996, the *Washington Business Journal* ran a story drawing comparisons between Philadelphia's experience and D.C.'s plight. Facing its own deepening fiscal crisis, the story reminded readers, Philadelphia had been placed under the supervision of a "state-financial overseer" (PICA 2016), and Center City, Philadelphia's downtown BID, had initiated its operations almost contemporaneously in 1990. Philadelphia's story gave license for optimism: "While Washington appears lost in its financial abyss, it doesn't have to search far for possible solutions," the reporter proclaimed (Lundegaard 1996). The article highlighted both the participation of the private sector, which "became actively and independently involved in the city's struggles by forming the self-taxing Center City District" and the privatization of public services, spending reductions, and investments in management technologies as key ingredients to Philadelphia's success (Lundegaard 1996). Only three years after Philadelphia's flirtation with bankruptcy, the city was solvent again, showing surpluses. In 1996, Washington, D.C., would finally follow in the footsteps of pioneer cities, such as Philadelphia (Feehan, Gomez, and Andreski 2005).

The Council finally passed the Business Improvement District Act of 1996—DC LAW 11-134—and amended it again in 1997—DC L12-0026—to include the possibility of using tax increment financing (TIF) in these districts.[20] In her 1997 opening statement, Jarvis, who had just recently taken over as chairperson of the Council, observed: "We were especially careful in drafting this legislation to ensure that small neighborhood corridors could easily create and manage BIDs" (Jarvis 1997a). In response to trepidations about the model, the legislation did delineate separate processes for different types of BIDs (Council of the District of Columbia 1997). Two categories emerged: (1) BIDs to be sited in the two downtowns (the "old downtown" and the Golden Triangle area) and in planned "Central Employment Areas" (CEAs) and (2) neighborhood BIDs for commercial corridors outside of those areas. The first, BIDs for the downtown areas and Central Employment Areas, required two petitions: one signed by owners who owned at least a 51 percent interest in the assessed value of nonexempt property and another signed by owners representing at least 25 percent of individual nonexempt properties.[21] The second category, BIDs for outside the Central Employment Area, downtown, or Georgetown, stipulated that 51 percent of the affected tenants had to officially agree in writing as well.[22] In addition, owners representing 51 percent, not 25 percent, of qualifying property owners had to agree. The 51 percent of assessed value remained unchanged.

These new rules seemed to respond to testimony highlighting the fact that neighborhood commercial corridors presented distinctive micropolitical climates, property ownership patterns, and retail environments as compared to those of the downtown or new, high-density neighborhood districts, such as Mount Vernon Triangle, NoMa, and what was to become Capitol Riverfront, which were already in the planning stages. But the D.C. BID Council, an umbrella organization for BIDs, in its fact sheet, "How to Start a Business Improvement District," has made it known that "all the [neighborhood] BIDs formed to date have had the first provision [regarding commercial tenants] waived, and the last provision [number of property owners] modified to twenty-five percent rather than fifty-one percent" (D.C. BID Council 2011). Consequently, tenants especially, as the Adams Morgan case study later in the book shows, have in practice been systematically disenfranchised. Moreover, by 2015, this section of the D.C. code was repealed, which effectively signaled that D.C.'s comparatively more inclusive legislation with regard to the BID establishment process would be officially rescinded and the link between property ownership and voice definitively strengthened (Council of the District of Columbia 2015).

In the end, the legislation also kept the board structure relatively open. As noted, rather than specifying mandatory set-asides of votes for ANC members, residents, or retail tenants, the legislation left this up to the discretion of individual BID organizations as long as the majority represented property owners. The neighborhood-level chapters later in the book, which detail the protracted process of creating the Adams Morgan Partnership BID, illustrate that the DCMPA chairman's statement as well as CAG's misgivings would prove well founded in anticipating the potential for "disharmony" created by a flexible BID structure that nevertheless privileged property owners. Moreover, in retrospect the business owners' warning against enabling an institution that would erode home rule and democratic governance and their warning that BIDs would add a "new layer of bureaucracy with the D.C. government's involvement," which in 1995 might have sounded unreasonable, also proved perceptive.

The City Council reports, testimony from the hearings, and newspaper articles examined here shed light on the intracity debates and point to the intercity policy conversations that informed D.C.'s BID establishment. As such, D.C.'s BID story, while specific, is not singular. Broader policy conversations in academia and policy circles, including conservative think tanks, such as the Manhattan Institute (MacDonald 1996b), were also instrumental in forging this BID-PPP governance model. As noted, a nested policy network had been working on the general concept of a district-based management structure since urban renewal.

Michael Porter's admonishment to economic development professionals, planners, and public officials that "the way for government to move forward is not by looking behind" is somewhat selective because it favors the interests of strong economic actors that stand to profit from this kind of ahistorical planning paradigm (Porter 1995, 67). This view turns a blind eye to the inequities already built into our urban political system and physical landscapes. It adopts an abstract, decontextualized, and marketized notion of urban governance rooted in public choice theory and salutes self-reliance, equality of opportunities, individual choice, and privatism. As the next chapter illustrates, the BID-PPP regime, whose governance strategy followed Porter's placemaking ethos without affirmatively addressing the legacy of discrimination embedded in D.C.'s property markets, ultimately distorted the city's development, leading to the figurative as well as physical displacement of low-income populations (Angotti and Morse 2016; McFarlane 2003, 2007).

CHAPTER 4

BID Urbanism Oils the Gentrification Machine

"Barry Says Home Rule Government Unworkable, Urges U.S. Takeover of District" read a headline in the *Washington Post* on February 3, 1995. Mayor Barry, long known as "The Mayor for Life," was publicly conceding that D.C. was insolvent. Not only that, D.C.'s mayor was asking "federal authorities [to] take over municipal welfare, medical, court and corrections programs, a move that would dismantle major parts of the local bureaucracy he helped build in the 1980s" (Schneider and Vise 1995a).[1] Barry's admission foreshadowed an intervention akin to that of a congressional oversight board. Barry, who had won the 1994 mayoral elections despite his 1990 crack conviction, was stepping into a changed political environment. His electoral victory, moreover, was compromised and signaled trouble for his incoming administration: middle-class residents, black and white, along with Washington's power elite, were looking for decisive action (Janofsky 1995).[2]

Over the ensuing months, the *Washington Post* and local papers, including the *Washington City Paper*, chronicled the evolving crisis as the nation's capital careened toward bankruptcy (Harden and Vise 1995; Melton 1995; Schneider and Vise 1995b, 1995c, 1995d). At this time, the "Gingrich revolution" was sweeping into Congress, and the Democratic Clinton administration in its campaign to "reinvent government" had officially embraced an entrepreneurial governance ethos, modeled on the New Public Management (NPM) tenets of devolution, privatization, and performance-based governance (National Performance Review 1995). D.C. was in the eye of the storm. While the Clinton administration was apparently slow to respond to the city's crisis, two Republicans, House Speaker Newt Gingrich and former congressman and Housing (HUD) Secretary Jack Kemp, took an active interest in using the nation's capital as a "showcase for conservative theories of governance" (Plotz 1995).

Two years after the 1995 takeover of the Fiscal Control Board, Congress enacted the National Capital Revitalization and Self-Government Improvement Act of 1997, which curtailed the mayor's and the City Council's authority. It also restructured the city's budget responsibilities. A 1997 study, echoing the findings from an earlier report released by a D.C. commission (the Rivlin Commission) in 1990, confirmed that D.C.'s "fiscal problems stem[med] largely from its nature as the nation's capital" and the structural constraints under which the city operated (O'Cleireacain 1997, 6; D.C. Commission on Budget and Financial Priorities 1990). The 1997 Act relieved the District of Columbia of some of the state-like fiscal burdens, such as the crushing pension obligations D.C. officials and representatives had highlighted in the 1995 congressional hearings prior to the authorization of the Control Board (Joint Hearing 1995). The law also removed many of the perennial budget problems that had in no small measure stymied home rule and facilitated the rebalancing of the city's fiscal position—but only after democratic rule had been revoked. By October 1997, a *Washington Post* article announced Barry's apparent political conversion from a pugnacious politician, used to "call[ing] the shots," to a "mild-mannered mayor" who had access to information but no longer had control of the city's agencies (Loeb 1997). Home rule had lasted barely two decades; ironically, the structural fiscal constraints that might have bolstered a locally elected regime were only posthumously ameliorated.

Chapter 3 illustrates how successive BID-enabling legislative proposals facilitated the delegation of decision-making power and political voice to property owners while diluting the voice of other district or neighborhood constituents and stakeholders. This chapter chronicles how BID urbanists reenvisioned the city. Through an analysis of the 1998 strategic plan, "The Economic Resurgence of Washington, D.C.: Citizens Plan for Prosperity in the 21st Century," and the 2004 comprehensive planning framework, "A Vision for Growing an Inclusive City," I detail the substance of BID urbanism. I look at what BIDs and their public and private partners aimed to accomplish and what they achieved, beginning with the leadership role the BID-PPP seized during the Control Board years (1995–2001) and then con-

solidated during Mayor Williams's administration (1999–2007). I then lay
out the geography of the strategic planning interventions in the two plans
and the vision of urbanity the BID-PPP pursued. Three themes emerge:
the initial erasure of D.C.'s identity as "Chocolate City," ironically sub-
merged through a discourse of "diversity" and "inclusion;" the consolidation of a safe, friendly, and connected space in the central city; and, ultimately, the reconstitution of the public realm as "third places" through
programming and pop-up placemaking tactics. The chapter closes with a
discussion of the dramatic demographic shifts that have occurred in the
city, especially in the downtown areas and the inner-city neighborhoods
targeted for strategic planning interventions, which in no small measure
revived urban renewal–era plans from the 1950s and 1960s (see map in figure 1, chapter 2).

BID Urbanism Begins

By April 7, 1995, the Senate had placed the city's fate once again in the
hands of federal officials in the form of the Control Board. Hearings on
the BID-enabling legislation were being held on the local city council level
during this same year. It was clear the Barry regime had lost "the capacity to
govern" effectively (Stone 1993). A transfer of power not only from the executive branch of D.C.'s government but also from the City Council to the
Control Board enabled BID-PPP urbanism in Washington, D.C., to gain a
sure footing. It also signaled a clear regime change from the "black nationalist" Barry era through the control board to a post–Control Board regime that
"self-consciously" sidelined "the racialized realities and dynamics" of the
District of Columbia (Harris 2010, 103). It marked the "ascension of a technocratic, managerial black leadership, exemplified by Anthony Williams,"
fully aligned with the BID-PPP regime that had consolidated its institutional
powerbase during the Control Board period (103). Ultimately, the transformation of D.C.'s urban regime then also signified a shift in the symbolic politics to rebrand the city's image.

In 1995, prior to the Control Board takeover, Mayor Barry, along with Herb
Miller, the developer of a Rouse-influenced mixed-use project in Georgetown, had organized the Interactive Downtown Task Force (IDTF). The
IDTF, unsurprisingly, promoted the latest iteration of the decades-old vision
of a vibrant ("living") downtown and noted the important role a BID would
play in implementing it.[3] Both, Councilmember Charlene Drew Jarvis and

the president of the International Downtown Association, Richard Bradley, were members of the task force. By late 1996, the *Washington Business Journal* reported, "The city's economic salvation depend[ed] upon a plan to attract tourists and office workers into the city in the evening" (T. C. Hall and Lombardo 1996). It also outlined a "three-point plan" to produce this new downtown: (1) creating "a Washington Center Alliance, a public-private group to implement the task force's plan"; (2) "forming a business improvement district"; and (3) establishing a "Tax Increment Finance District, using the same boundaries" (T. C. Hall and Lombardo 1996). BIDs, including the potential for neighborhood-based BIDs, had been enabled earlier that year. But the IDTF's downtown-focused vision represented only one element in the planning approach that was being articulated during this time. The broader, citywide vision that emerged during the next two years, which ultimately became the 1998 "Citizens Plan," was expansive in nature, incorporating strategic neighborhoods beyond the downtown core, many of which had previously been slated for urban renewal.

The Control Board and, subsequently, the administration of Mayor Williams brought to the city's urban governance regime an emphasis on strategic economic development, which ultimately shaped the comprehensive plan. Two important planning documents have guided the spatial development of the city since then. The "Citizens Plan" laid out the clear goals, objectives, and action steps that were to undergird the 2004 "framework" produced by Mayor Williams's Office of Planning (published in advance of the 2006 Comprehensive Plan). "In contrast to planning," however, Martin Kornberger observes, "strategy is a body of knowledge that aims at changing the balance of power in the present. It is not about the future, but a shared belief in the future" (Kornberger 2012, 90). In order to draw new residents, businesses, and consumers to D.C.'s neighborhoods and downtown districts, the 1998 strategic plan reimaged them as new, exciting, yet familiar urban places through the selective compilation of a "shared heritage" and an imagined future even before the comprehensive planning process had been completed.

The expansion of the municipal agencies engaged in planning was a positive development when considered in terms of its democratic possibilities, especially given Mayor Williams's rhetorical commitment to comprehensive planning. But the new regime's strategic planning approach also included a focus on increasing efficiency and competitiveness and institutionalizing predictable public-private partnership (PPP) arrangements.

The idea was to "give a good balance between insulation and input from the public, in order to get development done" (Jarvis 1997b). These proposals to rely on public-private partnerships, like BIDs as well as quasi-public economic development corporations, begged the question as to how and to what aims public resources and private power were to be deployed in the implementation of the plan.

In the initial restructuring period, key economic development consultants worked on the strategic plan, including Harvard economist Michael Porter, Marc Weiss, a senior-level HUD official in the Clinton administration, and BID advocates, such as Lawrence Houstoun and Richard Bradley. Councilmember Jarvis also continued to lend both political and research support during this period. High-profile planners were also involved. Two are of particular note: Richard Monteilh, who had left a high-level planning position as the director of the Metropolitan Atlanta Olympics Games Authority to head the Department of Housing and Community Development (DHCD) in D.C. (T. C. Hall 1998), and Andy Altman, who would lead the city's planning efforts as Mayor Williams's director of the reconstituted planning office. This team signaled the regime's commitment to investing in the necessary organizational infrastructure to enable a systematic approach to planning.

With the Control Board firmly in place, the two authors on the strategic plan, Marc Weiss and Richard Monteilh, were brought on board in 1997. This was a welcome change, as HUD had briefly stopped releasing Community Development Block Grant (CDBG) funds to the city's Department of Housing and Community Development, apparently to await a new management team (Weiss 2002).[4] The Control Board regime charged Monteilh and Weiss "with spending the money, all of the money (70 million dollars), as fast as possible" (Weiss 2002, 3). Thus, "before the plan was even completed," wrote Weiss in 2002, a "flurry of activity" indicated that the new regime "meant business" (7). Additionally, "to ensure designated public and private sector leadership responsible and accountable for [the] progress and success" of the forty action steps outlined in the 1998 "Citizens Plan," the regime created a number of key organizations to guide the development they envisioned (7). Thus, a new constellation of private and public actors, including historically powerful and newly formed organizations, constituted the new BID-PPP regime.

Political scientist Jon Pierre observes that if individuals and organizations "succeed" in regime formation, "they preempt the leadership role in their community and establish for themselves near decision-making mo-nopoly over cutting edge choices facing their locality" (Pierre 1998, 47). In D.C., this regime shift has proved durable. Over the next two decades, the economic and spatial development of the urban landscape would be co-ordinated through a network of actors, including city agencies, nonprofit agencies, and industry coalitions formed to aggressively market the city and highlight its "diverse" population, its historical heritage, its superb business location, and a new creative ethos. These organizations included the Wash-ington DC Economic Partnership (WDCEP), the Washington DC Conven-tion and Tourism Corporation, Cultural Tourism DC, the District of Colum-bia Building Industry Association (DCBIA), and the ten BIDs, including the powerful DowntownDC BID, by far the largest and most resource-rich BID.

The only two BIDs in existence in 1998 were two downtown BIDs, the DowntownDC BID in the "old downtown" and the Golden Triangle BID in the "new downtown," which encompassed the area of office development in the west end of the larger downtown area. Neighborhood-based BIDs—Georgetown, Capitol Hill, and Adams Morgan—were already in the plan-ning stages, and others, designed to be future centers of employment and growth—Mount Vernon Triangle, NoMa, the Capitol Riverfront, and the South West Waterfront—were also on the drawing board. The strategic planning process had already signaled all ten of the BIDs that exist today.

Many of these future BIDs were in proposed transit-oriented develop-ment (TOD) neighborhoods planned around improved and new stations that had been in various planning stages since the 1970s (Schrag 2014); most lay along the heretofore unconnected Green Line and would connect new growth areas to downtown, but a new Red Line station at New York Avenue would service the future NoMa area. This new strategic plan in fact revived old urban renewal plans (figure 1, chapter 2; compare with figures 2 and 3, this chapter), anchoring these plans back in the 1950s and 1960s when "stri-dently optimistic predictions [had] reappeared in executives' conferences and publications" about the "stability and the future" of central cities (Isen-berg 2004, 170).[5] This is how strategy works. It not only "represents an image of the future; it is also an engine that produces this very future" (Kornberger 2012, 94) while obscuring elements of the past. This "rhetoric of absence" (Kelly and Hoerl 2012), also characteristic of public choice theory, which sees change as "prospective," as previously noted (Halper 1993, 272), omits past racialized narratives mobilized by real estate industry interests that would stand to profit from an urban resurgence.

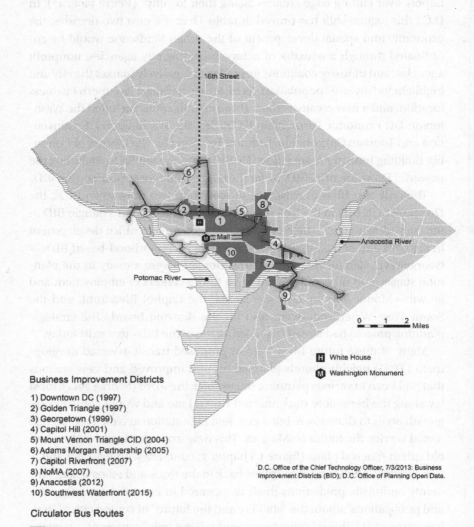

16th Street

Anacostia River

Potomac River

Mall

H — White House
M — Washington Monument

0 1 2 Miles

Business Improvement Districts

1) Downtown DC (1997)
2) Golden Triangle (1997)
3) Georgetown (1999)
4) Capitol Hill (2001)
5) Mount Vernon Triangle CID (2004)
6) Adams Morgan Partnership (2005)
7) Capitol Riverfront (2007)
8) NoMA (2007)
9) Anacostia (2012)
10) Southwest Waterfront (2015)

Circulator Bus Routes
▬▬▬

D.C. Office of the Chief Technology Officer, 7/3/2013: Business Improvement Districts (BID), D.C. Office of Planning Open Data.

FIGURE 2. Business Improvement Districts, Dates of Establishment, and Circulator Bus Routes

BID Urbanism and Leadership

Business improvement districts figured prominently in the "Citizens Plan" that was released a year after the downtown BIDs commenced operations. Noting the crucial importance of placemaking in postindustrial urban redevelopment, the report proclaimed that BIDs would "point the way" to D.C.'s "resurgence" (Asch and Musgrove 2015).[6] As a D.C. BID executive explained in 2006: "a good BID is a leadership organization, a community leadership organization, and the best BIDs all play that role." The idea is "to provide the basic services to all the businesses to get the buy-in, but at the end of the day your real value is you're thinking three dimensionally about the economic development challenges, and you're taking a leadership role in addressing those challenges and getting in front of them."[7] The BIDs were to function as urban management organizations, policy entrepreneurs, and planning agents (Stevens, Suls, and Avery 2016).[8]

Of particular note was the policy guidance that the downtown BID provided to redirect downtown development. D.C. BID executives interviewed in 2006 offered two examples, tax increment financing (TIF, see figure 3), which would allow the issuance of bonds to finance district-based improvements, and residential development.[9] Both would help bring about the "living city" vision that had eluded downtown over the previous decades. With regard to attracting retail, an executive observed that "BID leaders had put together the leadership for TIF for downtown," which, according to him, had enhanced the city's ability to once more compete in the regional market and to draw retail investment back into the city. "People are establishing BIDs because it is prerequisite to competition" was the conviction. Moreover, BID leadership, apparently drawing on Porter's (1995) insights, namely that inner cities offered a competitive advantage vis-à-vis suburban markets, advocated for urban reinvestment, including in retail. To do this, a BID executive remarked, "We had to disabuse retailers of the mythologies of urban areas and convince them to adapt their suburban model to denser populations." The BID-PPP coalition messaging communicated that D.C. did not have the capacity—either the financial resources or the professional staff—to accomplish what the BIDs in combination with TIF financing might and would achieve.

The importance of combining BIDs with TIFs was highlighted in a 1997 article published by *Legal Times*, which proclaimed: "Stirrings of Hope for Downtown DC . . . Despite the District's recent crises, hope now abounds. . . . Washington D.C. is one of the few cities in the world poised to capture the defining market forces of the 21st century" (Maszak, Gross, and Porter 1996). Coauthored by Stephen Porter, a member of the IDTF, the article laid out the tools available to the public-private partnerships that had been enabled through both the TIF and BID legislation. The oversight of TIF districts would reside in the Downtown Retail Committee, a subset of property owners appointed by the mayor. The combination of these tools enabled the new BID-PPP regime to deploy public subsidies, including through TIFs, payments in lieu of taxes (PILOTs), and tax abatement programs, to attract investment by private sector developers and real property owners who, in turn, through the Downtown Retail Committee were given direct control over the selection and oversight of projects to implement their vision of place. At a 2004 legislative hearing to extend TIF financing to strategic neighborhoods beyond downtown, Robert Gladstone, the founder of Quadrangle Development, founding chair of the DowntownDC BID, and chair of the Downtown Retail Committee, strongly endorsed the combined power of BIDs and TIFs to spur development. Of BIDs he observed, they had "great success in stabilizing the downtown, creating a more predictable investment environment, and changing downtown's perception. Over the last seven years the public and private sectors have invested heavily in downtown offices, hotels, housing, culture and entertainment venues" (Jack Evans 2004, 8). This predictability was achieved because BID advocates, representing the interests of property owners, developers, and corporate business interests, provided leadership and also ran the operations of or sat on the board of coordinating institutions.

BID executives identified downtown residential development as the second major challenge to a Washington, D.C., renaissance. In keeping with prevalent New Urbanist tenets, BID professionals and their allies in city agencies continuously advocated for downtown living and the amenities to support this development. To realize this laudable vision of a vibrant downtown required solving a crucial piece of the puzzle: how to catalyze residential development in an area perceived profitable for office space. A BID executive, interviewed in 2006, recounted that although the downtown had been zoned to allow residential uses since 1991, residential development was "not happening." Apparently, BID leadership suggested that "a slight tax-abatement" was in order "to take a little bit of the risk out, [so] they'd [developers] do it." He concluded, "we sort of solved that problem by providing the leadership." Furthermore, in negotiation with "a small group of developers," the city adjusted its regulatory framework, especially its zoning, and used its taxing authority as well as its substantial land ownership in downtown to support the downtown agenda (McCarthy 2008, 80–83). These were used both for large entertainment projects and to secure amenities crucial for residential development, such as a cinema, affordable studio space, and artist housing in the arts districts. In 2004, Gladstone proclaimed, "in just seven years we have gone from having the weakest office markets in the region to the strongest in the nation and from having no housing under construction to 3000 units" (Jack Evans 2004, 8).

Effective BIDs, then, work as analysts, and good center-city BIDs, according to the International Downtown Association, reposition downtowns as the engine driving not just downtown growth but regional growth. But, as noted, BIDs don't do this alone. They function as part of broader urban PPP regimes because, as private partners, they rely on the public authority of the municipal government to implement their placemaking ideas and ultimately their real estate strategy (Briffault 1999). Far from the "self-help" ethos BID proponents portrayed during the hearings for successive BID-enabling legislative proposals, the implementation of a strategic urban vision calls for coordinated governmental planning actions and targeted public investment in existing and potential BID districts. In D.C. the BID-enabling legislation empowered a network of professional BID-PPP leaders to guide the redevelopment of potential growth areas or central employment areas identified in the plans. Moreover, numerous people who worked to steer the redevelopment of D.C. have done so by moving back and forth between jobs in the public and private sectors within the BID-PPP regime.[10]

Many of the strategies outlined in the "Citizens Plan," particularly those contemplating the development of specific transit-oriented neighborhoods, as noted, had been conceived long before the release of the "Citizens Plan" and the subsequent "inclusive" comprehensive planning framework. Today, the geography of BIDs in D.C. incorporates areas with large-scale redevelopment projects, such as the Verizon Center Arena, the Convention Center, and Hope VI projects, which provided funds to leverage the redevelopment of public housing into new mixed-income and mixed-use neighborhoods. In the early years, after intense lobbying, BID leadership had successfully turned the tide and spurred on mixed-use development with significant residential components in the greater downtown area and beyond (Widdicombe 2010). Figure 3 locates where TIF and PILOTs have been used to subsidize development. And the assurance of a BID helped secure the Verizon Center development, which brought a major entertainment hub to downtown D.C., for example. In fact, writes Ellen McCarthy, the for-

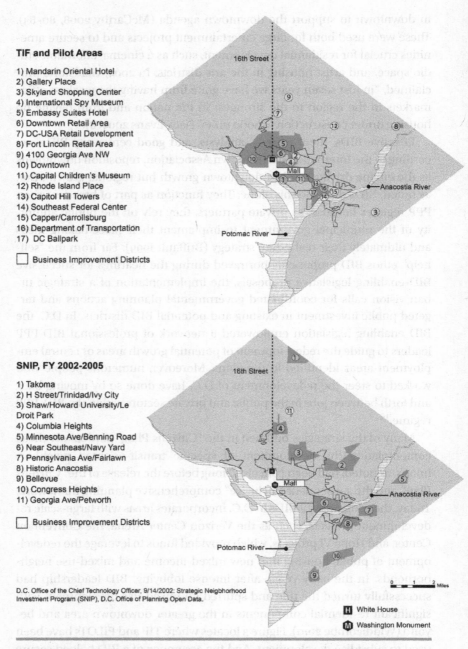

TIF and Pilot Areas

1) Mandarin Oriental Hotel
2) Gallery Place
3) Skyland Shopping Center
4) International Spy Museum
5) Embassy Suites Hotel
6) Downtown Retail Area
7) DC-USA Retail Development
8) Fort Lincoln Retail Area
9) 4100 Georgia Ave NW
10) Downtown
11) Capital Children's Museum
12) Rhode Island Place
13) Capitol Hill Towers
14) Southeast Federal Center
15) Capper/Carrollsburg
16) Department of Transportation
17) DC Ballpark

☐ Business Improvement Districts

16th Street

Mall

Anacostia River

Potomac River

SNIP, FY 2002-2005

1) Takoma
2) H Street/Trinidad/Ivy City
3) Shaw/Howard University/Le Droit Park
4) Columbia Heights
5) Minnesota Ave/Benning Road
6) Near Southeast/Navy Yard
7) Pennsylvania Ave/Fairlawn
8) Historic Anacostia
9) Bellevue
10) Congress Heights
11) Georgia Ave/Petworth

☐ Business Improvement Districts

16th Street

Mall

Anacostia River

Potomac River

0 1 2 Miles

D.C. Office of the Chief Technology Officer, 9/14/2002: Strategic Neighborhood Investment Program (SNIP), D.C. Office of Planning Open Data.

Ⓗ White House
Ⓜ Washington Monument

FIGURE 3. Strategic Interventions: Tax Increment Financing and Strategic Neighborhood Improvement Program Areas

mer deputy director of planning under Mayor Williams, "several Downtown developers agreed with the value of a BID" and signaled their "willingness to loan the money to start BID operations" in time for the opening of the arena (McCarthy 2008, 79).

The PPP-BID regime used signature projects, such as the Verizon Center downtown and later the Nationals Stadium in the Capitol Riverfront area (see DC Ballpark on figure 3)—highly subsidized by the public sector—to catalyze further development activity (Stevens 2016).[11] Fast forward to 2010 when the economic development director for the DowntownDC BID summarized the financial flows this way: "To date, the City made net economic development investments in downtown of approximately $300 million in projects totaling $2.3 billion, and total downtown private investment has been approximately $10 billion" (Widdicombe 2010). The continuous placemaking work BIDs provide, in turn, anchors these investments. The BID Council publishes reports every year with metrics that include the annual combined investment by BIDs in their districts' placemaking programs: Between 2010 and 2017 the eight BIDs that existed in 2010 have seen an average budget increase of 19 percent. In 2010 the investment of the eight existing BIDs, for example, stood at $22 million. In 2017 the number of BIDs had risen to ten, and "D.C. Business Improvement Districts," the Council report noted, had "invested over $30 million to make the District of Columbia's highest employment areas better places to live, to work and to visit" (D.C. BID Council 2017). BID urbanism has indeed created a "living downtown," a goal that had eluded the previous regime since the late 1970s.

BID urbanism has also activated D.C.'s urban core and the surrounding neighborhoods as a desirable place for newcomers to live, work, and play. The placemaking strategy, however, also entailed the spatial deracialization (Saff 1994) of D.C.'s core and of the strategic plan's target neighborhoods. In an apolitical employment of the concept of diversity (Modan 2008), new transportation networks were introduced as a connective tissue for these spaces, and temporary design interventions and programming to promote social gatherings were deployed to create a new sense of place also through experiential branding.

The "Creative Class," Diversity, and Erasure

BID urbanism is not just a downtown project. BID-PPP regimes seek to revalorize neighborhood after neighborhood to capitalize on the depressed land and property values created during earlier rounds of disinvestment and redlining (N. Smith 1996). To accomplish this, BID urbanism promotes a particular vision of urbanity, rooted in the reconstitution of an idealized nineteenth-century and early twentieth-century civic engagement, to produce a culturally enticing public realm. Even nineteenth-century boosters saw "physical improvements and additional services that went to business districts" as part of a placemaking repertoire because they "helped to fix the identity of these areas as places dedicated to order and, of course, of prosperity" (Monti 1999, 13–14). Alison Isenberg's history of the downtown improvement and Main Street movement highlights the initial work of public "housekeepers," bourgeois women who labored to improve downtowns, and explains how planners and business elites subsequently articulated commonly held, identifiable ideologies of place. They included "a clean and pleasing urban character, a uniting streetscape of entrepreneurs, and a dignified commercial corridor," Isenberg explains. "Together [these] made up the guiding principles of downtown investment as they emerged in the Progressive era" and then resurfaced in the 1950s and 1960s (Isenberg 2004, 50). These values, "clean, safe and friendly," have served as a clarion call for BID urbanism.

These values also guided the 1998 "Citizens Plan," which clearly asserted: "Place matters. It matters if we are going to grow the private sector. It matters if we are going to attract and retain residents in the city. We must have *real places—vibrant and welcoming places*—where businesses can take root, where the Industry Networks can thrive, and where people can *live and work and raise their families with dignity* and opportunity. To succeed in promoting neighborhood commercial districts, merchants need to be organized to provide *cleanliness, safety, and a pleasing environment* for shoppers, workers, visitors, and residents" (Monteilh and Weiss 1998, 40, emphasis added). The 1998 strategic plan advances a vision that runs through the literature on placemaking urbanism. It presents a positive, "pleasing," and orderly vignette of urban life.

This placemaking strategy, however, often works at odds with equity goals, such as inclusion, by disparaging or erasing the preceding identities of the city at large and of specific neighborhoods (Hopkinson 2012b; Modan 2007; Schaller and Modan 2005; Summers 2015). Thus, for example, this "place matters" passage presumed that D.C. and the neighborhoods that subsequently became subjected to specific planning interventions were not desirable or places where residents might be leading a "dignified" life. These underlying suppositions raise thorny questions about how we arrive at this end place and about whose place identities have to be erased or at least marginalized in order to create this new brand. Who is included in this strategic vision and how?

On the day Congress turned the city's governance over to the Control Board, the first imperative, as Republican representative Tom Davis announced, was to restore the "tarnished" image of Washington, D.C., in the national psyche. "That is why we called ourselves by the city's proper name, Washington, D.C.—the nation's capital—rather than "the District," noted one of the authors of the strategic plan (Weiss 2002, 5). In the strategic plan, the elevation of the city to its "proper" place as the nation's capital also signified the partial erasure of D.C.'s identity, that of "the District," home to many who did not necessarily see this as "a very demeaning term used only by regional insiders" (Weiss 2002, 5). In his 1996 State of the District Address, Mayor Barry explicitly countered this impetus to redefine D.C.'s identity in this way. He openly lambasted those he called "District bashers" and called for a "moratorium on District-bashing" by the media. Then he told D.C. residents to "Stand up for DC. Take pride in DC. Disagree without being disagreeable. This is our city" (Barry 1996). The mayor was walking a tightrope. While Marion Barry's political rhetoric focused on the current plight and future of D.C.'s residents, strategic planners turned their focus outward. Weiss, one of the main consultants on the "Citizens Plan," explained this choice to rechristen the District: "I often said that Washington, D.C. was the best city with the worst image in America. . . . This was compounded by racial animosity, as D.C. became Chocolate City" (Weiss 2002, 21). Weiss recognized how racist perceptions severed the positive associations many D.C. residents connected with their city. Rather than counter these kinds of views, the 1998 strategic vision purposely buried the idea of "Chocolate City," which as noted had since the 1970s performed a critical function as "a metaphorical utopia" that identified the District as a place of empowerment, African American entrepreneurial success, and cultural and artistic movements (Carroll 1998; Asch and Musgrove 2017). In her "Farewell to Chocolate City," Natalie Hopkinson, the author of *Go-go Live: the Musical Life and Death of a Chocolate City*, observed that in D.C. "blacks were not 'minorities,' with the whiff of inferiority that label carries; we were 'normal.' For the first time in my life, I felt at home" (Hopkinson 2012a). The strategic plan, however, proposed an urban imaginary of Washington, D.C., the nation's capital, with which white Americans in particular would identify. D.C.'s identity as the first "Chocolate City" finally succumbed to the "prejudice" located outside of the city (Weiss 2002, 2).

The prevailing consensus among Washington, D.C.,'s new leadership, as communicated through planning documents and city-marketing web-sites, insisted that Washington, D.C.,'s new image had to speak to and re-flect a broader audience, "the well-educated, culturally diverse workforce," that had for too long settled beyond D.C.'s boundaries, that is to say, in the suburbs (Monteilh and Weiss 1998, 4). Consequently, BIDs developed a dual focus: a "clean, safe and friendly" campaign and a place-marketing campaign to make sure visitors, shoppers, and potential residents felt safe, comfortable, and welcomed. This reimagining campaign, akin to the Main Street marketing postcards of the late nineteenth and early twentieth centu-ries, used promotional materials increasingly disseminated online to proj-ect Washington, D.C.'s image outward. Organizations such as Cultural Tour-ism DC, the Washington Economic Partnership, and the BIDs, which have overlapping board members, produced promotional materials both to mar-ket the city's heritage as located in both its monuments and museums on the National Mall and its neighborhoods. These organizations, such as the Washington Economic Partnership, are part of an organizational network that "connects public and private sectors, neighborhoods, and real estate communities to local, national, and international audiences."[12] Marketers, then and now, as Isenberg (2004) argues, hope to fix a new image of the city in people's minds, not as a "brick-and-mortar location but rather as a terri-tory within Americans' imaginations, a hopeful vision of urban commerce [and urban life] transformed" (43). And as a BID executive reinforced in 2006, their aim was to nudge tourists, potential residents and investors to venture beyond the monumental core into D.C.'s neighborhoods.

In his 2003 inaugural address, Mayor Anthony Williams promised "to bring 100,000 residents to the city within 10 years." The findings of several studies, including one by the Brookings Institution in 1997 and a 2003 re-port commissioned by the Office of Planning, supported this position. D.C., these studies cautioned, would only receive a limited fiscal boost from ad-ditional job creation unless it also attracted job-takers to live in the city. Therefore, one secure avenue of revenue growth was to increase the pop-ulation, and with it the pool of taxable income. Officially sanctioned, this view drove public policy under the Williams administration. However, at-tracting residents to the city was not a new idea. In fact, the administration was rearticulating goals already advanced in earlier urban renewal plans, including the infamous Southwest project of the 1950s. Downtown business interests and planners back then, as noted, had also sought to entice subur-ban commuters to settle in the City.[13]

The BID-PPP governance structure had finally created the institutions

and tools to pursue the measurable target set by the Williams administration (Office of Planning 2004, 29). To be fair, the stated aim as articulated in the mayor's 2004 "Inclusive City" framework was to attract a mix
of new residents, but the plans and projects primarily targeted middle-
income and higher-income consumers as part of the downtown and
neighborhood rebranding efforts. That this was an explicit goal might be
inferred from the fact that this demographics' contribution to the tax base
as measured in median income appears as a metric of success in various reports (Brown-Robertson et al. 2013), including BID annual reports.
A 2003 "Washington, D.C. Economic Policy Papers" report, which informed the comprehensive plan, specifically identified this target market
and noted, "new residents will, through self-selection, primarily consist
of childless individuals and couples, empty nesters, and the very wealthy"
(Shapiro and Bowers 2003, 17).[14] Thus, the BID-PPP needed to redefine the
common perception of Washington, D.C., as a "home of bureaucrats and
poor people" to create urban environments that would keep a new demographic interested in city living, especially by young professionals. The regime's planners thus turned their attention both toward "revitalizing" existing neighborhoods into chic destination neighborhoods and building
new high-amenity neighborhoods.

By 2006, the BID-PPP regime had named their target demographic following Richard Florida's lead (Florida 2003). The BID-PPP would officially
pursue a "creative class" strategy.[15] That year, Richard Florida was invited
by Steve Moore, who then served as the president and CEO of Washington
DC Economic Partnership (WDCEP) and as of this writing serves as executive director of the Southwest BID, to give the keynote address at WDCEP.
In 2010 the WDCEP and the city under Mayor Adrian Fenty released the
jointly produced "Creative Capital: D.C. Action Agenda." The deputy mayor
of economic development and planning, citing Richard Florida, described
this "creative class" demographic as the "most highly educated and ethnically diverse generation in U.S. history." The fact that they would continue
to bring "disposable income to support a vibrant arts scene, openness to
diversity and support for the creation of social and professional networks"
to the District made them a "robust" demographic to secure the city's
"longer-term prosperity" and "sustained economic growth" (Office of the
Deputy Mayor 2012, 13).[16]

Consequently, to refashion the city's association with "Chocolate City,"
the PPP-BID regime had to create a concept that would be "inclusive" of
this young, professional, to be sure increasingly culturally and ethnically

diverse, but still predominately white, target market. Its members, in particular, needed to see themselves reflected in the city's urban imaginary (Hyra 2016). "Diversity" became the signature concept to appeal to this population: "Diversity makes good economic sense," the "Citizens Plan" proclaimed (Monteilh and Weiss 1998, 37). Diversity, moreover, added spice and stimulation to the convenience of living and working in the region's urban heart (Modan 2008; Schaller and Modan 2011; Summers 2015). The reimaging campaigns, such as the one encountered on the website of the DowntownDC BID in early 2007, illustrates how this synergy worked. Appealing to the younger generation, a significantly growing segment of the nation's population, it portrayed a "Downtown (DC) . . . launched on a meteoric ascent to world class prominence, diversity and excitement" and declared, "Downtown is DC's hottest new residential neighborhood. . . . Here you'll find busy streets, bustling stores, happening restaurants and bars, new condos, movie theaters, museums, galleries."[17] Marketing materials, including on the websites of organizations such as Cultural Tourism DC and the Washington DC Economic Partnership (WDCEP), portrayed professional, clean-cut-looking individuals of indeterminate ethnicity, engaged in consumer activities: sitting at outdoor cafés, going shopping, or reclining in a grandiose hotel lobby (Schaller 2007). These branding strategies have been successful. The residential base in downtown has been steadily growing. Moreover, D.C.'s neighborhoods around the downtown core, including new growth areas, such as NoMa and Mount Vernon Triangle, as well as established neighborhoods, such as Shaw, Adams Morgan, and Columbia Heights, have been the destination for millennials moving into the city (P. Stein 2015).

In D.C.'s established, "historic" neighborhoods, local histories were mobilized to add a certain "funky" allure to create this new sense of urbanity (Schaller and Modan 2011) and also to consolidate the back-to-the-city trend. To steer new residents and consumers into existing neighborhoods around the center city core, an appeal to the "diversity" of D.C.'s heritage formed the backbone of these rebranding efforts. But, as Modan notes, the concept of "diversity" became increasingly "depoliticized" in the 2000s to reference lifestyle experiences (Modan 2008, 190). Whereas in the 1990s, she argues, "diversity" still "indexed social justice" where "inclusion" was deliberately linked to "equity," in the later iteration "diversity began to signify a commodified resource" (188). Through this reframing, "diversity" became an asset, which inserted and adapted its meaning to fit within the prevailing marketized, public choice, "voting with your feet" conception of neighborhood economic development. Diversity then became one of the local amenities new residents could acquire through their individual purchasing power. Brandi Thompson Summers's work on H Street echoes this finding. She notes: "In recent years, community organizations and government agencies have placed significant efforts into the rebuilding and rebranding of the H Street NE corridor—now called the Atlas District—privileging 'diversity' and the possibility of a global community" (Summers 2015, 299). Thus, the "cool aesthetics of blackness" and "black branding" in H Street and Shaw, respectively, and the "spice" of the Latinx barrio, in the case of Adams Morgan, became the language of place marketing, images summoned to imbue these particular places with a safe edginess (Hyra 2017; Modan 2008; Schaller 2007; Schaller and Modan 2011; Summers 2015). The discourse of "diversity" was not limited to specific neighborhoods but served to anchor D.C.'s entire urban space in a new imaginary, "to act," as Summers observes, as "the antidote to blackness" (2015, 300). As a result, marketing campaigns for existing neighborhoods built selectively on heritage versions of local history in order to re-present D.C. as a space of diversity.

In new growth areas BIDs have fashioned entirely new place identities to entice investment. Here BIDs have acted as if "their" neighborhood territory were a tabula rasa or "empty" space to be filled with meaning and enjoyment (N. Smith 1996). One recent example is what is now called the Capitol Riverfront area, where older public housing units were torn down as part of the process of remaking the area. The executive director of the Capitol Riverfront BID made clear the process of BID-centered neighborhood change in 2016, when he posed a rhetorical question to a group of planners: "Why would you establish a BID in a new growth area where nobody really lives, very few people are working and it's somewhat of a blank slate in terms of new development?" He proceeded to answer as follows: "Well you needed an organization to manage change . . . We speak in one voice, for all of our property owners, our residents, our office tenants, and our business owners. We needed to position this area for future investment so we could compete with the suburbs as well as other growth areas in the region" (Stevens, Suls, and Avery 2016; my transcription). This avowal that a unitary voice—"we speak in one voice"—removed from democratic deliberation or political representative processes can act on behalf of a neighborhood's multifaceted interests is built into the institutional model and goes unquestioned (Hochleutner 2003).[18] While this model sidesteps the fact that neighborhood politics are fraught with conflicting interests and power differentials, it is an effective vehicle to manage a cohesive brand to "reposition" neighborhoods as assets.

The Capitol Riverfront BID has created key planning frameworks, including more recently an Urban Design Framework Plan, to identify "major strategies to guide growth." The organization has worked hard to reimagine this area, and in the words of its executive director, "advocacy is huge": "We had to help people to understand where we were, what we were in real time, and where we were going to be when we grew up" (Stevens, Suls, and Avery 2016; my transcription). This BID is different from the Center City BIDs, such as the Golden Triangle BID and DowntownDC BID. By the turn of the century, these areas of D.C. were already "acceptable" because they were "part of the downtown grid and the downtown circulation patterns," such as "the Red Line . . . the preferred [Metro] line for office tenants in this city for years" (Stevens, Suls, and Avery 2016; my transcription). That is, they were already part of the mental image of the city with which suburban commuters felt a sense of familiarity. Unlike the downtown BIDs, Capital Riverfront had to create both a market identity, especially for real estate brokers and developers, and a sense of place.

The Capitol Riverfront BID could build on a few major assets: "We have accessibility from an elevated highway, [and] we sit on top of the Green Line," noted the BID's executive director. However, it seems even in 2016, the area still had an image challenge among real estate professionals, which the BID had to counter: "In talking to brokers in our fair city, they call it too urban, which means riders have to encounter the kids from Anacostia" he explained. Perhaps to neutralize this perception, the BID commissioned two studies in 2012 and 2017 to examine demographic trends along the Green Line. Citing the studies, the executive director in fact commented: "We are a very diverse line . . . I will show you more population is concentrating along the Green Line in the decade of the 2000s than any other" (Stevens, Suls, and Avery 2016; my transcription). This commentary works on two levels. It reinforces the narrative of "diversity" that was activated in the strategic plan; it also illustrates how selective amnesia and dog whistles can function in the new D.C. (Haney-López 2014). The speaker never uses racial categories to mark the "kids" or the people, who are part of "the downtown circulation patterns." These markers work with the audience's assumed knowledge of D.C.'s racial landscape. They juxtapose the "acceptable" Northwest predominately white neighborhoods along the Red Line with predominately black neighborhoods along the Green Line and in Anacostia. Allusions to the kids

from Anacostia invoke the image of D.C. ("black" and "urban") that planning for diversity has sought to suppress. In combination with industry code
words for preferred "growth populations," these references could be interpreted as dog whistles. They introduce a desired alternative urban vision
while reinforcing the racialized urban imaginaries that shape how some industry professionals still understand D.C. In fact, contemporary real estate
practices and planning strategies are reproducing iniquitous housing and
property markets. A 2012 report corroborates that racial steering and other
discriminatory practices have persisted in D.C.'s housing market (Lauber
2012).

The Capitol Riverfront area redevelopment is emblematic of the BID-
PPP regime. It was also made possible by active federal-local collaboration
through the PPP structure (Brandes 2005). The federal government and the
Williams administration coordinated the early efforts to reinvest in the area,
including the relocation of U.S. Navy offices to the area near the Metro station and the assemblage of land for redevelopment, much of which fell under federal jurisdiction (Mackinnon 2017; Price 2001). Mackinnon notes that
"at its founding" the Anacostia Waterfront Initiative, which comprised this
area as well, "involved the D.C. government, four local quasi-governmen-
tal corporations, and 14 Federal Agencies" (Mackinnon 2017, 427). In 2004
the Anacostia Waterfront Corporation (AWC) was legally enacted as an independent District entity to coordinate the investments on the Anacostia
River waterfront.[19] It, however, was dissolved in July 2007, and shortly af-
terward the Capitol Riverfront BID was enabled (Council of the District of
Columbia 2007). Its principal undertaking was "placemaking" as well as
managing and marketing the inventory of redevelopment sites. This placemaking enterprise as noted was represented as "placemaking in an area
where places did not exist." Yet, often in the targeted areas places did exist
prior to BID efforts in D.C. In the Capitol Riverfront BID area, in particular,
a neighborhood existed before the federally funded Hope VI program provided the leverage to redevelop the Arthur Capper Carrollsburg (ACC) public housing into a new mixed-use neighborhood (see location on figure 3).
Until Hope VI, this community had to live through years of neglect as crime
rates soared in the 1980s and 1990s.[20] As scholars, nonprofit organizations,
and public historians have documented, the ACC projects and surrounding
area, much like the Southwest urban renewal area of the 1950s, harbored
a community that feared displacement (Bockman 2013; Brandes 2005; Dubree n.d.). In 2002, many residents viewed the development with suspicion.
For example, one resident cited in a report documenting Hope VI projects

observed, "They say we're going to come back, but I just don't see it. I would love to stay here, but it doesn't look like it's going to happen." This resident's well-founded fears grew out of experience: "Where are the old residents of the 'Ellen Wilson' HOPE VI across the street? Now that HOPE VI is done there, it's mostly business people living there. Only 2% of the residents are black" (Center for Community Change 2003, 26).[21]

In the mid-2000s, after years of disinvestment, the 707 ACC public housing units were razed to make room for new buildings with the promise that they would be replaced at a one-to-one ratio (Cherkis 2005). This is a familiar urban renewal promise in D.C. and reminiscent of the Southwest story related earlier in the book. The promise is not to existing residents, however. It is a promise to replace units of housing. Uwe Steven Brandes, who interviewed AAC residents for his study, observed, "Several elderly citizen stakeholders . . . traced their personal and family history to the Southwest waterfront neighborhood from which they were relocated" (Brandes 2005, 415). This provides a glimpse into the kind of "serial displacement" that low-income, often African American, residents experience in D.C. (Fullilove and Wallace 2011). As has been the case with other Hope VI projects (Bockman 2011, 2013, 2018; Popkin et al. 2004), many of the original tenants were unable to return to benefit from the neighborhood's resurgence. This might have been foreseen, however. Apparently already as planned, 290 of the units did not correspond to the very low local median income of the residents (Center for Community Change 2003). The Capitol Riverfront development, consequently, is implicated in the kind of policy-induced serial displacement Fullilove and Wallace (2011) describe as one that repeatedly uproots vulnerable populations. Furthermore, with the recession of 2008, "flexibility" was built into the program to accommodate "workforce housing," relaxing the income eligibility requirements to allow people earning $82,800–119,025 to access subsidized units (Bockman 2011). An online real estate newsletter in 2011 also noted subsidies that were made available by D.C.'s Housing Authority to help these "moderate-income" households buy townhouses in the new Capitol Quarter built on ACC lots (W. Smith 2011).[22]

Today, luxury, high-density, mixed-use developments flank an award-winning park funded by the city but managed by the Capitol Riverfront BID.[23] The neighborhood features not one but two state-of-the-art parks, Yards Park and Canal Park, maintained and managed by the BID. According to the executive director of the Capitol Riverfront BID, D.C.'s regime, with Mayor Williams and Andy Altman at the helm of the Office of Planning, directed public investment to the tune of 1.4 billion dollars into the area.[24] Altman, in fact, headed the Anacostia Waterfront Corporation at its inception (Wilgoren 2005).[25] In 2014, according to the BID's estimates, gleaned from the U.S. census and posted on its website, the population was 68 percent white, 25 percent black, 4 percent Asian, and 3 percent Latinx; 56 percent of the population was representative of millennials (eighteen to thirty-four years old). It was also a well-off area, boasting a median income of $106,000 (Capitol Riverfront BID 2015). By 2016, the "Capitol Riverfront marketing video, used by stakeholders for attraction efforts," according to the BID's annual report, "was updated to communicate the latest neighborhood demographics, and the BID installed an advertising campaign in the D.C. Circulator with bright imagery to promote the Capitol Riverfront" (Capitol Riverfront BID 2016). Its tagline also communicates its new brand: "DC Amplified. Life Simplified." This reflects the new, "diverse" D.C. that BID urbanism has pursued since the late 1990s, and the Capitol Riverfront BID is not an anomaly.

The NoMa BID, also created in 2007, is situated in another new growth neighborhood, and a similar transformation has remade the district and its surrounding area in Northeast D.C. In describing this change, David Rusk of the D.C. Policy Center recently reminisced about what had been there and no longer is: "The row houses and apartments? Basically, all below Massachusetts Avenue are gone, torn down for office buildings, the Georgetown Law Center, and new hotels—The Hyatt Regency, the Washington Court, and the slyly-named The Liaison Capitol Hill" (Rusk 2017). With this development the demographics have changed as well, and "from today's vantage point" it is now composed of "two separate worlds, one largely white and high income, the other largely black and low-income (Rusk 2017). Like the Capitol Riverfront BID, the NoMa BID is also engaged in active rebranding efforts. In 2012 it successfully lobbied to have its Metro station renamed from New York Avenue to NoMa/Gallaudet U. Its website tagline in October 2108 read: "NoMa. City. Smarter."[26] This was accompanied by the message that "NoMa offers convenient luxury living just steps from the Capitol and Union Station. NoMA lives up to the reputation of a transit-oriented neighborhood. According to the BID's president 'fewer than 15 percent of residents drive to work'" (Hoffer 2015). The median household income, according to the Washington DC Economic Partnership, has risen steadily from $42,192 in 2013 to $54,482 in 2015 to $77,302 in 2018; 38 percent of the population was between twenty and thirty-four years old in 2018 (WDCEP 2013, 2015, 2018).

A 2015 article in the *Washington Post*'s real estate section declared:

"Where We Live: NoMa, the wrong side of the tracks no more." Unlike Rusk's (2017) reminiscence about what has been lost, the article asserts: "NoMa hasn't been NoMa very long. Before the name was conceived in the late 1990s and the new buildings followed in the new century, the area was largely desolate, known to many Washingtonians mainly as the site of the Greyhound station" (Hoffer 2015). Today, the author continues, "More hotels, more residential units, more stores, more restaurants and more offices are coming." In 2013, NoMa also secured fifty million dollars in public funding from the City Council for park construction (Wiener 2013).[27] New parks form crucial amenities for new neighborhoods. They serve as platforms for events and programming to create hospitable and sociable spaces for the "growth populations" described in the Capitol Riverfront BID reports.

D.C.'s BID geography is fairly contiguous and has expanded from the center outward, repositioning and inserting neighborhoods, old and new, firmly within the strategic image projected in 1998 of Washington, D.C., as "a world class city." These new "luxury" neighborhoods, which were clearly in the pipeline in 1998, also required a connectivity plan to ensure they did not become isolated as unconnected enclaves but rather part of an integrated identity in the geographic imagination of the city's new residents. Highlighted on the various BID websites are the mobility networks that connect potential residents and visitors to other parts of the city. NoMa is a case in point as its BID president made clear: "The Metro station, transit connectivity and proximity to downtown are big attractions" for these new residents (Hoffer 2015). The DowntownDC BID is another example. Its website offers not only the mass transit, Metrorail options, such as the "safe Red Line," and the "diverse" Green Line, but also highlights access to a highly subsidized D.C. Circulator Bus (DowntownDC 2013).

The Circulator is a public-private transportation partnership, only partially funded by four of the major BIDs; D.C. taxpayers shoulder most of the funding (Schwartz 2006).[28] Its routes initially focused on connecting the Georgetown BID to the two downtown areas (DowntownDC BID and Golden Triangle) and the city's monumental core, but since then the Circulator has come to connect all of the major BID areas to each other and to key tourist destinations as well as to Amtrak lines at Union Station (see figure 2). As the Capitol Riverfront BID's executive director noted: "We work with Circulator, but that accessibility is so paramount for us . . . improving local circulation, improving open space, knitting it together through a circulation pattern, and creating a civic framework where none existed" (Stevens, Suls, and Avery 2016; my transcription). Similarly, the Capital Bike

Share program, along with the necessary bike lanes, is concentrated in the BID areas while bypassing other outlying neighborhoods (Buehler and Stowe 2015). This circulation network, then, unites the BID geography and facilitates seamless movement through a new social landscape and a public realm teeming with activity.

Third Places and Pop-Ups

In its multipronged approach to placemaking, BID urbanism focuses on what a downtown Brooklyn BID executive in New York City called a "grounded focus" on the "people you want to come and stay" (APA-NYM 2017). Some of D.C.'s successful place entrepreneurs consciously use Ray Oldenburg's concept of "third place" to create "social" places in D.C. neighborhoods that provide opportunities to mingle and to anchor these new residents in place (Oldenburg 1999, 2001). In a 2012 interview, Constantine Stavropoulos, owner of Tryst, a highly successful café in Adams Morgan, a serial placemaking entrepreneur, and a key organizer of the neighborhood BID in Adams Morgan, was asked how D.C. had changed since 1998. He noted: "I think it's becoming more of a living city." Having come from "Philly," he continued, "I was always thinking, 'I'm in D.C.; it's just a stepping stone to somewhere else.' It wasn't until we opened Tryst that I really embraced D.C. as home" (Voelker 2012). For those unfamiliar with the old D.C., the city apparently seemed to lack "third places" in which to interact. But this depended on who was looking, what they were seeing, and what they desired (Hopkinson 2012b; Coghill Chatman 2015).

Certainly, D.C. had third places both in the private realm of cafés, restaurants, and churches, for example, and in the public realm, such as the drum circle at Dupont Circle and Malcolm X Park or the informal gatherings of Latinx high school students on Mount Pleasant Street. Michelle Coghill Chatman describes the network of Pan-African third places existing across the D.C. landscape that are threatened due to gentrification (Coghill Chatman 2015). In the same neighborhood where Stavropoulos created the Tryst phenomenon, El Tamarindo, an El Salvadoran restaurant, has been a 24/7 spot since the 1980s, and so have the Ethiopian cafés and restaurants lining 18th Street. Downtown had its own third places, such as d.c.space, where music, political poetry, and spoken word brought people together (Padua 2015). And the area that is Capitol Riverfront today from 1984 until 1999 was home to Tracks, which was "a gay nightclub" that attracted a "diverse cross section of the LGBT community, including whites, blacks, men and women,

Latinos and Asians," and where the "straight crowd knew it was a gay club but they couldn't find anything like it anywhere else" (Chibbaro 2013). Thus third spaces abounded in D.C., and someone familiar with this old D.C., if asked, would surely name numerous more third places.

The deliberate curating of third places to market neighborhoods to higher-income consumers unfamiliar with the city is expressive of BID urbanism, however. These third places are promoted to signal to newcomers the possibility that they might find a sense of belonging in the city's social landscape. Producers of third places, such as Stavropoulos, often become placemaking entrepreneurs, finding new terrain, neighborhoods in transition at the cusp of gentrification, in which to invest and replicate their success (Summers 2015).

Because BID-PPP urban regimes are invested in keeping their mixed-use environments vibrant, this placemaking trend, to create places of sociability, has increasingly encompassed the public realm. Building on the insights of Jane Jacobs, Holly Whyte, and more recently Jan Gehl, urbanists who have rightly sought to refocus attention on human-scale urban design and on street-level human interaction (Gehl 2007, 2010; Jacobs [1961] 1992; Whyte 1988). BIDs have also consciously turned to the temporary activations of their public spaces as part of their real estate strategy. In an ever-changing economic environment, BIDs clearly have to respond to market changes to maintain viable and profitable locations, and they are keen observers of their environments. Since the great recession (2008), BID urbanism has progressively relied on "programming," often employing "pop-up" economic development techniques. These, a D.C. BID planner explained in 2017, fall into at least two categories: pop-up retail to fill vacant storefronts and prevent the appearance of neighborhood decline and pop-up landscapes to produce a sense of "neighborhood" life and sociability in the public realm.

In D.C., pop-ups as such did not gain official traction until after 2010.[29] Consciously conceived "pop-up" activity appeared as part of the informal cultural industry, spearheaded especially by Philippa Hughes, founder of the Pink Line Project. The Pink Line Project paved the way beginning in 2007 when Hughes and friends "decided to do a 'happening'" and "found a raw space on the corner of 14th and Church Street" (Beete 2010). By 2010, the D.C. Office of Planning (OP) teamed up with the Washington DC Economic Partnership (WDCEP) to develop goals for an interim use strategy to "reverse negative association with vacant urban sites and spaces" (Driggins and Snowden 2012).[30] And in line with the city's "Creative Action Agenda," the OP subsequently developed a creative placemaking program, termed "Temporium," to activate vacant storefronts in Shaw, H Street, and Mount Pleasant through a partnership with cultural and design entrepreneurs (Douglas 2010, 2011). Apparently, during the recession, pop-up activities were thought to "sell condos, too," leading to "pop-up galleries-in-a-condo," which gave rise to "a new crop of impresarios . . . to connect the creatives with the capitalists" (Dawson 2010b).

From its early conception, Temporium has been a real estate-centric program, wherein the public sector "spearheaded an investment of resources into temporary or 'pop-up' retail stores and arts venues. Using vacant storefronts for weeks at a time allowed residents, entrepreneurs, and developers to see the potential of underperforming commercial streets to become vibrant retail corridors" (Driggins and Snowden 2012, 3). In 2014, the associate director for citywide planning at the Office of Planning in fact noted, "OP's mission is to guide real estate development in the District of Columbia" (Driggins 2014, 98). She added that OP began to "incorporate early initiatives that harness the arts and design for all neighborhood planning studies and projects" (100). Interestingly, the Office of Planning has cited this program as the forerunner of a new initiative, "Crossing the Street." Funded by the Kresge Foundation, it aims to "build D.C.'s inclusive future" and employs creative placemaking to involve communities in planning activities to stimulate "civic engagement" (Office of Planning 2016).

After Temporium began, there was an explosion of pop-up activity among BIDs. In effect, the pop-up retail strategy to activate storefronts, the continual programming of pop-up events, and the production of temporary mini-landscapes creates a synergy between the private and public realms. In neighborhoods such as NoMa and Capitol Riverfront, this kaleidoscope of new perspectives and experiences introduces novelty, as pop-up urbanism splinters the monotony of new-built environments and inoculates against boredom and isolation. For BIDs in "new" neighborhoods this activity is crucial: "These events bring people to our neighborhoods that ultimately lease rental properties, so it's a way to market our neighborhood and showcase our neighborhood," explained a Capitol Riverfront BID executive (Stevens, Suls, and Avery 2016; my transcription).

The Golden Triangle and NoMa BIDs have also explicitly turned to the production of pop-up landscapes to activate their public realm. In the Golden Triangle, movable seating elements on the sidewalks and on Farragut Square, the main "town square," give people a temporary sense of control over the structuring of their immediate individual or social space in an otherwise sterile office building environment (Stevens, Suls, and Avery 2016). Food trucks around the square and planned evening activities entice people both to stay after hours and to venture to this downtown office district. A Golden Triangle BID professional talked about these temporary placemaking strategies as a key way "to start to create identifiable places, attractive, comfortable public spaces" in places that "felt boring, same, monotonous" (Stevens, Suls, and Avery 2016; my transcription). In NoMa, for example, a temporary "Wunder Garden," similar to outdoor pop-up beer gardens found across Philadelphia's landscape (Schaller and Guinand 2017), disguises an empty lot to insert a precious social place in this densely built-up environment at least on an interim basis until the completion of the planned city-funded parks. In the NoMa's business plan for 2018–2022, pop-ups are specifically noted under branding and marketing activities "to address the needs of a growing residential population and ensure neighborhood vibrancy." The BID president praised the "collaborative" spirit of NoMa developers, who "frequently allow temporary use of undeveloped land they own for the public's benefit [such as film nights]" (Hoffer 2015).

Programming, according to a three-year research study conducted by Gallup on the Knight Foundation communities and profiled on the International Downtown Associations' website, is indeed a way to create an affective relationship between the space and those who come. This bond is what produces a sense of place (Gallup 2010). BID-managed urban districts thus intentionally draw people into carefully programmed experiences of place, or in hospitality literature parlance, into eventscapes that are meant to be "memorable and satisfy and exceed expectations" (Tattersall and Cooper 2014, 141). This BID urbanism weds James Rouse's "festival markets," which brought "bored suburbanites in droves to a restored city," with his management vision for the suburban mall and creates places where new residents indeed find that their part of the "city is fun" (P. Hall 2014, 384). Today's iteration of the festival market, with an intensification of placemaking, has become the eventscape that "caters to new lifestyle needs" in the city (Chang and Huang 2005). Temporary events and landscapes insert for a limited time an element of surprise into people's experience of the city and produce a sense of coziness, familiarity, and even nostalgia (Schaller and Guinand 2017). They create outdoor third places often through seasonal and ritualistic repetition (Schaller and Guinand 2017). By providing access to their parks, moreover, BIDs harness the creative energy of place entrepreneurs to create events, such as the now famous "Diner en Blanc" picnic, that lend an air of exclusivity, culture, elegance, and even mystery to quotidian life

(Judkis 2014a, 2014c, 2014b; Yates 2014; Dawson 2010a, 2010b). And the choreographed "lingering" it facilitates, in turn, is integral to the economic development and real estate repositioning strategy pursued by BID urbanists in D.C. (Stevens, Suls, and Avery 2016). Interestingly, in the D.C. region, this pop-up placemaking strategy has migrated to the Virginia suburbs, where a BID is trying to breathe life into Tysons Corner, a formerly sprawling landscape of parking lots, which has been turned into a new mixed-use neighborhood connected to D.C. via Metro through transit-oriented development (Aratani 2013, 2014; O'Connell 2013a, 2013b).

BIDs have used these artificially programmed social spaces as sites of revelry to reinforce the appeal of their neighborhoods. In D.C. these changes have come with a cost for longtime, especially low-income, residents. Urban design historian Emily Talen observes that both citizen- and business-led do-it-yourself (DIY) urbanism in the United States dates back to the nineteenth century. Even then "it was thought, [DIY urbanism] would make cities better places to live and better attractors of capital investment" (Talen 2015, 138). This motivation remains today (Oswalt, Overmeyer, and Misselwitz 2009, 2013; Schaller and Guinand 2017). The types of short-term interventions and activities in contemporary placemaking represent nothing particularly new then. With the 2008 recession, such activities reemerged more forcefully and were officially sanctioned as investment slowed and empty commercial spaces and vacant lots created blight across cityscapes. To activate urban places, planning consultants have also retooled and marketed tactics (Beekmans and Boer 2014; Lydon and Garcia 2015), such as street vending, food trucks, informal social gatherings in the public realm, that low-income communities have relied on to navigate economic insecurity and build social networks. The difference is that low-income youths and adults usually have had to pursue these kinds of informal social and income-generating activities under threat of harassment from public agencies as well as private improvement organizations (Kamel 2014).

The Underbelly of BID Urbanism

As BID urbanism induced a development and housing boom, the District and its private sector partners failed to address the increasingly disparate impacts of D.C.'s growth (Lauber 2012; Zippel 2016). By 2015, the city reached the goal to add 100,000 residents, which Mayor Williams had announced in 2003. A 2015 press release announced that D.C. had "added more than

70,000 residents since the 2010 census and just over 100,000 residents in the 15 years since the census in 2000" (Executive Office of the Mayor 2015). In 2015, a total of 672,228 people resided in the District, up from 572,059 in 2000. In this growth inheres a complicated story.

On April 13, 2018, a D.C. civil rights lawyer filed a class action suit against the city for "gentrification" (Schwartzman 2018; Delgadillo 2018). The lawyer represents members of CARE, an organization whose "members are all African-American's living East of the River" (*Matthews et al. v. D.C. Zoning Commission et al.* 2018, 2). The complaint, which the attorney has published as a PDF file, reads: "Over the past 12 years, and still continuing today, the District of Columbia has implemented a policy to attract the Creative Class ... this agenda disparately impacts other protected classes ... Adverse impacts noted in the Comprehensive plan such as displacement and gentrification have gone ignored" (2). Thus, the suit alleges that the "District Government has a clear preference for millennial creatives, making it somewhat harder for those residents that aren't notable assets" (26). The African American plaintiffs in the case do not only fear displacement, the lawyer observes, but are fighting the discrimination and dislocation that has accompanied gentrification: "their ways of life, which include gathering and holding court outside during day time hours," the complaint reads, "are increasingly being challenged by over policing and gentrifiers who have weaponized group listservs and apps like 'Nextdoor'" (2–3). The lawyer filing the suit traces these dynamics back to the administration of Mayor Fenty (2007–2011).

But the origins of the public-private redevelopment strategy that propelled D.C.'s drastic transformation, which the lawsuit addresses, reach further back in time to the 1998 "Citizens Plan" and the Williams administration's residential strategy. The question as to who would have the capacity to shape, participate in, and benefit from the type of place-based urbanism the "Citizens Plan" catalyzed was not adequately addressed. Despite the "inclusive city" moniker embossed on the 2004 "Framework," specific strategies to mitigate against rapidly rising land and property values, as well as rent and commercial lease rates that were doing the same, were not sufficiently incorporated into the subsequent budgeting, financing, and implementation of the various competing planning priorities (Rubin 2003).

Maps in the 2004 "Inclusive City" framework had documented a divided city, identifying 16th Street NW as a stark dividing line: generally speaking, east of this line poverty rates as well as unemployment rates appeared high and education levels low. This dividing line, as the neighborhood chapters

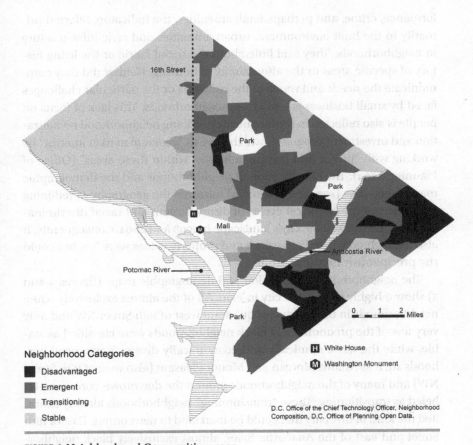

16th Street

Park

Park

H

Mall

M

Anacostia River

Potomac River

Park

0   1   2 Miles

Neighborhood Categories

H   White House
M   Washington Monument

Disadvantaged
Emergent
Transitioning
Stable

D.C. Office of the Chief Technology Officer, Neighborhood
Composition, D.C. Office of Planning Open Data.

FIGURE 4. Neighborhood Composition, 1990

show, has figured prominently in the urban imaginary of D.C. residents. It also became a main axis for the city's comprehensive planning vision and the plans for new transportation infrastructure, particularly the Metro's (mass transit) Green Line extension. To guide the concentrated investment laid out in the strategic plan and the 2004 "Framework," the city deployed a neighborhood indicator system based on 1990 census data, which classified neighborhoods into four categories: disadvantaged, emerging, transitioning, or stable (see figure 4).

The neighborhood indicators incorporated data on "infrastructure conditions, the quality of housing, and retail amenities, the local real estate market, crime rates, school performance, community facilities and parks as well as civic engagement" (Office of Planning 2004). Besides school performance, crime, and perhaps retail amenities, the indicators referred primarily to the built environment, urban amenities and civic infrastructure in neighborhoods. They said little about the social fabric or the living history of specific areas or the affordability of housing. Neither did they communicate the needs and wants of the residents or the particular challenges faced by small businesses already in neighborhoods. This lack of focus on people is also reflected in the language describing neighborhood revitalization and investment programs, which were to "generate market interest" by working with "public and private dollars . . . within these areas" (Office of Planning 2004). The classification of neighborhoods and the demographic map of 1990 data (see figures 4 and 5) mirrored the geography of redlining and reflected the historical cycles of disinvestment and racial discrimination that still marked the city's landscape in 1998 and 2004. Consequently, it also highlighted where land values and property values were low but could rise precipitously to realize profits.

The neighborhood composition and demographic maps (figures 4 and 5) show a highly segregated city in 1990. All of the almost exclusively white neighborhoods in the Northwest quadrant west of 16th Street NW and only very few of the predominately black neighborhoods were classified as stable, while the more ethnically and economically diverse parts, neighborhoods such as Adams Morgan and Mount Pleasant (also west of 16th Street NW) and many of the neighborhoods around the downtown core, were labeled as transitioning. These "transitioning" neighborhoods already exhibited the kind of diversity that could be marketed to newcomers. East of 16th Street and east of the Anacostia River, almost exclusively black neighborhoods were categorized as either emerging (if they abutted transitioning neighborhoods) or disadvantaged.

The classification system created a nexus between high property values, middle- or upper-class spaces, and social stability. Stable neighborhoods were considered to have "healthy real estate markets, above average home markets and positive social and economic indicators." Transitioning neighborhoods were characterized by "rapid development, rising property values, and the potential for displacement." Emerging neighborhoods, on the other hand, although they exhibited "moderately positive social and economic indicators," were considered as "underperforming compared to stable neighborhoods." Finally, disadvantaged neighborhoods were described as lacking in "private investment" and as having "low social and economic indicators" (Office of Planning 2004, 36).

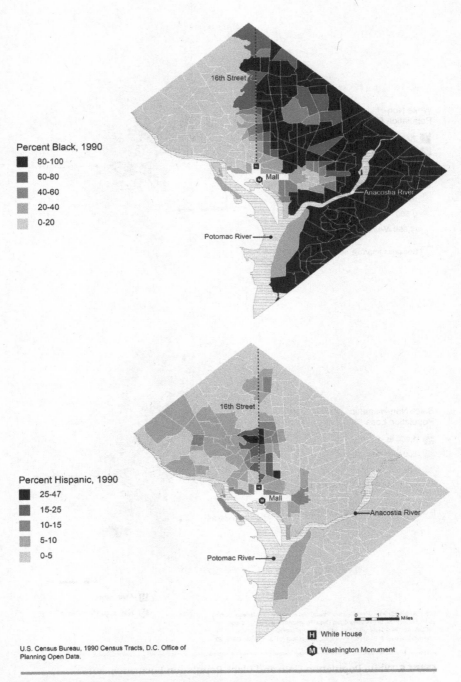

Percent Black, 1990

- 80-100
- 60-80
- 40-60
- 20-40
- 0-20

16th Street

H
M Mall

Anacostia River

Potomac River

Percent Hispanic, 1990

- 25-47
- 15-25
- 10-15
- 5-10
- 0-5

16th Street

H
M Mall

Anacostia River

Potomac River

0   1   2 Miles

H White House

M Washington Monument

U.S. Census Bureau, 1990 Census Tracts, D.C. Office of
Planning Open Data.

FIGURE 5. Percent Black and Hispanic Population, 1990

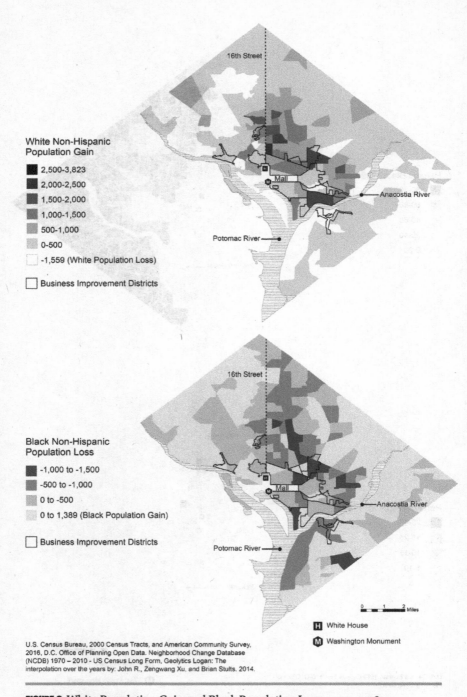

White Non-Hispanic
Population Gain

▪ 2,500-3,823
▪ 2,000-2,500
▪ 1,500-2,000
▪ 1,000-1,500
▪ 500-1,000
▪ 0-500
▫ -1,559 (White Population Loss)

▢ Business Improvement Districts

16th Street

Mall

Anacostia River

Potomac River

Black Non-Hispanic
Population Loss

▪ -1,000 to -1,500
▪ -500 to -1,000
▪ 0 to -500
▪ 0 to 1,389 (Black Population Gain)

▢ Business Improvement Districts

16th Street

Mall

Anacostia River

Potomac River

0 1 2 Miles

H White House

M Washington Monument

U.S. Census Bureau, 2000 Census Tracts, and American Community Survey,
2016, D.C. Office of Planning Open Data. Neighborhood Change Database
(NCDB) 1970 – 2010 - US Census Long Form, Geolytics Logan: The
interpolation over the years by: John R., Zengwang Xu, and Brian Stults. 2014.

FIGURE 6. White Population Gain and Black Population Loss, 2000–2016

While the 2004 framework maps did not overtly address race, the "Census 2010 Atlas" produced by the Office of Planning in 2012, unlike the 2004 framework, clearly draws these connections and illustrates that class and race/ethnicity continued to intersect in persistent ways even ten years later. The document visualizes them in starkly clear choropleth maps (Government of the District of Columbia 2012). The class-based inequalities expressed on the map with which the 2004 framework opened as a premise for its strategic foci masked the persisting racial disparities embodied in D.C.'s neighborhood geography at the time the "Citizens Plan" was released. Per capita income in 1999, for example, for Hispanics was $17,375 and for African Americans $17,734 whereas for whites it was much higher at $55,630 (U.S. Census 2000).

Downtown and its surrounding neighborhoods (Central Washington), areas identified as emerging along the Anacostia waterfront, and transitioning neighborhoods in the Central Washington and Mid-City planning areas, especially east of 16th Street NW, became strategic targets for successive place-based redevelopment and revitalization programs in accordance with the 1998 "Citizens Plan" and the 2004 "Comprehensive Planning Framework." Moreover, a spatial depiction of these investment targets in relation to the evolution of D.C.'s BID geography (compare figures 3, 4, and 7) demonstrates that the layered place-based interventions were originally focused particularly on transitioning neighborhoods situated around the downtown BIDs.

Ironically, the strategic intervention by the BID-PPP regime in areas first identified in the 1998 "Citizens Plan" and reconfirmed in the Comprehensive Plan accelerated the above-identified tendencies. Rather than fostering long-term integration and diversity, this BID urbanism has contributed to the continuing segregation of D.C. and its region albeit patterned into new neighborhoods, including the suburbs (Lauber 2012). Moreover, despite the District's overall population decline between 1980 and 2000, many of the transitioning areas had not lost but instead gained population, unlike areas with high concentrations of poverty east of the Anacostia River and parts of the Northeast quadrant of the city (Rubin 2003). Yet, neighborhood revitalization tools, such as TIF and PILOT financing, in conjunction with programs such as Great Streets and the Strategic Neighborhood Investment Program (SNIP) were initially concentrated in transitioning neighborhoods (see figures 3 and 4). This was done despite the warnings of displacement included in the 2004 comprehensive planning framework (Office of Planning 2004).[31]

Over the next decade, the census tracts adjacent to and comprised in the 1998 strategic action areas and later in the comprehensive plan consistently gained a significant number of whites while losing blacks and in some cases Latinxs as well. Although both the white and black populations declined between 1980 and 2000, a bifurcated trend emerged in the post-2000 years, wherein the city continued to lose African Americans while gaining whites. From this skewed pattern of population gains and losses depicted (see figure 6) in relation to the strategic planning interventions, it becomes apparent that another model of "diversity" and" integration" has been achieved "via what might be called the 'back door' route of gentrification" (Lauber 2012, 140).

The much celebrated achievement of multicultural "diversity" failed to acknowledge the ways in which the intersection of class and race was transforming D.C.'s landscape to benefit a younger, perhaps unprecedentedly more diverse, but still overwhelmingly white segment of the population. Together, figure 6 and figure 7, which show these demographic trends in another way, illustrate that those census tracts and areas where strategic investments were made have consistently lost black residents. In figure 7, only three comprehensive planning areas gained black population between 2000 and 2016; two of those, Four and Ten, are located east of the Anacostia River, a predominately black area before the advent of BID urbanism. The rapid demographic diversification of the census tracts around the downtown core placed African Americans, in particular, at risk of displacement (Lauber 2012). This trend subsequently pushed ever eastward even across the Anacostia River, at times cited as the last "dividing" line (O'Connell 2016). And the 2018 "gentrification" lawsuit brings into high relief the mounting pressure lower-income African Americans are feeling east of the river (*Matthews et al. v. D.C. Zoning Commission et al.* 2018).

In 2014, the Office of Planning analyzed the profiles of those moving into and those moving out of D.C. (Pate 2016). This "snapshot" confirmed the general trend in the areas that gained population over the past decade and a half: a net loss of African Americans and a net gain of white individuals, among whom young professionals with graduate degrees predominated. The Adams Morgan and Mount Pleasant area in the decade from 2000 to 2010, for example, disproportionally lost both Latinx and African American populations and gained higher-income whites; these trends, which almost doubled the median household income in Adams Morgan, have undermined the long-term survival and viability of these neighborhoods as diverse and potentially economically and racially integrative urban spaces.

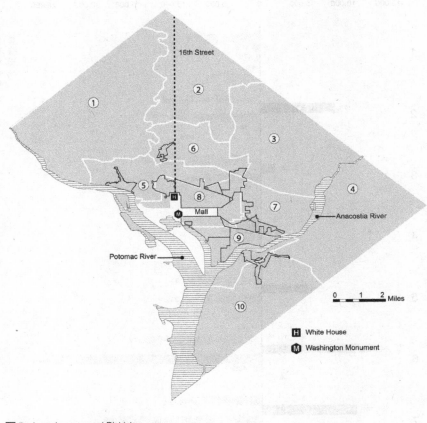

16th Street

① 1
② 2
③ 3
④ 4
⑤ 5
⑥ 6
⑦ 7
⑧ 8
⑨ 9
⑩ 10

Mall

M

←Anacostia River

Potomac River→

0   1   2 Miles

H White House

M Washington Monument

☐ Business Improvement Districts

▨ Comprehensive Planning Areas

1) Rock Creek West
2) Rock Creek East
3) Upper Northeast
4) Far Northeast and Southeast
5) Near Northwest
6) Mid-City
7) Capitol Hill
8) Central Washington
9) Lower Anacostia Waterfront
10) Far Southeast and Southwest

D.C. Office of the Chief Technology Officer, Comprehensive Planning Areas, D.C. Office of Planning Open Data. U.S. Census Bureau, 2000 Census Tracts, and American Community Survey, 2016, D.C. Office of Planning Open Data. Neighborhood Change Database (NCDB) 1970 – 2010 - US Census Long Form, Geolytics Logan: The interpolation over the years by: John R., Zengwang Xu, and Brian Stults. 2014.

FIGURE 7a. Comprehensive Planning Areas and Population Change, 2000–2016

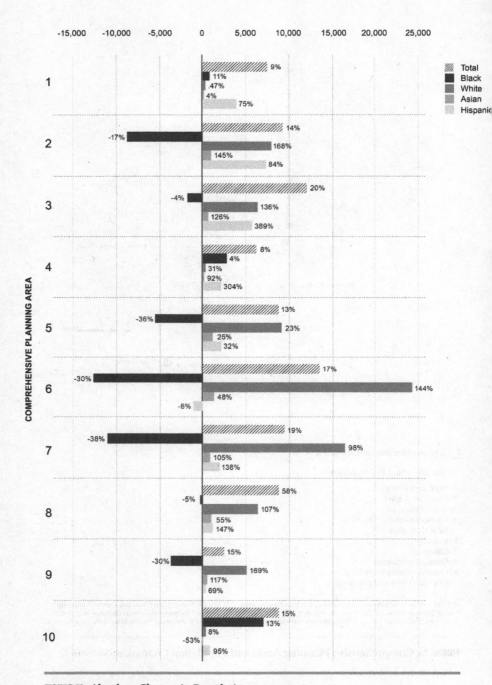

FIGURE 7b. Absolute Change in Population, 2010–2016

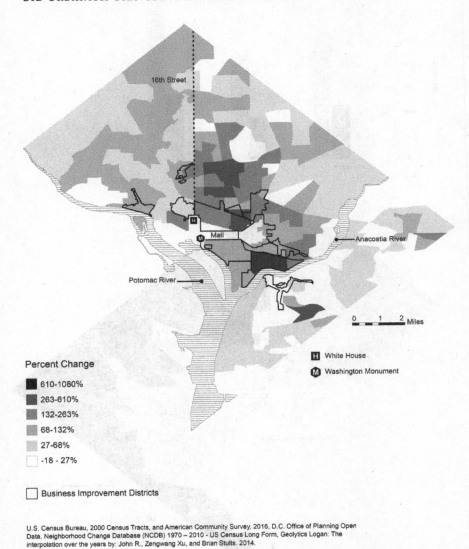

Percent Change

- 610-1080%
- 263-610%
- 132-263%
- 68-132%
- 27-68%
- -18 - 27%

Business Improvement Districts

U.S. Census Bureau, 2000 Census Tracts, and American Community Survey, 2016, D.C. Office of Planning Open Data. Neighborhood Change Database (NCDB) 1970 – 2010 - US Census Long Form, Geolytics Logan: The interpolation over the years by: John R., Zengwang Xu, and Brian Stults. 2014.

FIGURE 8. Change in Median Household Income: Census Tracts, 2000–2016

Figure 8, which shows the change in median income on the census tract level (in current dollars), indicates where low-income populations were especially vulnerable.

A look at figure 9 illustrates BID areas with a quarter-mile buffer and a graph showing the change in median household income (in 2016 inflation-

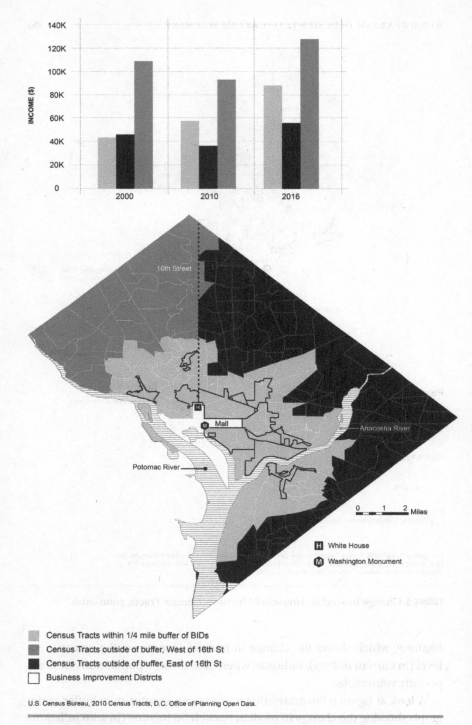

FIGURE 9. Change in Median Household Income, BIDs with ¼-Mile Buffer and Non-BID Areas, 2000–2016

adjusted dollars) in three different areas from 2000 to 2016. A striking picture emerges. The census tracts within this more broadly delineated BID area where BID urbanism concentrated its investments had an average median household income of about $57,788 in 2000; this area tracked a consistent and more pronounced increase in median household income (MHI) than "non-BID areas" between 2000 and 2016, rising to $87,992 in 2016. Thus, the median income in these census tracts increased 52 percent over this period. In non-BID areas east of 16th Street NW, on the other hand, which is where predominately black neighborhoods were concentrated, the average median household income changed less dramatically: in 2000 the MHI was $46,485 and rose to $56,639 in 2016, for an overall increase of 22 percent. In non-BID areas west of 16th Street, which comprises predominately white and wealthy census tracts in the Northwest quadrant of the city, the median income was much higher to begin with, but the areas evidenced a similar trend to the other non-BID area: the MHI was $108,671 in 2000 and reached $127,795 in 2016; the overall increase was 18 percent. This indicates that "stable neighborhoods" as might be expected witnessed no dramatic change. When one refines the analysis to highlight BID areas, looking at census tracts inside and adjacent to BIDs and then singling out the downtown and employment center BIDs, specifically, the increase in median income is even more apparent as compared to non-BID areas (figures 8 and 9). This seems to suggest that the concentrated redevelopment and rebranding activities have effectively attracted higher income, predominately white residents (see figure 6) to the areas where the BID-PPP focused its strategic investments.

Given the city's history, it was not unexpected that growth in D.C. has been unevenly experienced. This was, however, not a byproduct of the invisible hand of the market. To the contrary, scholars had predicted such outcomes for this type of targeted investment strategy. In 1985, a study of Washington, D.C., analyzing the impacts of what Asch and Musgrove (2015) identified as the "third wave" of gentrification, observed, "if revitalization is still in an early stage, the core could eventually re-segregate as blacks continue to be 'priced out' by higher-status whites;" moreover, the authors cautioned, "an extreme version of the displacement hypothesis predicts that revitalization will eventually produce not only a few whiter neighborhoods but a whiter city" (Lee, Spain, and Umberson 1985, 596). Two reports also surfaced in 2003, as the 2004 framework came under review and funding proposals passed through the City Council for the SNIP program. These warned against displacement, particularly in the Mid-City planning areas (both transitioning as well as emerging) around downtown and called for a deliberate focus on equitable development (Rivlin 2003; Rubin 2003). And the "Fair Housing" report published in 2012 confirmed this prediction: "parts of the city are becoming more racially and economically diverse largely through the in-migration of Caucasians with higher incomes than the African Americans they are replacing" (Lauber 2012, 16). Yet, while the imperative to "manage growth" in transitioning areas was recognized in the 2004 framework, no strategic anti-displacement policy was developed (Lauber 2012, 98).[32] To the contrary, the 2012 "Fair Housing" report prepared for the Department of Housing and Economic Development underlines the disparate racial outcomes of D.C.'s development trajectory in relation to the 2004 "Framework." The report highlights the juxtaposition between the lofty vision of the "Framework" and the shortcomings of the proactive policy proposals, goals, and objectives that were implemented presumably to achieve stable, integrated, and inclusive neighborhoods.

The reasoning behind BID urbanism adheres to a market-based ethos that valorizes competition, self-help, and property-based governance. This theory in fact persuades strong economic actors to influence and ultimately exploit market conditions that past urban policies have produced. The "Fair Housing" report cites widespread, persisting discrimination in the housing and mortgage markets and condemns D.C.'s governance regime for its failure to monitor these dynamics in the market and to proactively pursue fair and affordable housing policies (Lauber 2012). According to this report, not only African Americans in D.C. but also Latinxs suffered disparate impact under the urban regime's policies (Lauber 2012, 111). For example, in 2000, the city's building code enforcement officers swept through city neighborhoods "except for the District's wealthiest neighborhoods: Dupont Circle, upper Northwest, and Georgetown" to come up "with a list of the 27 worst buildings ... located in neighborhoods where the proportion of Hispanic residents was about four times the percentage of Hispanics for the city as a whole" (111). Not coincidentally, in Columbia Heights, one of the strategic neighborhoods, the city condemned buildings in the vicinity of the new Green Line Metro station and "DC USA," D.C.'s largest retail development projects at the time (see figure 3).

In D.C. as this chapter illustrates, BIDs fulfill key leadership roles; they have led or been instrumental in shaping the planning initiatives that have changed D.C.'s urban fabric. This BID urbanism has catalyzed or accelerated demographic shifts and produced new neighborhoods as mixed-use enclaves with public spaces and parks reconfigured in the words of a D.C.

BID executive as "expensive toys" for a new class of urbanites (Stevens, Suls, and Avery 2016). Guy Stuart (2003) shows how real estate interests bound, name, and brand districts in order to induce and steer gentrification and to manage risk. Thus, it should not be surprising that the BID-PPP regime in D.C. created a geography of BIDs wherein large BIDs, in conjunction with neighborhood-based business improvement districts (NBIDs), served to fuel gentrification: they empowered a select group of people to reposition the city's identity and make decisions about the provision of local services, place amenities, and programming to achieve their development aims. Unfortunately, as has historically been the case in D.C., these policies, subsidized by D.C.'s taxpayers, are not only class-inflected but also race-inflected policies. They do not address historical patterns of exclusion but renew skewed patterns of wealth creation. This chapter illustrates that BIDs are not simply self-help organizations that only pursue local objectives. Instead, their work is undoubtedly embedded in the wider planning agendas advanced by an institutional leadership network that constitutes a city-level PPP regime.

In March 2017, Anthony Williams, the former mayor of Washington, D.C., wrote: "Say what you want about Marion Barry, but he was a brilliant man who built a massive patronage system and following in Washington, D.C. He gave African Americans hope when the majority black city was fighting the city's white overlords in Congress. And he could deliver major economic projects, and most importantly, a fairer share of jobs" (A. Williams 2017). Williams's words are steeped in deep irony. His mayoralty, which followed at the heels of the Fiscal Control Board, ushered in the new era of municipal governance. Rooted in a "technocratic," post-racial worldview (Harris 2010), his administration in effect consolidated what I call the BID-PPP regime. But as the D.C. Fiscal Policy Institute has consistently argued, the fruits of this development, much of it supported by substantial government subsidies and various economic development tax programs, did not trickle down sufficiently to longtime D.C. residents; instead inequality has increased dramatically since the 1990s (Boivie 2017). In fact, the institute and other groups, including D.C. One—an organization working for racial and economic equity—advocated for legislation to introduce more transparency into the reporting of such projects, for strengthening first-source hiring requirements, and for union labor to be hired on these projects (D.C. Fiscal Policy Institute 2007).

In retrospect, Williams also questioned the efficacy and fairness of this type of regime: "Indeed, this style of data-driven governance," he acknowledged, "is seen as driving gentrification as it seeks to make cities more appealing to Millennials. It's their commutes that are getting easier, and their communities becoming more livable." Moreover, he added: "The poor and working-class African Americans. These communities feel alienated, lost, and overwhelmed in modern D.C." (A. Williams 2017).

The next four chapters turn to the neighborhood level to investigate the micropolitics of placemaking and to examine the complex ways in which BID urbanism can produce a sense of dislocation before displacement even occurs and distort local governance patterns, reinforcing exclusionary tendencies and projecting them into the future.

CHAPTER 5

Situating Adams Morgan
and Mount Pleasant

The politics of inter- and intra-neighborhood boundaries have been serious business in D.C., especially in the process of creating racialized property markets. They have also been instrumental in producing the racially disparate development outcomes delineated in the previous chapter. As Gregory Squires and Charis Kubrin (2006) note, privilege accrues in and through place, and boundaries and borders define place. The strategic and comprehensive planning documents of the BID-PPP regime in D.C. articulated a desire to resurrect an ill-defined or glorious "shared heritage." Yet, this notion of a "shared heritage" is contentious, burdened by what Leela Fernandes describes as the "politics of forgetting" (Fernandes 2004). This type of placemaking has not only given primacy to the aesthetics of the built environment through historic preservation, for example, but has also tended to "evoke . . . [a] very peculiar, selective, and imaginary time," which is frequently a place and time through which "we are all encouraged to identify with wealthy (most often white and male) elites" (Farrar 2011, 730).[1] This politics of forgetting often relegates more diverse social histories and practices of racism and discrimination to a past era and "sanitizes" local histories to appeal to a broad audience (Hyra 2017). These types of selective memory gloss over the complex social histories and contemporary lived experiences of exclusion, exploitation, perseverance, community solidarity, and basic quotidian survival practices that mark most neighborhoods (Farrar 2011). D.C.'s BID urbanism grafted onto these realities a vision of place that targeted a wished-for population identified in the 1998 "Citizens Plan."

This chapter situates the neighborhood case study in those aspects and moments of particular places that were remembered and referenced in contemporary talk around neighborhood "diversity," "revitalization," and "improvement" (Modan 2007). It begins with the early history of neighborhood development to highlight how contemporary politics of preservation and heritage function to fracture an understanding of the area's geographic space and identity that emerged later in the struggle over desegregation. From there, the chapter moves to community organizing efforts during the civil rights era, which gave Adams Morgan its name in 1955, a name that superseded the very localized identities associated with the period of restrictive covenants and citizens associations. This expansive view of neighborhood endured and transformed as the larger Adams Morgan and Mount Pleasant area developed into D.C.'s Latinx barrio, an identity that took on a specific salience in the context of increasing gentrification pressures. The chapter ends with a discussion of two previous "crises," one in 1991 and the other in 2000, which revealed the injustices, in this case faced by low-income Latinxs who lived in D.C.; the latter crisis exposed the deeply politicized placemaking ethos that the neighborhood BID (NBID) planning efforts exemplified.

Delineating Property Markets

Both Adams Morgan and Mount Pleasant have undergone several major demographic transitions since the early twentieth century. These processes concurrently brought changes to neighborhood commercial corridors (Henig 1982; Modan 2007; B. Williams 1988). Although the neighborhood signifier, "Adams Morgan," resonates deeply albeit differently with many residents and businesspeople, its early history is not one of a cohesive neighborhood. Like Mount Pleasant, the individual neighborhoods— Lanier Heights, Kalorama Heights, Washington Heights, and Meridian Hill (later Reed Cooke)—that later became identified as Adams Morgan were first developed as streetcar suburbs in the late 1800s to the early twentieth century. During the nineteenth century and up until the 1950s, this larger Adams Morgan area constituted a mosaic of subdevelopments and neighborhoods with distinct demographic, architectural characteristics and commercial identities. Sitting on a hill removed from the swampy lowlands, these five distinctive areas, as Henig (1982) notes, occupied prime land within the District's topography. Some of the elegant architecture dates back to the 1800s, but higher-density residential expansion, support-

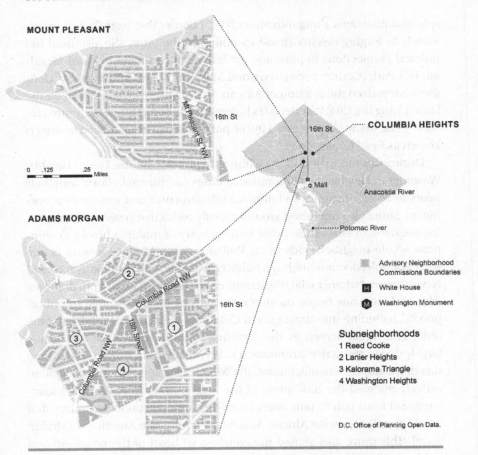

FIGURE 10. Adams Morgan and Mount Pleasant: ANC District Neighborhood
Boundaries, 1990

ing the development of the main commercial corridors, 18th Street, Columbia Road, and Mount Pleasant Street, took off in the early twentieth century
when electric streetcar lines linked the area to downtown and the federal
city. Prior to the 1950s, Mount Pleasant and three of the four neighborhoods
in Adams Morgan were predominately white and fairly wealthy.

Reed Cooke, which comprised portions of the old Meridian Hill, was already being forged through the interlocking politics of improvement and
displacement in the early twentieth century (Henig 1982). An advocate of
the City Beautiful, Mary Foote Henderson, a "Washington developer" who
"set the style for Washington's reinvention" during the gilded age of the
late nineteenth century (Conroy 2000), spearheaded the development of

splendid mansions along 16th Street NW, a border that later figured prominently in forging neighborhood identities. In the 1910s, she also used her political connections to persuade the federal government to build Meridian Hill Park (Conroy 2000), renamed Malcolm X Park in the 1960s.[2] Congress authorized the eviction of African Americans, who had settled on the land during the Civil War decades before Henderson requested the area for "her" park. Many, dispossessed by the park's construction, moved to what is known as Reed Cooke today.[3]

During this time, three of the white citizens associations, Lanier Heights, Washington Heights, and Kalorama, at times coordinated efforts with their peers in Mount Pleasant to lobby for infrastructure and service improvements. Some also organized around racially restrictive covenants, circulating petitions to ensure the racial homogeneity of multiple blocks to comprise whole neighborhoods (K. P. Williams 2015). Mount Pleasant is one such example, documented on a publicly available map (prologuedc.com).[4] Nevertheless, "where racial restrictions did not prevent them from doing so, African Americans began moving into many of these desirable neighborhoods," including into the adjacent Columbia Heights area; and for some time, 13th Street served as the "dividing line between black and white, largely due to restrictive covenants" (K. P. Williams 2015, 20). In response to this demographic encroachment, the Mount Pleasant citizens association actively pursued the movement of the neighborhood's eastern boundary westward from 14th to 16th Street to solidify a jurisdictional boundary that would clearly segregate African Americans from white Americans (Modan 2007). This move also shifted the commercial heart of the neighborhood to Mount Pleasant Street, reinforcing through its built environment and its physical and natural boundaries the urban "village" identity, which historic districting in the 1980s emphasized and contemporary heritage trails market (Cherkasky 2006).

New Deal policies and post–World War II policies precipitated the growth of the federal government, which brought on rapid population growth citywide. This growth flowed into centrally located streetcar-accessible neighborhoods, including into the Adams Morgan area (Henig 1982, 15).[5] The post–World War II era wrought additional changes as the civil rights movement assailed prevailing racial hierarchies, and court decisions began to dismantle the legal underpinnings of discrimination. As noted, in 1948, restrictive covenants were declared unenforceable in *Shelley v. Kramer*, and in 1954, the Supreme Court mandated the desegregation of schools. Furthermore, urban renewal planning in the 1950s into the 1960s unsettled the area's neighborhood identities for almost a decade (Henig 1982). These historical events reverberated through the neighborhoods. On the one hand, they hastened white flight into the suburbs and rallied efforts to secure existing neighborhood boundaries and character; on the other hand, they also deepened interracial coalition building to produce new and more open place identities (Huron 2014). The name Adams Morgan, which dates back to 1955, stands as recognition of community organizing to accelerate desegregation and a commitment to interracial solidarity. First hyphenated as Adams-Morgan, the name derives from the two neighborhood schools that had been educating whites and blacks separately until this time (Zapata and Gibson 2006).

Between Restoration and Solidarity

Even after *Shelley v. Kramer*, the Mount Pleasant and Kalorama citizens associations continued to lobby overtly for the continued protection of their interests and pursued a property owner–driven politics to "restore" historic neighborhoods well into the 1960s (Henig 1982, 16).[6] Asch and Musgrove (2015) observe that the Kalorama Restoration Society (KRS) was formed in 1959 to build on improvement processes already tested in Georgetown. Consequently, efforts to "restore" this neighborhood (and others as well) included a combination of individual renovation, developer activities, and government-sanctioned programs, such as historic districting (Asch and Musgrove 2015; Gale 1987).

D.C. politicians, the media, and developers, such as James Rouse, by now supported an alternative to the demolition-oriented urban renewal (Bloom 2004; Gillette 1999). Neighborhood "restoration" and "renewal" could be achieved by "more democratic and efficient means" through a synergistic partnership between public and private sector initiatives (Asch and Musgrove 2015). At the same time, the fortuitous political alignment that had halted urban renewal proved fleeting (McGovern 1998, 213) as some interest groups calling for preservation pursued more architecturally oriented revitalization strategies that ultimately undermined the goals of community activists seeking to secure the right of low-income communities "not to be excluded" from their neighborhoods and the city (Blomley 2016).

Between 1958 and 1962, according to Henig (1982), cantankerous discussions raged around an anticipated urban renewal designation in Adams Morgan, which revealed the simmering cleavages between the subneighborhoods. The Kalorama Citizens Association and the Kalorama Restoration Society, for example, lobbied for "a plan that would exclude their area" because an urban renewal label might affect property values (Henig 1982, 16). At the same time "organizations in predominately black sections," especially the Reed Cooke area, demanded that "conservation [not demolition] be emphasized" in order to avoid direct displacement (22). The ongoing difficult deliberations and the final defeat of the urban renewal plan in 1962 also signaled the definitive shift in urban policy on the national level (Griffith 1969).

Policy makers and planners were weary of the growing opposition to the old urban renewal model (N. Smith 1996).[7] As a result, developers, policy makers, and planners were increasingly turning to contextually guided restoration and redevelopment. These efforts were also welcomed by influential citizens associations in the wealthy sections of D.C., preparing and seeding the ground for coalitions that were to be built around preservation, revitalization, and placemaking (Asch and Musgrove 2015; McGovern 1998). But the urban renewal fight and the struggle for desegregation also served to build intercommunity cooperation across racial barriers, and the various subneighborhoods acquired an overarching place identity. Coalition building around concepts of "diversity" and "integration" inextricably linked with social justice came to define "Adams Morgan" for many residents and business owners for years thereafter. From this perspective the name itself exemplified that solidarity across class and race could bring about constructive outcomes on the neighborhood level (Modan 2008). These two tendencies, revitalization and solidarity, continue to collide.

The repercussions of the 1968 riots in the neighborhood precipitated widespread housing disinvestment. Prices declined, especially in neighborhoods abutting 16th Street NW. At the same time, young white people of middle-class backgrounds were beginning to move back into the city, and the Adams Morgan and Mount Pleasant area was one destination at this "urban frontier" (N. Smith 1996). Residents chose to settle or stay in Adams Morgan for multiple and sometimes crosscutting reasons: a specific appreciation of the area's demographic diversity, an admiration for its historic architectural composition, and a desire for urban conveniences, including the neighborhood's walkability and location in relation to downtown jobs (Henig 1982). In 2015, one longtime white resident, whose husband was born in the District, shared what she had "observed in that first ten years" after coming to the area in 1970: "People would move in, especially right after college," she noted, but "they would stay for a few years, and then they would either move away back to wherever home was or to some other city or

PICTURE 1. Raising the Adams Morgan flag on Adams Morgan Day 1982. Members of Adams Morgan Organization and other community activists raise the Adams Morgan "Unity in Diversity" flag. (Photo by Nancy Shia)

they would move out to the suburbs." Yet, "there was ... a really strong core of people who seemed to have no intentions of doing that." In her reminiscence, she encapsulated the tensions this incipient "back-to-the-city" catalyzed: how would these "newcomers" relate to and shape the neighborhood and its politics, especially with regard to longtime low-income residents, who, if they owned, had likely been denied loans to maintain their properties or, if they rented, were struggling to stay in the neighborhood? (Lloyd 2015).

Different groups proactively tried to contribute to what they saw as strategies to stabilize the neighborhood. Some focused on fighting crime and absentee landlords on the block level, while others, such as the Adams Morgan Organization (AMO), worked to build a broader, neighborhood-wide multiracial alliance to prevent displacement of low-income renters (Lloyd 2015). By the early 1970s, Adams Morgan was embroiled in the politics of gentrification, as anti-displacement activists watched the developments with trepidation (Lloyd 2015). In 1972, they organized the AMO to proactively confront gentrification. It launched a successful anti-redlining campaign and used a dormant D.C. law, which required if "a tenant was in a property and that property went up for sale, that property had to first be offered to the tenant," to support cooperative ownership of buildings (Lloyd 2015, 1099).

Even James and Patty Rouse famously became involved with "naïve" yet "stubborn" members of the Adams Morgan–based Church of the Savior with which they were affiliated (Shook and Ortmeyer 2012, 70), who had purchased two rundown apartment buildings in the early 1970s in order to rehabilitate them with and for low-income tenants. Since its approach was not at odds with his pragmatic outlook and belief in the efficacy of U.S. privatism, James Rouse supported this "Jubilee Housing" project to help demonstrate the feasibility of rebuilding cities through private socially oriented entrepreneurship (Gillette 1999). The Jubilee buildings along with limited-equity cooperatives the AMO supported (Huron 2014) created islands of affordability that endure in Adams Morgan today (Office of Planning 2015b). In an interview with James Lloyd, Frank Smith, a civil rights activist, AMO chairperson, and also former city councilmember, observed: "Middle-class and low-income African American and Hispanic community that's left over there now, primarily, and white community too, low-income white community, is a result of the anti-redlining campaign, the co-op movement that was financed by the anti-redlining campaign" (Lloyd 2015, 1103). In Adams Morgan, then, residents and business owners vigorously debated the threats of urban renewal and gentrification and called for multifaceted, sometimes contradictory, approaches to stem the twin ills: decline and gentrification (Henig 1982).

The ghost of "Georgetown," the first neighborhood to completely gentrify and displace a significant black population, loomed large in neighborhood discussions and continued to suffuse debates into the first decade of the 2000s. Opposing sides cited Georgetown as either a model for successful revitalization or an anti-model to illustrate the iniquitous outcomes of gentrification (Feaver 1974; Griffin 1974; Lippman 1974). Both Pierce and Liz Kaplan of the AMO conjured the creeping shadow of Georgetown (Huron 2014), as did city councilmember and local resident Tedson J. Meyers, who deliberately juxtaposed Adams Morgan and Georgetown, stating, "I don't want to see another Georgetown. . . . This is a working class community and we don't want to see it run into a chic neighborhood, but you can't stop all change" (Griffin 1974). The Adams Morgan motto, "Unity in Diversity," raised at the Adams Morgan Day Festival in 1982 (see picture 1), which also animates contemporary conversations, stands as a testament to AMO's interracial and cultural as well as cross-class organizing efforts.

Producing a "Worldly" Borderland

By the 1970s, the Adams Morgan and Mount Pleasant area had consolidated a reputation both as D.C.'s Latinx barrio (Cadaval 1998) and as a place where the world met. Due to accelerating demographic changes, the histories of the two neighborhoods in some ways realigned during this time. Situated between 16th Street and Rock Creek Park, the area was developing into a borderland space, distinct from the rest of the highly segregated District of Columbia with its sharply delineated black and white neighborhoods (see figure 5). In 1978 an article in the *Washington Post* affirmed the depiction that the Adams Morgan area represented a different kind of place in U.S. society due to its racial, cultural, and economic diversity (Lenz 1978).

Still, from its inception, the area's much hailed diversity was double-edged. The title of the article, "Concern in Washington's 'Latin Quarter': How Much Longer Can the Melting Pot Survive?" struck a foreboding tone (Lenz 1978). Pedro Lujan, a Peruvian-born community leader and business owner quoted in the article, remarked: "The government is paying a lot of money trying to get blacks, whites and Latinos to live and work to-

PICTURE 2. Two young dancers gather a crowd in the street at 18th and Columbia while they show their skills in the Latino Festival of 1985. (Photo by Nancy Shia)

TABLE 1. Percent of Census Tract Population by Ethnicity and Race (1970–2010)

Neighborhood Census Tracts	1970	1980	1990	2000	2010
NON-HISPANIC WHITES					
Mount Pleasant 27.1	29	37	34	30	43
Mount Pleasant 27.2	30	31	35	37	56
East Adams Morgan 38	16	22	29	35	53
East Adams Morgan 39	38	32	45	54	67
West Adams Morgan 40.1	54	64	81	80	80
West Adams Morgan 40.2	54	64	63	66	75
NON-HISPANIC BLACKS					
Mount Pleasant 27.1	66	49	40	32	25
Mount Pleasant 27.2	63	48	31	20	13
East Adams Morgan 38	74	64	48	33	19
East Adams Morgan 39	53	47	30	20	13
West Adams Morgan 40.1	32	21	6	6	4
West Adams Morgan 40.2	32	21	20	12	8
HISPANICS					
Mount Pleasant 27.1	4	8	21	28	24
Mount Pleasant 27.2	5	17	32	34	25
East Adams Morgan 38	8	11	21	28	20
East Adams Morgan 39	8	17	21	19	12
West Adams Morgan 40.1	11	11	10	8	9
West Adams Morgan 40.2	11	11	13	11	9

SOURCES: Neighborhood Change Database (NCDB) 1970–2010, U.S. Census Long Form, Geolytics Logan; John R. Logan, Zengwang Xu, and Brian Stults, "Interpolating U.S. Decennial Census Tract Data from as Early as 1970 to 2010: A Longitudinal Tract Database," *Professional Geographer* 66 (3) (2014): 412–20, http://www.s4.brown.edu/us2010/Researcher/Bridging.htm.

gether. . . . The Adams-Morgan, Mount Pleasant area is the only part of the city where this happens naturally, without a penny from the government" (Lenz 1978). But this coexistence was tenuous and not free of conflict, as whites with greater purchasing power continued to move into the neighborhood. Lujan also raised the specter of displacement: "Too many people from outside are moving into Adams-Morgan, and there will be a time when no Latinos live here." The "third" wave of gentrification rolling across the city was engulfing, especially the west side of Adams Morgan (Asch and Musgrove 2017). Similar media coverage about these kinds of tensions in Mount Pleasant would appear a decade later (Farhi 1990).

U.S.-supported wars precipitated a continual flow of immigrants to the D.C. metropolitan area and these neighborhoods in particular (Cadaval 1998). In Adams Morgan, Latinx immigrant entrepreneurs had already begun opening stores to cater to a growing local market in the 1960s and 1970s, and this trend continued. By the early 1980s, businesses, such as restaurants, began to market this "ethnic charm" to "outsiders" and "Non-Hispanics"

TABLE 2. Homeownership, Median Income, and Per Capita Income
by Ethnicity and Race, 2000

Neighborhood Census Tracts	Percent of Population	Homeownership Rate %	Median Income ($)	Per Capita Income ($)
WHITE (NON-HISPANIC)				
Mount Pleasant 27.1	30	43	53,839	38,847
Mount Pleasant 27.2	37	53	71,838	42,736
East Adams Morgan 38	35	58	59,271	51,980
East Adams Morgan 39	54	31	50,634	44,600
West Adams Morgan 40.1	80	51	60,417	65,404
West Adams Morgan 40.2	66	43	60,114	56,918
BLACK				
Mount Pleasant 27.1	32	22	31,768	21,098
Mount Pleasant 27.2	20	40	24,250	25,017
East Adams Morgan 38	33	12	26,959	19,672
East Adams Morgan 39	20	19	32,369	25,766
West Adams Morgan 40.1	6	29	41,625	36,316
West Adams Morgan 40.2	12	28	49,602	26,891
HISPANIC				
Mount Pleasant 27.1	28	12	27,065	12,202
Mount Pleasant 27.2	34	12	38,234	11,961
East Adams Morgan 38	28	9	33,269	15,569
East Adams Morgan 39	19	29	35,938	18,221
West Adams Morgan 40.1	8	26	60,500	37,952
West Adams Morgan 40.2	11	16	35,417	17,014
ASIAN				
Mount Pleasant 27.1	8	12	29,000	18,680
Mount Pleasant 27.2	7	19	49,167	21,427
East Adams Morgan 38	2	17	12,024	11,610
East Adams Morgan 39	3	12	35,278	28,275
West Adams Morgan 40.1	6	33	71,000	105,081
West Adams Morgan 40.2	6	10	34,844	22,662

SOURCES: Census 2000 Summary Files (SF 1) 100-Percent Data and Summary File 3 (SF– 3) Sample Data.

(Henig 1982, 16). Mount Pleasant attained this reputation a little later when Central Americans streamed into the neighborhood in the late 1980s. By 1980, about 13 percent and by 1990 19 percent of the population in the entire Adams Morgan and Mount Pleasant area was considered to be Hispanic. As table 1 shows, however, according to the U.S. census, individual census tracts in both of these neighborhoods had much higher concentrations of "Hispanic" residents, illustrating a pattern of intra-neighborhood segregation. It also shows the demographic transformation over time.

The area gained a nationwide reputation as being "worldly." In 1985 the *New York Times* noted a new wave of East African refugees opening up restaurants on 18th Street in Adams Morgan, "a multiethnic neighborhood whose business listings often provide a tip to the latest influx of immigrants or political refugees" (*New York Times* 1985). And another *New York Times* article in 1986 pronounced: "Mount Pleasant's commercial district is not large, but it is worldly" (Toner 1986). Dubbed the "'Rainbow Ward' with Clouds," this area was being noticed both for its diversity and stubborn inequalities (Toner 1986). At this time, Vietnamese immigrants also settled in Mount Pleasant, and by 1990, a *Washington Post* reporter observed, "a sizable Asian community lived in the area, particularly in Mount Pleasant" (Farhi 1990). Following this residential trend, businesses and community, social service, and media organizations, serving diverse immigrant groups, but especially Central Americans, increasingly clustered in the larger Adams Morgan and Mount Pleasant area as well as in Columbia Heights, creating social networks that reached across neighborhood boundaries and even into northern Virginia and Maryland. But the area was also "at a crossroads," burdened, on the one hand, by a "sense of white dominance in civic affairs," including "a campaign to 'clean up' Mount Pleasant Street," and on the other hand, by the "lack of minority participation at community meetings." Given disparities in wealth and education, Pedro Lujan, who had warned about these impending conflicts in the 1970s, asked: "'Now, how is that second group going to stop the other one from taking over?'" (Farhi 1990).

"A City on the Cusp of Growth"

On May 5, 1991, "simmering tensions" erupted in open conflict in D.C. as the "Mount Pleasant riots" spread through D.C.'s Latinx barrio. Images of police in riot gear and overturned smoking cars in Adams Morgan and Mount Pleasant flickered across television screens around the world. Twenty years later, on May 5, 2011, Pedro Aviles, a local activist who became the executive director of the Latino Civil Rights Task Force charged with investigating the root causes of the riots, recollected the events: "I think that the—there was a sense of ownership of the neighborhood in the city, but that went out the window after the [police] shooting of Daniel Gomez because of the accumulated frustration, the sense of alienation that was being experienced by members of the community had reached a limit" (Nnamdi 2011). In his retrospective assessment, Aviles implied that prior to the 1991 riots, Latinxs had still felt "a sense of ownership" over this part of the city. After all, in the 1970s Latinxs had been organizing to brand Adams Morgan as the "Latin Quarter," and the 1980s witnessed the consolidation of both a strong, collective Latinx presence and a parallel "worldly" identity in the larger Adams Morgan and

Mount Pleasant area. But Aviles's powerful statement also forcefully reiterated that, for many in the neighborhood, displacement from the everyday life of the city began before individuals or groups of people were physically uprooted through gentrification: a process of dislocation in place actively undermined this sense of belonging (Fullilove 2005; Davidson 2008).

In a 2011 *Washington Post* opinion piece, former Mayor Sharon Pratt, who had in 1991 just become mayor of the nation's capital, remarked that in hindsight the riots "presaged a city on the cusp of growth" (Pratt 2011). However, Pratt's 2011 explanation that D.C. had been "a city on the cusp of growth . . . [which indeed has] grown by light years since those days in 1991," carried deep irony. In 1990, Adams Morgan and Mount Pleasant were "transitioning" neighborhoods where "rising property values and the potential for displacement" were already converging and uprooting lower-income residents and some small businesses (Office of Planning 2004).[8] Although this dynamic was already in plain view, highlighted by academics, newspaper articles, and activists, Pratt only retroactively recognized this bifurcated development, acknowledging that despite the growth, it was "still a divided city" (Pratt 2011).

The policy response to the riots at the time exemplified the shifting community development terrain necessitated by increasing federal retrenchment in the 1980s and the concomitant ascendance of governance ideals built on community entrepreneurialism in the 1990s (Cummings 2001). Pratt, for example, applauded "Latinos" for not relying on "a benevolent government" to solve their problems in the early 1990s: "Though I cannot condone riots," she wrote, "I recognize that it was important that Latinos became empowered through their own efforts." However, this genre of localism, as we will see, ultimately reinforced rather than ameliorated inequities both citywide and on the neighborhood level because it made local organizations responsible not only for solving historically entrenched problems of discrimination and economic marginalization but also for improving dismal housing conditions.

Between Empowerment and Entrepreneurialism

The self-help initiatives Pratt identified in her piece included the birth of several Latinx organizations, including the aforementioned Latino Civil Rights Task Force and the Latino Economic Development Corporation (LEDC), a local community development corporation (CDC). As previously noted, many CDCs, as did LEDC later, had an activist history, dating back to both civil rights social movement organizations of the 1960s and the era of federal funding through the Equal Opportunity Act's Special Program. Typically, they were driven by a mission to "revitalize poor or at-risk communities," with a focus, not primarily on revitalizing physical places, but on improving the lives of people (Vidal 1996, 149). But the growth and development of CDCs, like LEDC, also suggested the progressive "institutionalization of minority insurgency" as activists sought to access funding (Marquez 1993).

LEDC's founding mission, for example, was to "economically empower" low- and moderate-income Latinxs in the D.C. area, specifically in Mount Pleasant and Adams Morgan. Early on, LEDC sought to ameliorate bleak housing conditions in the neighborhoods through tenant organizing work, to inform tenants of their rights, and to secure long-term affordability by supporting limited-equity cooperatives in select buildings. The agency also sought to develop planning processes and programs that would politically strengthen the voice of Latinx entrepreneurs and residents in the neighborhoods. LEDC's story, however, exemplifies how a shift to entrepreneurial governance and BID urbanism strains grassroots organizations as they reorient their work from community empowerment to pursue social justice goals to neighborhood revitalization through place-improvement strategies (DeFilippis and Saegert 2012). Almost from its inception, LEDC was inserted in the market-oriented, nonprofit, business model that had emerged in full force in the late 1980s and gained strength during the Clinton administration.

Accepting government funding as part of the federal Community Development Block Grant (CDBG) program incorporated CDCs, including LEDC, squarely within federally articulated urban policy priorities mediated through urban regimes (Vidal 1996). This meant that CDCs, initially "one of the few politically viable antipoverty approaches," necessarily began to "embrace the value of self-help and promoted private-public partnerships" (Cummings 2001, 424). By 1998, in fact, the BID-PPPs regime as noted also reoriented the work of the D.C. Department of Housing and Community Development (DHCD), which managed the disbursement of CDBG funding (chapter 4). LEDC received significant funding through the Home Purchase Assistance Program (HPAP), which promoted traditional homeownership, and shifted its housing focus by de-emphasizing collective strategies while expanding individually focused programs. Yet, due to rising property values, placing qualified low- and moderate-income families in a traditional homeownership position in the organization's target area was difficult. Tellingly, LEDC was beginning to follow the movements of its low-income and small business constituency by extending its mission-rooted programs to Latinxs citywide and into the suburbs. This change in geographic scope revealed the organization's inability to solve broader societal problems of housing discrimination and income inequality on the neighborhood level (Athey 2000).

BID Urbanism and the Housing Crisis

Not even a decade after the riots, the new BID-PPP regime's focus on place-making increasingly positioned LEDC at a crossroads, as it, like other CDCs in the city, became a vehicle to implement the city's new strategic plan. LEDC increasingly aligned its programmatic repertoire with the "Citizens Plan," managing an array of placemaking activities, including commercial corridor beautification and a facade improvement project.

The vision enshrined in the 1998 "Citizens Plan" focused on creating places to attract new high-income residents, draw tourists beyond the monumental core into neighborhoods, and woo industries, such as the technology sector. While it celebrated D.C. as a capital city rooted in the nation's democratic traditions, a city "By the People, for the People" (as the watermark on the downloadable document attests), the plan spoke to a particular people: the "well-educated and culturally diverse workforce" to strengthen the tax base. This particular vision of cultural diversity turned a blind eye to vexing questions of discrimination, economic inequality, and deep poverty that continued to define the lifeworld of many Latinxs in LEDC's target area (Orloff 1993).[9] LEDC's local geographic area, although recognized as one of the already "transitioning" neighborhood areas where "displacement was likely" (Office of Planning 2004), became subject to the city's place-based initiatives. It already exhibited the kind of "diversification" that the plan exalted. Indeed, the "Citizens Plan" seemed to revive some of the tenets that guided Nixon's urban policy. The city's resurgence would require the production of places where incoming white residents would feel comfortable and where they might assert or recognize their sense of place as part of a greater "diversity" (Metzger 2000).

A brief look at the events that unfolded in 2000 illustrates LEDC's increasingly betwixt-and-between position in relation to its mission and constituency. The "Citizens Plan" homed in on strategic assets both downtown and in surrounding neighborhoods, including not only Mount Pleasant and Adams Morgan but also adjacent Columbia Heights (Weiss 2002). By 1999, the targeted investment by the public sector, in partnership with developers, industry groups, CDCs, and philanthropic organizations, were becoming highly visible (Weiss 2002, 5). The long awaited Metro station on the Green Line opened in Columbia Heights. The new station finally linked this "Mid-City" planning area to the downtown and federal core and to other redevelopment areas (Good Jobs First 2002). At the time, this neighborhood across 16th Street NW was still identified as predominately African American, but buildings around the new Metro station and near the site of the DC-USA Retail project (see figure 3, chapter 2) also housed Central American and Vietnamese immigrants. Shortly after the station's opening in 2000, the District government, which was selectively stepping up code enforcement, placed nearby rental apartment buildings on a condemnation list, citing their uninhabitable conditions (Howell 2013). This "Hot Properties Initiative" (Lauber 2012) sparked public outrage and community organizing.[10] A coalition of organizations and community activists spearheaded by the Central American Resource Center (CARECEN), an immigration legal clinic, organized the political actions, including demonstrations, legal workshops, and meetings with administration officials, to stay the eviction of the tenants, 59 percent of whom were Latinxs.[11] Concurrently, the Washington Lawyers Committee filed a lawsuit against the city, charging discrimination in the selection of the buildings. Moreover, by deeming the buildings uninhabitable, they noted, the city had also attempted to skirt the "first right of refusal" tenants have in D.C., namely the right to make an offer to buy their building when it is put up for sale (Gallaher 2016; Howell 2013).[12]

Local CDCs, LEDC among them, occupied a paradoxical position. Dependent on the city for funding, they walked a tightrope in a politically volatile situation. In order to be part of the broader political conversation as the crisis unfolded, LEDC worked largely behind the scenes, its staff providing technical assistance to help train potential tenant associations.[13] Other organizations, such as CARECEN and the Civil Rights Task Force, openly organized the tenants, the media, and the public. Given the District's political context and policies, these community activists, housing coalitions, and nonprofit agencies explicitly and in retrospect rightfully charged that the government's action was discriminatory. A 2012 Fair Housing report highlights the Columbia Heights case, citing a 2006 court decision, which had concluded that "tenants had presented enough evidence" to show that "the District had discriminated against them on the basis of 'place of residence'" and "intentionally targeted Hispanic neighborhoods when it implemented the Hot Properties Initiative" (Lauber 2012, 112).

During the housing crisis, activists publicly articulated the complex political, social, and economic life space immigrants in general, and undocumented immigrants in particular, had to navigate in D.C. They brought to
the public's attention the crucial network of bilingual legal, youth, health,
and human services nonprofit organizations that worked in this specific
geographic area (Nnamdi 2011). A neighborhood represents not only a place
of residence, they cogently argued; it also embodies social commitments
and support networks, and cultural spaces—in short, the needs, struggles,
and hopes of the diverse communities that shape it.

The housing crisis, like the 1991 riots, signaled the unbalanced development process underway in D.C. While middle-class African Americans and
Latinxs were moving into the area in small numbers (Modan 2007), the majority of newcomers to Mt. Pleasant and Adams Morgan were and continue
to be white and high income. Moreover, census data show (see tables 1 and
2) that Latinxs and African Americans in this area have historically been
represented disproportionally among low-income populations. This inequitable distribution of wealth, as measured by median household income
and homeownership rates, is quite evident, and it is these groups of people
who comprise the most recent population losses in the various neighborhoods' census tracts (Office of Planning 2015a). BID urbanism, instead of
investing to stabilize these neighborhoods, reinforced and exacerbated displacement trends already underway (see table 1 for demographic changes).

Feelings of Impending Loss

While Kalorama Triangle and Mount Pleasant had already been declared
historic districts, preservation-minded residents in Adams Morgan began to
advocate for historic districts in Washington Heights and Lanier Heights in
the first years of the 2000s (Trieschmann 2005, 2008). This meant reassert-
ing nineteenth- and early twentieth-century neighborhood boundaries and
identities, thereby promoting the fragmentation of the larger area into its pre-
1955 constellation. Not everyone welcomed this move to separate out sub-
neighborhood identities that predated the fight for desegregation because it
would supplant the activist history symbolized in the Adams Morgan name,
treating this period as "an aberration" (Farrar 2011, 729). In fact, some heritage narratives emphasize this notion: in *Adams Morgan: Then and Now*, for
example, the era associated with the struggle for solidarity across boundaries of class, race, and culture, which to be sure was not free of conflict, has
become framed as a historical anomaly (Zapata and Gibson 2006).

Through its structure, the narrative implies that the neighborhood now gentrified has returned to some kind of original state. "It prides itself on being the polar opposite of the homogenous cookie-cutter suburbs," the authors write, "yet it itself was once a suburb." Acknowledging gentrification, they observe, "it rightfully decries and fears gentrification as being right around the corner," but, they suggest, "it has been doing so for nearly five decades." Finally, the writers conclude, "despite the fact that before the neighborhood was rich it was poor, and before it was poor, it was originally rich" (Zapata and Gibson 2006, ix). This narrative uses juxtaposition to indicate that Adam Morgan may just be returning to the kind of neighborhood it perhaps was meant to be. The sense of place associated with political activism to reckon with the past and perhaps rectify past injustices and imagine an alternative future, however, becomes bookended by its past suburban, well-off identity and its gentrified, also wealthy, future. This storyline, like the strategic plan, normalizes a particular progression of history, suggesting both that there is no alternative future to gentrification and that gentrification may simply reflect a restoration of the neighborhood to its "original" state of being.

Adams Morgan as a space gives meaning to and emotionally emplaces people's lived experiences of "diversity" in ways not captured by these kinds of heritage narratives. Like the strategic plan, they often fail to address how their accounts work to purge from the present the lived experiences of people still there (Hayden 1997). A Latinx resident who participated in a 2006 mapping workshop at LEDC, for example, drew and named "Adams Morgan" as his neighborhood but during the discussion remarked: "Actually, where we live, they want to call the neighborhood Washington Heights. They don't want to be from Adams Morgan because of the diversity. Historic Washington Heights or Kalorama Heights, they don't want to be with Adams Morgan." The Adams Morgan name embodies for many, like this resident, a personal experience of "diversity" that is political and emotional; moreover, it is unstable and threatened. But the anger with which this participant infused his account to communicate the emotional significance of "Adams Morgan" is rarely captured in heritage tourism literature hailing the area's "historic" diversity.

The Adams Morgan name in 2006 interviews and workshops was still associated with ongoing struggles against the displacement of low-income tenants and businesses. Thus, the remembrance of "Adams Morgan" is crucial to the notion that solidarity is complicated and grows out of contested struggle for social integration grounded in class, racial, and cultural diversity. Diversity in this old sense (Modan 2008) meant a complex social fabric made up of people, businesses, and places, shaped by the interactions they sustain with one another. As table 1 illustrates, the 2000 U.S. census already indicated that the African American populations had declined precipitously and the Latinx population was declining as well in parts of Adams Morgan. Mount Pleasant at the same time became home to a higher concentration of Latinx residents, suggesting an eastward movement. The more complex, vertical diversity, comprising the economic and racial diversity, that Adams Morgan and by now also Mount Pleasant exemplified was actively under threat in these transitioning neighborhoods as the strategic plan was rolled out.

CHAPTER 6

Neighborhood Identities Collide

By carving out a fixed jurisdictional district, BIDs set neighborhood boundaries. They demarcate territory and, in the process, create a set of local constituents. At the same time, the work of BIDs is to increase local economic
activity; therefore, the work of BIDs is not merely to create a "clean and safe"
environment but also to create a marketable image in order to attract people willing to invest and spend their money in the district. This economic
development strategy seeks to invite in people who both add "vitality" to
the local economy and enhance the valuation of local properties. However,
neighborhood boundaries, onto which business improvement districts may
be grafted, are socially constructed and often embedded in historical conflicts. Since the 1960s, Mount Pleasant and Adams Morgan have served as a
prism of urban "diversity" in which shifting notions of community and ur-
baneness have been applied to build a sense of identity to support revitalization proposals and to expand as well as circumscribe social and physical
belonging (Modan 2007).

   Neighborhood politics have been, and continue to be, fraught with tensions among the diverse residents, businesses, and property owners because they constitute overlapping communities that hold contrary visions of place, progress, and development (McGovern 1998; Modan 2007;
Schaller and Modan 2005; B. Williams 1988). These often remain in dialogue, albeit sometimes obliquely, with different eras of a neighborhood's
life, including the palimpsest of preceding territorial tactics and strategies

that shaped how people might exercise the right to define and claim neighborhood spaces (Harvey 2005; Schaller 2007).

In 1998, the strategic "Citizens Plan" outlined an action agenda to create "real places." Apparently the neighborhoods targeted in the plan were not sufficiently "vibrant," "welcoming places" for the kind of businesses, visitors, and above all new residents the city needed to attract (Monteilh and Weiss 1998). But what exactly makes a place "real"? How do we define a neighborhood place? What are its boundaries, its identity? What makes a place pleasing, and to whom? Whom is it supposed to welcome in? The "Citizens Plan" seemed to suggest that targeted neighborhoods, like Mount Pleasant and Adams Morgan, were not yet "real places." The ultimate question then is who is given or who seizes the authoritative voice to determine which and whose answers to the above questions should guide planning interventions and influence regulatory processes.

To implement its placemaking vision, D.C.'s recently installed BID-PPP regime funded the Latino Economic Development Corporation (LEDC) to spearhead a neighborhood BID (NBID) in its geographic target area. Aligned with the placemaking objectives articulated in the 1998 "Citizens Plan," the NBID's purpose was "to offer increased cleanliness, safety, and a pleasing environment for shoppers, workers, visitors, and residents" (Monteilh and Weiss 1998, 46). LEDC, as noted, originally formed in 1991 to counteract the discrimination and address the lack of affordable housing and limited economic opportunity many Latinxs, especially recent Central American immigrants, faced in the neighborhoods. As it was being integrated into the emerging placemaking regime, however, the organization found itself in a difficult position, trying to pursue its mission—to serve its low-income, Latinx constituents—while responding to the BID-PPP's policy priorities.

This chapter develops a micropolitical analysis of placemaking dynamics that were unfolding in the Mount Pleasant and Adams Morgan area during the period the NBID proposal was being considered (Marcus 1999, 46). A micropolitical analysis is "premised on the supposition that the relative autonomy of groups ... produces goal diversity based on differing interests and ideologies" (46). These collective interest formations, in turn, have spatial implications as differentiated groups translate their meaning making into fairly coherent "ideologies of place" (Modan 2008). Using locally produced maps, related focus group discussions, as well as place narratives from community Internet forums, this chapter examines how different groups perceived, experienced, and ultimately imagined their neighborhood space.[1] These divergent perspectives coexisted uncomfortably in the Adams Morgan and Mount Pleasant area, and the analysis illustrates the power dynamics at play when LEDC was asked to graft a neighborhood business improvement district onto the area.

The data show how neighborhood improvement politics in the Mount Pleasant and Adams Morgan area were driven by discourse communities (Modan 2008) that also coalesced into coherent interest groups to employ their access to power to structure places in accordance with their understanding of neighborhood history and identify formation. They also illustrate how some groups, usually those well positioned economically and politically to effect change, unfortunately may exercise "selective amnesia" (Farrar 2011) or the "privilege of unknowing" (Sedgwick 1988) when they, whether wittingly or unwittingly, fail to proactively recognize the historically layered injustices embedded in the social and economic geographies of their neighborhoods. But by selectively mobilizing place histories, norms, or aesthetics to create a sense of place, their placemaking activities can serve to replicate exclusionary development patterns (Fullilove 2005; Till 2012). The chapter then focuses on bringing to the surface some of the history and power disparities that the "privilege of unknowing" left unarticulated in the placemaking politics and vision promoted in the "Citizens Plan" (Sedgwick 1988).

The data span from the late 1990s to the early 2000s to show continuities in the ideologies of place various groups of people expressed over time and elucidates the contentious micropolitics of place, especially with respect to the three commercial corridors (see figure 11).[2] Mount Pleasant Street is a five-block-long shopping corridor of largely low-lying brick buildings on both sides of the street but also with multistory residential and mixed-use buildings. One of these buildings, Adelante, is a limited-equity cooperative organized by LEDC. There were and still are about 60 businesses on the street; at the time, most were immigrant-owned businesses. Despite the ongoing residential gentrification on both sides of Mount Pleasant Street, this commercial corridor has remained fairly stable over the past twenty years; yet 2000 and 2006 civic group mapping participants and local business owners identified major redevelopment east of the neighborhood on 14th Street as a harbinger of more significant changes to come to the corridor. The Columbia Road and 18th Street are longer corridors. At the time of the BID-proposal, there were approximately 330 businesses. Except for short stretches of one-story commercial buildings, Columbia Road is pre-

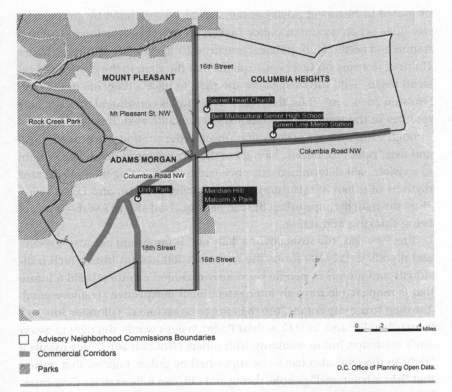

Advisory Neighborhood Commissions Boundaries

Commercial Corridors

Parks

D.C. Office of Planning Open Data.

FIGURE 11. Mount Pleasant and Adams Morgan ANC Districts with Neighborhood Commercial Corridors

dominately lined with multistory, mixed-use buildings. Until very recently many perceived Columbia Road east of 18th Street as a mixture of Latinx mom-and-pop stores and chain stores while the 18th Street corridor from Columbia Road to Florida Avenue, which is characterized by mixed-use townhouses, comprises the center of the neighborhood's nightlife. The Adams Morgan and Mount Pleasant area is home to the types of cultural, architectural, and even political heritage that placemaking-focused initiatives can mobilize to create a sense of place.

The Right to the City and Boundary Work

French philosopher Henri Lefebvre emphatically argued that the "right to the city" must be understood holistically (Lefebvre, Kofman, and Lebas 1996). It should not be bestowed based on economic or political power or rooted in historical privilege; nor should it be claimed by groups who use their access to urban policy makers to uphold exclusionary cultural frames and aesthetics or political practices. Unfortunately, it often is. James Holston, drawing on Lefebvre, explains that the right to the city should instead begin "with the struggle for the right to have a daily life in the city" (Holston 2009, 248). Thus, the "right to the city" is constituted through daily routines in the ways social relationships are cultivated. It is also asserted through extraordinary actions that unsettle the present, such as the 1968 and 1991 "riots." To "declare" a right to the city means to defend one's right to a visible, self-determined existence while coproducing the multifaceted rhythms of urban life (Holston 2009; Lefebvre, Kofman, and Lebas 1996). Thus, the right to shape urban life can be conceived also as a verb—a way of being, thinking, and acting.

This focus on "the struggle for a daily life" is important because a secure and dignified daily life forms the necessary foundation from which individuals and groups of people previously excluded can then build a future that is more stable from an intergenerational perspective (Fullilove 2013). The right to the city entails "the right not to be excluded" (Blomley 2016, 20) from urban life and, in D.C. activist Pedro Aviles's words, the right to assert one's existence, but in solidarity with others (Nnamdi 2011). This means a "right to the city" also has to be supported by public policies that ensure that "less advantaged" people, young and old, can fully exercise their capabilities and can live, work, and play in the city unencumbered by fear and insecurity as well (Fainstein 2011; Nussbaum 2003).

Because BID urbanism is rooted in public choice theory, with its emphasis on entrepreneurial localities competing in a self-regulating market of places as the most efficient form of local governance (Tiebout 1956), it specifically denies the openness of place that inheres in Lefebvre's notion of the "right to the city" and instead reifies the production of multiple, strictly defined jurisdictions. This mode of boundary work plays into economic development planning paradigms, including BID urbanism, that aim to enhance gentrification processes in urban property markets because "pioneer" neighborhoods, for branding purposes, must "have a boundary" to separate them "from the territory beyond" (Stuart 2003, 149).

Yet this kind of boundary work disrupts or seeks to suppress the "transbordering" activities that economically less secure individuals and groups deploy, such as street vending, picnicking on a plaza, or setting up DIY street furniture to socialize at the street corner, both to negotiate their economic survival in the city and to enrich the experiences of urban life (Irazábal

2014b). This transbordering mode of placemaking is generally unstable because low-income residents, street entrepreneurs, artists, immigrants, and Latinx youth, for example, who engage in these practices are often criminalized. Unlike with the pop-up or tactical urbanism promoted by urbanists today, which draws on Lefebvre's insights and calls for rule breaking and DIY interventions to simulate this informality (Kageyama 2011), higher-income placemakers in alliance with local officials frequently and specifically vilified or sought to control the "transgressive" (Irazábal 2014b) activities low-income residents and entrepreneurs pursued in the public realm. Lefebvre's notion of the right to the city nevertheless corresponds more closely to precisely the nonconforming practices of everyday life—often treated as disruptive by public authorities and elite economic interests—through which people on the margins (Hooks 1984) have staked a deeply existential survival claim, including a poetic, artistic, and cultural presence in urban life (Losada Romero 2016; Purcell 2014).

Mapping Neighborhood Space

In 2000 as previously described in chapters 4 and 5, the housing crisis around the newly opened Green Line Metro station highlighted the precarious position of low-income tenants under this BID-PPP regime. LEDC was keenly aware that only eight years after the "riots," conflict continued to simmer in the area as civic organizations in Mount Pleasant were targeting "antisocial" behavior they attributed to Latinx residents and merchants, and nightlife revelry in Adams Morgan was straining neighborhood life there. These conflicts played out primarily on the three main commercial corridors described above and named in the NBID proposal.

To better understand the situation and potentially build political bridges, LEDC proposed (and received funding for) a visioning project to "develop a social geography" of neighborhood life. LEDC sought to create a "forum to learn about the perspectives [of those] who [did] not have a voice in civic organizations." The idea was to highlight "how these perspectives differed from [those of members of local] civic organizations," including also the ANC (Latino Economic Development Corporation 2000), which at the time represented pivotal local actors pursuing place "improvement" strategies (Modan 2008; Schaller and Modan 2005). Inspired by Kevin Lynch's work, *The Image of the City*, first published in 1960, LEDC sought to uncover the kinds of "mental maps" of neighborhood space different groups of residents might reproduce on paper and in group conversations about the maps.

Accordingly, the organization's staff conducted a series of mapping work-shops during which facilitators, without predefining the contours of specific neighborhoods or privileging particular place-names, asked mapmakers to draw their "neighborhood space" on butcher-block paper; they also asked participants to use different-colored markers to indicate the institutions and organizations they viewed as important and to identify spaces they used for specific activities, such as socializing and shopping.

To find participants and to ensure these potential mapmakers would feel relatively at ease in what might prove to be difficult conversations about the dynamics of racial, ethnic, cultural, and class relations, LEDC reached out to people through already established social networks.[3] The participants included locally elected officials and civic group members, Latinx residents of a housing cooperative, professional staff from community development organizations, teenagers from local youth centers, and Latinx seniors attending a daytime center in Adams Morgan, but the maps here were coded as follows: (1) ANC commissioners and civic group members; (2) Latinx residents and community-based development professionals (limited-equity co-op tenant association members, participants at a senior center, and local organization staff); and (3) youths (Latinx and Vietnamese youth). To deepen the analysis, the discussion in this chapter also draws on written posts from community Internet forums on which the writers tended to represent leading civic organizations and residents who were actively engaged in local politics and already technologically networked and connected in the late 1990s and early 2000s (Schaller and Modan 2005).

From "Transbordering" to the Politics of Selective Amnesia

Different groups produced quite distinct neighborhood maps. The visual renderings and narratives illustrate differences, not only how individuals but also groups of people defined their neighborhood's boundaries and identities. Borders appeared as a main theme in the neighborhood maps: not just their presence and fixity, but also their relative absence or flexibility. Two seemingly antithetical conceptions of neighborhood boundaries emerged from the data. While Latinx and youth participants drew trans-bordering neighborhood boundaries, civic group members seemed to reify officially recognized neighborhood borders (figure 10).[4] Thus, unlike civic group members, who ascribed distinct identities to the Adams Morgan and Mount Pleasant neighborhoods, Latinx and youth mapping workshop participants did not tend to strongly delineate the Adams Morgan and Mount

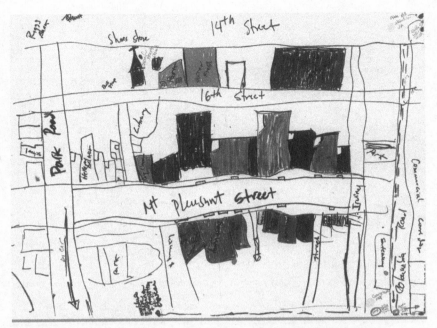

FIGURE 12. Map by Latino Community Development Professional, CDC, 2000

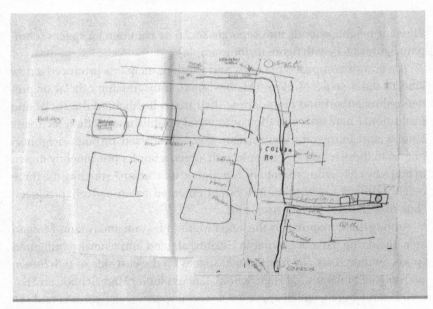

FIGURE 13. Map by Latino Senior Center Participant, 2000

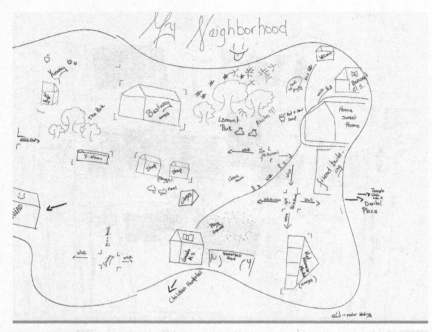

FIGURE 14. Map by Asian American Youth, 2000

Pleasant neighborhoods into separate social or commercial spaces (compare figures 12–15 with figure 10, for example).

The groups composed of Latinx and youth participants produced a new kind of open sense of place (Massey 1994), transgressing official or predefined neighborhood boundaries. Their maps highlighted the social and institutional networks and the commercial establishments that, for many Latinxs and immigrant youth (figures 12–14), crossed through neighborhoods. In these maps, for example, 16th Street, a border prominently drawn in maps by civic group members, functioned as a "seam," stitching the three neighborhoods together as 16th Street emerged as an actively produced "line of exchange" (Lynch 2005, 100).

Among these mapmakers the larger Mount Pleasant and Adams Morgan area, including parts of Columbia Heights, aligned into a newly configured space, anchored also by institutional spaces on the east side of 16th Street, such as Bell Multicultural High School, Lincoln Junior High School, and Sacred Heart Church, which appeared as social spaces (see figures 12 and 14). In fact, many youths in the area went to these schools, and many Mount Pleasant and Adams Morgan residents, especially, but not exclusively, Lat-

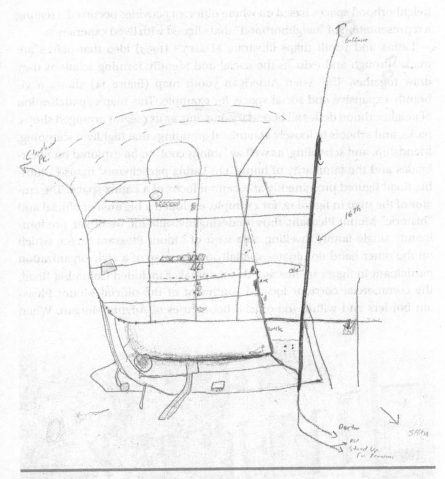

FIGURE 15. Map by Civic Group Mount Pleasant, 2000

inxs, attended mass or participated in activities at Sacred Heart Church and gathered for soccer games on the weekends. Additionally, throughout the 1980s and 1990s politically active residents of diverse backgrounds gathered in institutional spaces for music, such as Sweet Honey in the Rock and Izalco, and for spiritual solidarity and political organizing, including support of the sanctuary congregation at All Souls Church, which continues to be active today (Cohen and Mills 2017). Thus, the mental maps Latinxs and youth reproduced on paper included these institutions and talked about them as crucial social spaces. The mapmakers of maps 13 and 14 drew neighborhood spaces based on where different activities occurred, creating a representation of "neighborhood" that aligned with lived experience.

Latinx and youth maps illustrate Massey's (1994) idea that places are made through and exist as the social and identify-forming relations they draw together. The Asian American youth map (figure 14) shows a vibrantly expansive and social space, for example. This map's spatialization of neighborhood defies all boundary drawing, as its creator arranged shops, parks, and schools in loosely assembled groupings that highlight shopping, friendship, and schooling, as well as "things cool" to be explored on rollerblades and the familiarity of home. On Latinx participants' maps Columbia Road figured prominently as a central focus of a Latinx space. The creator of the map in figure 12, for example, excluded a big area of official and "historic" Mount Pleasant, thus rendering invisible the wealthier, predominantly single-family dwelling area west of Mount Pleasant Street, which on the other hand dominates spatially on the map of a civic organization participant in figure 15. Instead, this mapmaker included Columbia Road, the commercial corridor located southwest of the official Mount Pleasant borders and within the official boundaries of Adams Morgan. When

PICTURE 3. People gather outside Zodiac Record Shop on Columbia Road in 1982. Zodiac was a popular place that sold music from every country in Latin America. (Photo by Nancy Shia)

asked about Columbia Road, one participant, drawing an equivalency between two of the area's commercial corridors in terms of their sense of place, explained: "it feels like Mount Pleasant Street." Latinx participants also talked about individual businesses, such as Zodiac on Columbia Road, which played important roles in the Latinx community. "Zodiac was the only place in 1985 that you could get Spanish music," one participant underlined (Modan 2007; Schaller and Modan 2005). In and of itself the comment about a record store, now closed, may not carry much significance to an outsider; but in the history of Adams Morgan, Zodiac and its owner Daniel Bueno were emblematic of the social and entrepreneurial networks inextricably connected to the perception of the Mount Pleasant and Adams Morgan area as D.C.'s Latinx barrio (Cadaval 1998, 78).[5]

Finally, the commercial corridors on these maps appeared as places not just for consumption activities but also for socializing, establishing and maintaining social networks, and negotiating a livelihood, including as ambulatory vendors. This kind of "textured" understanding of urban life, which unfolds in the public realm to reinforce a cultural identity and to earn a livelihood, countered and collided with the ideology of place held among many civic group members, however, who envisioned and sought to impose a different kind of order on the street and in urban life (B. Williams 1988).

Boundary Work and the Politics of Selective Amnesia

The maps by civic group participants, in contrast to those by Latinx and youth mapmakers, anchored neighborhood identities in place, deploying the fixity of borders to carve out specific neighborhoods. Their maps, such as figure 15, generally reaffirmed the official boundaries of the two neighborhoods (see figures 10 and 11), which were also used as markers for the neighborhood BID proposal. The similarity between the boundaries ANC participants drew and the official "representations of space" (Lefebvre 2011) published by the ANC is not surprising, given that their official responsibilities were circumscribed by these boundaries. Civic group participants drew "edges" (Lynch 2005) that set apart each neighborhood, Adams Morgan or Mount Pleasant, from adjacent neighborhoods, especially from Columbia Heights. These kind of edges, notes Lynch (2005), distinguish two "regions" and direct "the observer in the inside-outside sense" to create a distinct territorial identity linked to civic belonging, ownership, and ultimately privilege (100). The mapmakers, in this sense, assumed a clearly bounded insider positionality on the local, or perhaps "urban village," scale within the context of the larger city, echoing also historic districting and heritage vernacular (Lynch 2005; Cherkasky 2006).

Neighborhoods from this viewpoint can function as differentiated areas of the city, and the edges they create can mark "neighborhood turf" (Modan 2008). These mapmakers, however, drew various types of edges, communicating discrete meanings relevant to understanding the politics of neighborhood transition. While boundaries, such as Rock Creek Park, and topographic variation, such as the Harvard Street "ravine" between Adams Morgan and Mount Pleasant, were depicted as uncontested, static, "natural" boundaries, 16th Street was portrayed both as a physical and social border separating people (see figure 15; Schaller and Modan 2005). At the time, according to the Office of Planning 2000 census figures, the population in the census tracts abutting the east side of 16th Street was characterized as 40 percent black, 46 percent Hispanic, 5 percent Asian, and 7 percent white. By comparison, in Mount Pleasant census tracts west of 16th Street, as table 1 illustrates, whites comprised a higher proportion of the population at 34 percent, and by this time only 26 percent of the residents were black, while 31 percent were identified as Hispanic and 7 percent as Asian. An undertow of race and class seemed to operate here to delimit place identities.

Unlike the Latinx and youth mapmakers, these civic group mapmakers did not talk about the institutions along or east of 16th Street as central spaces bringing neighbors together. Among civic group participants they simply served as landmarks in the built environment that "need not be entered"; that is, they served as "clues of identity and even of structure" to demarcate place from afar (Lynch 2005, 48). In the group discussion, one participant explained that 16th Street has "a lot of institutional space that prevents us from being over there with people from the other side of the street, schools, playground, big church—places where people can come together, go to church or school—but as neighbors it separates us." While the speaker apparently attempted to build a narrative bridge to the "other side" by evoking these institutions, he inadvertently subtracted the people who went to church, school, and the playgrounds on that side of 16th Street from the designation "neighbor."

Through their comments and maps, civic group participants clearly delineated east of 16th Street as an outside space. A Mount Pleasant civic group member, for example, remarked in 2000: "16th St. is a demarcation line. What goes on over there is usually kept over there." Mapmakers also used signifiers, such as "criminal element" and "different kinds of activities," placing these "over there" in relation to 16th Street (Schaller and Modan

2005). Similar language suffused the community Internet forum serving Mount Pleasant. Only a year after the housing crisis, in July 2001, a post on the forum, titled "Come Visit the Border," read: "We are just blossoming!! We are a group of homeowners in the 3100 Block of 16th Street. We are protecting the border of Mt. Pleasant. And with new owners coming in you owe it to yourself to take a pleasant walk down our block and see all the improvements." This call to neighbors by a "group of homeowners" exemplifies a kind of selective amnesia that newcomers sometimes demonstrate when talking about "improving" and "protecting" neighborhoods in a historically decontextualized way. A decontextualized placemaking discourse such as this one "omits events [both past and present] that defy seamless narratives of [local] progress and unity" (Hoerl 2012, 180). It in fact reconfirms what legal scholar Audrey McFarlane has called "operatively white" ideologies of place (McFarlane 2009, 165). In this case the writer of the quasi-public statement, wittingly or not, conjures an image from the early twentieth century when the citizens association had successfully lobbied to shift the neighborhood's eastern boundary from 14th Street to 16th Street to ensure a homogenous, white population and secure property values in Mount Pleasant. Thus, this call to "protect the border," even if unconsciously, illustrates how the privilege to "unknow" history can be mobilized (Sedgwick 1988).

Taken together, the Internet post and the mapmakers' discussion might be read as examples of dog whistle politics in which class and race either intersect or become conflated but reinforce racial constructs (Haney-López 2014). The discourse and visual renderings expressed an unspoken, perhaps unintentional, "hostility toward non-white," predominately Latinx and black spaces, and also spatially marginalized the lower-income spaces of Columbia Heights, bordering the ethnically and racially "more diverse" and higher-income ANC districts of Adams Morgan and Mount Pleasant, where whites by this time constituted at least a third of the population along the border and in specific census tracts over 50 percent of the population (see table 1). This is precisely how selective amnesia works. The coded language normalizes, depoliticizes, and deracializes notions of neighborhood improvement, placemaking, and gentrification through the trope of the "blossoming" property owners, paving the way for "the new property owners coming in" (Modan and Wells 2015).

The post and maps also illustrate how the production of the gentrification "frontier" was functioning in D.C.'s transitioning areas. Columbia Heights, as noted, was one of the strategic areas into which the BID-PPP regime sought to guide the back-to-the-city movement (N. Smith 1996).

By 2000, the investment in the Green Line station in Columbia Heights, it seems, was beginning to pierce through the mentally constructed boundary. According to a civic group mapmaker, "more recently the criminal element has been brought down because of the Metro station."[6] Another participant nodded in agreement and added: "Before the Metro came in, I didn't have occasion to go over there very much, now I'm going over there every day. It feels safer, looks safer." Pointing to the map (see figure 15), the speaker continued: "[But] it's a little peninsula, 'cause [the Metro's] the only place to go, you or me have no other reason to go there." The massive public and private investment in the area just across 16th Street in conjunction with BID urbanism further downtown (see figure 3) was successfully creating a breach in the mental barrier between these neighborhoods, one that white residents had historically produced. Nevertheless some newcomers discursively maintained this border through a "rhetoric of absence" that ignored persisting racial and class-based inequities and forged a sense of solidarity and privilege using the language of property investment and neighborhood fortification ("come visit . . . you owe it to yourself" or "we are protecting the border"). This kind of selective amnesia, however, contributes to the "maintenance of existing power relations" (Kelly and Hoerl 2012, 5).

In contrast, to the Latinx and youth mapmakers, civic group members generally framed the public realm, especially sidewalks, plazas, and streets, as paths or specific venues rather than "nodes" where a variety of informal social activities, such as the pleasures of running into friends, talking on the street, rollerblading on the basketball court, and listening to mariachi musicians in front of a local restaurant, might take place (Lynch 2005). Thus, from this viewpoint, people "hanging out idly" signaled people were "up to no good." The civic conflation of hanging out in public space with disadvantage, drunkenness, and suspicious or illegal activities is problematic. The fact that apartment dwellers, and many low-income Latinx tenants live in apartments, had no backyard in which to congregate made their "hanging out" a highly visible activity, particularly to passersby who judged them without taking notice of the privilege of privacy a backyard bestows (Modan 2007; Schaller and Modan 2005). Moreover, in describing "people entering stores, people buying things, having a purpose" as "more comforting," civic group participants valorized consumption-oriented activities and drew an artificial boundary between the social and private life of the residential space and the public commercial life of a neighborhood space (Schaller and Modan 2005, 403).

This marketization of the public realm undermines the right of others to "inhabit" the space, to assert a sense of personhood unrelated to economic activity (Purcell 2014). One civic group participant noted: "It's depressing that people don't have any other things to do with their time." Thus, "non-productive" activities by Latinxs, in this case, were branded as suspect.[7] Although this attitude superficially seems to contradict today's efforts to reproduce non-work-related social interaction in the public realm, it fully aligns with the aims BID urbanism pursued in D.C., namely to produce places that would attract similar-minded, higher-income residents and visitors to D.C.'s historic neighborhoods. This necessitated the displacement of different, often racialized street cultures from the public realm (Hopkinson 2012b; Modan 2007; Schaller and Modan 2005; Summers 2015).

Regulating Livelihood and Belonging

In 2000, several discussions raged on the neighborhood Internet forum around both alcohol consumption and the regulation of alcohol sales on Mount Pleasant Street. The Mount Pleasant Neighbors Alliance MPNA, founded in 1992, a year after the riots, with the mission to improve the neighborhood's "quality of life," was now actively trying to curtail alcohol sales and entertainment sponsored by local businesses. Its members, some of whom had been ANC commissioners, understood D.C.'s political geography and utilized political as well as bureaucratic channels to accomplish their goals. As part of these efforts and with the support of the local ANC, MPNA pressured largely immigrant-owned businesses to sign "voluntary" agreements to accept specific terms of operation and to supervise certain activities in front of their premises.[8] These activities echoed an earlier "cleanup campaign" in 1990. Only a few months before the "riots," a *Washington Post* reporter had observed, "the main street has become a repository for the neighborhood's conflicting agendas and a symbol of its gnawing tensions" (Farhi 1990).

The renewed efforts in the late 1990s and early 2000s followed a similar pattern and paradigm, but they also ignited controversy on the local Internet forum. The ANC and MPNA were "protesting" every liquor license renewal, ostensibly to hold businesses accountable for their sales practices. According to the MPNA and ANC representatives, "the only way that a non-seller [could] participate in an ABC [Alcoholic Beverage Control Board] proceeding [was] as a complainant, a petitioner, and a protestant . . . one way to resolve the protest [was] through modification of the seller's behavior as recorded in a Voluntary Agreement, which [would] become part of the li-

cense term." Other residents, however, who found out that a particularly beloved corner market had been targeted, criticized this practice and pointed
out that the "protest" had forced the market's owners to incur unwarranted
costs. After much questioning about the blanket use of the voluntary agreement, an ANC commissioner acknowledged that the form letter might indeed have been "a blunt instrument." The voluntary agreement, it seems,
was the brainchild of a relatively small group of people. Nevertheless, the
episode illuminates the ways in which residents, perhaps ignorant of or un-
concerned about the costs to small business owners, were operating from
their class privilege to gain control over and reshape the character of "their"
neighborhood's main street.

During this Internet-based discussion, one person directly highlighted
the fact that most of the businesses on the corridor were immigrant owned
and perhaps catered to and attracted a clientele that did not reflect the desires of some of the property owners on the west side of the commercial corridor:

> I am a first time contributor to the Mount Pleasant Forum. I live and work in
> Mount Pleasant and have been a resident of either MP or Adams Morgan for
> the last twenty-five years. I congratulate the Forum and have some quick com-
> ments, both the pro and con, about the latest edition. As a resident of Hispanic
> origin, I am appalled at the behavior of certain residents and groups who "pro-
> test" every single liquor license in the MP neighborhood. I have heard and re-
> corded stories of immigrant storeowners who have struggled mightily to put
> together their version of the American Dream. Most of these small retailers are
> very responsible, concerned and hard working.
>
> They are routinely harassed, called before the Liquor Board and forced to spend
> untold amounts of money to defend themselves . . . And yet what I most love
> about this neighborhood is the progressive neighborly spirit. The belief that we
> all of us can co-mingle and live together even if we are different. . . . Those who
> do most of the protesting [as is usually the case] have least to do with Mount
> Pleasant businesses and find their food, beverage and entertainment needs
> somewhere else. ANC commissioners, . . . for whom I have an enormous re-
> spect, having been an ANC commissioner at one time, trot out convoluted and
> often times tortured logic to justify a policy that is blatantly and obviously bi-
> ased, unjust and just plain silly.

This writer, unlike most contributors to the forum, identified himself ethnically and then proceeded to firmly inscribe himself as a community mem-

ber and political voice in the area; he was someone who lived, worked, and was actively engaged in neighborhood affairs. By situating himself squarely within both the unofficial and official power structures of the place (he had been an ANC commissioner), the author established his legitimacy to question the authority, motivations, and actions of not only the ANC but also, from his perspective, the few residents who were undermining the "progressive" and "neighborly" spirit of the neighborhood as well as the livelihood of small business owners. Indeed, the writer reframed "those who do most of the protesting" as outsiders, people whose consumption behavior in fact did not contribute to the neighborhood and its local economy. This letter may not immediately have stopped the practice since the "routine" technique to control local business owners continued through nearly the first decade of the 2000s, but in 2009 residents who were particularly exasperated with the live music ban allied with business owners to successfully contest the voluntary agreement, which also ended prohibition of live music (DC Jobs with Justice 2009).

The Dog Whistle Politics of Everyday Life

If the right to the city entails the right not to be excluded from the city (Blomley 2016), then uncovering the ways in which "normalcy" and the "presumptions of innocence" (McFarlane 2009) or conversely the presumption of criminality are mobilized in conversations about everyday activities in the public realm reveals how class, racial, and cultural privilege are often operationalized simultaneously in pursuit of individualized or collective placemaking goals. This was also reflected in the relatively insular Internet discussions, in which writers at that time seemed to assume a largely middle-class and English-speaking audience (Schaller and Modan 2005). The above-mentioned conversations about regulating businesses paralleled a discussion around menacing behavior, such as "public drunkenness," "harassment," "hanging out," and "threatening stares," all of which served as justification for the increased regulation and policing of businesses and particular groups of people who used the commercial corridor. The debate offered an example of the kind of dog whistle politics that can emerge when local groups feel empowered to "improve the neighborhood" even if it means criminalizing and ejecting people of color or poor people and the entrepreneurs who serve that unwanted market (Haney-López 2014).

In 2000, one forum writer remarked, for example: "About the groups of men who hang out all day on the fence . . . They like to stare threateningly at white males who walk by, and of course they make disgusting comments to any woman who walks by. I imagine most women reading this would feel way safer on any Georgetown street than on Mount Pleasant Street. In Georgetown, they (meaning residents and businesses) do not tolerate drunken loiterers harassing pedestrians. This is not a racist or cultural attack but a discussion about making our street safe for us and our children." The speaker, a self-described homeowner who "recently moved into the neighborhood," implies through his appeal to safeguard "our street for us and our children" that the other readers are like him and shows his discomfort with different people and distinct modes of using neighborhood space, construing and constructing young Latinx men as threatening, potential criminals (Schaller and Modan 2005, 405).[9] In the post, the writer conflates the young Latinx men hanging out on the fence, many of whom were local high students, with some of the older men, who indeed suffered from alcoholism and spent time on the street. These two groups of people were treated as one and the same, and as a consequence the commentary painted an undifferentiated portrait that distorted the reality of the situation.

Moreover, in the context of the forum, the writer never mentioned the words "Latino" or "Hispanic": these ascriptions were understood. However, another post, which was supportive of the writer's position, drew the connections quite clearly, referencing the Mount Pleasant riots: "Does the current behavior spiral to sitting on your car while you are in the local store, then maybe blocking your way in a doorway . . . Is it alright for these folks to urinate and crap on your property, pass out on the sidewalk, scare your kids and yes, even start another riot." This last post revealed the racializing discourse that was really taking place as a subtext of the broader conversation. It overtly linked Latinxs to the fear of urban disorder. The original poster also discursively proclaimed the right to lay a physical claim to neighborhood space when he jokingly suggested that he had "seriously considered getting several of [his] male friends to 'occupy' the fence for an afternoon" (Schaller and Modan 2005, 405). The micropolitics of place, as Modan's 2007 book title so succinctly summarizes, can truly be a war over turf.

Interestingly, this string of conversations invoked Georgetown as a place of safety: "Women reading this would feel way safer on any Georgetown street than on Mount Pleasant Street." In setting up a comparison between Mount Pleasant and Georgetown, the wealthy, predominantly white neighborhood it became during the first wave of gentrification in the early twentieth century, the original writer revealed his ambitions for the neighborhood.

Yet, Georgetown, as a place symbolic of white (male) privilege and wealth, as noted, was also frequently used as a counterpoising vision of place, but as an anti-model, a model against which neighborhood activists concerned about gentrification squarely and with pride defined "working-class" Adams Morgan and Mount Pleasant (Huron 2014). A woman who grew up in Adams Morgan and lived in Mount Pleasant, perhaps to deflate the image of Georgetown that the Internet writer was trying to project, observed with a hint of sarcasm: "women were harassed in Georgetown, too!" Then she added: "Frankly I felt harassed EVERYWHERE." Harassment of women, which this commentator cogently noted, although undeniably present in Mount Pleasant, was as pervasive in other places in D.C. The discussion on the Internet about the young men "hanging out," however, patently racialized and exclusively linked the behavior to Latinx men. And, in this case, Georgetown was framed as an aspirational place: apparently clean, orderly, and safe.

The mapping, focus group, and forum data from the early 2000s illustrate the complicated layering of boundaries and ideologies of place that produced separate senses of place for different populations in the larger Mount Pleasant–Adams Morgan area. They also signaled the ways in which the NBID establishment was likely to reinforce precisely the social, political, and economic boundaries that the visioning process was trying to bridge. Planning paradigms rooted in a marketized conception of urban placemaking reinforce the ideologies of place held by local officials, local elites, usually high-income property owners, but also some renters as well as placemaking entrepreneurs. This circumscribed concept suppresses a more open notion of place, one that recognizes the different place identities that overlap and intersect in the urban landscape irrespective of jurisdictional boundaries. It suppresses the power of place Dolores Hayden defines as "the power of ordinary urban landscapes to nurture public citizens' public memory to encompass shared time in the form of shared territory" (Hayden 1997, 9). Yet, "how we attend to the past through the medium of the built environment"—and I would add political, economic, and social environment—"has implications for our future" (Farrar 2011, 723). In the entrepreneurial conception of neighborhood revitalization, the politics of selective amnesia or "the privilege of unknowing" can empower economically advantaged residents (and businesses) because they are more readily able to channel their resources to redefine neighborhood life (Sedgwick 1988).

Needless to say, LEDC's visioning process was held in a difficult climate and by its very existence countered the underlying premise of the potential neighborhood BID with its restrictive governance structure. The BID's very definition as a taxing district meant that it would require the drawing of clear jurisdictional boundaries, boundaries that would be used to mar-ketize specific place identities. This boundary work, as I have shown, was not value free. It was political. At the same time, neighborhood conflicts are not reducible to simplistic oppositions. The commentary offered by the self-identified "Hispanic" resident, who eloquently noted that, despite all, he in fact "loved the progressive neighborly spirit" of the broader neighbor-hood, reinforces the notion "that we all of us can co-mingle and live together even if we are different." LEDC's visioning process was an attempt to engage in this kind of broader conversation about the different ways neighborhood residents experienced their neighborhood lifeworld. And LEDC's visioning process in fact provided an important planning engagement with a multi-plicity of stakeholders in the area. It could have served as a way to facilitate a deeper and more inclusive debate about placemaking politics around the merits or demerits of an NBID more broadly, but a community-engagement process to build on this limited, yet instructive, visioning process in relation to the NBID proposal was not funded (Reardon and Forester 2016). Never-theless, as the next chapter discusses, the BID project for the moment pro-ceeded apace.

CHAPTER 7

BID Urbanism and the
Politics of Exclusion

BIDs are flourishing in cities across the United States and internationally, and increasingly BID-PPP regimes have incorporated neighborhood-based BIDs (NBIDs) specifically into their economic development tool kit. Despite the fact that BIDs frequently spawn controversy and often exacerbate local power struggles related to placemaking, advocates within the BID move- ment continue to promote them as an effective and democratic economic development and "revitalization" strategy, not only for downtowns but also for residential city neighborhoods.[1] Their expansion has been actively spon- sored by the public sector, which subsidizes their creation with general fund tax receipts.[2] In some of these areas, earlier BID organizing had been met with skepticism (Alpert 2008).[3] Lest we think this tide might be receding, in 2016 Mayor Muriel Bowser of D.C. officially launched an "Emerging BID demonstration grant program" to support the establishment of additional neighborhood-based BIDs, including in the target areas that were identified in D.C.'s 1998 "Citizens Plan" (Regan 2016; see figure 3).[4]

This chapter describes the NBID establishment process in the Mount Pleasant and Adams Morgan area. The discussion juxtaposes two inter- pretations of "the right to the city," the Lefebvrian and the public choice versions (Harvey 2013; Purcell 2014). The NBID process illustrates how an expansive notion of "the right to the city," which holds that the "less advan- taged" should be able to participate fully and stand to benefit from neigh- borhood revitalization (Fainstein 2011), became subverted by the public choice notion that those who (ostensibly) pay for the good life should profit.[5] The account highlights the predicament of the Latino Economic Development Corporation (LEDC) during the original organizing phase as the process evolved. Ultimately, after LEDC stepped away from the project, NBID organizing marginalized the voices of "immigrant" or Latinx merchants, while also splintering and spatially peripheralizing the area's expansive sense of place as Mount Pleasant broke off and East Columbia Road merchants were largely ignored.

The interpretation of who constitutes the people rightfully empowered to make decisions through the BID structure is inspired by the public choice model underlying its legal concept: people who pay should retain majority voice to influence local plan making.[6] This perspective contrasted starkly with and undermined the understanding of community development associated with the early work of community development corporations (CDC) and the advocacy planning movement of the 1960s, which attempted to deliberately empower or give voice to area inhabitants and "stakeholders" who were often silenced in public discussions and planning deliberations because they could not command the economic, political, or symbolic capital necessary to influence neighborhood planning decisions (Arnstein 1969; Davidoff 1965). These two conceptions of community development clashed during the NBID development process.

To reiterate, the legal structure for BIDs in D.C. had been defined in the 1996 enabling legislation, which set up two legal typologies for BIDs: one for the downtown and central employment areas and the other for traditional neighborhoods. The approval process for the NBID in the Adams Morgan and Mount Pleasant area required the submission of a business plan as well as an affirmative petition from at least 51 percent of all of the property owners and the agreement of enough property owners to represent at least 51 percent of the assessed value. Most important, the legislation stipulated the need for demonstrated support from 51 percent of merchants. The requirement to petition merchants intended to give voice to a group of stakeholders often excluded from the formal procedural requirements in cities, such as New York City and Philadelphia.[7] In D.C., the merchant petition reflected a political compromise after the initiative to enable BIDs faltered twice (see chapter 3). Just like their downtown counterparts, however, NBIDs in D.C. require the majority of board members to be property owners.[8]

What follows here builds on Gerald Frug's pointed question: "Why are these people, and not others in the neighborhood, given decision-making power?"(Frug 2010, 14). One could also ask: How do these specific people, and not others, acquire that decision-making power? These questions may seem deceptively simple, but they are acutely important because the leadership that takes over the organizing of an NBID also determines the boundaries and membership of the district, silencing some voices, while strengthening others. The fact that the BID model pivots on a collectivity built around property ownership is not made explicit in the BID policy discourse. Actually, among BID professionals in D.C. as well as in New York City, an amorphous concept of "the business community" has been invoked as the obvious sponsor to spearhead local economic development planning. This notion was embedded in the name. But the name "business improvement districts" represents a confounding use of language because it conflates the "business community" into a singular interest group masking the differentiated positions of influence and power tenants have in relation to property owners (J. E. Davis 1991).

This is where John Emmeus Davis (1991) has argued that the disaggregation of interests at the neighborhood level, especially in relation to property rights and tenure status, becomes important.[9] In the story of the development of NBIDs, whether in D.C. or elsewhere, it is critical to examine these interests. Multiple cleavages exist among businesses. In addition to the tenure divide (owner / renter), various kinds of products and services businesses sell on a given commercial corridor may work at cross-purposes with one another (nighttime / daytime businesses) and businesses cater to different market segments (low-income / higher-income consumers).[10] The livelihood of merchants leasing their space depends on the local economic environment, the specific products and services they provide, and the markets they target and serve. Additionally, while commercial property owners or developers holding property for accumulative purposes primarily seek to extract value from their property investments, commercial property owners, who are also tenants or have a particular relationship to an area, may simultaneously seek to pursue profits and maintain neighborhood stability. Building on Davis (1991), an additional frame of reference in examining business interests in relation to commercial districts might include both the kinds of accumulative or profit-making activities that prospective business owners (whether property owners or tenants) pursue through their relationship to a neighborhood and the kind of use-value they create to shape this neighborhood's character, contributing to a sense of "authenticity" (Zukin 2011). Sharon Zukin describes this process as realizing a certain "balance" wherein a neighborhood's "origins and its new beginnings" continue to coexist (2011, 246).

The Nascent NBID

Neighborhood business improvement districts, as noted, were part of the 1998 strategic plan, the "Citizens Plan," developed under the auspices of the Fiscal Control Board in the mid-1990s. This plan, in turn, guided the city's funding priorities.[11] As such, NBIDs were part of the overall action agenda for strategically promoting place-based economic development. In 1998, Neighborhood BIDs in the so-called transitional areas of D.C. were as of yet nonexistent (Asch and Musgrove 2015).[12] To piece together the origination

D.C. Office of Planning Open Data.

FIGURE 16. Adams Morgan Partnership Boundaries

story of the Adams Morgan Partnership Business Improvement District was not a simple endeavor because its eventual birth in 2005 proceeded in fits and starts. Not surprisingly, this is not a story with a linear or fixed storyline.

To help restore D.C.'s prosperity, the recently established BID-PPP regime expected community organizations, such as LEDC, to participate in implementing the strategies delineated in the "Citizens Plan." To move the citywide plan forward necessitated what geographer Deborah G. Martin called supportive "neighborhood policy regimes" (Martin 2004, 394). Thus, the examination of urban development politics "requires analysis of the behind-the-scenes supporters of community development at a neighborhood scale, rather than solely the local state and its elite business allies" (395). As noted, the plan signaled that "community development corporations and community-based organizations" were to play a "key role" in these neighborhood regimes (Monteilh and Weiss 1998, 46). As discussed, however, LEDC was working in a context where low-income Latinxs, in particular, continued to be largely invisible or actively sidelined from formal plan-making decisions (Nnamdi 2011). To suppose that LEDC should spearhead a BID and the kind of placemaking outlined in the "Citizens Plan" was from the outset problematic. It ignored the micropolitics of place in which the organization worked (chapter 6). Yet, the citywide political coalition and the policies and action steps that had been elaborated in the strategic plan informed and, ultimately, sustained this NBID project.

Already in 1996, prominent councilmembers from Ward 1, where Adams Morgan and Mount Pleasant are located, and Ward 2, which covers downtown, Georgetown, and Dupont Circle, and the chairperson of the council promoted NBIDs. In this case, the NBID was not just a local economic development initiative but part of the broader implementation of BID urbanism in D.C. According to accounts from D.C. BID professionals, the idea for the neighborhood BID emerged while the enabling legislation was being pursued in the City Council. In 2006, one BID professional with intimate knowledge of the dynamics that unfolded explained that the Ward 1 councilmember "was always pushing it ... and was trying to get everybody together, he and one or two people." This professional also intimated that the promotion of this particular NBID coincided with the desire to support the larger political goal of "moving the [BID] legislation" through the council. That is, the NBID was, from its inception, politically tied to the BID movement's broader advocacy activities. Yet, this kind of approach poses a dilemma because, as the BID professional observed, "the BID has to come from the local leadership ... It can't come from a council member. The council member isn't the right vehicle. If the politicians propose a BID, it obviates why you are doing it in the first place." The establishment of this particular NBID as well as how subsequent NBID proposals emerged in D.C., however, suggests this was and perhaps continues to be precisely the case.[13]

This reality controverts the democratic principles for which advocates hail the model, namely that NBIDs should theoretically grow out of a "collaborative" and "consensus driven" partnership (Grossman and Holzer 2015, 55). Seth A. Grossman and Marc Holzer (2015) speak of BIDs as "unique PPP examples," which "fundamentally reinforce practices that support successful democratic governance and community and economic development" (55), an ideal reiterated also by D.C. BID professionals. "It's about bringing the business community folks together, the building owners together to form something that works to address their issues," one executive observed. From this, we might conclude that the right way to go about organizing and building an NBID public-private partnership is not just to get local buy-in but to submit the "form and substance" of the BID idea to debate and have a dialogical decision-making process (Frug 2010). Grossman and Holzer's definition of "consensus," which seeks "to identify and support agreement rather than an orientation toward resolving disagreements," however, denies the difficult work of engaging controversies and opposition; it reflects a consensus-making through which "the outcome may gravitate towards the interests of those forcing the agenda" rather than a consensus-building approach (Connelly and Richardson 2004, 8).

In the complex neighborhood context that Adams Morgan and Mount Pleasant presented at the time different interest groups (older immigrant merchants, new entrepreneurs, various resident groups, and diverse property owners) held divergent views about the neighborhoods' identities and future. Thus, the strategic and consensus-driven process that the NBID model presupposed in actuality produced exclusionary tendencies, valorizing one vision of the future while suppressing others. And the maelstrom of discontent eventually caught up with LEDC.

Preparing the NBID

Under the auspices of the 1998 "Citizens Plan," the NBID project in the Adams Morgan–Mount Pleasant area received budget priority and was funded through the newly reconfigured Department of Housing and Community Development.[14] In accordance with the plan's objectives to "offer increased cleanliness, attractiveness, public safety and security, streetscape improvements, and coordinated marketing campaigns," LEDC had already been harmonizing its work with the kinds of commercial corridor and Main Street programs the plan envisioned as necessary to "succeed in promoting neighborhood commercial districts" (Monteilh and Weiss 1998, 46). The plan's strategic focus on attracting and keeping new, higher-income residents in the city, however, conflicted with LEDC's mission to empower low- to moderate-income Latinx residents and small businesses already there.

For one of the lead-in programs, LEDC had adapted the four-point Main Street model (promotion, organization, design, economic restructuring) of the National Trust for Historic Preservation (NTHP). LEDC promoted its programmatic focus under the slogan PODER, or "power" in Spanish. The NTHP designed and evaluated the Main Street model in the late 1970s to counteract the decline of downtown districts and "to preserve these [districts'] historic structures and community histories" (Gates 2005, 2). By 1980, with the creation of the National Main Street Center, the model was well on its way to becoming a formal program, supported both through federal and philanthropic funding (Feehan and Feit 2006; Gates 2005). "Their objective," notes Jennifer Gates (2005), also "was to create an organization that would empower states to develop and fund their new program for implementation at the local levels" (3). In addition, the International Downtown Executives Association (IDEA), the forerunner of the International Downtown Association (IDA), which subsequently developed and disseminated the business improvement district model, actively supported this Main Street initiative.

The work of Main Street programs more generally, and LEDC's commercial corridor work in Adams Morgan, were and remain part of a broader urban policy advocacy movement linked to the politics of BID development and expansion (Isenberg 2004).[15] The four-point program already identified the ambition to reorganize local governance arrangements in order to effect the economic restructuring of neighborhood Main Streets; it presaged the NBID model. The Main Street funding pattern usually built in the prerequisite that its programs eventually be spun off and managed by an independent, self-sustaining organization in the future. Thus, in keeping with this philosophy, the establishment of a model neighborhood BID in the Adams Morgan and Mount Pleasant area would secure a stable, recurring funding stream and eventually obviate the reliance on grant funding.

LEDC's neighborhood business improvement district project was conceived as a replicable model to help consolidate the citywide BID urbanism that Mayor Williams's administration pursued in line with the "Citizens Plan" and funding priorities identified by the D.C. Department of Housing and Community Development. In early 2000, a press release announced the following: "LEDC was chosen, through the District's Strategic Economic Development Plan, to undertake the pilot neighborhood BID development project for the city. LEDC's BID will encompass both Adams Morgan and Mount Pleasant. Upon successful completion of the effort, LEDC will prepare a how-to manual on neighborhood BID development for the District government so that other interested neighborhoods will have an easier time getting their BIDs set up."[16]

LEDC's executive leadership approached the NBID project thoughtfully and grappled with the implications of this programmatic trajectory. At the same time, staff members were also debating what an NBID might signify for LEDC's target neighborhoods. The main cleavages that emerged in the organization became clear during a staff meeting in 1999 and the numerous follow-up conversations. They can be traced to the very different theoretical positions from which different staff members built their arguments. Given that the area was already "transitioning," gentrification became the pivot around which the discussion developed. Those supporting the NBID concept gave primacy to economic arguments reminiscent of the public choice paradigm: they saw gentrification as a natural outcome of economic growth and the functioning of private property markets. They also separated LEDC's competencies into discrete programmatic areas—housing, commercial corridor revitalization, and small business development—and defined the commercial corridor elements as primarily the domain of "business." Staff members who argued against the NBID viewed gentrification as a process, not rooted in the aggregate decisions of individuals in urban property markets, but as an outgrowth of policy decisions, past and present. They interpreted the policy statements emanating from the city's plans, as well as the investment strategies and action steps that the regime, with a newly elected Mayor Williams, was taking, as actively supportive of gentrification.[17]

As the internal discussion about the specific NBID proposal continued, it finally centered on the question of who should take part in the planning for this institution. A proposal to include nonprofit organizations, residents, tenant associations, and small businesses and to commence with a public forum that would uncover both the strengths and the weaknesses of NBIDs, however, proved a nonstarter. DHCD community development block grant

(CDBG) funding did not contemplate such extensive "planning" activities at the time. LEDC applied for funding in accordance with the DHCD program and the legal precepts set out in the BID-enabling legislation. It proposed a process that adhered to the legislative requirements, which at least rooted it in the notion that the BID needed to grow out of the broad participation of merchants. LEDC thus tried to develop its NBID model in a way that would allow it to stay true to its mission and fulfill its responsibility to its primary programmatic constituents, in this case merchants on the commercial corridors.

The "Model" Encounters Strains

The two neighborhoods, as noted, when defined through their jurisdictional boundaries, comprised very different commercial corridors (see figure 11). Overwhelmingly minority-owned and immigrant-owned small businesses clustered on Mount Pleasant's very short but hotly contested main commercial stretch (see chapter 6).[18] The two main commercial corridors in Adams Morgan functioned spatially as different worlds, serving different populations. The northern side of Columbia Road east of 18th Street was characterized as a Latinx or immigrant space with mom-and-pop stores and restaurants while chains were seen as dominating the southern side. Columbia Road west of 18th Street comprised a mixture of neighborhood-serving businesses and restaurants that were seen as serving multiple markets. The 18th Street corridor from Columbia Road to Florida Avenue represented the highly contentious entertainment district due to its burgeoning nighttime economy.[19]

A crucial aspect of LEDC's early work on the project was both to carry out its mission and to build leadership capacity among merchants on the commercial corridors. In theory, the NBID-enabling legislation supported this aim because in addition to property owners, 51 percent of tenant-merchants would have to agree to its establishment. LEDC's NBID planning approach differed for the two neighborhoods. For Adams Morgan, LEDC hired the person who had initially researched BIDs for the organization and had coordinated early conversations with BID professionals in D.C. around the NBID concept. In Mount Pleasant, as noted, LEDC had already launched multiple programs simultaneously to empower both local merchants and groups of people who were often absent or "invisible" in official public political forums, such as Advisory Neighborhood Commission (ANC) meetings. Different bilingual staff members coordinated these conversations, worked with the business association, supervised a grant-based Façade Improvement Program, and managed the visioning-mapping activities.

In both neighborhoods LEDC initiated the NBID process by working to reinvigorate two business associations, the Adams Morgan Business and Professional Association (AMBPA) and the Mount Pleasant Business Association (MPBA). Through technical assistance and direct organizing, for example, LEDC staff worked to broaden and strengthen their membership base. The Adams Morgan business association had been viewed as fairly ineffective, and its leadership had been characterized by BID advocates as a few "old-timers" and "contrarians" who were not easily budged in their opinions.[20] A 1998 election passed the AMBPA's leadership into the hands of a relatively new merchant, someone who was willing to take the BID idea under consideration. With this process in motion LEDC also received and managed funding for both associations to lead pilot beautification projects. By 1999 LEDC had identified concrete elements of an Adams Morgan–Mount Pleasant NBID plan to solicit further city funding and create organizing resources. Materials from this time reveal the scope of the proposed BID planned activities: supplemental street cleaning, security, street-scape improvement, and marketing, as well as coordinated cultural events such as street festivals or holiday parties, and "notably, over 50 percent of the budget for the proposed NBID was apportioned to security" (Schaller and Modan 2005, 398). These traditional "clean and safe" activities seemed oddly predefined (Schaller and Modan 2005).

The idea for a combined Mount Pleasant–Adams Morgan NBID ran into trouble fairly early when business owners in Mount Pleasant expressed reservations. An influential business owner, with establishments in both neighborhoods and a former president of the Mount Pleasant Business Association, voiced his misgiving regarding the BID model. He also intimated that there was disagreement among LEDC's leadership, particularly with respect to the benefits Latinx business owners (he used the phrase "negocios hispanos") would accrue through an NBID.[21] Moreover, the ongoing tensions in the relationship between the businesses and some of the civic organizations in Mount Pleasant reinforced suspicions among businesses that an NBID would not serve their interests. During informal follow-up conversations, two business owners specifically cited their fear of displacement as having tilted the scale against a BID. As early as 2001, LEDC abandoned the idea of pursuing an NBID that would include Mount Pleasant.

Different groups of residents and business owners in Mount Pleasant, as noted in chapter 6, were deeply engaged in the politics of placemaking on the corridor.[22] In this case, interestingly, conflicting ideologies of place converged in a broadly held skepticism of an Adams Morgan and Mount Pleasant NBID. Some civic groups were concerned that Mount Pleasant might lose its "village" identity by a closer association with Adams Morgan. In retrospect, the local councilmember's chief of staff recollected, there was a general consensus among these organizations that Mount Pleasant should conserve and develop its own identity. Other residents and organizations were also clearly concerned about how the BID model might impact local small businesses. Even some years later, when the idea of an NBID reemerged, a Mount Pleasant Main Street report, funded by reStore D.C., which documented a mini-charrette to envision strategies for the commercial corridor, reiterated this view, concluding: "we do not recommend a BID at this time due to the tenuous nature of some of the businesses" (Mount Pleasant Main Street Program 2005). In the early 2000s, the organizational dynamics in Mount Pleasant, where social justice–focused groups were also deliberately working to assure a more expansive notion of the right to the city (Modan 2008), made the NBID project impossible. But perhaps this stay in the development of a Mount Pleasant BID was only a temporary one (Nadeau 2017). By 2015 when I conducted follow-up research, the BID idea had been picked up again. Recently, District Bridges, a Main Street organization "bridging" Columbia Heights and Mount Pleasant, formed. Its mission is to "help our growing neighborhoods stay cleaner and safer." It remains to be seen whether this will transform into a BID. Its development along with other BID districts would create an almost contiguous BID geography covering the central city and the surrounding Mid-City planning areas. This development speaks to the long-range strategic vision that inheres in BID-PPP regimes and the continued change in governance relations these coalitions pursue through BID urbanism.

Sidelining Latinx and Old-Timer Merchants

At the critical juncture when Mount Pleasant broke away, LEDC also underwent a leadership change and lost a number of key staff members working on the NBID and commercial corridor revitalization projects. Thus, the strongest proponents of the NBID were no longer there to drive the process forward. Nevertheless, LEDC hired Progressive Urban Management Associates (PUMA), a well-known BID consulting firm, to assess the feasibility of the NBID concept for Adams Morgan. Its 2002 report identified several challenges and concluded that a "reasonable level of skepticism and mistrust" existed "within the district." The report noted: "Divisions are found in a variety of realms" (PUMA 2002, 2).[23] These divisions echoed findings from the mapping exercises (see chapter 6) and delineated almost identical fault lines: "Geographic (Columbia vs. 18th Street); Cultural (Latino/ethnic vs. 'gentrified' mainstream); Use (business vs. residential)" (2). Deeming the neighborhood "too fractious," it also echoed earlier calls by LEDC staff members to develop a more inclusive process to build support within the business community and among other constituents. Moreover, it suggested that the "preceding segments [representatives of the various divisions] must be represented within a potential BID governance structure." Thus, rather than abandoning the project, LEDC held several stakeholder meetings, especially with businesses owners, to assess their support.

The PUMA report, which included a draft budget detailing specific line items, once again predefined the potential NBID's scope of work, prioritizing safety and cleaning services. As part of the meetings, LEDC also presented the potential assessment formula undergirding this potential budget and put both up for discussion. Creating a feasible and acceptable assessment for relatively low-density, mixed-use commercial districts was (and is) difficult, however. Adams Morgan's irregular commercial spaces added to the conundrum because they comprise ground floor, semibasement, and walk-up spaces in townhouses. As a result, to create a viable budget, the assessment formula, at $0.21 per $100 of assessed value, represented the highest rate levied on neighborhood commercial properties thus far.[24] LEDC showed merchants these numbers and also informed them that property owners would be able to pass the NBID fee through to their tenants. In response, a former LEDC staff member observed, sectors of the merchants, especially the smaller immigrant business owners on East Columbia Road, withdrew their support. Following on the heels of the Mount Pleasant Business Association's withdrawal, this increasingly negative assessment of the NBID concept among many of its constituents contributed to LEDC's decision to finally let go of the whole project. These setbacks did not sound the NBID's death knell, however.

The new leadership of the Adams Morgan Business and Professional Association (AMBPA) sprang into action. The resources that had paid for cleaning, beautification, and other commercial corridor enhancement services had also dried up, and the new leadership recognized the NBID as a way to sustain these initiatives. The center of gravity for the NBID organizing shifted to the business association. By 2000, one of the AMBPA's prominent leaders, a relatively new business owner on the corridor and a tireless advocate of the NBID initiative, was making his mark as a place entrepreneur in D.C. In fact, Constantine Stavropoulos, owner of the Tryst Café (see chapter 4), was profiled in the *Washington Business Journal* in 2003 as the driving force behind the BID and "a leader to be reckoned with in D.C.'s politically charged business community" (McCalla 2003).[25] In 2006, one downtown BID professional observed, until "he became the leader and said 'I think this is a good idea' . . . the BID in Adams Morgan was going nowhere." Stavropoulos worked in close collaboration with the local councilmember's office to get the NBID off the ground (McCalla 2003).

Carving out Mount Pleasant from the NBID, where the voices of immigrant-owned and particularly Latinx-owned businesses were highly concentrated, reduced the influence of the remaining Latinx merchants inside the newly reconfigured and smaller BID geography. This new geography now comprised only the commercial corridors officially identified with Adams Morgan: 18th Street and Columbia Road. This choice of borders for a revised NBID proposal failed to consider that the remaining Latinx merchants, who were largely concentrated on the east side of Columbia Road, did not necessarily define themselves as part of Adams Morgan per se, but of a larger Latinx space that reached beyond official neighborhood boundaries (Schaller and Modan 2005). The new NBID boundaries ignored this broader sense of place, produced through cultural, social, political, and consumption-oriented spatial practices that had been captured in transbordering narratives about D.C.'s Latinx barrio (Cadaval 1998; Lenz 1978) as well as during LEDC's mapping workshop (see chapter 6).

Given the oppositional sentiment evident among these East Columbia Road merchants, it seems the leadership of the AMBPA briefly considered redrawing the NBID boundaries to exclude the remaining cluster of Latinx merchants. However, economic considerations intervened. The large Safeway supermarket, which would have been cut out of the catchment area, was key to the BID's budget projections due to the size of the assessment it represented. Despite obvious and previously identified tensions, the steering committee that formed to lead the BID efforts apparently did not include Latinx business owners from East Columbia Road.[26] One of the ANC commissioners interviewed in 2006 indeed noted that "a lot of the businesses, who . . . headed up the BID . . . [were] relative newcomers." He argued, "if you have a relative newcomer have this idea, which by itself is not controversial and should be beneficial to all businesses," there needs to be extensive communication and cross-cultural work that is done or it's going to be "a tough one." Although he was not critical of the BID model, from this ANC commissioner's perspective the organizing efforts that proceeded did not include the kind of explicit outreach and intercultural work that LEDC had indeed tried to pursue.

In the zeal to establish a BID, the "newcomer" businesses, moreover, failed to proactively recognize the investment in place "older" merchants and their customers had made in the 1970s and 1980s to co-constitute a Latinx space and lifeworld (Cadaval 1998), one that still existed but was unable to politically assert its presence. The same ANC commissioner observed that "for a lot of longer-term businesses . . . you know somebody who has been at that corner of 18th and Columbia, and who was synonymous with Adams Morgan, to have somebody come in and say 'well we need to do this and this to run our businesses correctly,' I think they felt was an awful bit of white intrusion." This "form of forgetting," which undermines "social justice and collective empowerment" (Kelly and Hoerl 2012, 4), ultimately translated into an affirmation of both class and ethnically circumscribed privilege (McFarlane 2003). Several interviewees, including business owners, the ANC commissioner, and a former chief of staff to a D.C. councilmember, corroborated the sense that the NBID was conceived and really desired only by a few, relatively new businesses catering to an emerging demographic who were working in line with the BID-PPP regime's priorities including and asserting their right to make decisions for the governance of the corridors.

The NBID can additionally be viewed as a reflection of the changing character of a neighborhood in which both the interests of an older generation of entrepreneurs, specifically Latinx merchants but also older daytime and evening businesses, were being sidelined by newer, entrepreneurial placemaking interests, who were fueling the nighttime economy. Some very vocal business owners of this newer generation supported Adams Morgan's regional recognition as an entertainment destination and were also attracting a younger crowd into its neighborhood spots. These new placemakers' interests aligned with the strategic plan's focused support of "neighborhood tourism" and the aim to stimulate "entertainment" as well as "cultural and specialty retail activities" (Monteilh and Weiss 1998, 10). In a 2006 interview, a former city official involved in the process assessed the situation as a "divide" that "was further delineated as an old-timer versus a newcomer dynamic." He added, "a lot of the actual business owners don't really have a say. It becomes the newcomer business owners, the landlords and then a third entity of people who I view as having this power play." The needs of this newer generation of placemaking businesses, he intimated, coincided with the interests of many, if not all, of the property owners. Moreover, their placemaking activities dovetailed closely with the goals of "a third entity of people," namely the city's BID-PPP regime stakeholders. Years later, a daytime business owner who had served on the NBID's board of directors to try to shift its programmatic priorities, angrily told me: "Anything on Columbia Road to the east, all the Latino businesses, never considered, never. It was: how does it affect nightlife? That was all that the BID was ever about." This support of the nighttime economy, which would be reflected in the NBIDs budget priorities of "safe and clean," eventually created internal friction for the organization but persisted perhaps because it mirrored city policy (see chapter 8).

"Fixing" the BID

In the end, the element that made D.C.'s NBID legislation relatively progressive was irreparably damaged. Due to the impossibility of building consensus among 51 percent of the tenants, the BID organizers made the decision to seek an exemption from this requirement. In this, they were apparently following the lead of the other BIDs (D.C. BID Council 2011). With this action, however, BID proponents undermined the experiment for which LEDC had sought support: to create a model that would include majority support from merchants. It follows that the most expedient way to ensure a BID establishment process is successful is to narrow the field of participants to property owners and a cohort of business owners whose activities parallel development trends that property owners or developers view as profitable because support from these tenants can give legitimacy to the BID as a "business" organization.

The Adams Morgan case is also instructive because it highlights that individual property owners may not necessarily see NBIDs as serving their immediate interests either. The ownership patterns in Adams Morgan, including the high proportion of absentee landlords, also complicated the establishment process. Thus, by early 2004, I was told, the Adams Morgan Partnership had managed to gather only 11 percent of the necessary 25 percent of property owners and 15 percent of the necessary 51 percent of the assessed value. Finally, in late 2004, a neighborhood resident, an early advocate who had actively worked to create the BID, offered to rescue the faltering petitioning process by doing the legwork necessary to get the BID passed. To support his efforts, the District government, through its reStore

D.C. program, designated grant dollars and lent technical assistance for the preparation of the grant proposal and the final organizing push (commercial District Technical assistance Program 2002).

A final power struggle seems to have emerged within the AMBPA with the election of the new board of directors. Behind the scenes, one property owner, who was apparently holding out the last 2 percent needed to reach the threshold so the partnership could submit the application and petitions to the city, was lobbying to have preferred people placed on the board. The compromise resulted in a shared chairmanship of Adams Morgan Partnership's board of directors. In June 2005, the partnership submitted the application. Because of the difficulties in gaining consensus and increasing worries about factions who were "trying to get the ear of the local D.C. council member," the BID legislation was introduced on an emergency basis, and the amendment legally registering the BID passed in July 2005.[27]

This NBID process highlights that a keen understanding of current urban policy priorities, access to political capital, and an effective network of people and agencies with resources within the BID-PPP regime are required to move an NBID proposal across the finish line. In order to finally gain approval for the BID, the AMBPA, as described, had to leverage crucial resources through a network of BID advocates in the private and public sectors.[28]

When Theory Meets Practice

Advocacy literature and scholarly works, rooted in public choice theory, portray BIDs as a return to localized control over resource allocation, thereby enhancing local democracy (Hoffman and Houstoun 2010; Grossman 2010). I return to the quotes from the beginning of the chapter to reiterate the contradictions that can emerge when this theoretical framing meets with the practicalities of establishing an NBID. As noted earlier, in 2006 two BID executives generally talked about BIDs as representing "democracy at a lower level" because they let "the people spend money to influence" what happens in their district. The other executive in the same conversation added that BIDs are "about bringing the business community folks together, the building owners together to form something that works to address their issues." This abstracted notion of "folks coming together" belies the complexity inherent to the micropolitics of placemaking in ethnically, culturally, and economically diverse and fragmented neighborhood spaces (see also Gross 2010).

BID proponents and BID practitioners held these contradictions remarkably in tension with one another: on the one hand, when talking generally or abstractly about BIDs, they characterized the BID process as local democracy at work; on the other hand, in referencing the Adams Morgan process, several BID professionals suggested that D.C.'s legislation, designed with the intention of being relatively inclusive by explicitly including merchants, was inefficient. In 2006, one BID executive in reference to Adams Morgan, for example, conceded that he "knew there was no way to organize a BID [in Adams Morgan] because [of] two things: because one was the way the legislation was written required 51 percent of the tenants to agree. It took them over 6 years—even without doing the requirement—to dig up the 51 percent of the assessed value and 25 percent of owners [note: the 51 percent requirement for NBIDS was dropped]; it took them that long, it took them, what, almost 10 years." The final process, in fact, had more to do with fulfilling the obligatory but adaptable "legal" requirements than with a democratic—let alone an inclusive and deliberative—process.

In a letter to the city, the Adams Morgan Partnership confirmed the position that "even if the BID hearing was crowded with BID opponents (instead of the one opponent who did attend), this would have no impact on the ultimate approval of the BID unless those opponents could demonstrate that the BID requirements had been violated. Undoubtedly, some property and/ or business owners oppose the BID in concept, but the proper legal process was followed to create it, and only testimony speaking to a flawed process would be germane at the hearing" (Adams Morgan Partnership 2005b). Herein, the Adams Morgan Partnership outlined not only a different ethos from the one that was originally articulated by LEDC, but also one that is disseminated by BID policy proponents. Interestingly, the Adams Morgan story seems to have served as a cautionary tale for other neighborhoods. A 14th and U Street NW BID faltered in 2008 due to vociferous public opposition by merchants (Alpert 2008). We should therefore continue to scrutinize the notion that BIDs, and NBIDs in particular, enhance local democracy or represent the "publicization" of the private sector through a collaborative public-private partnership rooted in trust relationships (Grossman 2010; Grossman and Holzer 2015). In fact, as the next chapter shows, BIDs can devolve into organizations that serve the needs of a limited set of constituents; yet, they shape the identity and sense of place of their respective districts.

CHAPTER 8

BIDs as Clubs

In a 2015 interview, a locally elected official from the Advisory Neighborhood Commission summed up his view of BIDs: "Some of the challenges are that they, the BID itself, is by its founding structure captured by certain business interests and not others. So, by its charter, this may be a matter of D.C. law, landlords automatically always have a majority of the votes on the BID." The ANC commissioner's comments underscore that neighborhood business improvement districts (NBIDs) are political institutions and represent a circumscribed set of interests while pursuing placemaking strategies that impact neighborhood life more broadly, especially when landlords, as he saw it, "fill their property with whoever comes along first and is willing to pay the highest dollar without any regard for what kind of business they may operate." By this time, the Adams Morgan NBID had been in operation for ten years.

This chapter follows up on the line of questioning proposed by Frug's cross-examination of "the kind of private power that the government is sanctioning by creating a BID" (Frug 2010, 12); the concern again is: "Whose private power is it? In other words, who runs the organization and makes its decisions?" Additionally, to reiterate how the kind of power that BIDs wield is legitimated, the chapter examines how BID proponents outlined this power, how it was carried out, and how stakeholders perceived its implementation. The chapter illustrates how NBIDs might splinter neighborhood interests and exacerbate existing tensions by drawing an artificial boundary between residential and commercial spaces. Moreover, I show how the timing of an NBID establishment process may empower select interest groups, who then shape the priorities and trajectory of the organization's work. The chapter proceeds as follows: First I examine the arguments BID advocates used to persuade stakeholders, both business owners and property owners, to find common cause in creating a unique and competitive place in D.C. and to accept the NBID as the appropriate vehicle to achieve this. The subsequent sections examine how different stakeholders, including residents and merchants, perceived the BID's marketing work in the context of Adams Morgan's already-established nighttime economy. I discuss how these priorities benefited subgroups of the BID "club," creating internal tensions; some business owners in fact talked about a club-within-a-club dynamic. The last section of the chapter analyzes these internal power struggles in relation to the city's strategic priorities.

BIDs can be understood as governance "clubs" that sidestep democratically elected decision-making bodies (Warner 2011). These "clubs" enhance the private role in placemaking because they create local dominions where a territorially defined real estate levy funds local goods and services. To justify the model, advocates and BID professionals, including urban planners, draw on economic arguments rooted in public choice theory to stress that they exemplify a grassroots solution to local problems.[1] Built specifically on the Tiebout model for the provision of "local public goods" and Buchanan's "economic theory of clubs" (Tiebout 1956; Buchanan 1965), BIDs reframe neighborhoods as "economic units" (Cummings 2001) rather than the expression of ideologies of place that have been produced through the historical layering of social, political, and cultural processes (Lefebvre 2011).

The BID's regulatory framework translates principles of public choice theory into operational submunicipal governance arrangements. To accomplish this, the legal structure of BIDs permits a select group of "stakeholders" to harness their collective resources to develop competitive place-amenities and place-identities. Through the geographically specified assessment districts, these groups function something like membership clubs that make decisions within the different areas they control. The individual clubs then provide "club goods" or common goods, such as sanitation, programming, project management, and urban design services. While advocates and public officials talk generically about BID members as "businesses," the benefits reaped by the investment of the assessments should, by definition and decree, accrue to the property owners ultimately responsible for paying them.[2] Accordingly, actual "voice" on their governance boards, as shown in chapter 3, is structured to ensure that property owners maintain at least a majority of votes in these territorial clubs.[3] Thus, BIDs revert to nineteenth-century notions of democracy that tied together property ownership, citizen responsibility, and civic engagement (Levy 2001; Mallett 1994; Monti 1999).

Theoretically, when they successfully restructure a district and restyle its urban image to draw in new residents and visitors, these localized public-private partnerships catalyze a productive synergy among consumers and producers of place (Oates 2006, 33). BIDs also function as "territorial enterprises for jurisdiction-users," such as residents, tourists, and regionally based visitors, for whom they create these environments to enjoy (Vanberg 2016, 831). This is not contradictory, however, because the increase in this consumer demand is likely to raise property values and lease rates, which accrue back to the "club members" (Armstrong et al. 2007).

The assessment provides BIDs with the capacity to manage these place-based revitalization strategies in cooperation with but also independently of the municipal government. As a result, local club politics, policies, and programmatic priorities are responsive to the broader strategic planning visions advanced by BID-PPP regimes, especially when these enhance their economic well-being. This strategic orientation dovetails with the consensus-making model (Connelly and Richardson 2004) underlying the BID-PPPs, which centers on organizing consent among property owners and interested allies and avoids disagreements (Grossman and Holzer 2015, 55). This kind of consensus paradigm is in keeping with the strategic thinking behind D.C.'s "Citizens Plan" in that it "offers a platform for envisaging a big picture that represents a shared future uniting people beyond the differences and conflicts of today" (Kornberger 2012, 91). BID urbanism in D.C. summoned a "shared heritage" to undergird its plans and projected this past into the vision of an "inclusive" future (Monteilh and Weiss 1998; Office of Planning 2004). The BID-PPP regime in fact failed to acknowledge or analyze how the governance strategies and planning tools they deployed would intersect with the inequities and inequalities of the present to condition future outcomes. The public choice discourse used to sell BIDs as an implementation strategy obfuscates the club constraints that inhere in this governance model, embodied both in its legal form and in its primary function to feed the growth machine (Frug 2010; Molotch 1976). As the contentious micropolitics with regard to the Adams Morgan BID illustrates, this kind of approach suppresses real and existential power struggles.

Selling the BID to the Club

Drawing on the national "clean and safe mantra," local BID movers used the motto "Clean, Safe, and Organized" to contextualize their Adams Morgan plan in the larger BID movement. Outreach materials, including letters to the local property owners and business owners dating from 2004 and 2005, respectively, highlighted the benefits of becoming part of the NBID. These letters reinforced the private versus public rhetoric that belied the fact that this particular NBID initiative had been part of the city's broader BID-PPP regime as far back as the 1990s. Moreover, the letters show how the broader BID policy discourse, which purposively conflates business owners' interests with those of their landlords, could be mobilized to obfuscate the differential interests and power relations in the neighborhood.

One prevalent organizing strategy is to emphasize common cause in the face of government incapacity and to stress the need for self-help initiatives, such as a BID, to counter government neglect (see also chapter 3). In 2004, a letter went out to Adams Morgan property owners, signed by Stavropoulos, the proprietor of Tryst Café (1998) and The Diner (2000), who had been profiled in the *Washington Business Journal* as "kicking [his] leadership role into high gear" by "organizing a business improvement district for the eclectic mix of Adams Morgan businesses" (McCalla 2003). As president of the business association, he introduced the NBID initiative, noting, "The Adams Morgan Business and Professional Association (AMBPA) has spent nearly two years developing a Business Improvement District (BID) for you, our businesses and our community" (Adams Morgan Partnership Steering Committee 2004). The letter accentuated that the steering committee had "worked on the many issues of critical concern to our community, issues like public safety, maintenance of our sidewalks, streets and alleys, inadequate parking and traffic congestion, [and] the public's perception of our community." The main thrust of the letter simultaneously highlighted the civic engagement of local (tenant) business owners and communicated the view that the municipal government was neglecting the Adams Morgan "community." Because the government was providing "insufficient city services" and paying "inadequate attention to our community's needs," the NBID was crucial: "We are convinced that the BID is precisely what is needed to help us address our common issues," the steering committee argued. The BID, the letter explained, would be an "an organization—run by local property owners and businesses"—that could "provide the necessary time, resources, and organization to develop sustainable solutions." In presenting the formation of the NBID as an opportunity to develop tailored, self-sustaining responses to local problems rooted in an ethos of self-help and mutuality, this advocacy strategy echoed key tenets of public choice theory that had also been mobilized to support the BID-enabling legislation in the 1990s (see chapter 3).

Compared to the formal tone of the letter to property owners, the letter to business owners set its more informal tone in the inclusionary salutation: "Fellow Merchants of Adams Morgan" (Adams Morgan Partnership Steering Committee 2005). The letter dates to 2005, and by this time the NBID efforts apparently no longer needed the votes of merchants and just required that "commercial property owners sign petitions indicating their support for the BID." Accordingly, this letter exhorted business owners "to urge" their landlords "to sign the BID petition."

To persuade business owners of the efficacy of the model, the letter also detailed more precisely the types of services the NBID would provide. To do so, it posed a rhetorical question underscoring that some BID services mistakenly thought of as the government's responsibility were not: "You may be thinking 'Shouldn't my property taxes already be paying for these services?' No—cleaning sidewalks and the first 18 inches of the street is a property owner responsibility," it read. The NBID members, however, would be "collectivizing" this individual yet clearly defined obligation that ultimately fell on business owners "to make sure it gets done right." In a conversational question and answer style, this letter, like the one to property owners, makes two main points, namely that the services to be provided by the NBID were not the purview of the government but the charge of individuals and that they would go beyond what the government might provide to assure "the comfort of our visitors and shoppers." The letter to business owners, moreover, clearly pronounced the idea that business owners comprised the party most directly affected by, and ultimately accountable for, the relative cleanliness of the district. This required the collaboration of all.

Accordingly, one of the main talking points to justify the BIDs in D.C., and one frequently cited in the public choice literature, focused on the need to eliminate the ability of some business owners to "free ride" on the efforts of others (Grossman and Holzer 2015). Toward that end, the letter to business owners specifically opened with a reminder that the NBID steering committee was a group of "six business owner/operators who [had] spent years working to improve the community." But "despite past successes" the model was no longer sustainable, "doomed to be minimal and sporadic."

The NBID would bring about equity [no free riding] in this collective effort. At the same time as it suggested that the NBID would more fairly spread the costs across the broader community, the letter to business owners failed to clearly explain that assessments could and probably would be passed down to them; therefore, it did not address who would ultimately assume the cost of services.

To marshal support, BID organizers also implied that Adams Morgan was at risk of suffering reductions in government services. A BID contract with the city, they suggested, would "lock in" baseline service levels (Adams Morgan Partnership Steering Committee 2005).[4] The business plan and NBID application reiterated this issue. It asserted that "for many years the District of Columbia government has suffered severe financial short falls," and "diminished public resources have made it difficult to provide its commercial areas with a level of service that enables them to compete with suburban shopping areas" (Adams Morgan Partnership 2005a). While this may have been the case in the late 1990s when the NBID was first proposed, by 2005 the city had a balanced budget and apparently a budget surplus "with a $1.6 Billion Fund Balance" (Gandhi, Spaulding, and McDonald 2015; Office of the Chief Financial Officer 2006). The BID application for Adams Morgan, however, continued: "It is obvious, therefore, that any additional or improved services must be a result of self-help initiatives." The letters and the plan picked up on and disseminated an austerity discourse prevalent in the earlier discussions leading up to the approval of D.C's first BID-enabling legislation in 1996 and in urban policy circles more broadly. Moreover, BID advocates and public officials frequently use this discourse both to explain the inability of BID-PPP regimes to fund redistributive equity initiatives and to exhort local stakeholders to be entrepreneurial in their dealings with the city in order to remain competitive (Brash 2011).

In trying to convince business and property owners that an NBID was needed, its advocates also situated Adams Morgan regionally, listing districts that had already taken this step to "take the future in their hands" (Adams Morgan Partnership Steering Committee 2005). Consequently, echoing the language of the citywide BID-PPP regime (chapters 3 and 4), they presented the submunicipal BID districts in D.C. as Tiebout localities competing in a larger market of communities vying for consumers and investment. The letter to property owners, for example, again mentioned the "1000 BIDs" working nationwide also invoked by BID advocates in the 1990s and named four existing D.C. BIDs, "the effects and contributions of which

178   CHAPTER EIGHT

are ongoing and evident: cleaner, safer, faster growing and more successful business communities."⁵ Similarly, the letter to business owners emphasized that "virtually all of the shopping, cultural, dining, and nightlife destination neighborhoods in the region with whom we compete already have
BID or BID-like organizations in place."⁶ Similar to the argument BID advocates presented during the 1995 BID-enabling hearings, namely that D.C.
would be left behind (chapter 3), the implication here was that Adams Morgan would be left behind.

Interestingly, neither letter mentions that the municipal government
was actively supporting the efforts—with public monies—to establish this
particular NBID and promoting BIDs more generally as part of its strategic
plan (Monteilh and Weiss 1998). Yet, the letter to the business owners con-
veyed the message that the NBID would give property and business owners a "seat at the table" and a "full-time voice for our commercial district in
any conversations with the city." Thus, the steering committee explicitly announced the NBID as a vehicle to become part of the city's power structure.
The NBID would ensure that the interests of Adams Morgan were heard in
the broader policy discussions affecting the development of the city and, by
extension, the competitive environment in which the neighborhood district
had to continually redefine its position (Porter 1995; Monteilh and Weiss
1998). The NBID would also become a member of a larger club of BIDs that
was coordinating placemaking with the various city agencies and with other
private sector organizations involved with rebranding and marketing the
city and its neighborhoods. The letters did not enumerate further in what
ways Adams Morgan compared or not with these very different business
environments. Furthermore, the letters did not acknowledge the different
business environments that existed in Adams Morgan, and they did not delineate specific responses to the needs of the different commercial development challenges faced by Adams Morgan area merchants. This indicates
that the Adams Morgan Partnership had no tailored plan to address the district's various subdistrict identities. Rather the NBID plan presented a fairly
formulaic "clean and safe" approach.

The recruiting letters reframed the neighborhood as the domain of property and business owners. Ultimately, its advocates portrayed the NBID as
an opportunity for local property owners to coordinate with businesses to
take on the communal responsibility for the management of "our precious
assets—*our businesses, your properties* and *our entire community*" (Adams
Morgan Partnership Steering Committee 2004; emphasis in original). The
"precious assets" involved not just individual commercial properties or

businesses but embraced the entire "community" (Adams Morgan Partnership Steering Committee 2004). The NBID organizers expertly drew on
the notion that BIDs represent both a collectivization and "publicization" of
private sector engagement and local economic development by creating a
"hybrid capacity for mutually beneficial community and business development" and "an avenue of public impact, participation, and organization for
invested private actors" (Grossman 2010, 365). The "community" here was
defined as the invested private actors, which in this case became framed
as the "business community" more broadly. The letters communicated the
unifying message: the NBID would pursue the mutual interests of a club
of property and business owners. The positive externalities of their collective investment, presumably a safer, cleaner, and interesting place and increased sales revenues and property values, would accrue to this larger
community. Yet, once the NBID was authorized, its actual work brought to
light multiple, often contradictory, interests at work in neighborhoods, including on their local commercial corridors.

Selling Adams Morgan

Even before the Adams Morgan Partnership NBID came into existence in
2005, the area, especially the 18th Street corridor, had acquired a reputation
as a nightclub destination, and tensions between residents and tavern or
"nightclub" owners were running high.[7] The long organizing process to create the BID (1997–2005) coincided with a transition on the 18th Street commercial corridor, negatively affecting the neighborhood's "quality of life" in
the eyes of many residents and merchants. Although the ANC had successfully advocated for a moratorium on liquor licenses to curb the number of
nightlife establishments, it also removed itself from the BID debate. One of
the commissioners, interviewed in 2006, explained the ANC's reasoning
this way: "I think we'd like to see many of the ultimate goals of the BID, but
as people started to divide and there ended up being these huge fights over
if we were to have the BID and what the BID would look like, I think the ANC
was like, we are not taking a position on that, we are not being taxed for it,
we are not the ones who are having to write a check every month or every
quarter to the BID." Thus, in the early 2000s, the only elected local governance body in Adams Morgan, unlike in Mount Pleasant, indirectly ratified
both an artificial line between the neighborhood's residential and commercial areas and the public choice rationale that those who "pay" for local services should ultimately decide how the funds are deployed.[8] Yet, residents

are inextricably linked to life on commercial corridors. Their perceptions and experiences of these spaces condition daily routines and habits, and these, in turn, can reshape neighborhood commercial environments and atmospheres. In this case, the transformation of 18th Street, according to some residents, redefined how people lived in the larger neighborhood space. Moreover, from what daytime storeowners, such as clothing retailers, as well as evening businesses, such as older, sit-down restaurants, told me, these changing habits affected their livelihood and ability to stay open.[9]

One of the NBID's stated goals during its organizing campaign had been to manage the nighttime economy through its "safe and clean" programs "to convey to the public the impression that the area is 'under control' and being managed" (Adams Morgan Partnership 2005a). This also reinforced the NBID's aim to "enhance the image of the neighborhood as a destination for visitors." The general consensus among placemakers is that a successful place-marketing strategy not only has to persuade potential outside consumers to come, spend their money, and share their experience, but it also has to mobilize the consent of local stakeholders to participate, even if passively, in the production of place (Kearns and Philo 1993, 3; Mele 2000). Thus, in order to reposition the neighborhood, the NBID's role was to market and package its district's place identity as a saleable good (Kearns and Philo 1993). The outside target market, however, is often a consumer group seeking a romanticized or fetishized place experience that makes invisible and may eventually work to erase some of its quotidian rhythms, in the process producing an entirely different kind of urban space (Lefebvre 2011).[10] In 2006, the image of Adams Morgan projected through the government agency responsible for the Main Street and BID programs was the following: "From unusual stores to diverse ethnic cuisines, funky furnishings, to one-of-a-kind finds, this urban neighborhood is an attraction in itself. Like its inhabitants, the flavor of Adams Morgan is spicy and alluring."[11] On the face of it, this marketing language draws on Adams Morgan's reputation as an ethnically diverse neighborhood. But in this framing, the neighborhood turns into a commodity to be sold to visitors, ready to consume the atmosphere, and residents become pieces of the landscape, rather than community members with their own interests and concerns (see Schaller and Modan 2011). It is also questionable which inhabitants are adding the spice. It is unlikely the marketing campaign meant the new gentrifying, largely white residents but instead was leveraging stereotypes of "spicy" Latinxs and perhaps Africans, given the visible presence of Ethiopian establishments at the time. The language, exoticizing its "alluring" inhabitants, fur-thermore, called to mind, wittingly or not, an image of Adams Morgan as a local habitat to be experienced, not of a neighborhood that residents might call home (see Schaller and Modan 2011).

Building on Adams Morgan's ethnicized identity, the 2006 marketing language harnessed the neighborhood's "diversity" to attract new urbanites or visitors to this edgy "one-of-a-kind" place. But some of the longtime resi-dents and merchants pointedly resented this superficial understanding and selling of diversity. A longtime business owner observed: "When we came here there was a larger diversity in terms of people and shops, fewer restau-rants, more retail, more of a place to find things that was [sic] not American. It has lost that homey kind of community to us and it's heading more to-ward a mainstream kind of [place]." Diversity, then, in Adams Morgan has been changed into a flatter, commodified notion of diversity that avoids necessary but potentially divisive questions about economic disparity and its relationship to the politics of class, culture, and race (Modan 2008). In addition, the marketing effort directed the focus of attention to visitors and away from people already in the neighborhood, although many were un-happy with the commercial corridor's path of development (see Schaller and Modan 2011).

In 2006, one year after the establishment of the NBID, residents and day-time merchants seemed to feel besieged by the changing commercial atmo-sphere. While both groups expressed an appreciation for the cleaning ser-vice that the NBID provided because they no longer had to deal with the mess left by their neighbors' nighttime patrons, they were concerned about the general trajectory of development reframing Adams Morgan's identity. A number of mapping workshop respondents, for example, assuming the question "What image would you want other people to have of the neigh-borhood?" referred to marketing, articulated their answers accordingly.[12] One mapping participant, for example, offered the following assessment: "If I were marketing this place I'd show a girl coming out of Shake Your Booty [shoe store], Rumba [Café], with drinks on the table, I'd have all the diverse shopping and eating, drinking, having a good time. I wouldn't take that picture on Saturday night, where that same girl is throwing up into a garbage can!" These participants recognized that this kind of "marketing" was associated with expanding the entertainment-oriented economy, and they used sarcasm to underline the point. The above speaker, echoing the place-marketing language from the official neighborhood marketing websites, first painted a positive image of a temporally layered commercial corridor with diverse offerings (i.e., daytime, evening, and nighttime life), which he promptly undermined by evoking an image from the nighttime, weekend economy. The person having a good time while responsibly enjoying the neighborhood's daytime retail and evening entertainment options is embraced in the description, but that person abruptly wears out her welcome as she loses control and vomits, pathetically ending her own fun: she is not only reflecting badly on the neighborhood but literally soiling it, and this latter discreditable picture is not to be taken (see Schaller and Modan 2011). Yet, the latter picture in the eyes of many merchants and residents represented the lived reality masked by the advertised image of the neighborhood.

Marketing the neighborhood as a place for revelry and play seemed to undermine the functioning of its public realm, including its commercial corridors, as a civic space. Reflecting on the transition, the aforementioned merchant complained, "kids from the outside, they don't know how to behave, they have no manners." This rude behavior marked nighttime consumers as "outsiders," who did not belong to Adams Morgan and whose behavior was offensive and antisocial, which violated rules of hospitality.[13] Young people who behaved in ways that their home communities would never tolerate were trashing Adams Morgan (see Schaller and Modan 2011). A longtime merchant on 18th Street—she and her husband had been on the commercial strip for seventeen years when I spoke with her in 2006—also explained, "during the nighttime, liquor and drugs bring in an element of danger." Another respondent simply and curtly asked: "What image would I want? To draw them in, or keep them away?" So while the NBID's cleaning services were appreciated, its marketing efforts were seen as continuing to facilitate this often unwanted redefinition of Adams Morgan's place identity. In the eyes of these residents, however, the proliferating taverns and nightclubs were seen as stripping Adams Morgan of its distinctive identity. When asked in 2006 how he assessed the NBID's work, an ANC commissioner corroborated this view: "I think it [the NBID] has some good things, but it looks too outerly—well you know you have 16,000-plus people here. Yes, you want to bring people in but you also need to focus on the people who live here." The most acute tensions generated by the NBID were rooted in its outward focus and this temporal (daytime/nighttime) split, which was producing two distinct and seemingly incompatible neighborhood spaces (see Schaller and Modan 2011).

The Nighttime Economy and Spaces of Avoidance

The pulsating heart of Adams Morgan, which converged at the 18th Street and Columbia Road intersection, according to 2006 mapping workshop participants and neighborhood merchants, became unavailable during specific periods; they were adjusting their movements in reaction to the new visitors. Most residents with whom I spoke during this time talked about having lost access to the heart of their neighborhood during weekend evening hours, a time when residents had traditionally patronized the many restaurants lining 18th Street. When looking at the maps during the group discussion, one participant noted: "18th Street is the center of all our maps. Maybe psychologically" (see figure 17, for example). Another participant described a shifting pattern of behavior and an emerging ambivalence about her affective relationship to the neighborhood space as follows: "Lots of people coming into 18th Street affect how you walk around—changes how you live on the weekends, patterns change. I've not been willing to give up that I actually feel pretty safe. Interestingly I feel it more as the neighbor-

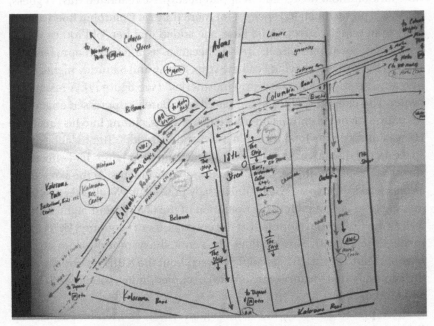

FIGURE 17. Map by Adams Morgan Mapping Participant, 2006

hood becomes more affluent. . . . It's a different sense of community. It feels less safe now." Residents, such as this respondent, expressed conflicted feelings toward their commercial corridor. This person talked about having felt safe at one time before the nightlife took over. At the same time, her commentary embodied the desire not to give into a new awareness of insecurity as she expressed an unwillingness "to give up" on her lingering feeling of safety (see Schaller and Modan 2011). In contrast to the BID urbanist narrative, rising "affluence," in the mind of this person, intersected strangely with an unsettling sense of anxiety related to both safety and community. Many of the residents and merchants who had observed and experienced the transformation of the corridor firsthand also highlighted this dynamic (Schaller and Modan 2011).

The influx of people onto 18th Street produced a new kind of spatial awareness. It not only altered the way you "walk around" and "how you live on the weekends"; it distorted people's daily patterns of urban life. During another mapping group, the conversation similarly turned to the perception that residents had had to reorient their spatial understanding of the neighborhood. A longtime resident, for example, noted: "I spend a lot of time on Columbia Road," and in apparent surprise reiterated this: "I guess, oh, this is pretty much it. I spend a lot more time on Columbia Road apparently than on 18th Street." A bit later, she added that her "old routes would have been down 18th Street." This is because, as a fellow mapmaker described it: "18th Street, what I call the strip, Friday and Saturday nights turns into any frat street, any crazy strip in America" (see figure 17). A restaurant owner who catered to "locals" lamented with barely suppressed anger that his patrons avoided coming on weekend evenings, cutting into his business. He was unsure how long he could survive this trend.[14] The neighborhood space, in the mental maps of many residents and merchants, had effectively shrunk as residents adjusted their habits and movements. At the same time, as the clean initiative was being universally praised, it was also seen as legitimating or at least enabling the operation of the taverns and nightclubs (as well as the further development of the entertainment economy) by trying to manage their negative externalities (the vomit, the disorderly conduct, etc.). In 2006, then, the misgiving people voiced about the NBID revolved around the centrality that visitors (consumers) occupied in its vision (see Schaller and Modan 2011).

In a presentation to the Washington (DC) Economic Partnership (WDCEP) by a representative of the newly minted NBID, before and after photos illustrated how place marketing could virtually (through the use of web-based media and increasingly social media) erase the actual people "inhabiting" a neighborhood space. The "before" picture showed an African American man walking down a littered Columbia Road with a group of Latino men standing in the background; the "after" picture replaced this scene with an image of an unpopulated Caribbean beach, a fantasy (Latinx / Caribbean) space. The NBID was playfully promoting the Adams Morgan entertainment district as an untouched, tropical landscape. This was likely done as a kind of joke and with a very specific audience in mind: D.C.'s placemaking and economic development powerbrokers at the WDCEP.[15] These kinds of placemaking images, however, circulate the idea that neighborhoods are playlands onto which visitor-consumers can project their desires. Moreover, it mobilized the area's Latinx or "ethnic" and "spicy" image while erasing the people, especially working-class residents and daytime merchants, struggling to stay in the neighborhood (see Schaller and Modan 2011).

BIDs, to create a sense of place, refashion urban districts into eventscapes that perform emotional work (Furman 2007; Tattersall and Cooper 2014). But turning neighborhoods into eventscapes not only enacts erasure; it also elicits negative affective responses. In the eyes of NBID critics, the young, mostly suburban, visitor-consumers were somehow liberated from commonly accepted norms of civil behavior in the public realm by the "civic" engagement of NBID members because NBID clean teams would sweep in to remove the evidence of their self-indulgent partying, to wipe the slate clean for the next party (see Schaller and Modan 2011).[16] In this vein, the NBID critics perceived the "clean and safe" programs as reinforcing an undesirable, seemingly ever-expanding trend in Adams Morgan, alienating both residents and daytime merchants. Indeed, until recently, this latter perception bore itself out in the continued support of the entertainment district concept by the city agencies responsible for regulating activities on the corridor. This came not without costs as the sense of this neighborhood space's publicness diminished over this time.

Paying for the "Public Life" in Whose Interests?

BIDs "pay for the public life," Paul Levy asserted in 2001. Yet, the question remains: who defines the character of, and shapes, this public life and to what end? More pointedly, "who actually pays for what" on the neighborhood level should be examined more closely (Levy 2001). In this case, the security, one of the club goods provided by the NBID, was irrelevant to many of its members, especially daytime businesses, who felt they were paying for services that benefited neither their operations nor their bottom line. But the entertainment and nighttime economy was viewed by the city as a key economic engine, and the city was invested in its expansion (see Ocejo 2014 for similar dynamics in New York). In 2005, to stave off complaints from residents without stifling the operations of nightclubs or taverns, Councilmember Graham, a chief advocate of the Adams Morgan Partnership BID, sponsored a bill to allow businesses and BIDs to hire reimbursable police officers through the Metropolitan Police Department (MPD). In 2008, the city amended the 2005 act to specifically subsidize security for the nightclub economy (Alcoholic Beverage Regulation Administration 2017; R. Smith 2010; Metropolitan Police Department n.d.). In a 2014 interview, a BID executive director explained, "It's a cost share . . . so that additional officers can be hired by ABC [Alcoholic Beverage Control] businesses [with a liquor license] and also BIDs." In the case of the NBIDs, such as the Adams Morgan Partnership, "the Alcohol Beverage Regulation Administration, or ABRA, . . . pays 50 percent, and NBIDs pay the other 50 percent." Through successive ABRA amendments, the BID-PPP coalition has continued to communicate the public policy message that nighttime entertainment districts, including the production of eventscapes through outdoor special events and pub crawls, are worthwhile endeavors to be funded by taxpayers more generally, not just BID assessments and ABC businesses.[17]

In Adams Morgan a 2014 notice transmitted through the general counsel of the Alcoholic Beverage Control Board, Martha Jenkins, responded to residents' grievances regarding the disrespectful behavior visitors exhibited, grievances residents and merchants had already raised in 2006. The ABC Board acknowledged, "destination patrons don't care about their behavior because they don't live there," but the board countered this with an economic development argument, asking the ANC to view the problem in light of the broader development goals the city needed to pursue. "Lest it gets lost in the greater discussion," the notice continued, "the Board makes clear that it appreciates the balance that must be struck between the interests of the residents in the neighborhood, and the interests that promote a nightlife economy" (Alcoholic Beverage Regulation Administration 2014, 11). The District's economy, it noted, depended on "a thriving and safe nightlife [that] can act as an economic engine by attracting new businesses and restaurants, diversifying the range of cultural offerings, creating employment opportunities, and increasing tourism" (11). The city's BID-PPP regime, however, seemed to selectively prioritize the needs of those consumers of place it viewed as integral to the economic growth of the city while other nightlife cultures were actively suppressed. Hopkinson (2012b), for example, describes how the regime, relying on a heightening perception of insecurity and disorder disseminated through the media, actively displaced D.C.'s Go Go scene from the city. She discusses in particular the evolution of historically black U Street into the "new" and "hip" entertainment district it is today.

In Adams Morgan, the feeling that the NBID-city partnership placed priority on the functioning of the nighttime economy seemed not to have abated by 2015. One of the neighborhood's ANC commissioners interviewed that year lamented that the Office of Planning had apparently accepted the continued promotion of Adams Morgan as a destination: "they've literally used words like entertainment district, which we found problematic."[18] In Adams Morgan, the spending that these consumers brought to the NBID district, however, in the eyes of some observers benefited a small group of alcohol-serving businesses as well as those property owners able to capitalize on the higher rents the greater profitability of this entertainment business model affords. These two interest groups, by extension, reaped the direct benefits of the ameliorative NBID services. In this manner, they turned the area, especially the 18th Street corridor, into a club realm. Ironically, it also appears the liquor license moratorium had contributed to the dynamic because it artificially inflated the price of these licenses, creating a positive feedback loop by creating a high barrier to entry for restaurants.

NBID Clubs and the Problem of Clique Politics

The Adams Morgan BID illustrates an example of how the club dynamic of a neighborhood-based BID can undermine rather than build cohesion or consensus. As a "transitioning" neighborhood with a regionally recognized entertainment district, this NBID brings into high relief the contradictions embedded in the model. During interviews in 2015, daytime tenant businesses articulated their dissatisfaction with the distribution of power in the NBID. Daytime merchants, in fact, expressed resentment because as members (sometimes involuntary) of the BID club, they had to pay the fees, but they were unable to effectively make themselves be heard or shape the direction of the NBID's work. Ironically, even a new generation of entrepreneurs who sought to cater to the growing demographic of higher-income residents saw themselves disempowered by the NBID structure and internal politics as well. The tenant businesses profiled in this section saw themselves as a new generation of placemaking entrepreneurs who had at one time or another been actively involved with the NBID but ended up disappointed, feeling stymied in their efforts.

The 2015 ANC official's quote at the beginning of the chapter makes clear how this dynamic unfolds. Highlighting that a BID is "by its founding structure captured" by property interests, he additionally noted there have been huge tensions even within the BID because "landlords, even absentee landlords, hire a broker just to fill their property with whoever comes along first and is willing to pay the highest dollar." Some landlords, he argued, demonstrated a lack of consideration for the overall health of the neighborhood and local business environment. Instead, a profit motive appeared to trump "any regard for what kind of business they [the new tenant] may operate" despite the fact that "the adjacent businesses suffer in the externalities of that mightily." At the same time, the official implied that adjacent businesses felt "powerless to actually get the BID itself to promote a different way of thinking about things." Interviews with business owners that same year corroborated the official's assessment. These respondents made clear that they highly respected the NBID's executive director and staff, including its clean team, but they questioned and pointedly criticized the institutional priorities that the NBID's programs represented at the time.[19]

Without detailing the particular cleavages in Adams Morgan, the ANC official noted that tenant businesses suffered from the "negative externalities" produced by the choices some of the landlords made to maximize their properties' profitability. A business owner on the corridor put it more bluntly: "there is a number of properties that have sat vacant since you were last here, and they're the same properties. And we've actually lost more spaces than we've really turned around and gained." The vacant storefronts, daytime merchants noted, impacted the feeling of interconnectedness and a sense of place that they [desperately] wanted to preserve to attract and keep their clients, including local residents.[20]

It is also worth listening to these merchants to get a sense of how they viewed their entrepreneurial role in the neighborhood and D.C. more broadly. One owner, when asked about how she got started in D.C., and in Adams Morgan more specifically, exclaimed: "I love D.C.! I want to raise my kids in D.C. [We] live downtown. We're really big urban people." Her statement served to signal her long-term commitment to "urban" life in D.C. Another owner similarly placed her entrepreneurial activities in the context of her personal story: "Some background about me very quickly is that I grew up in the Midwest. When I moved out here, I had moved to Arlington first, like every other red state transplant, right? And then, I moved into Adams Morgan." She "started out in politics," she noted, but during the recession when "budgets were being slashed," she did what she "had wanted to do for a long time": she opened a store. Unlike the first business owner, who described herself as "urban," this owner situated herself as one of many newcomers who took a circuitous route through the suburbs before settling in the city. Another owner recounted that his business "had moved here in 2005," and about five years later he "took an apartment next door." "So," he noted, "I live and work here." He had been optimistic because "the first few years it looked promising . . . looked like the neighborhood was transitioning in a positive direction as far as attracting a lot of people from other neighborhoods for dining and evening entertainment and even retail during the daytime and on weekends." In the context of a transitioning neighborhood, then, the interests of older tenants and newer tenants, as well as daytime and nighttime businesses and owners of buildings do not always overlap, creating a difficult and sometimes tense environment as the different options for gaining an economic foothold or achieving and increasing profitability can work at cross purposes (J. E. Davis 1991).

Entrepreneurs such as the ones profiled here were homing in on the business possibilities that accompanied the District's and the neighborhood's demographic trends. Some saw affordable opportunities in Adams Morgan and "a very friendly, neighborhoody kind of place," especially in comparison to some of the more recently established neighborhood entertainment districts, such as U Street, closer to the downtown core. These daytime merchants specifically situated their entrepreneurial aspirations in the larger back-to-the-city trend. "I know D.C.'s audience, the young people who were coming and gentrifying and working really hard and not really making that much money, living in group houses, but very educated, very diverse. I wanted the audience to be me, like a 20-something," one owner explained. Another echoed this approach. Even though she had "intended for this store to go on U Street or some trendier block with more retail" since "there was no retail here," she explicated her choice of Adams Morgan as follows: "I started reading up on the demographics in this neighborhood, like the percentage of 18-to-35-year-olds was higher. There was more discretionary income . . . They tend to be more single, young professionals and they spend more on apparel than almost every other sector." Some of these new Adams Morgan–based entrepreneurs, then, could be classified as members of the very same creative class and segment of the millennial generation so coveted by the city's growth coalition. And they sought to cater precisely to the kind of population that D.C. policy had targeted since the late 1990s.

Indeed, in 2015, a *Washington Post* article exuberantly proclaimed the success of this residential strategy: "By now, everyone knows that millennials love D.C., and D.C.—the former mayor included!—seems to love its newly arrived millennials" (P. Stein 2015). The increase of these young consumer citizens ran contrary to the nationwide trend as D.C. continued to gain millennials even during the recession (Frey 2013). But D.C., according to one of the business owners, had not caught up with New York or San Francisco in terms of having "fun, funky parts of a city" that would cater to this "massive influx of people." Adams Morgan, as these entrepreneurs had observed, reflected a great location through which to reach this target market.[21] Moreover, Adams Morgan, because of its peculiar commercial spaces—second- and third-story floors or basements of townhouses—still offered relatively affordable leases for these kinds of start-ups.

These seemed to be precisely the type of daytime businesses that might support the Adams Morgan NBID, whose third major priority had been to stimulate the daytime economy. They knew the new "audience"—"the young people who were coming and gentrifying" D.C.—and in their own assessment they were media savvy and effective networkers and marketers.[22] Yet, this relatively new generation of daytime merchants also expressed irritation with the NBID. Their grievances related to the types of club goods, primarily the cleaning, safety, and marketing services, the NBID prioritized in its funding plans. They and other daytime entrepreneurs appreciated the focus on cleanliness, but their neighbors' business models created the filth, danger, commercial vacancies, and shabby facades that were particularly noticeable during the day. These negative externalities, only partially addressed through the NBID services, constrained their own entrepreneurial aspirations.

These owners stressed the difficulty they had finding a voice in an organization dominated by antagonistic interests.[23] One owner, who had served on the board in the early years of the NBID, described his experience as "a waste of time." He noted: "all they would talk about is how it [any subject that would come up] affects nightlife." He described his attempt to voice the concerns that daytime merchants might have as follows: "you'd let the conversation go on for 15 minutes, and then I'd say, excuse me, there are some of us that open at two, three, four, six in the afternoon; have you considered us?" His interpretation of the response to this question was a declarative "no." Daytime businesses, then, felt sidelined, their voice drowned out by the nightlife interests. Another business owner, after bemoaning the lack of marketing for the daytime economy, confirmed this perception in a separate interview: "I think my other frustration, too, is that unfortunately the BID is overly dominated by the interests of the bar owners."

The issue of marketing further illustrates how club politics functioned to curtail both the "community" engagement that NBID organizers highlighted in their original appeal for the NBID and the private business ambitions of daytime owners. A business owner explained: "For the most part, I find that the most successful businesses here get involved in and then distance themselves from the BID. And these businesses are also owned by young people, like they're the next-generation businesses." Another business owner expressed the feeling of having been silenced or of having run "into road blocks."

A brief examination of an 18th Street streetscape improvement project, completed in 2012, highlights how a failure to proactively address the particular needs of daytime businesses resulted from a lack of both strategic and holistic thinking. The project program, which was designed to enhance pedestrian traffic on the corridor, proceeded without planning for the eventuality that the actual construction might impact the profit margins, especially of the small daytime businesses on the corridor. A transportation planner involved in the project had apparently suggested that the Adams Morgan Partnership spearhead a strategic planning process. Yet, a respondent close to the project described the NBID's board as not inclined to engage in this kind of broader planning initiative. Instead, a person knowledgeable of the dynamics confirmed in 2015 that members of the board "were just not interested in taking the time, you know, to sit down and really think hard about the future. . . . It just wasn't the right time." Yet, business owners talked about the construction phase as "a turning point" for daytime retail (not the recession), because daytime traffic declined.

The dynamics that played out in Adams Morgan in the immediate post-construction period contradicted a 2012 Office of Planning study, which recommended that "the Adams Morgan Partnership and the D.C. Department of Small Business should reach out to property owners to begin a dialogue about the need to maintain a mix of businesses that will keep the district viable" (Office of Planning 2012). The inattention to the daytime business environment apparently persisted. As one of the 18th Street business owners observed, there was no real initiative to proclaim, "Adams Morgan was back." When asked whether there had been a relaunch of the neighborhood's presence after finalization of the streetscape improvement, another owner just shrugged and said: "You would think that there could have been and should have been, but there was not." After a question probing whether daytime businesses had brought their concern to the NBID, she responded: "Yes, but we'd get the same answer we always get, there's no money available. There's money available for nightlife security, but there's never money, none ever for marketing and promotion, branding, anything." It also seems that even though there are several large hotels just a short walk away, the NBID did not pursue a concerted effort to market Adams Morgan immediately following the project completion to hotel employees who inform guests about local retail and dining options. Yet, according to one business owner, hotel guests had been an important source of income for daytime retail. "I don't know where they're sending those people nowadays," he noted, "but we used to see five, ten, fifteen buyers, not just people [who] walked in the door, but realized sales five, ten, fifteen times a week from people that are staying at the Hilton, Marriott, and Omni Shoreham." Recapturing these consumers would have required a proactive, collective marketing effort to reinsert the neighborhood's presence into the habitual frame of reference of hotel employees. This was particularly true, as one business owner noted, because in the interim years, besides Dupont Circle just down Columbia Road and Connecticut Avenue, other areas, such as U Street and H Street, had emerged as new neighborhood destinations, creating a more competitive environment for Adams Morgan.

The BID concept of common responsibility and shared cost burden is hard to maintain in the context of such complex neighborhood commercial environments where the interests of different stakeholders obviously collide rather than productively intersect. The daytime business owners, perhaps not unexpectedly, questioned the NBID's budget priorities. Despite its recent efforts to redirect its attention to stimulating the daytime economy, several of the business owners interviewed in 2015 still felt that they were "subsidizing" services that supported the nightlife economy. One business owner angrily exclaimed during the interview: "I'm subsidizing the nightlife businesses. That's all that's going on. It's taking from us to prop up their business expenses. Okay?" These businesses felt that they had "pleaded," "volunteered," "prodded," and "begged," but in their view this had not gotten them an encouraging or positive response "over the years."

To be fair, the acting NBID's executive director at that time was trying to balance the interests that are heard by the board of directors and to increase participation from the entrepreneurial daytime businesses in the board's activities, especially on a marketing committee explicitly organized to address these simmering concerns. One of the women business owners, whose entrepreneurial motivation included the desire to "be a part of making D.C. a better place," highlighted her recruitment as an attempt to diversify the board: "I've been showing up for those meetings for so long, and I'm a female business owner, and I'm on Columbia Road. A lot of them are from 18th Street, so I was added for diversity ... because I really was participating and [asking] how do we shape this?" This particular business owner had hoped that the NBID might play a planning role in the neighborhood. "My dream," she noted, "would be to really be a part of a BID in the sense that I would have that curatorial role. That would be something I would love to do because I constantly look at retail around the city and think—'this kind of business would fit here.'" The time to effect such change had not yet been ripe during her tenure on the board. However, it seems the focus of the BID was perhaps beginning to transition.

Some of the entrepreneurs with whom I spoke in 2015 have since abandoned their Adams Morgan locations. Ironically, when I returned to the neighborhood on June 7, 2016, the faces of one of these entrepreneurs and of another Columbia Road daytime business owner graced the bus stop where I disembarked. These oversized posters were part of a new branding campaign launched by the NBID. The motto read: "Adams Morgan Runs on Small Businesses: Get to Know the Faces behind Them." The Adams Morgan Partnership's logo on the poster carried the tagline, "An Independent Streak a Mile Long." Even though some of them are no longer in the area, the consternation and knowledge some of these business owners had shared during their tenure in the neighborhood seemed to have informed new marketing strategies.

Other recent developments in Adams Morgan may portend change. They have, according to a 2018 *Washington Business Journal* article, thrown the NBID into "turmoil" (Cooper 2018). The NBID had been looking forward to the opening of the Line Hotel, a long-awaited luxury boutique hotel on East Columbia Road. Its addition signified both a boost to the daytime economy and a significant increase in the BID's assessment-based budget. An agreement with the ANC also required the hotel to contribute to the redesign and refurbishment of Unity Park just across a narrow street (see approximate location on figure 16, chapter 7).

The hotel's inclusion in the NBID seems to have upset the power dynamics on its board. A letter written by two members of the hotel's development and investment team to the NBID's board, submitted also to a local newspaper, apparently "charge[d] that the BID's services [were] provided in 'disproportionate amounts' to the businesses on 18th Street" (Kramer 2018a, 1). According to Kirk Kramer of the *Current* newspapers (2018a), these investors, who were voting members on the NBID's board, also wrote: "We can no longer tolerate this lack of equity of BID resources, priorities and funding." At the same time, the hotel's representatives have been criticized by the NBID board for not disclosing a significant reduction in the property's assessment by the city, an action that would negatively affect the NBID's budget projections, challenging its capacity to reduce assessment rates for all the properties in the district (Kramer 2018b).

This internal dispute reveals the power large property owners can exercise in NBIDs. Whereas smaller daytime business owners had pointed out the internal governance problems for several years and critiqued the NBID's "club" dynamic, their voices were drowned out. Not until the initiatives by the executive director to diversify the board and to create the new marketing campaign, "An Independent Streak a Mile Long," finally took hold were the needs of daytime businesses elevated and given priority. On the other hand, the new development's outsized assessment contribution, even with the abatement, potentially makes the hotel's development team, which for now has two votes on the board (Kramer 2018b), formidable actors within the NBID moving forward. This transition in focus and power within the NBID could mean that Adams Morgan may yet be the right place to invest for the type of daytime entrepreneur, interviewed in 2015, who had sought to cater to the new residential demographic and tried to shift the conversation and the NBID's priorities.

The Adams Morgan case illustrates that the regulations determining how a submunicipal local governance partnership is institutionalized can distort decision-making processes. NBIDs, which by now provide local public goods and services essential to local economic development, may come to principally benefit subgroups in the club because the logic that those who pay should decide is built into the institution (Levy 2001). Often BIDs also build in a weighted voting system, which means those who own more and pay more gain additional votes and influence on the board (Christopherson 1994). In his reporting on the Line Hotel in Adams Morgan, Kramer (2018a, 2018b) highlighted a pertinent discussion around potentially restricting board membership (votes) to one per business. This rule, if applied, would remove one of the Line Hotel's votes.

As the discussion so far has illustrated, NBIDs can influence how the public realm of a local commercial corridor functions in the larger neighborhood space. NBID-enabling legislation, which dictates that voice is allocated in relation to property ownership, then also interferes with the ability of differently situated constituents to be effectively heard in local decision-making processes. Therefore, the recognition "of whose private power" the "government [is] sanctioning" is crucially important because the provision of club goods through NBIDs can have repercussions that reverberate across the entire neighborhood space, not just the commercial corridor. They do not just impact the commercial corridors for which they are held contractually responsible; they also project a sense of place for the wider neighborhood. Thus, it is crucially important that NBIDs ascertain how this image might affect various groups who live, work, and do business there.

Creative Placemaking

In 2012 the local Advisory Neighborhood Commission (ANC) decided to confront the development pressures in the neighborhood, including the perception that the commercial corridors had become divorced from the rest of the neighborhood. Working with volunteer groups supported by Catholic University's (CU) School of Architecture and Urban Planning to "Envision Adams Morgan," the ANC collected baseline data and conducted an online community survey to begin to formulate a vision for Adams Morgan. Beginning in 2014, the city's Office of Planning (OP) supported and supplemented these neighborhood efforts to create a framework with specific action steps that could guide future developments in the area.

The visual representation of a communitywide workshop, published in the OP's 2015 preliminary "I AM: Ideas for Adams Morgan: Adams Morgan Vision Framework," anchored Adams Morgan in its activist history (Office of Planning 2015b, 27). At least among the workshop's participants, the history of solidarity and organizing embodied in the Adams Morgan name still resonated broadly. At the center top of the image, for example, several people were drawn, holding a sign "SI SE PUEDE [it is possible]" with the tagline "This is where our story started. Latino history!" Other key words, "economic diversity," "diversity of housing," "Latino street vendors," "solidarity," "more inclusive of our youngest and oldest residents," underscored that the social justice–oriented conception of diversity remained integral to the area's neighborhood identity (27). At the same time, Latinx participation in the initial process, especially the community workshop, was disproportionally low, and outreach activities by the Office of Planning revealed that Latinx merchants on East Columbia Road still felt marginalized.

In 2015, OP sought to counteract the relative invisibility of Latinxs in the planning process. Under the auspices of its Kresge Foundation–funded program, "Crossing the Street: Building D.C.'s Inclusive Future through Creative Placemaking," OP hired a team of Chilean consultants, Ciudad Emergente, with expertise in tactical urbanism. Creative placemaking starts from the idea that the arts function as powerful contributors to local economies and can be used to build sociability and empathy to strengthen community-based social capital (Nicodemus 2013; Markusen 2013). The "Crossing the Street" program was designed both to undergird the development of a "Cultural Plan" element for D.C.'s Comprehensive Plan and to promote community building in neighborhoods experiencing rapid demographic and social change (Office of Planning 2017). Perhaps the kind of process contemplated in "Envision Adams Morgan," in which public officials and planning agencies take the lead in facilitating a broader planning process, signifies a more effective publicization of neighborhood planning (Grossman 2010). According to OP's creative placemaking documents, "this change presents an opportunity for the District to devise innovative ways for stakeholders not only to manage growth but also to interact with one another in meaningful ways and, in doing so, strengthen communities" (Office of Planning 2017). This approach, however, seems to avoid viewing ongoing transformations through a critical lens by not directly addressing the iniquitous development trends embedded in "this change."

In Adams Morgan, the OP's creative placemaking initiative revolved around the goal "to redefine Unity Park [a small urban park on Columbia Road east of 18th Street] as a multicultural park through events and programming" and an associated action step to conduct a "community charrette [a participatory community design workshop] for a new park design" (Office of Planning 2015b, 10); both were articulated in the Vision Framework. The aim to incorporate Latinxs in the communitywide conversations to envision Adams Morgan thus became linked to the refurbishment and programming of Unity Park. The proposal for the park's redesign had been part of an agreement among various partners, including the ANC and "other" community leaders, the Office of Latino Affairs, and the Line Hotel developers; these discussions dated back to 2008 (Developer 2012; Lieberman 2016). The creative placemaking program now offered the opportunity to follow through on the charrette, to test out programming ideas for the park, and to collect qualitative data regarding people's perception about neighborhood change while also creating an intercultural and engaging eventscape (Ciudad Emergente 2016a).

Ciudad Emergente (Emerging City; CEM) used a "tactical urbanism" methodology by which "short-term actions in public space" are planned "to inform long term planning processes" (Ciudad Emergente 2016a, 11). In 2016, Ciudad Emergente deployed their "Okuplaza" method, akin to other tactical urbanism interventions (Ciudad Emergente 2016a; Lydon and Garcia 2015; Sadik-Khan and Solomonow 2016), to transform Unity Park into a "Latin American city plaza" for two days. The "Latin American city plaza" concept signaled a variation on the original idea (Ciudad Emergente 2016b, 22), which had been to create a Latinx space to draw attention also to the presence of the Latinx subdistrict on East Columbia Road. Thus, the creative placemaking initiative was not anchored in this local Latinx reality but internationalized as an abstracted "Latin American" space "to succeed in bringing in a multicultural audience" to the park. The aim was to create "a unique sensory environment" and a platform to engage multiple voices in a conversation about place in "a space that was comfortable for everyone," thereby promoting "multicultural civic engagement" (10).

This creative placemaking and tactical urbanism combine DIY urbanism and participatory planning to activate people and place. In this case, the name "Okuplaza Fest D.C." forged a cool association with the worldwide Occupy movement and seemed to evoke Lefebvre's notion of "the right to the city," inhabiting the space not just for revelry but also to create a participatory process for change. Okuplaza, the report notes, brought a wide variety of people into Unity Park to celebrate together and gather data about the perspectives people might have on neighborhood change, how they thought they might be better neighbors, and what ideas they might have to reimagine Unity Park as a public space. The Ciudad Emergente project report summarizes the data around this question in vague terms, observing "individuals were seeing Adams Morgan as a more diverse neighborhood, but it is also clear that the attendees of the Okuplaza Fest are seeing important changes in the neighborhood, regarding a shift in local business and restaurants, and an increase in infrastructure development, and gentrification" (Ciudad Emergente 2016a, 115). It is unclear from the documentation how productively this conversation about neighborhood change will feed into longer term transformative planning to manage or perhaps redirect trends in the neighborhood's transition and to secure Adams Morgan's economic and cultural diversity.

Adams Morgan has an affordability crisis. OP's 2015 Neighborhood Profile observed that the neighborhood only "has 349 rental units, or just under 4 percent, that are subsidized affordable housing for low-income households" and notes that this falls "below the citywide average of approximately 13 percent" (Office of Planning 2015a, 18). Many residents, as the 2015 Framework highlighted, expressed the desire to safeguard Adams Morgan's celebrated identity—"unity in diversity." The preliminary Framework, on the one hand, recognized this desire to safeguard Adams Morgan as an economically and culturally inclusive neighborhood; on the other hand, the report used Porter's (1995) competitive advantage conception of neighborhood development as a path to get there. In two places the report reiterated the importance of maintaining the neighborhood's competitive position given citywide development trends (emphases added):

> In order for Adams Morgan to *sustain itself* and in many ways reinvigorate the *competitive advantages of the past* as an ethnically diverse and culturally rich community, residents must draw upon the neighborhood's multiculturalism, diversity and activist sensibilities *to thrive in today's changing social and economic environments.* (Office of Planning 2015b, 21; emphases added)

The report also stated:

> The vision framework tells a narrative of the neighborhood by unpacking its important cultural and historical aspects and building on them to ensure Adams Morgan *retains relevancy and competitiveness* in the context of a *growing city.* (26)

The report concluded that Adams Morgan might best be reenvisioned as "a family friendly and age-friendly neighborhood with robust amenities" (2). The ANC's proactive initiative and strategic action steps, in so far as they also reflected the demands of the increasingly high-income residential base, may shift the development dynamic on the commercial corridors in a new direction. Adams Morgan might yet be the right place to invest for daytime entrepreneurs who cater to D.C.'s new higher-income residential demographic, at least as long as the quirky, and relatively affordable, commercial floor plans keep the larger, chain stores at bay.

But the use of tactical urbanism or creative placemaking to achieve equity and a more just city is still untested (Fainstein 2010). Unless clear linkages are created between "creative placemaking as planning" and aggressive policies and actions to redress the displacement of working-class culture, commerce, and residents, the strategy may fail to maintain the kind of vertical economic, racial, and cultural diversity Adams Morgan has represented. Instead, creative placemaking may come to be construed as leveraging the public realm, the arts, and artists to reposition neighborhoods, such as Adams Morgan, as high-income residential markets and upscale consumer destinations. Interestingly, NBID members' interests may today more clearly dovetail with the BID-PPP's desire to keep millennials in the city as they age into a new lifecycle and lifestyle. This may be the competitive alliance necessary to finally rebrand Adams Morgan as a daytime and evening economy (Office of Planning 2015b).

Yet, in its radical iteration tactical urbanism, which creative placemakers, such as Ciudad Emergente, seem to claim as their inspiration, should work to achieve a Lefebvrian "right to the city." Producing planning processes through which people come to visualize their place in specific neighborhood spaces and in the city more broadly is not sufficient. This means, placemakers working in this paradigm should fundamentally question and counter prevailing development strategies and trends in ways that make the city livable not just for people active in the creative sector (Office of Planning 2018), such as artists, but also for low-income, working class people and the small business owners they serve.

BID Urbanism beyond D.C.

From the vantage point of 2017, the changes to D.C.'s economic fortunes and urban landscape since the late 1990s have been astounding. But this transformation was planned and predictable, and astute, critical observers, including a *Washington City Paper* reporter, foresaw it. David Plotz's article from June 2, 1995, exemplifies this critical viewpoint, although at the time it may have been meant as a satirical commentary on an absurd and, in many ways, tragic situation. Beginning with the usurpation of home rule by Congress, he described the scene: "The mayor is gone. A city manager is running the government now, a real, honest-to-god administrator who can perform his job unencumbered by patronage or rhetoric." Then he presented a vignette of D.C.'s future: "The streets are clean for the first time in years. Garbage trucks make daily rounds through your neighborhood—and even collect your newspapers and bottles for recycling. . . . The city is adding thousands of middle-class families every year" (Plotz 1995). In uncanny ways today's Washington, D.C., as interpreted through the eyes of this reporter reflects the "urban jewel" that Mayor Marion Barry evoked in his call for federal help and the city that Republican Newt Gingrich promised at that time (Vise and Schneider 1995). But, unfortunately, it also reflects some of the more disturbing aspects of Plotz's predictions: "All the poor have vanished. Some fled when they were wiped off the welfare rolls. . . . Most were forced out by a massive gentrification triggered by tax incentives and the abolition of rent control. When real estate prices climbed sky-high, their rents tripled. They packed up, trekked across the city line, and leased apartments in the new suburban ghettos" (Plotz 1995). Given the foci of the governance and planning strategies that emerged during the Control Board period, Mayor Williams's administration, and subsequent administrations since then, the fulfillment of these predictions, one could say, went as planned (Lee, Spain, and Umberson 1985; Metzger 2000; Schaller 2007). The population has grown steadily, and because of who came and who left, this made the city wealthier and whiter. And D.C. undeniably has become one of the "success" cities when measured in terms of economic growth metrics, such as budget, population growth, and real estate values (Gandhi, Spaulding, and McDonald 2015).

For many of the residents and small business owners who wondered how displacement and neighborhood change happened so fast, BIDs may have been hidden players in driving Washington, D.C.'s "resurgence," their role in oiling the gentrification machine unclear or obfuscated by the way advocates marketed BIDs. From the discussion in this book, it should be clear that BIDs in D.C. and other cities do much more than simply "supplement" or "augment" existing public services. Yet, they continue to be promoted simply as a grassroots, "clean and safe" strategy, especially for neighborhoods beyond the downtown core. The evolution of BID policy in D.C. illustrates that NBIDs continue to be crucial vehicles to catalyze and manage "improvement" strategies in neighborhoods that have not fully transitioned. Parts of Anacostia, east of the river, and Congress Heights, which are still predominately African American, for example, are the next "frontier"—to use Neil Smith's terminology—in the gentrification that has been rolling across the city (N. Smith 1996).

As noted, public choice theory underlies the BID model. But D.C. is still a highly segregated city; and as the 2012 "District of Columbia Analysis of Impediments to Fair Housing Choice, 2006–2011" notes, D.C. is not a city where housing choices can be exercised freely in a "free market." Not only have property and housing markets there been historically shaped by iniquitous racial policies, but these and other "distortions" continue to shape its housing market today (Lauber 2012). The idea that people should be induced, through placemaking, to vote with their feet and buy into the place they desire belies the fact that this choice is historically conditioned. Because the racial wealth gap, which includes Latinxs, persists today, policies rooted in a market-based conception of the choice to move, or the choice to stay, are not consistent with an equal opportunity doctrine (Lauber 2012). The contemporary competitive collection of fairly contiguous, branded neighborhoods, which aestheticizes race and culture, has been built on top of this geography; this form of place valuation, however, only reinforces what Modan (2008) calls "a systematic depoliticization of ethnicity/race and class, [where] issues of inequality are displaced from the public discourse" (203), both on the neighborhood and the city levels. This is in keeping with the public choice worldview, which, as Halpern (1993) notes, "seeks to strengthen the bonds of property" and to "preserve the status quo" (270) while arguing that "uncompensated redistribution is wrong . . . without a reasoned justification for the initial distribution" of economic benefits, derived especially from property in the United States (275).

During his unsuccessful 2013 mayoral candidacy, Councilmember Jack Evans, one of the key figures in the D.C. BID movement, proclaimed that the strategies that had been so successful in Ward 2, where the Georgetown, Golden Triangle, and Downtown BIDs are located, should serve as a model for the city: "BIDs are business improvement districts that we have successfully used in Ward 2, everywhere. And east of the river, a lot of times businesses don't have the money to support a BID. So I will be doing legislation in January to create BIDs that are government-sponsored for a three- to five-year period, with all the other attributes of BIDs. And BIDs are fundamentally two things: Clean and safe" (Hughes 2103). Since that time, the Department of Small and Local Business Development has indeed developed several grant programs that fund "clean teams" for BID as well as other non-BID commercial corridors.[1] And Mayor Bowser's announcement in 2016 that the city would fund an "emerging BID" demonstration project speaks to the continued faith policy makers and planners have in BID urbanism. Some of the "newly" proposed NBIDs are areas that were identified in the 1998 "Citizens Plan," including in Anacostia, Congress Heights, and the H-Street corridors (see figure 3, chapter 4), but never successfully organized. The BID-PPP regime has redoubled these efforts now.

While some may see the availability of public funds to these smaller NBIDs as leveling the playing field to enhance equity goals, the NBID institution is still legally an organization run by and for property owners. The continued conflation of the interests of "businesses [that] don't have the money to support a BID" with those of local and prospective property owners masks the institutionally defined purpose BIDs are supposed to play. In 2016, a story in the *Washington Post* pointed out: "While the District's overall population boomed from 2000 to 2010, its black population dropped by 39,000, prompting the current mayor to create the first-ever position of African American affairs director. There are only 300 Chinese Americans left in what remains of Chinatown, and half of them are battling a development project that would force them out" (O'Connell 2016). Although BIDs are not mentioned, if one reads between the lines, their work suffuses the discussion about D.C.'s development trajectory in the article: "The growth of the District during the past 30 years is the story of one mega-project after another. The MCI Center (now Verizon) opened in Chinatown in 1997. The new convention center opened in 2003. Nationals Park by the Navy Yard opened in 2008 . . . with another under construction on the Southwest waterfront" (O'Connell 2016). As discussed in chapter 4, these are all BID-managed areas. The BIDs, however, did not just provide supplemental cleaning, safety, and marketing service as the law initially intended. They oversaw and continue to direct the development of these areas.

The 2016 article also tells the story of Jennifer Bryant, who is but one example of the kind of serial displacement that BID urbanism has wrought. Having been displaced from Shaw, she ended up in Congress Heights, where a similar dynamic is playing out: "I see the beginnings of that in my neighborhood, and it scares me that I won't be able to stay." She told the reporter: "It is kind of a state of panic, knowing that you have to buy or you will be displaced" (O'Connell 2016). Indeed, the real estate blog *Urban Turf* noted that Congress Heights along with Anacostia "ranked Nos. 1 and 3 in the city by price appreciation" (*Urban Turf* staff 2015). It is also a neighborhood where one of the new, emergent BID projects is receiving technical assistance from seasoned BID professionals, including the former IDA president and retired DowntownDC BID leader. BID urbanism, then, is implicated in spreading "panic" in D.C. among those unable to afford to purchase into the places they already inhabit or in which they invested their entrepreneurial energies during times of neglect and disinvestment (O'Connell 2016). This dynamic fuels the sense of dislocation low-income residents and small businesses may feel, not unlike that expressed by Latinx residents and small businesses in the Adams Morgan and Mount Pleasant area during the LEDC-led neighborhood visioning and BID establishment processes. It is the anxiety that settles in before physical displacement (Fullilove 2005). And it is a well-founded sense of panic, rooted in experience.

LEDC's story should serve as a cautionary tale about neighborhood-level BIDs, especially to those public officials, planners, and organizations interested in fostering economic development activities that help the "less advantaged" stabilize in place and grow their economic prospects (Fainstein 2011; Krumholz 2011). A fundamental contradiction is built into the BID model, which gives primacy to the interests of property owners while ostensibly championing grassroots development. Instead, BIDs have been mobilized to sideline a community development ethos that had been founded on the pursuit of both political and economic empowerment. The outcome to date has increased inéquity under the rubric of inclusion and diversity. In the new D.C., abstractly speaking, many of the census tracts that have seen an influx of new residents have become more "diverse" as whites have moved in and as might be measured through statistical indexes, such as a diversity index (Furman Center for Real Estate and Urban Policy 2011; Lauber 2012). But this "diversity" has meant the disproportionate displacement of low-income, especially African American residents, who have not been able to respond to or withstand the rapid transition the city's strategic planning approach was meant to induce in their neighborhoods. It has also increased income inequality (Naveed 2017).

Mildred E. Warner (2011) argues: "A city is more than a collection of clubs. Any system can sustain only so much fragmentation before it breaks apart" (164). However, BIDs are no longer individual clubs that simply fragment the city into "delectable" islands of wealth (Zukin 1995, 134). BID urbanism is intended to extend the club economy and governance ethos and particular urban aesthetics across entire urban geographies (Sorkin 1992; Zukin 1995, 2009, 2011). D.C. is evidence of this trend. The work BIDs performed in the urban core—the central city and the Mid-City neighborhoods, such as Shaw, LeDroit Park, Adams Morgan, Mount Pleasant, and Columbia Heights—has bled into adjacent neighborhoods even if they as of yet have no BID. In disturbing ways the underlying rationale of BID urbanism in D.C., including the rebranding efforts that have emerged from it and the strategic focus on transitioning neighborhoods, harkens back to ideas articulated in the mid-twentieth century to theorize conditions under which inner-city neighborhoods might be reintegrated. One such idea, as noted, was that the majority of "middle-class whites would support integration only if they remained in the numerical majority and maintained 'cultural dominance'" (Metzger 2000, 14).

In D.C., "diversity" and "integration" have been achieved through the "back door" of gentrification, a process that continues seemingly unabated, and that does not bode well for the goal of achieving long-term integration (Lauber 2012, 138). In D.C., this wave of gentrification was planned. Professional planners, downtown advocates, and economic development consultants focused strategic actions on those neighborhoods that were already economically, ethnically, and racially diverse, where "diversity" had meant reaching across differences in class and race. Unfortunately, maintaining this vertical integration—meaning ethnic, racial, and class diversity—did not emerge as a funded or proactively pursued policy priority. Instead, the BID-PPP regime articulated and implemented the explicit policy priority to attract the creative class, especially the millennial, young professional class, to the city to secure both the profitability of D.C.'s urban space and its tax base.

The goals of the 1998 "Citizens Plan" have been realized. Washington, D.C.'s population has been steadily growing, increasing the city's tax base. Placemaking has been a resounding economic success if one narrows the target population (those made to feel a sense of ownership over, and belonging in, the city) to young professionals and higher-income residents and consumers, including visitors. Hip food trucks—some with ethnic-themed fare, pop-up parklets, communal movie nights, and free concerts are creating managed, highly programmed eventscapes to provide an experientially variable and exciting public realm. These eventscapes perhaps represent a fun and exciting way to rebuild community, but they have come at the expense of low-income individuals, families, and small businesses that have lost the capacity to assert a right to the city. Their economic, political, and social lifeworld and right to a dignified urban life were actively marginalized or suppressed, and their neighborhoods, instead, were largely "revitalized" for a new audience. The creative placemaking paradigm has emerged also to confront the exclusionary tendencies as well as equity gaps created by BID urbanism thus far. Policy makers might draw lessons from Frank Smith's assessment of Adams Morgan (see chapter 5), where the cooperative movement and a people-focused community development paradigm secured long-term stability at least for some (Lloyd 2015, 1103; see also Huron 2014).

"We Are Actually like Small City Governments"

Predictably, BIDs and the professionals behind them have become fully integrated into the governance of cities, and not just in D.C. This is testament to the porous boundary between the public and private sectors that is inherent to PPP governance and characteristic of these newly consolidated, pro-growth urban regimes (Beauregard 1998; Brash 2011; Lyall 1986; Sagalyn 2007). BIDs have in fact taken ownership of their districts in ways perhaps not foreseen by residents and business owners, who were not paying close attention to this new governance vehicle. BIDs no longer operate in the shadows of planning, raising crucial questions the planning profession needs to address. Some BIDs are even more boldly proclaiming the control they exercise over their turf. At an American Planning Association event in Washington, D.C., in 2016, two BID executives and a representative of the D.C. BID Council repeatedly referred to "their" neighborhoods. One executive proclaimed the following: "We are much more nimble than the district government and able to procure services—faster, quicker, more efficiently.... *We are actually like small city governments*, providing much more enhanced city services in our area ... DPW [Department of Public Works] *does not come into our neighborhood* and take trash out of trashcans anymore, and this is pretty much the same in all BIDs. ... We take it to a collection spot of dumpsters, and they touch that, but *you don't see the trash trucks coming through our neighborhoods*" (Stevens, Suls, and Avery 2016; emphases added to my transcription). By 2016, the District government had effectively relinquished crucial territory and major assets, such as public parks, to these BIDs.

Where BIDs early on might have sold themselves as merely "clean, safe, and friendly" organizations, formed to enhance and supplement city services, BID executives are no longer shy about openly claiming the governance space they have come to occupy. It is worth reiterating what this BID executive told APA planners in 2016: "As mayors change, council members change, and ANC representatives change, the BID can be seen as the go-to representative or the constant institutional organization for that neighborhood" (Stevens, Suls, and Avery 2016; my transcription). Unlike democratic governance cycles, BIDs from this perspective provide continuity and predictability for the real estate development community as well as for the new residents and businesses they wish to attract. They mitigate the risks to investment by repositioning real estate markets and keeping abreast of and developing a new and evolving urban lifestyle. The question of what is sacrificed and whose voices are sacrificed in the process remains a crucial one, however. BIDs are still unelected representatives, and the unitary voice they purport to represent is a fiction; this fiction suppresses the multiplicity of voices that contest and shape a sense of place. This multiplicity should not only be represented in planning processes but should also benefit from planning's outcomes.

. I turn again to Gerald Frug. In 2010, he raised the question of why "the almost automatic answer when one seeks to create an organization to improve neighborhood life" is still: "Let's create a BID," not just in Philadelphia, but also in D.C., and in New York City and elsewhere. And, "whose private power" lies behind contemporary placemaking trends? Policy makers as well as planners continue to be "seduced" by the BID model and its placemaking ethos. In Northern Manhattan in New York City, an area comprising West Harlem, Washington Heights, and Inwood, since 2013 there have been rumors of BID expansion plans covered in the *Daily News* that would extend across Broadway from the 130s to 218th Street and major cross streets along the way (Feiden 2013). This BID initiative would, not coincidentally, connect Columbia University's campuses as well as medical and sports facilities. While these are rumors for now, the "progressive" de Blasio administration in fact is expanding the organization of BIDs in tandem with his administration's controversial mandatory inclusionary housing (MIH) rezoning proposals, which form an integral component of the mayor's affordable housing plan but which to date have only been proposed for predominately low-income communities of color (Pratt Center 2018).

One such neighborhood is the predominately Dominican area of Inwood.[2] In Inwood, the MIH zoning plan, which recently passed, allows the production of thousands of market-rate housing units in exchange for limited affordable housing units whose income eligibility criteria, however, do not respond to the needs of the local low-income population (Rickenbacker, Krinsky, and Schaller 2018; S. Stein 2018). The neighborhood's median income is much lower than the regional median income the MIH program uses to create its affordability guidelines (New York City 2018a, 3–36). Therefore, the projected high-income residents who will move to Inwood will be crucial to make MIH work in Inwood (Rickenbacker, Krinsky, and Schaller 2018, 33). As in D.C., this dynamic will likely serve to "diversify" Inwood through the backdoor of an accelerated gentrification process abetted no less by this self-described progressive regime's policies (Stein 2018).

In Inwood, a BID has had trouble getting off the ground for years, but it now seems to be squarely on the city's agenda as part of this rezoning plan and in the eyes of many was treated as a foregone conclusion.[3] Parallel to the rezoning process, as part of a broader "Inwood Planning Initiative" marketed by New York City's Economic Development Corporation (EDC), the New York City's Department of Small Business Services (SBS) funded the nearby Washington Heights BID—the BID seeking to expand into Inwood mentioned in the 2013 *Daily News* article—to extend its services to Inwood. SBS provided $1.23 million to organize BID-like placemaking programs: these included the standard BID playbook, marketing, sanitation, banners, and events as well as business courses (Pichardo 2017). In 2018, to show the kinds of "investments" the city was ostensibly making in the small businesses in the area, SBS presented these BID initiatives at several community board meetings during the mandatory Uniform Land Use Review Process (ULURP), which is the public review process the city has to follow to approve a rezoning. In this manner, city agencies established a direct link between the rezoning plan and this preliminary BID-like work.[4]

BIDs are stealthy creatures. They are called "business" improvement districts and are marketed as serving merchants on commercial corridors. Yet, as we have seen, BIDs are designed to give property owners, not tenant-businesses, an organized voice in the management of an area's commercial environment as well as in the land use planning and urban design decisions that might guide future development. In Inwood, unlike in Adams Morgan, property ownership is highly concentrated. To channel development and enhance the profitability of a district, as the story of D.C. has shown, BIDs draw boundaries. These boundaries, however, frequently are arbitrarily created not necessarily to reinforce a sense of place recognizable to different resident groups or small business owners, but to secure the interests of property developers. It is not surprising that the pre-BID marketing website "Up in Inwood," designed to profile Inwood's creative community and public amenities, such as its flagship Inwood Hill Park, to lure people uptown, sports a map that overlaps with the rezoning area and not with Inwood boundaries recognized by longtime residents and business owners. These indications suggest that in Inwood the local political leadership, including the council members, community board members, and other BID interests as part of the de Blasio administration's governance coalition, is pursuing BID urbanism in keeping with the preceding Bloomberg administration (Brash 2011; Zukin 2011). This strategy includes bringing on board creative placemakers through the Washington Heights BID, which received a grant from the Department of Small Business Services supposedly "to foster a sense of community." These initiatives, according to SBS Commissioner Gregg Bishop, "will go a long way towards revitalizing key commercial corridors" (Pichardo 2017). Funds were allocated to artists and arts organizations to program the public realm, especially Inwood Hill Park, and create marketing banners for Inwood's commercial corridors (Pichardo 2017; Washington Heights BID 2018). These are standard BID activities that may have little to do with the actual needs of the hundreds of independently owned businesses on the commercial corridors. It is these businesses, now at high risk of displacement, that over the years through periods of active disinvestment have created the kind of Jane Jacobs vibrancy that is rapidly vanishing in New York City (Moss 2017).

Inwood is still a unique, vibrant neighborhood in which small businesses, especially immigrant-owned and neighborhood-serving businesses, have been able to survive. The city's own data show that Inwood still had over 316 businesses on three of its major commercial corridors in 2016 (Department of Small Business Services 2016). But 98 percent of these businesses, the majority of which were independently owned, leased, and most felt extreme pressure from ever-increasing lease burdens (Department of Small Business Services 2016). As in Adams Morgan and other entertainment districts in D.C., in this environment high-revenue businesses, such as restaurants and clubs, which have been gaining a presence on Inwood's corridors, are more likely to survive increasing rent burdens than neighborhood-serving daytime businesses.[5] In early 2018, the three merchant members of the prospective BID listed on the site were two club owners and a Community Board 12 member, and at the time one of the most prominently displayed courses for business owners was "how to obtain a liquor license." A pattern similar to the one in Adams Morgan may be emerging, then, where the interests of the outwardly focused businesses, such as destination restaurants and bars, are prioritized (Rodriguez 2018). Finally, the rezoning opens up land on the waterfront currently zoned for manufacturing uses to high-rise residential development with a waterfront esplanade. A BID, covering the entire rezoning area, as suggested by the Up in Inwood map on the marketing website, could function akin to the Capitol Riverfront and NoMA BIDs in Washington, D.C.

The BID urbanism model is traveling, seemingly like wildfire, across the globe, actively promoted by policy entrepreneurs through international conferences, short purposeful study tours, and BID consultants (Ward 2012; Cook 2008). This focus on replicating "best practices" eschews a critical engagement with difficult and controversial questions, including how historical privilege is considered and treated in planning practice. If indeed public-private partnerships, and BIDs in particular, continue to be heralded by urban planners and policy makers as a means to democratize urban restructuring and community development (Grossman 2010), then it also remains essential that we continue to scrutinize the validity of claims that BIDs represent a democratic grassroots, merchant-focused revitalization strategy.

Planners are ethically charged with seeking "social justice by working to expand choice and opportunity for all persons, [while] recognizing a special responsibility to plan for the needs of the disadvantaged and to promote racial and economic integration"; at least this is the profession's aspiration.[6] Following Fainstein's reminder that "planners, policy makers and political activists cannot wipe out history and act as if they start from scratch" (2011,

28), this book has situated Washington, D.C.'s business improvement districts both historically and contextually in the micropolitics of place. The history in D.C. and trends in New York City suggest that planners, policy makers, community development professionals, and small business owners as well as residents should be wary of being captivated by the aesthetics and excitement of placemaking or of being seduced by the discourse of grassroots democracy, which disguises the inherently undemocratic nature of BIDs. As noted throughout the book, this isn't happening just in D.C. But given the experience of D.C. and New York (Zukin 2011), the extension of BID urbanism to cities such as Detroit, where BIDs are also on the march, should be approached with caution (Haimerl 2014). In Inwood, residents and business owners continue to organize. And, as in D.C., they hope to file a lawsuit charging that the placemaking policies pursued by New York City's urban regime have produced racially disparate outcomes (see also Angotti and Morse 2016).[7]

BID Urbanism, the Internationalization of Eventscapes

BIDs are emblematic of global trends in BID urbanism: the intensification of placemaking and the ubiquitous production of eventscapes in central cities, urban neighborhoods, and also, more recently, the suburbs. In 2003, the conservative mayor of Hamburg, Germany, Ole von Beust, threw his support behind business improvement districts. The "Anglo-Saxon model," the mayor observed in his speech, enables "people to take their fate into their own hands; the state retreats, self-reliance takes over, and problems are solved more quickly." Tellingly, Beust invoked the BID model in a speech calling for a systemic political and cultural change in Germany that would be rooted in market principles. Local citizens had to take on more responsibility for the "shaping of their city" (Beust 2003). And BIDs, he concluded, provided a perfect opportunity. After enabling BIDs in 2015, Hamburg became recognized as the German pioneer city in the movement.

In 2012, I arrived in this harbor city on a sunny day to investigate the introduction of business improvement districts. My intention on the first morning was to see whether I could find Hamburg's BID areas without looking at a map that outlined their boundaries. So, I began to wander through the downtown area looking up, searching for the telltale banners that might have indicated that I had actually entered a BID area. But there were none. It was not until a few hours later when a researcher from the Hafen University of Hamburg took me on my first guided walk through the downtown BIDs that I realized that I had been looking in the wrong direction; I should have looked down instead of up. As we moved through several contiguous BID areas, the subtle changes in the hues of the sidewalk pavement came to light.

Accustomed to New York City, Washington, D.C., or Philadelphia, where BID districts are often easily identified by the ubiquitous signs that guide and welcome visitors, U.S.-trained eyes may fail to recognize where one BID district in downtown Hamburg ends and another begins. No banner calls out a BID identity or a neighborhood brand. Instead, in Hamburg, the quality and the shade of the stone differentiate the various districts to bestow distinct identities. The overall policy objectives articulated by several BID stakeholders, namely to harness private resources to impel a redefinition of the urban space in this city and to reposition particular districts, however, echo the goals of downtown BIDs in the United States.

BID initiatives in Hamburg were also part of a BID-PPP regime. BIDs there dovetailed with a PPP project initiated in 2001 and completed in 2006. Under the slogan *lebenswerte* (livable) and *lebendige* (vibrant) city, this public-private partnership reconstructed the Jungfernstieg, the main boulevard along one of the city's waterfronts (Vollmer 2011; Michel and Stein 2015). With this investment, the PPP sought to reclaim the Jungfernstieg's history as an elegant promenade in order to propel Hamburg back onto the world stage as a destination city. The design concept, which reorganized and repaved in light, expensive stone larger open spaces, streets, and sidewalks, was to bestow the area with a cosmopolitan "Mediterranean" flair. Accordingly, the approval of BID-enabling legislation in 2005 was timely. The city could focus its attention on the infrastructure below grade, and BIDs could finance the publicly visible public realm in the adjacent districts. Several BID projects in line with the overall urban design aesthetic for downtown have worked to maintain the visual impact of the Jungfernstieg's light stone. To further boost a sense of local uniqueness, several BIDs have also planted exotic and costly trees. These extravagant design elements provide the basis for district character, reaffirming the investors' interest in establishing the inimitability of place and to confer a sense of corporate identity.

The aim of these downtown BID projects, I was told, is to revalorize, that is, to achieve the "up-scaling" (*Veredelung*) of the inner city. In homing in on recognizable brands, "top labels, like Tiffany, Ferragamo, Hermès, Neuhaus, Lacoste," my guides from both the public and the private sector situated the districts as globally competitive shopping environments with ca-chet and an exclusive air. In line with Hamburg's wider rebranding efforts, my guides echoed the language found in widely available marketing litera-ture and news outlets (Hirschbiegel 2014; Iken 2015).

BID projects have deliberately created destination districts that facilitate *flanerien* (strolling), but not only on foot. The idea, a Hamburg planner clar-ified, is also to force automobiles and by extension passengers to slow down to allow the gaze to capture the scene: "In the districts . . . we have reduced the speed. . . . That means driving slowly so that you can see the stores from the car as well." And "cruising," a word inserted in English into conversa-tions otherwise in German, was used by both a BID project manager and a planner, invoking the notion of traveling without a destination in mind but on the lookout for something new and exciting. The explicit design intent is to make it easy for visitors to see and to be seen. In this manner, visitors be-come part of the production of postindustrial urbanity (Bookman 2013).

Interestingly, the language defining this newly constituted urban space both weds this northern European harbor city to a southern cosmopolitan identity and draws on historical local references. In Hamburg, it is not the "cool aesthetics of blackness" or the Latinx "spice" that is evoked to create a unique place brand. Instead, allusions to Italian cities and "Mediterranean flair" echo through newspaper articles and marketing literature, pointing to the conscious use of a branding discourse that arouses a sensory imag-ination (Bookman 2013): the Mediterranean Sea, a cool breeze, the aroma of Italian piazzas, perhaps. At the same time, this re-presentation of Ham-burg also plays on the city's memories, invoking nineteenth-century el-egance and flânerie, complete with "men in stiff hats parading in front of stores . . . and children playing on the street . . . streets full of life" (Hirschbie-gel 2014). What may be tongue-and-cheek references to the past reinforce an unambiguously class-inflected (not to speak of gendered) vignette of ur-banity, one being materially reincarnated in the present, a class-inflected image sharpened by the multiple invocations of Milan (N. Smith 2002), the fashion capitol of Europe, a quintessentially cosmopolitan city, as a com-parative association. Yet, this re-presentation does not go uncontested.

In 2010, "Not in Our Name, Marke [Brand] Hamburg!" published a man-ifesto. Like the 2018 lawsuit in D.C., it called out Florida's "creative class" strategy. The manifesto warned: "A specter is wandering through Europe since the U.S. economist Richard Florida has shown us the calculations that only those cities in which the creative class feels comfortable will prosper" (NION 2010). Not unlike in D.C., BID urbanism in Hamburg created its cosmopolitan brand in pursuit of a particular demographic, it seems. Critical media outlets and anti-gentrification activists have pointed out that the creative city and creative placemaking policies are driven by a BID-PPP regime that fails to recognize the necessary foundations for a truly creative city, one where artists are not used as "decoys" (*Lockvoegel*) to lure investors, residents, and consumers and ultimately to displace the working-class city (NION 2010). As in D.C., BID advocates and city officials have used selective amnesia, evoking the nineteenth-century city without remembering its stark inequalities, to reposition Hamburg as a postindustrial powerhouse. The activists behind "Not in My Name" remind us: "The City is not a brand. The city is not a business. The city is a body politic and a community."[8]

In an environment of ever-growing disillusionment with democratic governance, BID urbanism, however, further undermines peoples' faith that they can have a say over matters of concern. BID urbanism penetrates into and transforms our capability to shape how we navigate our everyday survival, our daily routines, and our sense of belonging and rootedness in urban life. In the conception of Lefebvre's right to the city, based on a pragmatic sense of solidarity, people should be guaranteed a commonly shared right to the city they inhabit (NION 2010). Recently, U.S. national-level planning conversations have explicitly linked "equity" and "placemaking," and corresponding concerns are emerging among public sector BID officials in rapidly gentrifying cities (APA 2016). The true "publicization" (Grossman 2010) of public-private partnerships would require centering solidarity into public policy debates and targeting investments deliberately on equitable economic growth. It also necessitates the proactive rethinking of property regimes, turning to community land trust, cooperative building groups, and other forms of property ownership that temper speculative dynamics, for example, to establish the possibility for the cocreation of urban life and to ensure a right to stay (Hovde and Krinsky 1996; Schaller 2018). Only a city that can meet the daily needs of its population inclusively can begin to function as an integration, rather than a polarization, machine (Feldtkeller 2012).

NOTES

Introduction. BID Urbanism in Washington, D.C.

1. In 2012, a member of the Chamber of Commerce in Hamburg, Germany, described Paul Levy, the founder of Philadelphia's Center City BID as highly charismatic. In 2017, Seattle stakeholders described Dan Biederman, New York City's BID policy entrepreneur, in similarly enthusiastic terms.

2. In fact, as I note in chapter 4, this centrifugal force is also reaching back into the suburbs in the D.C. region to areas such as Tyson's Corner (Aratani 2013). "The version of regime theory propounded here," writes Stone, wherein BIDs form part of broader BID-PPP regimes, "holds that public policies are shaped by three factors: (1) the composition of a community's governing coalition, (2) the nature of the relationships among members of the governing coalition, and (3) the resources that the members bring to the governing coalition. Of course, this does not mean that the governing coalition operates in a social and economic vacuum; the socio-economic environment is a source of problems and challenges to which regimes respond" (2).

3. New York and D.C. follow the nonprofit model. Multiple institutional forms exist, including BIDs as municipal authorities. Philadelphia started out with BIDs as municipal authorities but changed its laws to enable BIDs to be formed as non-profit organizations as well. Philadelphia's neighborhood BIDs allow the assessment of BID fees from residential properties as well (City of Philadelphia 2013).

4. Incredibly, Richard Florida has only recently recognized and acknowledged that this monopsonistic vision has been detrimental to the overall development of cities, precipitating what he now calls a new crisis (Florida 2017).

5. When I refer to "urban renewal," unless otherwise explained, I mean the period of the late 1940s to the late 1960s, which was met with organized resistance

both to the use of eminent domain and the razing of designated areas to make room for redevelopment. Hyra (2012) marks this period from 1949 to 1974: this bookmarking captures the Housing Act of 1949 and the year urban renewal was retooled during the Nixon administration (Pritchett 2008).

Chapter 1. Framing BID Urbanism and Placemaking

1. These PPP regimes can also produce common goods to enhance equity through community land trusts (Hovde and Krinsky 1996), the support of cooperative building groups (H. Müller 2015), and planning processes that are based on an outcomes-oriented paradigm and commit to producing social value (Schaller 2018).

2. Hackworth (2007) cites Hayek in his discussion of neoliberal governance.

3. Suzanne Scotchmer (2002) describes this dynamic and demonstrates how spatial jurisdictional boundaries allow the benefits of local public goods, including supplemental ones, to be capitalized in land.

4. See for example, the differing accounts of Sandra Cisnero's decision to paint her San Antonio house, located in a "Germanic" historic district, purple (J. N. Rodriguez 1997; Lowry 1997).

5. The focus on regimes facilitates an analysis of the qualitatively different institutional arrangements that organize in response to supra-local and other, evolving ideological frames. I rely here both on Harvey Molotch's conceptualization of the growth coalition (1976, 1993) and Clarence Stone's urban regime (1993). Molotch notes that "Stone concentrates on politician coalition-builders and why they gravitate toward the growth faction; I focus on the actions of growth entrepreneurs and how they link up with political actors (among others)" (Molotoch 1993, 32). In analyzing the establishment of BIDs and the consolidation of the BID growth coalition, I move between these two perspectives, at times examining the work of elected officials, including members of Congress, while at other times directing my analytic focus on the BID entrepreneurs.

6. Whiteness and blackness are socially constructed categories that have changed over time. Freund (2007) explains: "In the late nineteenth century, racial science was harnessed to describe the wave of so-called new immigrants to the United States. . . . In the eyes of self-described whites (or 'Americans'), the new immigrants were culturally and even biologically distinct, thus described alternatively as nonwhite, 'almost white,' or 'in between.' In popular discussions as well as policy debates over immigration, the term 'race' sometimes stood in for nation, at times it was treated as heritable, at times it was viewed as acquired. . . . If the new immigrants had occasional defenders in the planning profession, most urban experts still viewed blacks and other unambiguously 'nonwhite' populations as a categorical threat to sound development" (55).

7. Modan (2007) dissects and examines discourses of place and analyzes how these overlapping and competing ideologies of place structure social relations as well as power in the Washington, D.C., neighborhood of Mount Pleasant.

8. McFarlane (2009) observes: The "vestigial oppression of slavery has evolved to a norm of presuming black deviance, lack of wealth, disadvantage, and presumptions of guilt; and an economic structure whenever Blackness is inscribed on the physical landscape to mean places that are less desirable and to be avoided. . . . Taking race and class into account seems to demand exploration of the significance of Blackness and affluence within an existing societal structure that has evolved from white supremacy to a seemingly less-virulent, or more-benign, white norm—one in which normalcy, wealth, advantage, and presumptions of innocence are still implicitly predicated on Whiteness and in which an economic structure of white privilege and advantage is inscribed into the geography of the physical landscape. . . . [But] Blacks with money are privileged in certain limited circumstances to be operatively white" (165).

9. Fullilove and Wallace (2011) argue that previous urban policies have both patterned displacement (cultural, economic, and political displacement) over time, creating a path-dependency, and have embedded racist mindsets in our collective social imagination about who belongs in the public realm, malls, or commercial establishments, mindsets that also pattern placemaking norms in local communities. See also McFarlane (2009).

Chapter 2. Urban Governance and Planning before BIDs

1. A recent class action lawsuit filed in D.C. makes precisely this argument (*Matthews et al. v. D.C. Zoning Commission et al.* 2018).

2. Racial categories, such as "white" and "black," are obviously socially constructed, but because they were deployed to steer investment, create property markets, and structure employment opportunities, especially in the early twentieth century, they continue to be relevant categories to examine planning and policy outcomes. See Freund (2007).

3. Georgetown did not become part of the District of Columbia administration or Washington, D.C., until the establishment of the territorial government in 1871.

4. The District's population grew from 73,492 in 1860 to 230,402 in 1890 (Manning 1998, 332). The black population grew from 14,307 in 1860 to 75,572 in 1890 (Horton 2003, 71). Congress declared slaves in the District freed in July 1862, contributing to the in-migration (Gillette 1995, 67).

5. An excellent source on this topic is Masur (2010).

6. This framing of D.C. as a city inhabited by bureaucrats and the poor reappeared in 2003 to advocate for the new residential growth strategy adopted by the BID-PPP regime (Shapiro and Bowers 2003).

7. Indeed, writes Fauntroy, "racial conservatism has played a considerable role in driving many of the policy decisions that were made in the pre-home rule era" (Fauntroy 2003, 66).

8. In 2015, my colleague Susanna Rosenbaum and I developed and team-taught a course that critically examined the nation-building role world's fairs played in circumscribing notions of citizenship and national belonging.

9. The National Association of Real Estate Boards, founded in 1908, changed its name in 1915. Today it is the National Association of Realtors. In other cities these inimical policies targeted other "nonwhite" populations. See Hannigan (1998). The Federation of Citizens Associations and, more specifically, property owners seemed quite content to keep the District under federal control due to the influence they exercised over the commissioners and the District committees. See editorials in the *Washington Post* on April 17, 1903, and January 8, 1928 (Proquest Historical Newspapers, 1877–1990).

10. PrologueDC, a public history project, has mapped a significant portion of this geography (http://prologuedc.com).

11. Derek Hyra (2017) elucidates the history of Shaw in particular.

12. The "1919 Race War in Washington," during which a white mob assailed black residents in a Southwest neighborhood, served as a stark reminder of the length to which whites would go to enforce racial hierarchies (Asch and Musgrove 2017, 231). The "Race War in Washington" was not an isolated incident; white mobs assaulted black communities across the country, using extreme violence (Fain 2017).

13. Cummings (2001), in tracing the "genealogy of market-based community economic development," argues that the shift toward market ideology was so effective is because it resonated with such diverse and to some extent contradictory currents of thought.

14. The University of Richmond's "Mapping Inequality" project has digitized many of these maps. To find out whether your neighborhood was redlined, see "Mapping Inequality: Redlining in New Deal America" (https://dsl.richmond.edu/panorama/redlining/#loc=4/36.71/-96.93&opacity=0.8).

15. A recent research article in the *Journal of Planning Education and Research* by Dan Trudeau examines New Urbanist developments in suburban jurisdictions and illustrates that this discomfort persists even today (Trudeau 2018).

16. *Berman v. Parker*, No. 348 U.S. 26 (Supreme Court 1954). The Fifth Amendment states: "No person shall be . . . deprived of life, liberty, or property, without due process of law; nor shall private property be taken for public use, without just compensation." See, for example, the Cornell University Law School interpretation (https://www.law.cornell.edu/constitution/fifth_amendment). For more on the "discourse of blight" and the impact of Berman, see Pritchett (2003).

17. In Adams Morgan, as I relate later in the book, the fractured nature of the neighborhood's micropolitical life both exposed a surprisingly reactionary local politics with respect to property, race, and revitalization and ushered in an era of organizing across historical racial boundaries. While residents in Adams Morgan ultimately thwarted the urban renewal plan, residents of Shaw, with the astute guidance of civil rights activist Reverend Walter Fauntroy, produced an exemplary community-driven plan.

18. The commuter tax, in the view of the Brookings Institute, is warranted, given that D.C. functions both as a state and as a municipality.

19. Fauntroy (2003) notes, "A complicating factor at the time was that organized business interests in the District were segregated. Consequently, the most power-

ful business interests—the Federal City Council and Washington Board of Trade—were still all-White, further marginalizing Black interests in the District" (49).

20. This reframing of urban policy provided a rationale to redirect federal aid away from high-poverty areas to moderate-income communities, which were more likely to have the internal capacity to improve. Deploying a "triage planning strategy" based on a neighborhood lifecycle analysis akin to the HOLC and FHA underwriting standards, this policy re-racialized investment patterns without overtly using racial criteria (Metzger 2000, 16).

Chapter 3. The Push for BIDs

1. Writing in 1998, Beauregard noted the fragmented nature of these growth partnerships. However, at this point BID urbanism has been able to consolidate the initially fragmented project-based PPPs by managing and guiding overall planning for a district beyond the time frame of any given project and providing municipal-like services to ensure the environment retains a certain service standard. Beyond that, BIDs also ensure continual placemaking services.

2. Seigel continues: "This was certainly in order. But the way it was handled and financed was by starting the process of emasculating renewal and switching into these other *high-need* and also *high-publicity* fields of action" (emphasis in original). He also criticized federal policies underwriting suburbanization as "those twin bugbears of downtown—the huge Federal highway programs and immense funding for single family housing via FHA."

3. Lyall (1986) notes that President Carter's 1978 "National Urban Policy" focused specifically on public-private partnerships to deal with "economic problems as well as social conditions of the older central cities. It recognized that to revive central-city economies, basic transformations had to occur in the conditions for doing business, investing in facilities, and providing jobs" (5).

4. Oliver Carr, a controversial downtown developer whose family real estate history reaches back to the late 1800s, and David Childs of Skidmore, Owings & Merrill, known for his corporate architecture, sat on this task force.

5. See also Jerry Knight's article "Ways and Means to Make City Core an Exciting Place," *Washington Post*, July 26, 1982.

6. See also U.S. National Crime Prevention Council (1974). The planned downtown urban renewal area (1969) for which Downtown Progress lobbied spanned from 5th and 15th streets NW and Pennsylvania Avenue to Massachusetts Avenue NW.

7. McGovern (1998) notes the gentrification pressures that downtown development was exerting on surrounding neighborhoods in the late 1970s and the 1980s.

8. McCarthy (2008), who served both as executive director of the D.C. Downtown Partnership (1985–1988) and as planner in leadership positions at the Office of Planning—deputy director for development review, historic preservation, and neighborhood planning (2000–2003) and director of Office of Planning (2004–2007) and interim director (2014–2015)—describes the politics of this rezoning

process. The main players she highlights, besides developers and the city, are the Greater Washington Board of Trade, the Preservation League, the Citizens Coalition for Planning, and affordable housing advocates, such as the Downtown Cluster of Congregations. Small business interests do not appear in this narrative.

9. See also a 1984 HUD report: "Another major public/private partnership venture undertaken in FY 1983 was the Downtown Retail Development Conference which CPD sponsored in conjunction with the International Council of Shopping Centers (ICSC) and 20 other supporting partners organizations. This first-of-its-kind Downtown Retail Development Conference brought together all partners involved in the development process. Nearly 500 mayors and city officials, real estate developers, lenders and retailers participated. The conference focused on the complex downtown retail process and what is required to make downtown retail ventures successful. Because of its success, a second conference is planned for FY 1984" (HUD 1984, 14).

10. A letter penned by George Brady, president of the National Corporation for Housing Partnerships, is an earlier example of advocacy for entertainment-oriented development (Brady 1975): it encourages Mr. Knox Banner of the Downtown Progress to support this development because it would include a "skating rink about the size of the rink at Rockefeller Center and would be surrounded with restaurants and stores." He compares this to the FBI building development, which he deplores as being "a dead space and probably forever."

11. In 2006, a downtown BID manager pointed to before and after aerial pictures depicting the parking lots that pockmarked the district's landscape before the creation of overlapping BID and TIF districts.

12. This zoning regulation represented the first step to create new neighborhoods, such as Penn's Quarter and Mount Vernon Triangle, but it did not build in safeguards to protect the small businesses characteristic of some of the downtown's subareas such as Chinatown, for example (Lou 2013).

13. Hodos (2010) notes that the South Street / Headhouse District (SSHD) created in Philadelphia in 1992 was raising similar questions in neighborhood stakeholders' minds. Conflicts emerged during the 1998 reauthorization process: "complaints were about what they perceived as a democratic deficit embedded in the model, which gave residents no voice in the development of their neighborhood's commercial corridor" (Hodos 2010, 201).

14. This procedure combined provisions in New York City's legislation with that of Philadelphia.

15. Ex officio means that this member serves by virtue of occupying the office of councilmember, ANC commissioner, and so forth. Should the person no longer occupy this office (councilmember or commissioner, for example), the individual replacing the officeholder would then occupy the ex officio membership seat on the BID.

16. Porter was a consultant for the city's 1998 strategic plan, "The Citizens Plan."

17. New Orleans is often cited as the first city in the United States to enable BIDs.

18. Note that written testimony was submitted to Mr. Joe Sternlieb, committee clerk for the Committee on Economic Development on Bill II-464, "Business Improvement Act of 1995." Sternlieb later became a downtown BID executive and then the executive director of the Georgetown BID. As noted previously, there is a blurring between the public-private spheres that is evident in these PPP regimes. BID movement advocates have moved across the BID landscape to install and strengthen BID urbanism. Similar patterns are evident in New York. One need only follow the career paths and institutional relationships of de Blasio officials, such as Carl Weisbrod and Maria Torres Springer, for example.

19. One witness testifying at the hearing specifically cited the report (Neighborhood Development Assistance Program 1995). Lawrence Houstoun "is a business improvement district and public space consultant living in Center City Philadelphia" (Houstoun 2010). In addition, Richard Bradley, from the International Downtown Association, also noted: "There are more than 1,200 BIDs operating in over 600 communities in North America (in some cities, like New York there are multiple districts)" (International Downtown Association 1995).

20. BIDs differ from tax increment financing: TIFs can add another layer of financing. The BID assessment, unlike in TIF financing, is not linked to future potential tax receipts but to a formula based on the assessed value of taxable properties in the BID-managed district.

21. Some properties, such as those of nonprofit organizations and government facilities, are exempt from paying assessments. This is a fairly standard provision in BID legislation.

22. Georgetown is explicitly mentioned in the legislation because influential local voices (developers and Councilmember Jack Evans, the sponsor of the bill) had been actively advocating for a BID since the late 1980s. Yet, resident associations and representatives of small businesses in Georgetown voiced their discomfort as well as opposition to the legislation.

Chapter 4. BID Urbanism Oils the Gentrification Machine

1. As negotiations with congressional Republicans proceeded, Mayor Barry stepped back from this option, seeking a bailout instead.

2. Janofsky (1995) noted: "According to a count of early votes, in Ward 6, a predominantly black middle-class area, Mrs. Schwartz [a white, Republican candidate] drew unusually large support: Mr. Barry led her there by just 5,751 to 4,776 votes. By contrast, in Ward 8, a largely black but lower-income area, in which Mr. Barry lives, he led in the early count by 5,572 to 496."

3. The IDTF chair, Herb Miller, was a major developer in D.C. and a close ally of the Barry administration. He had been working on the "living downtown" vision since 1982. His corporation's investments in the downtown Gallery Place project, often cited as the anchoring project for the downtown revival, were subsidized through tax increment financing (TIF). As such, it is difficult to separate private benefit from public good (T. C. Hall and Lombardo 1996).

4. According to Weiss (2002), the funds were being sequestered due to investigations into the Barry administration's questionable disbursement practices and his administration's failure to spend the money.

5. Isenberg (2004) traces how the International Downtown Executives Association (IDEA) and "The American Council to Improve Our Neighborhoods (ACTION), [which] drew its members from the leadership of such associations as the Mortgage Bankers Association of America, the Chamber of Commerce of the United States, the National Association of Home Builders, the Congress of Industrial Organizations, the National Urban League, and the U.S. Savings and Loan League," promoted the idea that developers and planners would have to respond to white, middle-class, suburban aesthetics and, specifically, white women's sense of place to undergird this renaissance.

6. Asch and Musgrove (2015) argue that the fourth wave of gentrification can be dated to the post–Control Board period. I concur with the timing but argue that BIDs were institutionally crucial to consolidate this fourth wave.

7. A D.C. BID executive in an interview in 2006 drew parallels to powerful BIDs in Philadelphia and New York. He noted, "Downtown D.C. is a leadership organization like Center City Philadelphia" and "downtown Manhattan [The Downtown Alliance] under Carl Weissbrod." These organizations, he argued, "use the institutional infrastructure as a platform to lead discussions in the business community."

8. Of a large-scale placemaking urban design project along Connecticut Avenue, one of D.C.'s major avenues, the Golden Triangle BID professional observed: "The BID organized a group of stakeholders for federal agencies, local agencies, property owners, business owners, and the nearby residents. We brought them all together. We did an RFP through an architecture firm and had the stakeholders select a concept design to create a beautiful plan that we then could take to the city, and keep in mind a lot of these stakeholders were the city. Let's build this, and in return it would maintain a large section of the BID" (Suls 2016).

9. Briffault (1997) provides a thorough discussion of TIFs: "Property tax revenues generated by the frozen assessed valuation level will continue to flow into local government coffers; any additional revenues resulting from growth in the area's assessed valuation will be reserved to pay for economic development programs for the area. The TIF authority—either the municipality itself or a local economic development entity—will issue bonds" (8).

10. This is only a sampling of this network of relationships: Gerry Widdicombe, who came from Office of the Deputy Mayor of Planning and Economic Development to the DowntownDC BID, has been in leadership positions in the DowntownDC and the Mount Vernon Triangle BIDs. Similarly, Joe Sternlieb, who was involved in the writing of the BID legislation at the City Council, has been at the DowntownDC and the Georgetown BIDs as well as on the PPP coordinating the Circulator Bus. Steve Moore, who was at the Rouse Company, where he worked on the Faneuil Market Place in Boston, South Street Seaport in New York, and Philadelphia's Market Street East, was also deputy executive director at the

DowntownDC BID and the president and CEO of the Washington DC Economic Partnership and became the executive director of the latest business improvement district, the Southwest BID. Similar patterns can be found in New York City and Philadelphia.

11. Hyra (2017) delineates the various projects that were completed to consolidate an entertainment district in downtown, whose development impacts as predicted (Schaller 2007) would extend into adjacent neighborhoods and beyond.

12. Washington DC Economic Partnership, "About Us," https://www.linkedin.com/company/washington-dc-economic-partnership/, last accessed October 15, 2018. See also DC Radio, *The Economic Partnership Business Buzz*, https://dcradio.gov/programming/the-economic-partnership-business-buzz/, last accessed October 15, 2018.

13. Downtown business interests, which often also had properties in the suburbs, developed a consensus "to make the downtown attractive and safe for white, middle-class, suburban women" (Isenberg 2004, 174). In the late 1990s, the target market may have shifted, but the governance institutions and planning paradigms in development in the 1950s had finally matured and could be transformed into actionable strategy to remake the central city.

14. Shapiro and Bowers (2003) linked this finding to the state of the D.C. public school system, noting that those families who could afford to pay for private school might settle in the city.

15. See the various policy statements and Action Agenda plans the D.C. government developed: Office of the Deputy Mayor of Planning and Development (2007, 2012); District of Columbia, Office of Planning (2010). See also the news release from the Washington DC Economic Partnership on September 29, 2006 (WDCEP 2006).

16. The report noted, "These qualities, among others, make this demographic the basis for the robust creative class Florida describes, one that supports the labor demands of the District's growing Creative Economy" (Office of the Deputy Mayor 2012).

17. "Growth in the number of 20-to-34 year-olds increased sharply between the 1990s and the 2000s and was widespread because it stemmed from changes in the national age structure" (Myers 2016, 929). For commentary on D.C.'s image see the DowntownDC website (https://web.archive.org/web/20070208022853/http://www.downtowndc.org:80/).

18. Hochleutner (2003) uses public choice theory to build a tautological or self-confirming argument in support of this kind of stakeholder democracy, one that justifies weighting or restricting voting to those who pay.

19. Brandes (2005) writes: "The District of Columbia Anacostia Waterfront Corporation Act . . . passed by the City Council in 2004, creates a District government-chartered Corporation charged with the development, promotion and revitalization of the Anacostia River waterfront. With a board that includes both Mayoral appointees as well as ex-officio members from both the District

and Federal agencies, the Corporation is a city-created entity poised to become a development partner for both municipal and federal agencies" (427).

20. The blog *JDLand* by Jacqueline Dubree (n.d.) provides an archive of before and after photographs documenting the area's transformation. See "Capitol Quarter," *JDLand*, http://www.jdland.com/dc/capquarter.cfm; "Capper/Carrollsburg Redevelopment," *JDLand*, http://www.jdland.com/dc/capper.cfm.

21. See Johanna Bockman's analysis of D.C.'s Ellen Wilson HOPE VI project in Capitol Hill, which has had a BID since 2001 (Bockman 2015, 2018).

22. Will Smith (2011) noted: "The primary restriction is that a buyer's household income fall between 80 and 115 percent of the Washington area's median income. . . . It doesn't matter if the buyer is single or married; so long as the total household income falls within that range, the requirement is met. The home must also be owner occupied and a primary residence. Notably, the buyer does not have to be a current D.C. resident nor a first-time home buyer."

23. D.C. has a complex park governance structure, and many parks and squares do not fall under the city's jurisdiction.

24. These data come from a Capitol Riverfront BID presentation (Stevens, Suls, and Avery 2016): (1) PILOT for federal DOT-$70M; (2) PILOT for SE Federal Center (Yards) -$98M; (3) PILOT for Arthur Capper Carrollsburg—$35M; (4) HOPE VI Funding Arthur Capper Carrollsburg—$50M; (5) Nationals Park Financing—$680M; (6) Canal Park Construction—$14M; (7) 11th Street Bridges Construction—$300M; (8) SE Water/Sewer Assessment District—$13M. The presentation can be accessed at https://planning-org-uploaded-media.s3.amazonaws.com/document/tuesdays-at-apa-jun16-impact-of-bids-in-dc.pdf. The Capper PILOT runs until 2037 (see The Code of the District of Colombia, "§ 47-4611. Payments in lieu of taxes, Capper/Carrollsburg PILOT Area," https://beta.code.dccouncil.us/DC/council/code/sections/47-4611.html#).

25. Altman's career illustrates the blurring of lines between public and private development that characterizes BID urbanism: After leaving D.C., where he headed the Office of Planning and guided the development of the Waterfront through the quasi-public development corporation, he moved to Philadelphia to repeat a similar pattern. He is also the founder and principal of Fivesquares Development, a real estate development company in D.C. founded in 2015 (https://sap.mit.edu/news/andrew-altman-joins-mit-school-architecture-and-planning).

26. NoMa Business Improvement District, https://www.nomabid.org.

27. Its sister nonprofit, NoMa Park's Foundation—with a shared board, offices, and staff—has raised additional philanthropic dollars to acquire land for parks.

28. See also Jenkins (2005). Fares on the Circulator Bus are only $1.00. Thus, the Circulator could be viewed as subsidizing the mobility costs for high-income residents as well as visitors in the city's core while residents in the outlying neighborhoods incur higher costs on the traditional public transit system; this may explain why a *Greater Greater Washington* article in 2016 asserted that the creation of the route to east of Anacostia (comprising some of the poorest areas in the D.C.) "was a political move" (Alpert 2016). The Anacostia BID came on line in 2012.

29. In Philadelphia a similar search for the concept revealed a first mention of pop-up landscapes or venues in the public realm in 2011 (Schaller and Guinand 2017). This post-2008 emergence of pop-ups and their increasingly higher concentration is also chronicled by industry pioneers (Baras 2016).

30. "The report found that the creative economy supports 75,000 jobs and generates $5 billion in revenue in Washington, particularly in media, culinary arts, and design" (Driggins and Snowden 2012, 3). Renan Snowden, the coauthor of this report, has since moved to the Capitol Riverfront BID, where she is vice president of planning and development (https://www.capitolriverfront.org/about/about -the-bid/staff, last accessed January 13, 2017).

31. The neighborhood revitalization programs include BIDs, Main Streets, and more recently independent Clean Teams, perhaps as precursors to BIDs. The Strategic or Target Neighborhood Investment Program was subsequently legislatively reinforced in 2004 as L15-131: "to reduce the scattershot nature of past economic development investment efforts in the District's neighborhoods by creating the critical mass of investment and activity necessary to bring about a significant impact in each neighborhood. The legislation requires the Mayor to designate 6 neighborhoods into which the District will pour significant and concentrated economic development resources. The legislation required the District to concentrate initial investments in 2 neighborhoods at a time so the District's efforts remain focused and significant.—Established a non-lapsing account whose dollars shall not revert to the General Fund" (Brazil 2003).

32. This is also what the 2018 lawsuit charges (*Matthews et al. v. D.C. Zoning Commission et al.* 2018).

Chapter 5. Situating Adams Morgan and Mount Pleasant

1. Increasingly, to attract young professionals of diverse cultural backgrounds, also in response to demands from community groups, this placemaking is turning to creative placemaking strategies and diverse programming in the public realm to enhance the "vitality" of neighborhood districts (Office of Planning 2016).

2. The contention over the park's name has apparently reached an impasse or a compromise (Izadi 2012; Prince of Petworth 2014).

3. For great images then and now, see Zapata and Gibson 2006). See also the Smithsonian Archives (http://siarchives.si.edu/blog/hidden-women) and Evers (2007).

4. See, for example, PROLOGUE DC (prologuedc.com).

5. Henig (1982) notes that unlike Georgetown, where the citizens association lobbied for and received protective zoning to prevent "random development," Adams Morgan saw rapid commercial development and densification.

6. Newspaper articles from 1948 show that the Mount Pleasant Citizens Association sought to continue to enforce restrictive covenants "(Citizens Unit Studies Plan to Circumvent Covenant Ban," *Washington Post*, October 11, 1948; "Race Covenant Rule Disappoints Many," *Washington Post*, May 4, 1948.

7. See Neil Smith (1996) for an analysis of the urban renewal plan in the Society Hill area of Philadelphia, which deliberately incorporated restoration and preservation.

8. The 2004 Comprehensive Planning Framework, as explained in chapter 4, used 1990 census data to categorize neighborhoods.

9. The way people relate to urban space is conjugated through the various ways their identities are shaped (race, culture, class, sexual orientation, etc.). These in turn shape their memories of place and produce ideologies of place that take on collective significance. Thus, people can create overlapping "lifeworlds" and produce multiple place identities in the same area.

10. I attended meetings in 2000 organized or attended by the following: D.C. government agencies, the mayor, D.C. Coalition for Housing Justice, the Washington Lawyers Committee, the Council of Latino Agencies, and the Committee for Indigenous Solidarity.

11. Two Latinx leaders closely connected to the El Salvadoran community spearheaded the public political efforts; one, a young man in his twenties from the Latino Civil Rights Task Force, had experienced eviction firsthand as a young boy. The other was the well-known leader of CARECEN, a community-based organization with deep roots on Mount Pleasant Street. Asian American Youth Leadership Empowerment and Development (AALEAD became another key organization, organizing tenants in the buildings.

12. Exercising "first right of refusal" is already an uphill battle, and it takes sustained effort and savvy financial brokering to purchase and renovate seriously dilapidated buildings. Another loophole, the 95/5 loophole, also existed to circumvent this law. It allowed owners to sell 95 percent of their building to outsiders while holding on to 5 percent, only to sell that at a later date; in this maneuver, "the transfer of 95 percent ownership in a building didn't qualify as a sale under the law, and so tenants never had a chance to make the purchase themselves" (Wiener 2015; see also Howell 2013).

13. According to its own history, "CARECEN began its Housing and Community Action Program, which helps renters in the District defend their rights as tenants," in 2000 (see http://www.carecendc.org/about/history/, accessed July 15, 2016). Up to this point among the Latinx organizations in D.C., housing and tenant organizing had been under the purview of LEDC.

Chapter 6. Neighborhood Identities Collide

1. The Mount Pleasant Forum discussions were, at the time, also available at the public library.

2. The data analysis in this chapter draws on work with Gabriella Gahlia Modan, who was a research fellow at LEDC at the time. Selected passages are from a joint article (Schaller and Modan 2005), elucidating the mapping data from 2000, and a joint conference presentation (Schaller and Modan 2011) for the 2006 mapping data analysis. The mapping workshops are also discussed in Modan's book *Turf*

Wars (2007). Interestingly, the earlier work foreshadowed the issues that indeed emerged as the NBID process proceeded between 2000 and 2005. I also draw on conversations among LEDC staff. When I talk about LEDC staff, I include Gabriella Modan.

3. LEDC conducted the initial mapping exercises in 2000. We then replicated the methodology in 2006, one year after the establishment of the neighborhood business improvement district in Adams Morgan. Data from the 2006 workshops and interviews are further discussed in chapters 7 and 8. The identities of the individual mapmakers and interviewees were anonymized.

4. When I use the notion of "official" here, I am referring to the Advisory Neighborhood Commission (ANC) boundaries.

5. In her book Cadaval (1998) makes clear that this Latinx identity was differentiated and not conflict free, given the Latinx community's diversity.

6. While the strategic planning focus in Columbia Heights broke down investment barriers, selective amnesia continues to function through planning documents that legitimize this gentrification. The 2000 housing crisis demonstrates that BID urbanism at the time eschewed a clear equity-oriented, historically rooted placemaking ethos. Property values in Columbia Heights rose sharply, 63 percent, between 2004 and 2005 alone. Due to its architectural heritage, moreover, the area was also recognized as a conservation area in the 2006 Comprehensive Plan, and gentrification has been visibly moving eastward across 16th Street, as evidenced in the renovation of row houses and the proliferation of fairly expensive restaurants (see also figures 3, 5, and 6).

7. Works by Summers (2015) and Hopkinson (2012b) highlight how African American everyday lived culture was framed as criminal and progressively evicted from D.C.'s public realm.

8. In 1997, at least 70 percent of the businesses were minority owned, which in this case meant Latinx, African American, or Asian owned. And at least 50 percent of the businesses were Latinx owned (LEDC 1999).

9. At the time, the fence was a hangout place for high school students from Bell Multicultural High School, located on the east side of 16th Street. This is not to say that "harassment" did not occur on the commercial corridor. But the extent of it, at least in my experience as a white female who has walked on these commercial corridors since the early 1980s (at all hours), was highly exaggerated in the forum discussions. Other women, as Modan highlights in *Turf Wars*, felt similarly: one in particular, wrote a retort to this poster: "White boys do it too," calling out the hidden but racializing discourse the original post precipitated.

Chapter 7. BID Urbanism and the Politics of Exclusion

1. The Jackson Heights BID expansion proposal in Queens, New York, was highly controversial; it was especially opposed by small, largely Latinx, business owners. In the Inwood neighborhood of Northern Manhattan in New York City, a BID has had trouble getting off the ground for years but is now being pushed

as part of a rezoning plan by the de Blasio administration. And a group recently launched an anti-BID Facebook page in New York City (see https://www.facebook .com/vozantibid/, last accessed January 28, 2018).

2. In New York City, under Mayor Bloomberg's administration (2001–2016), for example, this expansion of small BIDs was actively promoted and supported, and today NYC has over seventy BIDs. During 2002–2011, the administration created twenty-two BIDs "in all five boroughs," apparently "more than any other administration" (see City of New York 2011). The de Blasio administration is also expanding the organization of BIDs in tandem with his administration's controversial mandatory inclusionary housing (MIH) rezoning proposals.

3. The first attempts to create NBIDs in the 14th and U Street areas failed in 2008. On H Street a BID had been under discussion at least since 2006, indicating that NBIDs were not unquestioningly welcomed when viewed from a "grassroots" or local perspective. See Lee (2016) for an NBID establishment dynamics in Los Angeles.

4. The proposed emerging BID areas included Historic Dupont Circle Main Street, H Street Main Street, Shaw Main Street, Congress Heights Community and Training Development Corporation, and the Mid-City Business Improvement District.

5. For the former expansive definition, see, for example, Fainstein (2011), Harvey (2013), and Purcell (2014). For the more restrictive definition, see, for example, Houstoun (1994, 1997, 2010) and Levy (2001). Houstoun (1997) cites the Times Square BID president in New York City as stating, "We control the money, we get things done, and we are outside democratic oversight and accountability" (15). This discourse suffused the conversations of BID professionals in D.C. as well, perhaps not quite as bluntly. Even then this notion is misleading since business owners—that is, tenant merchants—almost always pay.

6. The legal foundation of the BID, rooting the model in the antecedent of the special district, requires this (Briffault 1999).

7. New York City's and Philadelphia's processes seem to be evolving, especially where neighborhood-based BIDs are concerned. New York City's Department of Small Business Services, for example, is focusing on persuading some business owners of the model during the early BID organizing stages to preempt vocal and public opposition.

8. In the Adams Morgan Partnership model, nine seats of the fifteen-member board of directors are reserved for property owners and six for tenant businesses. Additionally, the board has four nonvoting members: Lanier Heights Citizens' Association; ANC 1C; Reed-Cooke Neighborhood Association; and one ex officio member from the Metropolitan Police Department, Third District.

9. John Emmeus Davis (1991) focuses on the analysis of residential property relations. He relates two dimensions of property interests: accommodative interests, shaped also by attachment to place and "the use value" individuals ascribe to their neighborhood, and accumulative interests, conditioned by the exchange values that owners can derive from their property. Thus, he distinguishes among property

capitalists, whose interests are accumulative, owner-occupiers, who have both accommodative and accumulative interests, and tenants, whose interest are mostly accommodative.

10. J. E. Davis's work (1991) presents a framework to analyze this kind of differentiated interest group formation in the context of neighborhood development.

11. The plan with some of the funding outlays is available at DC Watch (http://www.dcwatch.com/govern/dhcd981c.htm#OPPORTUNITY:%20TARGETED%20ECONOMIC, last accessed March 8, 2016).

12. As noted, the Northwest quadrant of D.C. west of Rock Creek Park (Adams Morgan and Mount Pleasant lie east of this park) was composed of almost exclusively white and wealthy neighborhoods and defined as stable.

13. By 2008, the next Ward 1 councilmember also promoted a BID in the ward for 14th and U Street, and the Adams Morgan Partnership organizers worked with groups there, but up until recently the NBID drive was unsuccessful (Alpert 2008). Similarly, BID expansion in Northern Manhattan was being driven by the Department of Small Business Services with the advocacy by the local councilmember and allied interests. See Lee (2016) for an analysis of Los Angeles.

14. See also DC Watch (http://www.dcwatch.com/govern/DHCD1998.htm, last accessed January 15, 2016).

15. Isenberg (2004) links the development of BIDs and the ethos they advance to Progressive Era politics around Main Street improvements and late nineteenth-century initiatives spearheaded by women's clubs (309).

16. Capital Area Asset Builders Corporation Newsbriefs (http://www.cdsc.org, February 19, 2000 [cached]). "CAAB was founded in 1997 by several non-profit organizations that shared a common goal to support the development of Individual Development Account (IDA) programs in Washington, D.C." LEDC was an early member of CAAB as it developed its own Individual Development Accounts program (http://www.caab.org/en/who-we-are, last accessed July 2016).

17. At the time, I was a staff person at LEDC and obviously actively engaged in these conversations, and it is probably clear on which side of the argument I stood as a staff member at the time.

18. In 1997, according to LEDC data, at least 70 percent of the businesses were minority owned, which in this case means Latinx, African American, and Asian owned. At least 50 percent of the businesses were Latinx owned.

19. The characterizations are very broad and obviously fail to adequately capture all of the nuances; I have drawn on the mapping workshops and discussions in 2000 and 2006 to reproduce these broad-stroke descriptions. Interestingly, this characterization coincides with the BID consultant report from 2002 (hired by LEDC) and a 2012 retail report as well (PUMA 2002; Office of Planning 2012).

20. Henig (1982) provides a thorough discussion of earlier, similar dynamics, indicating a recurring struggle over the organization's control.

21. In 2016, an executive-level staff member at that time concurred that the board had never come to unequivocally embrace the idea of the BID.

22. During this time residents and merchants were also building bridges,

organizing together to invalidate the "voluntary agreements" that civic organizations had imposed on merchants (see chapter 6). Additionally, the Multicultural Coalition, founded in 1993, was actively vigilant and was organizing around issues of gentrification, which intensified during this period from 1994 to 2006. See, for example, Modan (2008).

23. The Denver-based Progressive Urban Management Associates (PUMA), a national consulting firm, specializes in the creation of BIDs. PUMA's president Brad Segal visited Adams Morgan "to accomplish the following objectives: Meet with property and business owners to discuss the pros and cons of forming a BID. Provide recommendations for moving forward, including the identification of next steps, sequencing and costs" (PUMA 2002, 1).

24. A D.C. BID professional explained in 2006 that the assessment formula for the NBID could either be based on square footage or on assessed value. The relatively low commercial density made it difficult to arrive at a workable formula based on square footage. It would have required very high assessments (in comparison to high-density downtown districts) to raise budgets sufficiently to fund the BID's operations. For comparison, see the annual reports published by the D.C. BID council (http://www.dcbidcouncil.org/publications/).

25. BID advocates, including the local council member, described Stavropoulos literally as a "saint" for having taken on the role of lead organizer. John McCalla (2003) wrote: "'If he had done nothing more than open Tryst, he would have made a lasting and valuable impression,' says Josh Gibson, an ANC commissioner and Tryst regular, and the author of the 'saint' comment on the DCWatch Web message board. 'When you consider The Diner and throw in his presidency of the business association, and his work on the creation of the BID, he's clearly been one of the top people in the community.'"

26. Adams Morgan Partnership Steering Committee, "Letter to Business Owners," April 7, 2005. Four of the signatory businesses had only recently opened in Adams Morgan: Tryst (1998), Blue Room (1999), All About Jane (2000), and The Diner (2001). The other two had been there much longer: Idle Times Books (1981) and Fleet Feet (1984). Two of the signatories were associated with businesses owned by Savropolous—Tryst and The Diner. It appears that none of the business owners on the steering committee represented Latinx businesses during the organizing drive in 2004 and 2005.

27. The fact that the BID was passed on an emergency basis was to complicate the renewal process five years later. See Code of the District of Columbia.

28. The nascent NBID received crucial pro bono professional support from a retired businessman, who helped write a grant proposal and researched and wrote the business plan and by-laws to help create the governing structure. D.C. official and government agencies as noted lent their support, including also the Office of Tax and Revenue, which made corrections to inaccurate property-use records and furnished the list of properties with assessment information to develop the tax basis for the BID.

Chapter 8. BIDs as Clubs

1. I have had discussions with planners both in New York City and Washington, D.C., and managers of BID programs at city agencies (in 2015, 2016, and 2018), who had not critically assessed the premise of the BID model or the implications of BIDs for some of the merchants they were trying to organize in support of one; nor had they thought of the role BIDs play in the context of BID urbanism and the growth coalitions it serves more broadly.

2. During conversations in D.C. and NYC with several representatives of different government agencies, I repeatedly had to ask for clarification to tease out whether they were referring to the role of tenants or commercial property owners in the BID establishment process. This conflation is problematic since landlords and tenants often have conflicting interests. It is, however, reflective of the policy language used to promote BIDs. The preferred nomenclature is businesses, business community, etc.

3. Just as a reminder: enabled by state legislation, BIDs are most often formed as nonprofit organizations responsible for a specific geographic area; and unlike other nonprofits, they are able to levy mandatory assessments on district properties, enforceable by liens, giving them a predictable funding stream to be reinvested in a specific place.

4. The "Letter to Business Owners" explained: "Commercial property owners sign petitions indicating their support for the BID. Once we have petitions from owners representing 51% of the assessed commercial value of the neighborhood, the BID is created and becomes binding on all property owners. Property owners pay at a rate of $0.21 per $100 of assessed value. Fully 82 percent of property owners will pay less than $4 a day for BID services, 61 percent will pay less than $3 a day, 37 percent will pay less than $2 a day, and 15 percent will pay less than $1 a day." . . . Without a BID, the city can cut the level of services it provides at any time, and we would have no recourse. With a BID, cutbacks in covered city services would be illegal."

5. The "Letter to Property Owners" stated: "There are well over 1,000 BIDs throughout the country and currently four in Washington D.C.—The Downtown BID, The Golden Triangle BID, The Georgetown BID, and The Capitol Hill BID— the effects and contributions of which are ongoing and evident: cleaner, safer, faster growing and more successful business communities."

6. The "Letter to Business Owners" named five D.C. BIDs: Downtown, Georgetown, Capitol Hill, the Golden Triangle, and Mount Vernon Square (*sic*); and five suburban districts: Bethesda, Clarendon, Silver Spring, Rosslyn, and Wheaton.

7. In the early 1990s several businesses focused on attracting nighttime revelers opened, much to the chagrin of many of the nearby residents. Some of these establishments were restaurants that also functioned as nightclubs, yet apparently they did not meet the food consumption requirements. I use the term "nightclub" here to distinguish these establishments for the club goods discussion.

8. The ANC reinserted itself into the debate ten years later when it spearheaded the *Envision Adams Morgan* process, a planning process facilitated by the Office of Planning (2015).

9. Daytime merchants and evening businesses—that is, restaurants and delis, for example—saw their interests as overlapping. I have placed them in the category of daytime here.

10. Parts of this section, specifically the discussion of marketing language, draw on a joint conference presentation with Gabriella Modan (Schaller and Modan 2011).

11. Accessed October 12, 2006, on the RestoreDC's Main Street website for Adams Morgan (http://restore.dc.gov/restoredc/cwp/view.asp?a=14; no longer active link). For more on the DC Main Streets Program see D.C. Department of Small and Local Business Development, https://dslbd.dc.gov/node/443942.

12. This question was posed before asking participants to share their thoughts about the NBID as part of the neighborhood mapping discussions. The notion of marketing was not specifically raised by the facilitators.

13. These sentiments were echoed on the Adams Morgan online listserv, where comments about drunken yelling and ensuing fights on the streets adjacent to the commercial corridor abounded during this time. The Adams Morgan listserv is an unmoderated Yahoo group, which in 2005 had about 1,500 members, by 2009 apparently counted about 2,500 members, and by 2016 had reached 4,215 members. See "What's Your Neighborhood Listserv?" (*DCist*, http://dcist.com/2005/05/whats_your_neig.php); "Best Neighborhood Listserv" (*Washington City Paper*, http://legacy.washingtoncitypaper.com/bestofdc/peopleandplaces/2009/best-neighborhood-listserv); and (Adams Morgan Community, https://groups.yahoo.com/neo/groups/AdamsMorgan/info, last accessed July 15, 2016).

14. This beloved restaurant did eventually close in 2013 and moved to U Street, but apparently with the intention of returning.

15. The WDCEP is "a nonprofit public-private partnership organization whose core purpose is to actively promote and support economic development." The cochair of WDCEP's board, for example, is Robert Lake from Roadside Development LLC. A quick search of Robert Lake and Roadside in the *Washington Business Journal* reveals the myriad of projects in which Roadside has invested over the years in D.C., particularly in its emerging neighborhoods (see WDCEP, www.wdcep.com/about, last accessed July 11, 2016).

16. The revelers' behavior, which was frequently identified as linked to people coming from the Maryland and Virginia suburbs, is more than tolerated and managed; it is enabled because their activities are seen as enhancing the tax base. This stands in contrast to the suppression of the Go Go scene described by Hopkinson (2012b).

17. This Reimbursable Police Officers (RPO) program has evolved over time. The 2017 notice (Alcoholic Beverage Regulation Administration 2017) explains that the reimbursable has been extended from two to seven days. It also "assists licensed

establishments to defray the costs of retaining off-duty MPD officers to patrol the surrounding area of an establishment or an outdoor Special Event or Pub Crawl Event for the purpose of maintaining public safety, including the remediation of traffic congestion and the safety of public patrons, during their approach and departure from the establishment or Special Event or Pub Crawl Event."

18. Two daytime merchants and an ANC commissioner alluded to the fact that the ABRA turned a blind eye to some of the "bad actors" on the commercial corridor. In doing so, they were encouraging rule breaking, specifically the requirements to balance food and alcohol consumption.

19. This was a common theme during interviews: the institution was problematic, not the people employed by the BID.

20. In transitioning neighborhoods, such as Adams Morgan, where nighttime entertainment is ascendant, property owners may indeed want to speculate or take a risk, keeping their storefronts vacant to potentially capitalize on higher capacity businesses (J. E. Davis 1991).

21. In 2010, 47 percent of the population fell between the ages of 18 and 34; 32 percent between the ages of 35 and 54. The population was characterized by greater "educational attainment" than 2000, and median household income had jumped from $48,000 in 2000 to $84,000 in 2010. It has steadily climbed since then; in 2013 it reached $91,000. Although the median age changed little, "discretionary" income had grown tremendously in this time span (Office of Planning 2015a).

22. As noted by the second business owner, who had opened her store in a second-floor space in 2007: "I also went out of my way to cultivate things that a lot of business owners hadn't." She told me she had been featured in *Washingtonian Magazine*'s "Best Of" issue for 2011, 2014, and 2015; was a runner-up *City Paper* winner in 2012, 2013, 2014, and 2015, and runner-up *Washington Post Express* winner. The other owner has been featured in the *Washington Times*, the *Huffington Post*, and the *Washington City Paper*.

23. By July 2016, all three of these daytime businesses, although they catered to the more upscale professional residential market, had closed their locations in Adams Morgan and reopened their businesses elsewhere. One moved online and was searching for a new location. Another has three locations, Dupont Circle, Mount Vernon Triangle, and Union Station, but abandoned the Adams Morgan one; and the third moved to Georgetown.

Conclusion. BID Urbanism beyond D.C.

1. According to the Department of Small and Local Business Development, $2,106,700 of grant funding was awarded by DSLBD for eighteen clean teams in 2014. See the agency's website (http://dslbd.DC.gov/service/clean-teams).

2. Over the course of fall 2017 and spring 2018, I contributed to documents and an alternative plan created by groups that form part of Uptown United, including Unified Inwood. These groups were opposing the EDC's plan as proposed and

presented an alternative plan. (See also Clarke et al. 2017; Rickenbacker, Krinsky, and Schaller 2018).

3. See the website created by the Washington Heights BID for Inwood (https://www.upininwood.nyc), which only recently went live.

4. One presentation was held on February 6, 2018 (New York City 2018a). Community Boards are comparable to D.C.'s ANCs, but they are appointed and not elected. Also, members can be drawn from people who live, work, or pray in the district. They are not necessarily residents.

5. Ocejo (2014) offers a similar analysis about the transition of neighborhood commercial corridors in New York City: the Lower East Side, the East Village, and the Bowery.

6. See the American Institute of Certified Planners (AICP) Code of Ethical and Professional Conduct, https://www.planning.org/ethics/ethicscode/.

7. See Inwood Legal Action (https://www.gofundme.com/inwood-legal -action). The groups that had come together under the Northern Manhattan Is Not for Sale umbrella, which also created the Uptown United plan, are raising funds for two potential lawsuits: an Article 78 lawsuit challenging the city's environmental impact analysis and a "Fair Housing" lawsuit.

8. "Eine Stadt ist keine Marke. Eine Stadt ist auch kein Unternehmen. Eine Stadt ist ein Gemeinwesen."

BIBLIOGRAPHY

Abramowitz, Michael. 1991. "Drawing the Line on Developers' Dollars." *Washington Post*, April 30. https://www.washingtonpost.com/archive/politics/1991/04/30/drawing-the-line-on-developers-dollars/59b19d68-b028-499d-bf45-bf52417a2eda/?utm_term=.b9b868408dff.

Adams Morgan Business and Professional Association, AMBPA. 1995. Statement by Hilda Rivas and Pat Patrick, President, Regarding Bill 11–464: The Business Improvement Districts Act of 1995. Committee Report, Council of the District of Columbia. kwiktag ~ 062 318 257 DC Council. http://dcclims1.dccouncil.us/images/00001/CP11/062318257_1.PDF.

Adams Morgan Partnership. 2005a. "Adams Morgan Partnership, Inc. Business Improvement District Initiative: Application and Business Plan."

———. 2005b. "Letter in Response to July 28 Supplemental Testimony Given in Opposition to the Creation of the Adams Morgan Business Improvement District," October 17.

Adams Morgan Partnership Steering Committee. 2004. "Letter to Property Owners." November 22.

———. 2005. "Letter to Business Owners." April 7.

Alcoholic Beverage Regulation Administration, Alcoholic Beverage Control Board. 2014. "Adams Morgan Moratorium Zone Notice of Emergency and Proposed Rulemaking." Martha Jenkins, general counsel, Alcoholic Beverage Regulation Administration. District of Columbia. https://abra.dc.gov/node/860552.Alpert, David. 2008. "U Street Biz Debate BID." *Greater Greater Washington*, September 17. http://greatergreaterwashington.org/post/1248/u-street-biz-debate-bid/.

———. 2016. "The D.C. Circulator Isn't a Waste of Taxpayer Money. In Fact, Some

Argue It's Too Cheap." *Greater Greater Washington*, June 8. https://ggwash.org
/view/41940/the-dc-circulator-isnt-a-waste-of-taxpayer-money-in-fact-some
-argue-its-too-cheap.

Angotti, Tom. 2008. *New York for Sale: Community Planning Confronts Global Real
Estate*. Cambridge: MIT Press.

Angotti, Tom, and Sylvia Morse, eds. 2016. *Zoned Out! Race, Displacement, and City
Planning in New York City*. New York: Terreform.

APA (American Planning Association). 2016. "Policy and Advocacy Conference:
Education and Event Lineup." Washington, D.C. https://www.planning.org
/policy/conference/schedule.htm.

APA-NYM (American Planning Association, New York Metro Chapter). 2017. "Panel
Discussion on Impact of BIDs on NYC." Economic Development Committee.
New York. March 7. https://www.nyplanning.org/events/panel
-discussion-impact-bids-nyc/.

Aratani, Lori. 2013. "Pop-up Development May Be the Bridge to Tysons Corner's
Future." *Washington Post*, July 30. 1415491177.

———. 2014. "Tiny Pop-up Park in Tysons Seen as Herald of Big Things." *Washington Post*, December 21.

Armstrong, Amy, Ingrid Gould Ellen, Amy Ellen Schwartz, and Ioan Voicu. 2007.
"The Benefits of Business Improvement Districts: The Case of New York City."
Furman Center Policy Brief. New York: Furman Center for Real Estate & Urban
Policy, New York University.

Arnstein, Sherry R. 1969. "A Ladder of Citizen Participation." *Journal of the American Institute of Planners* 35 (4): 216–24.

Asch, Chris Myers, and George Derek Musgrove. 2015. "'We Are Headed for Some
Bad Trouble': Gentrification and Displacement in Washington, D.C., 1920–
2014." In Hyra and Prince, *Capital Dilemma*, 107–36.

———. 2017. *Chocolate City: A History of Race and Democracy in the Nation's Capital*. Chapel Hill: University of North Carolina Press.

Athey, Lois. 2000. "Housing: The State of Latinos in the District of Columbia."
Washington D.C.: Council of Latino Agencies.

Avila, Eric. 2004. "Popular Culture in the Age of White Flight: Film Noir, Disneyland, and the Cold War (Sub)Urban Imaginary." *Journal of Urban History* 31 (1):
3–22. https://doi.org/10.1177/0096144204266745.

Baras, Jeremy. 2016. *Popup Republic: How to Start Your Own Successful Pop-up
Space, Shop, or Restaurant*. Hoboken, N.J.: John Wiley.

Barras, Jonetta Rose. 1998. *The Last of the Black Emperors: The Hollow Comeback of
Marion Barry in the New Age of Black Leaders*. Baltimore: Bancroft Press.

Barry, Marion. 1996. "Marion Barry's 1996 State of the District Address." *Washington Post*, March 25. http://www.washingtonpost.com/wp-srv/local/longterm
/library/dc/barry/96speech.htm.

Beauregard, Robert. 1998. "Public Private Partnerships as Historical Chameleons:
The Case of the United States." In *Partnerships in Urban Governance: European*

and American Experience, edited by Jon Pierre, 52–70. Houndmills, Basingstoke, U.K.: Macmillan.

Beekmans, Jeroen, and Joop de Boer. 2014. *Pop-up City: City-Making in a Fluid World*. Amsterdam: BIS.

Beete, Paulette. 2010. "We're Talking with Philippa P.B. Hughes: D.C.'s Pink Line Project." *NEA Arts Magazine*, 2010. https://www.arts.gov/NEARTS/2010v2 -arts-capital/were-talking-philippa-pb-hughes.

Bell, Clement Julian. 2015. "Primed for Development: Washington, D.C.'s Great Society Transition, 1964–1974." In Hyra and Prince, *Capital Dilemma*, 45–65. New York: Routledge.

Beust, Ole von. 2003. "Halbzeit in Hamburg—Handeln im Bund: Eine Bestand-saufnahme." Speech Erster Bürgermeister und Präsident des Senats der Freien und Hansestadt Hamburg. https://www.ueberseeclub.de/resources/Server /pdf-Dateien/2000-2004/vortrag-2003-09-22.pdf.

Blomley, Nicholas. 2016. "The Right to Not Be Excluded: Common Property and the Struggle to Stay Put." In *Releasing the Commons: Rethinking the Futures of the Commons*, edited by Ash Amin and Philip Howell, 89–106. London: Rout-ledge.

Bloom, Nicholas Dagen. 2004. *Merchant of Illusion: James Rouse, American's Salesman of the Businessman's Utopia*. Urban Life and Urban Landscape series. Columbus: Ohio State University Press.

Bockman, Johanna. 2011. "Priced out of Public Housing." *Public Sociology Association* (blog). February 11. https://gmupublicsoci.wordpress.com/2012/03/25 /priced-out-of-public-housing/.

———. 2013. "Who Is to Blame? Canal Park, History, and Community." *Sociology in My Neighborhood: D.C. Ward 6* (blog). January 14. http://sociologyinmy neighborhood.blogspot.com/2013/01/who-is-to-blame-canal-park-history -and.html.

———. 2015. "Home Rule from Below: The Cooperative Movement." In Hyra and Prince, *Capital Dilemma*, 66–86.

———. 2018. "Removing the Public from Public Housing: Public-Private Redevel-opment of the Ellen Wilson Dwellings in Washington, D.C." *Journal of Urban Affairs*, May, 1–21. https://doi.org/10.1080/07352166.2018.1457406.

Boivie, Ilana. 2017. "Lessons from the Waterfront: Economic Development Projects Must Do More to Lessen D.C.'s Worsening Income Inequality." Washington, D.C.: D.C. Fiscal Policy Institute.

Bonilla Silva, Eduardo. 2010. *Racism without Racists: Color-blind Racism & Racial Inequality in Contemporary in America*. 3rd ed. New York: Roman and Little-field.

Bookman, Sonia. 2013. "Branded Cosmopolitanisms: 'Global' Coffee Brands and the Co-Creation of 'Cosmopolitan Cool.'" *Cultural Sociology* 7 (1): 56–72. https:// doi.org/10.1177/1749975512453544.

Bovaird, Tony. 2004. "Public-Private Partnerships: From Contested Concepts to Prevalent Practice." *International Review of Administrative Sciences* 70 (2): 199–215.

Brady, George, Jr., president, National Corporation for Housing Partnerships. 1975. "Letter to Knox Banner, Downtown Progress," regarding Federal Home Loan Bank Headquarters, March 26.

Brandes, Uwe Steven. 2005. "Recapturing the Anacostia River: The Center of 21st Century Washington, D.C." *Golden Gate University Law Review* 35 (5): 411–28. https://digitalcommons.law.ggu.edu/cgi/viewcontent.cgi?article=1910& context=ggulrev.

Brash, Julian. 2011. *Bloomberg's New York: Class and Governance in the Luxury City.* Athens: University of Georgia Press.

Brazil, Harold, chair, Committee on Economic Development. 2003. "Targeted and Concentrated Neighborhood Investment Act of 2003." Council of the District of Columbia. http://lims.dccouncil.us/Download/599/b15-0128-COMMITTEE REPORT.pdf.

Brenner, Neil. 2004. "Urban Governance and the Production of New State Spaces in Western Europe, 1960–2000." *Review of International Political Economy* 11 (3): 447–88. https://doi.org/10.1080/0969229042000282864.

Briffault, Richard. 1997. "The Rise of Sublocal Structures in Urban Governance." *Minnesota Law Review* 82: 503.

———. 1999. "A Government for Our Time? Business Improvement Districts and Urban Governance." *Columbia Law Review* 99 (2): 365. https://doi.org/10.2307 /1123583.

———. 2010. "The Most Popular Tool: Tax Increment Financing and the Political Economy of Local Government." *University of Chicago Law Review* 77: 65–95.

Brooks, Richard Rexford Wayne, and Carol M. Rose. 2013. *Saving the Neighborhood: Racially Restrictive Covenants, Law, and Social Norms.* Cambridge, Mass.: Harvard University Press.

Brown, Graham, Insun Sunny Lee, Katherine King, and Richard Shipway. 2015. "Eventscapes and the Creation of Event Legacies." *Annals of Leisure Research* 18 (4): 510–27. https://doi.org/10.1080/11745398.2015.1068187.

Brown-Robertson, LaTanya N., Daniel Muhammad, Marvin Ward, and Michael Bell. 2013. "An Analysis of Neighborhoods in the District of Columbia." Draft report prepared for the June 3, 2014, D.C. Tax Revision Commission Meeting. http://media.wix.com/ugd/ddda66_c74ec09aada64ff7200a2fd76f49817a.pdf.

Buchanan, James M. 1965. "An Economic Theory of Clubs." *Economica* 32 (125): 1. https://doi.org/10.2307/2552442.

Buehler, Ralph, and John Stowe. 2015. "Bicycling in the Washington, D.C. Region: Trends in Ridership and Policies since 1990." In Hyra and Prince, *Capital Dilemma*, 180–206.

Cadaval, Olivia. 1998. *Creating a Latino Identity in the Nation's Capital: The Latino Festival.* Latino Communities series. New York: Garland.

Capitol Riverfront BID. 2015. "Capitol Riverfront BID: 2015 Perceptions Survey."

https://www.capitolriverfront.org/_files/docs/2015_perception-survey
-results-final-for-web.pdf.

———. 2016. "Annual Report." https://www.capitolriverfront.org/_files/docs
/crbid_2016_annual_report.pdf.

Carroll, Kenneth. 1998. "The Meaning of Funk." *Washington Post*, February 1.

Cazenave, Noel A. 2011. *The Urban Racial State: Managing Race Relations in American Cities*. Lanham, Md.: Roman and Littlefield.

Center for Community Change. 2003. "A HOPE Unseen: Voices from the Other Side of HOPE VI." Field study prepared for ENPHRONT (Everywhere and Now Public Housing Residents Organizing Nationally Together). http://nhlp.org /files/greenbook4/Chapter12/FN%20176%20CCC,%20A%20HOPE%20Unseen %20—%20Voices%20from%20the%20Other%20Side%20of%20HOPE%20VI %20(2003).pdf.

Chang, T. C., and Shirlena Huang. 2005. "Recreating Place, Replacing Memory: Creative Destruction at the Singapore River." *Asia Pacific Viewpoint* 46 (3): 267–80. https://doi.org/10.1111/j.1467-8373.2005.00285.x.

Charenko, Melissa. 2015. "A Historical Assessment of the World's First Business Improvement Area (BIA): The Case of Toronto's Bloor West Village." *Canadian Journal of Urban Research* 24 (2): 1–19.

Cherkasky, Mara. 2006. "Village in the City: Mount Pleasant Heritage Trail." Edited by Jane Freundel Levey. Distributed by Cultural Tourism D.C. http://www .culturaltourismdc.org/portal/c/document_library/get_file?uuid=20532956 -f4a0-4420-9176-4182a4f8f2de&groupId=701982.

Cherkasky, Mara, and Sarah Shoenfeld. N.d. "Mapping Segregation in Washington DC." *Prologue D.C.* (blog). Accessed January 17, 2017. http://prologuedc.com /blog/mapping-segregation/.

Cherkis, Jason. 2005. "The Cost of Leaving: Left in the Rubble of the Arthur Capper Exodus: Bags of Clothes, Rusting Grills, Children's Toys, and a Cautionary Tale." *Washington City Paper*, May 20. http://www.washingtoncitypaper.com/news /article/13031018/the-cost-of-leaving.

Chibbaro, Lou. 2013. "Glory Days." *Washington Blade*, April 25. http://www .washingtonblade.com/2013/04/25/glory-days-tracks-gay-nightlife-staple-of -80s-90s-remembered-fondly/.

Christopherson, Susan. 1994. "The Fortress City: Privatized Spaces, Consumer Citizenship." In *Post-Fordism: A Reader*, edited by Ash Amin, 409–27. Studies in Urban and Social Change. Oxford: Blackwell.

Citizens Association of Georgetown (CAG). 1995. "Testimony of Stephen Kurzman, President, Citizens Association of Georgetown, on Bill 11–464, The Business Improvement Districts Act of 1995." District of Columbia. http://dcclims1 .dccouncil.us/images/00001/CP11/062318257_1.PDF.

City of New York, Office of the Mayor. 2011. "Mayor Bloomberg Announces Creation of New Business Improvement Districts on Atlantic Avenue in Brooklyn and in Chinatown in Manhattan." September 27. http://www1.nyc.gov/office

-of-the-mayor/news/343-11/mayor-bloomberg-creation-new-business
-improvement-districts-atlantic-avenue-in.

City of Philadelphia Department of Commerce and Drexel University's Center for
Public Policy. 2013. "Starting a Business Improvement District in Philadelphia."
https://business.phila.gov/media/Starting-A-BID-in-Philadelphia-FINAL
.pdf.

Ciudad Emergente (CEM. 2016a. "Okuplaza FestDC: A Creative Placemaking Intervention to Promote Community-Building." December 1. https://issuu.com
/ciudademergente_cem/docs/161122_reporte_final_okuplaza_fest_.

———. 2016b. "Okuplaza FestDC: A Creative Placemaking Intervention to Promote
Community-Building (Report Synopsis)." Summary Report.

Clarke, Maggie, Paul Esptein, Allegra LeGrande, Cheryl Pahaham, Nancy Preston,
Susanna Schaller, Philip Simpson, Maria Luisa Tasayco, and David Thom. 2017.
"The City's Flawed Process and Results in Planning Inwood's Future." *Urban
Matters*, November 29. Center for New York City Affairs at the New School.
http://www.centernyc.org/planning-inwoods-future.

Code of the District of Columbia. Part B, Section 2-1215.51 to 2-1215.61. https://
code.dccouncil.us/dc/council/code/titles/2/chapters/12/subchapters/VIII
/parts/B.

Coghill Chatman, Michelle. 2015. "At Eshu's Crossroad: Pan-African Identity in a
Changing City." In Hyra and Prince, *Capital Dilemma*, 239–54.

Cohen, Matt, and Alexa Mills. 2017. "Houses of Worship Are Re-Creating a
Decades-Old Support System to Protect Immigrants." *Washington City Paper*,
March 2.

commercial District Technical assistance Program (cD-TaP). 2002. "cD-TaP Adams
Morgan Grant Application."

Congress, 104th Cong. 1995. "H.R. 1345 (104th): District of Columbia Financial Responsibility and Management Assistance Act of 1995." GovTrack. https://www
.govtrack.us/congress/bills/104/hr1345.

Connelly, Stephen, and Tim Richardson. 2004. "Exclusion: The Necessary Difference between Ideal and Practical Consensus." *Journal of Environmental
Planning and Management* 47 (1): 3–17. https://doi.org/10.1080/0964056042000
189772.

Conroy, Sarah Booth. 2000. "A Socialite's Lost Dreams for 16th Street." *Washington
Post*, December 30. https://www.washingtonpost.com/archive/politics/2000
/12/30/a-socialites-lost-dreams-for-16th-st/0bd4fbfe-f399-4037-b979
-e35b69835109/?utm_term=.d63b0f6a4b19.

Cook, Ian R. 2008. "Mobilising Urban Policies: The Policy Transfer of U.S. Business
Improvement Districts to England and Wales." *Urban Studies* 45 (4): 773–95.
https://doi.org/10.1177/0042098007088468.

Cooper, Rebecca. 2018. "Turmoil at the Adams Morgan BID as Line Owners, Legacy Board Members Face Off." *Washington Business Journal*, April 2.

Council of the District of Columbia. 1995. Report of the Committee on Economic
Development. Testimony at Public Hearing on Bill 11–464, The Business

Improvement Districts Act of 1995. kwiktag ~ 062 318 257 DC Council. http://
dcclims1.dccouncil.us/images/00001/CP11/062318257_1.pdf.

———. 1996. Business Improvement District Act of 1996.

———. 1997. Business Improvement Districts Amendment Act of 1997. https://code
.dccouncil.us/dc/council/laws/docs/12-26.pdf.

———. 2007. Capitol Riverfront Business Improvement Amendment Act. D.C.
Official Code 2–1215.58. http://lims.dccouncil.us/Legislation/B17-0208
?FromSearchResults=true.

———. 2015. Business Improvement Districts Amendment Act of 2014.

Crew, Spencer R. 2003. "Melding the Old and the New: The Modern African American Community, 1930–1960." In *Washington Odyssey: A Multicultural History of
the Nation's Capital*, edited by Francine Curro Cary, 208–29. Washington, D.C.:
Smithsonian Books.

Cummings, Scott L. 2001. "Community Economic Development as Progressive
Politics: Toward a Grassroots Movement for Economic Justice." *Stanford Law
Review* 54 (3): 399–493. https://doi.org/10.2307/1229464.

Davidoff, Paul. 1965. "Advocacy and Pluralism in Planning." *Journal of the
American Institute of Planners* 31 (4): 331–38. https://doi.org/10.1080
/01944366508978187.

Davidson, Mark. 2008. "Spoiled Mixture: Where Does State-Led 'Positive' Gentrification End?" *Urban Studies* 45 (12): 2385–2405.

Davies, Mark S. 1997. "Business Improvement Districts." *Washington University
Journal Urban & Contemporary Law* 52: 187–224.

Davis, Christopher H., and Darrell D. Jackson. 1990. "The Sunset of Affirmative
Action: City of Richmond v. J. A. Croson Co." *National Black Law Journal* 12 (1):
73–87.

Davis, John Emmeus. 1991. *Contested Ground: Collective Action and the Urban
Neighborhood*. Ithaca, N.Y.: Cornell University Press.

Dawson, Jessica. 2010a. "Along City Sidewalks, New Windows on Art." *Washington
Post*, January 1.

———. 2010b. "Art of the Deal: 'Pop-Up' Shows Sell Condos, Too." *Washington Post*,
January 15.

DC BID Council. 2011. "How to Start a Business Improvement District." http://
static1.1.sqspcdn.com/static/f/1025641/19002369/1340908357627/Starting-a
-BID.pdf?token=k%2BvogJvqGtJfnFwEx3tl4ED3DsY%3D.

———. 2017. "2017 DC BID Profiles: A Report by the DC BID Council." www.dcbid
council.org/storage/bid-reports/BID%20Profiles%20Report%202017.pdf.

D.C. Chamber of Commerce. 1995. Testimony by Sheldon Repp at Public Hearing
on Bill 11-464, "The Business Improvement Districts Act of 1995." Committee
Report, Council of the District of Columbia. kwiktag ~ 062 318 257 DC Council.
http://dcclims1.dccouncil.us/images/00001/CP11/062318257_1.pdf.

D.C. Commission on Budget and Financial Priorities (Rivlin Commission). 1990.
"Financing the Nation's Capital: The Report of the Commission on Budget and
Financial Priorities of the District of Columbia."

D.C. Fiscal Policy Institute. 2007. "Meeting D.C.'s Challenges, Maintaining Fiscal Discipline: Reforming Economic Development Programs to Promote Job Creation and Fiscally Responsible Use of Public Funds." Washington, D.C.: D.C. Fiscal Policy Institute.

DC Jobs with Justice. 2009. "Continuing the Dream: Organizing for Local Justice in 2008." January 11. http://www.dcjwj.org/continuing-the-dream-organizing-for-local-justice-in-2008-2/.

D.C. Public Services and the Environment Committee. 2012. "Adams Morgan Historic Hotel: Adams Morgan Community-Driven PUD Amenities." Developer Presentation of Amenities Specifically Requested by the Community. ANC1C, Public Services and the Environment Committee.

DeFilippis, James. 2004. *Unmaking Goliath: Community Control in the Face of Global Capital*. New York: Routledge.

DeFilippis, James, and Susan Saegert, eds. 2012. *The Community Development Reader*. 2nd ed. New York: Routledge.

Delgadillo, Natalie. 2018. "D.C. Is Being Sued for Gentrifying. Here's What to Know about the Case." *DCist*, June 15. http://dcist.com/2018/06/dc_is_being_sued_for_gentrifying_he.php.

Demarest, Michael, Peter Stoler, and Robert T. Grieves. 1981. "He Digs Downtown." *Time*, August 24.

Department of Small Business Services, New York City. 2016. "Neighborhood 360: Inwood Manhattan Commercial District Needs Assessment." https://www1.nyc.gov/assets/sbs/downloads/pdf/neighborhoods/n360-cdna-inwood.pdf.

Developer. 2012. "Adams Morgan Historic Hotel: Adams Morgan Community-Driven PUD Amenities." Developer Presentation of Amenities Specifically Requested by the Community. District of Columbia: ANC 1C Public Services & the Environment Committee.

Didier, Sophie, Marianne Morange, and Elisabeth Peyroux. 2013. "The Adaptative Nature of Neoliberalism at the Local Scale: Fifteen Years of City Improvement Districts in Cape Town and Johannesburg." *Antipode* 45 (1): 121–39. https://doi.org/10.1111/j.1467-8330.2012.00987.x.

Douglas, Danielle. 2010. "For Artists, Storefront on a Shoestring." *Washington Post*, July 12, Local Business section. http://www.washingtonpost.com/wp-dyn/content/article/2010/07/11/AR2010071102972.html?referrer=emailarticle.

———. 2011. "Pop-up Retail Gains Favor in D.C. with Garment District, Mount Pleasant Temporium." *Washington Post*, March 6, Business section. http://www.washingtonpost.com/wp-dyn/content/article/2011/03/06/AR2011030602666.html.

DowntownDC. 2013. "BID Provides DC Circulator Testimony." 2013. https://www.downtowndc.org/news/bid-provides-dc-circulator-testimony/.

Downs, Anthony. 1977. Opening Up the Suburbs: An Urban Strategy for America. New Haven, Conn.: Yale University Press.

Dreier, Peter, John H. Mollenkopf, and Todd Swanstrom. 2004. *Place Matters:*

Metropolitics for the Twenty-First Century. 2nd ed. Studies in Government and Public Policy. Lawrence: University Press of Kansas.

Driggins, Kimberly C. 2014. "Strengthening Economic Development: Arts and Culture Temporiums—Washington, D.C." *Community Development Investment Review: Creative Placemaking* (Federal Reserve Bank of San Francisco) 10 (2): 98–100.

Driggins, Kimberly C., and Renan Snowden. 2012. "Revitalizing Neighborhoods through Temporary Urbanism." *Public Sector Digest*, December.

Dubree, Jacqueline. N.d. *JDLand* (blog). http://www.jdland.com/dc/index.cfm. Accessed January 17, 2017.

Dupont Circle Merchants and Professionals Association. 1995. Statement of L. Page (Deacon) Maccubbin Regarding Public Hearing Business Improvement Districts Act of 1995 Bill 11–464. Committee Report, Council of the District of Columbia. kwiktag ~ 062 318 257 DC Council. http://dcclims1.dccouncil.us /images/00001/CP11/062318257_1.pdf.

Elstein, Aaron. 2016. "Shaping a Neighborhood's Destiny from the Shadows: Business Improvement Districts Were Created to Rescue a Dirty, Crime-Ridden City. With Order Restored, Some Say It's Time to Bid Them Goodbye." *Crain's New York Business*, September 18. http://www.crainsnewyork.com/article /20160918/REAL_ESTATE/160919896.

Evans, Jack, chair. 2004. "Report on Bill 15–306, the 'Retail Incentive Act of 2004.'" Committee on Finance and Revenue, Council for the District of Columbia. http://lims.dccouncil.us/Download/637/B15-0306-COMMITTEEREPORT.pdf.

Evans, Judith. 1996. "D.C. Wants to Join the Boom for BIDs." *Washington Post*, January 13.

Evers, Donna. 2007. "Of Castles and Condos: Mary Foote Henderson's 'Castle' May Be Gone, but Her Legacy Remains." *Washington Life Magazine*, March. http:// www.washingtonlife.com/issues/march-2007/historical-landscapes/.

Executive Office of the Mayor, District of Columbia. 2015. "District's Population Climbs Again." Press release. https://mayor.dc.gov/release/district's -population-climbs-again.

Fain, Kimberly. 2017. "The Devastation of Black Wall Street." *JSTOR Daily* (blog), July 5. https://daily.jstor.org/the-devastation-of-black-wall-street/.

Fainstein, Susan S. 2010. *The Just City*. Ithaca, N.Y.: Cornell University Press.

———. 2011. "Planning and the Just City." In *Searching for the Just City: Debates in Urban Theory and Practice*, edited by Peter Marcuse, 19–39. Questioning Cities series. London: Routledge.

Farhi, Paul. 1990. "Living on Mount Pleasant Street." *Washington Post*, October 7.

Farrar, Margaret E. 2011. "Amnesia, Nostalgia, and the Politics of Place Memory." *Political Research Quarterly* 64 (4): 723–35.

Fauntroy, Michael K. 2003. *Home Rule or House Rule: Congress and the Erosion of Local Governance in the District of Columbia*. Lanham, Md.: University Press of America.

Feaver, Douglas B. 1974. "'Happy People' Spend Day Celebrating Spanish Heritage." *Washington Post*, July 28.

Federal City Council. 1995. Written Statement by Kenneth R. Sparks, Executive Vice President, to D.C. City Council Regarding Bill 11-464, District of Columbia Business Improvement Act of 1995. http://dcclims1.dccouncil.us/images /00001/CP11/062318257_1.PDF.

Feehan, Dave, and Marvin D. Feit, eds. 2006. *Making Business Districts Work: Leadership and Management of Downtown, Main Street, Business District, and Community Development Organizations*. Haworth Health and Social Policy series. New York: Haworth Press.

Feehan, Dave, John Gomez, and Jeannette Andreski. 2005. "International Downtown Association Celebrates Five Decades of Downtown Advocacy." *Downtown News Briefs*.

Feiden, Douglas. 2013. "Major Expansion of Business Improvement Districts Is Planned for Northern Manhattan." *N.Y. Daily News*, April 25. http://www .nydailynews.com/new-york/manhattan/progress-bidness-wash-hts-article -1.1326741.

Feldtkeller, Andreas. 2012. *Zur Alltagstauglichkeit unserer Städte: Wechselwirkungen zwischen Städtebau und täglichem Handeln*. Berlin: Schiller.

Fernandes, Leela. 2004. "The Politics of Forgetting: Class Politics, State Power and the Restructuring of Urban Space in India." *Urban Studies* 41 (12): 2415-30. https://doi.org/10.1080/00420980412331297609.

Florida, Richard. 2003. "Cities and the Creative Class." *City and Community* 2 (1): 3-19.

———. 2017. *The New Urban Crisis: How Our Cities Are Increasing Inequality, Deepening Segregation, and Failing the Middle Class—and What We Can Do about It*. New York: Basic Books.

Forester, John. 1993. *Critical Theory, Public Policy, and Planning Practice: Toward a Critical Pragmatism*. SUNY Series in Political Theory. Albany: State University of New York Press.

Freund, David M. P. 2007. *Colored Property: State Policy and White Racial Politics in Suburban America*. Historical Studies of Urban America. Chicago: University of Chicago Press.

Frey, William. 2013. "Millennial and Senior Migrants Follow Different Post-Recession Paths." *Brookings Op-Ed* (blog), November 15. https://www.brookings.edu /opinions/millennial-and-senior-migrants-follow-different-post-recession -paths/.

Friedmann, John. 2010. "Place and Place-Making in Cities: A Global Perspective." *Planning Theory & Practice* 11 (2): 149-65. https://doi. org/10.1080/14649351003759573.

Frug, Gerald. 2010. "The Seductions of Form." *Drexel Law Review* 3 (1): 11-17.

Fullilove, Mindy Thompson. 2005. *Root Shock: How Tearing Up City Neighborhoods Hurts America, and What We Can Do about It*. New York: One World/Ballantine Books.

———. 2013. *Urban Alchemy: Restoring Joy in America's Sorted-Out Cities*. Oakland, Calif.: New Village Press.

Fullilove, Mindy Thompson, and Rodrick Wallace. 2011. "Serial Forced Displacement in American Cities, 1916–2010." *Journal of Urban Health* 88 (3): 381–89. https://doi.org/10.1007/s11524-011-9585-2.

Furman, Andrew. 2007. "The Street as a Temporary Eventscape." *International Journal of the Humanities* 5 (9): 77–84.

Furman Center for Real Estate and Urban Policy, NYU. 2011. "State of New York City's Housing and Neighborhoods 2011: Indicator Definitions and Rankings." New York: Furman Center for Real Estate and Urban Policy. http://furman center.org/files/sotc/Indicator_Definitions_and_Rankings_11.pdf.

Gale, Dennis. 1987. *Washington, D.C.: Inner-City Revitalization & Minority Suburbanization*. Philadelphia: Temple University Press.

Gallaher, Carolyn. 2016. *The Politics of Staying Put: Condo Conversion and Tenant Right-to-Buy in Washington, D.C.* Urban Life, Landscape, and Policy. Philadelphia: Temple University Press.

Gallup. 2010. "Soul of the Community." John S. and James L. Knight Foundation. https://www.knightfoundation.org/sotc/.

Gandhi, Natwar M., James Spaulding, and Gordon McDonald. 2015. "Budget Growth in the District, 1999–2013." In Hydra and Prince, *Capital Dilemma*, 159–79.

Gates, Jennifer. 2005. "A Study of Inactive Main Street Communities." PhD diss., University of Pennsylvania. https://repository.upenn.edu/cgi/viewcontent. cgi?article=1026&context=hp_theses.

Gehl, Jan. 2007. "World Class Street: Remaking New York's Pubic Realm." New York City Department of Transportation. http://www.nyc.gov/html/dot/downloads/ pdf/World_Class_Streets_Gehl_08.pdf.

———. 2010. *Cities for People*. Washington, D.C.: Island Press.

Georgetown Business and Professional Association. 1995. "Statement of Michael N. Williams on Behalf of the Board of Directors of the Georgetown Business and Professional Association in Support of Bill 11–464, 'Business Improvement Districts Act of 1995.'" Presented to Committee on Economic Development of the District of Columbia, December 6. http://dcclims1.dccouncil.us/images/00001/ CP11/062318257_1.pdf.

Giant Food Corporation. 1995. Written Statement to Mr. Joe Sternlieb, Committee Clerk for the Committee on Economic Development, on Bill 11-464, 'Business Improvement Districts Act of 1995.'" Presented to Committee on Economic Development of the District of Columbia. http://dcclims1.dccouncil.us/im-ages/00001/CP11/062318257_1.PDF.

Gillette, Howard. 1995. *Between Justice and Beauty: Race, Planning, and the Failure of Urban Policy in Washington, D.C.* Philadelphia: University of Pennsylvania Press. http://site.ebrary.com/id/10492017.

———. 1999. "Assessing James Rouse's Role in American City Planning." *APA Journal* 65 (2): 151–67.

————. 2012. *Civitas by Design: Building Better Communities, from the Garden City to the New Urbanism*. Philadelphia: University of Pennsylvania Press.

Glantz, Aaron, and Emmanuel Martinez. 2018. "For People of Color, Banks Are Shutting the Door to Homeownership." *Reveal*, Center for Investigative Reporting, February 15. https://www.revealnews.org/article/for-people-of-color -banks-are-shutting-the-door-to-homeownership/.

Glasze, Georg. 2003. "Private Neighbourhoods as Club Economies and Shareholder Democracies." *Belgeo* 1: 87–98.

Goldfield, David R. 2011. *Encyclopedia of American Urban History*. Thousand Oaks, Calif.: SAGE.

Good Jobs First. 2002. "Economic Development in Washington, D.C.: High Costs, Unclear Benefits, Missing Safeguards." Washington, D.C.: Good Jobs First. http://www.goodjobsfirst.org/sites/default/files/docs/pdf/dc.pdf.

Gotham, Kevin Fox. 2000. "Urban Space, Restrictive Covenants and the Origins of Racial Residential Segregation in a U.S. City, 1900–50." *International Journal of Urban and Regional Research* 24 (3): 616–33. https://doi.org/10.1111/1468 -2427.00268.

Government of the District of Columbia. 2012. "District of Columbia: Census 2010 Atlas." Washington, D.C.: Office of Planning, Citywide & Neighborhood Planning, and State Data Center. https://planning.dc.gov/sites/default/files/dc /sites/op/publication/attachments/Atlas%202010%20RGB%20color_part1.pdf.

Graham, Wade. 2016. *Dream Cities: Seven Urban Ideas That Shape the World*. Stroud, U.K.: Amberley.

Grant, Jill L. 2007. "Two Sides of a Coin? New Urbanism and Gated Communities." *Housing Policy Debate* 18 (3): 481–501. https://doi.org/10.1080/10511482.2007 .9521608.

Griffin, James. 1974. "The Phantom In: City Councilman Tedson Meyers on Neighborhoods and the City." *Washington Post*, April 28.

Griffith, Reginald Wilbert. 1969. "The Influence of Meaningful Citizen Participation on the 'Urban Renewal' Process and the Renewal of the Inner-City's Black Community." Master's thesis, Massachusetts Institute of Technology.

Gross, Jill S. 2010. "The Aramingo Avenue Shopping District: Stakeholders Bridge or Border Divide." *Drexel Law Review* 3 (1): 171–92.

————. 2013. "Business Improvement Districts in New York: The Private Sector in Public Service or the Public Sector Privatized?" *Urban Research & Practice* 6 (3): 346–64.

Grossman, Seth A. 2010. "Reconceptualizing the Public Management and Performance of Business Improvement Districts." *Public Performance & Management Review* 33 (3): 361–94. https://doi.org/10.2753/PMR1530-9576330304.

Grossman, Seth A., and Marc Holzer. 2015. *Partnership Governance in Public Management: A Public Solutions Handbook*. New York: Routledge.

Hackworth, Jason R. 2007. *The Neoliberal City: Governance, Ideology, and Development in American Urbanism*. Ithaca, N.Y.: Cornell University Press.

Haimerl, Amy. 2014. "Biz Improvement Zones: A Concept That's Picking Up." *Crain's Detroit Business*, January 24.

Hall, Peter. 2014. *Cities of Tomorrow: An Intellectual History of Urban Planning and Design since 1880*. 4th ed. Hoboken, N.J.: Wiley-Blackwell.

Hall, Thomas C. 1998. "D.C. Resolves TIF: Retail `Projects Ripe.'" *Washington Business Journal*, February 2.

Hall, Thomas C., and John Lombardo. 1996. "Business Reacts to D.C. `Interactive.'" *Washington Business Journal*, December 16.

Halper, Louise A. 1993. "Parables of Exchange: Foundations of Public Choice Theory and the Market Formalism of James Buchanan." *Cornell Journal of Law and Public Policy* 2 (2): 229–78.

Halpern, Robert. 1995. *Rebuilding the Inner City: A History of Neighborhood Initiatives to Address Poverty in the United States*. New York: Columbia University Press.

Hamowy, Ronald, and Friedrich A. von Hayek. 2011. *The Constitution of Liberty: The Definitive Edition*. Collected Works of F. A. Hayek, vol. 17. Chicago: University of Chicago Press.

Haney-López, Ian. 2014. *Dog Whistle Politics: How Coded Racial Appeals Have Reinvented Racism and Wrecked the Middle Class*. New York: Oxford University Press.

Hannigan, John. 1998. *Fantasy City: Pleasure and Profit in the Postmodern Metropolis*. London: Routledge.

Harden, Blaine, and David A Vise. 1995. "Race and the Bottom Line in D.C." *Washington Post*, March 19.

Harris, Daryl. 2010. "The High Tide of Pragmatic Black Politics: Mayor Anthony Williams and the Suppression of Black Interests." In *Democratic Destiny and the District of Columbia: Federal Politics and Public Policy*, edited by Ronald W. Walters and Toni-Michelle Travis, 103–17. Lanham, Md.: Lexington Books.

Harvey, David. 2005. *A Brief History of Neoliberalism*. Oxford: Oxford University Press.

———. 2008. "The Right to the City." *New Left Review* 53: 23–40.

———. 2013. *Rebel Cities: From the Right to the City to the Urban Revolution*. London: Verso.

Hayden, Dolores. 1997. *The Power of Place: Urban Landscape as Public History*. Cambridge, Mass.: MIT Press.

Healey, Patsy. 2013. "Circuits of Knowledge and Techniques: The Transnational Flow of Planning Ideas and Practices." *International Journal of Urban and Regional Research* 37 (5): 1510–26. https://doi.org/10.1111/1468-2427.12044.

Henig, Jeffrey R. 1982. *Gentrification in Adams Morgan: Political and Commercial Consequences of Neighborhood Change*. Washington, D.C.: Center for Washington Area Studies, George Washington University.

Hilzenrath, David S. 1988. "Group to Study Concept of D.C. Business Tax Zone:

Study to Focus on Special Business Tax Zone." *Washington Post*, November 12. ProQuest Historical Newspapers ed., section E.

Hirschbiegel, Thomas. 2014. "Alter Wall: Braucht Hamburg Noch Eine Luxus-Meile?" *Morgenpost*, June 24. http://www.mopo.de/nachrichten/neues -shopping-center-alter-wall—braucht-hamburg-noch-eine-luxus-meile -,5067140,27586588.html.

Hirt, Sonia, and Diane L. Zahm, eds. 2012. *The Urban Wisdom of Jane Jacobs*. Planning, History and Environment series. London: Routledge.

Hochleutner, Brian R. 2003. "BIDs Fare Well: The Democratic Accountability of Business Improvement Districts." *New York University Law Review* 78 (1): 374–401.

Hodos, Jerome. 2010. "Whose Neighborhood Is It, Anyway: The South Street/Headhouse District." *Drexel Law Review* 3: 193–207.

Hoerl, Kristen. 2012. "Selective Amnesia and Racial Transcendence in News Coverage of President Obama's Inauguration." *Quarterly Journal of Speech* 98 (2): 178–202.

Hoffer, Audrey. 2015. "Where We Live: NoMa, the Wrong Side of the Tracks No More." *Washington Post*, February 6, Real Estate section.

Hoffman, Daniel, and Lawrence O. Houstoun. 2010. "Business Improvement Districts as a Tool for Improving Philadelphia's Economy." *Drexel Law Review* 3 (1): 89–107.

Holston, James. 2009. "Insurgent Citizenship in an Era of Global Urban Peripheries." *City & Society* 21 (2): 245–67. https://doi.org/10.1111/j.1548-744X.2009 .01024.x.

Hood, John M. 1996. *The Heroic Enterprise: Business and the Common Good*. Washington, D.C.: Beard Books.

Hopkinson, Natalie. 2012a. "Farewell to Chocolate City." *Washington Post*, June 23, Sunday Review section.

———. 2012b. *Go-Go Live: The Musical Life and Death of a Chocolate City*. Durham, N.C.: Duke University Press.

Horton, Lois. 2003. "The Days of Jubilee: Black Migration during the Civil War and Reconstruction." In *Washington Odyssey: A Multicultural History of the Nation's Capital*, edited by Francine Curro Cary, 65–78. Washington, D.C.: Smithsonian Books.

Hou, Jeffrey. 2010. "'Night Market' in Seattle: Community Eventscape and the Reconstruction of Public Space." In *Insurgent Public Space: Guerrilla Urbanism and the Remaking of Contemporary Cities*, edited by Jeffrey Hou, 111–23. New York: Routledge.

Houstoun, Lawrence O. 1994. "Betting on BIDs." Washington, D.C.: Urban Land Institute.

———. 1997. "BIDs: Business Improvement Districts." Washington, D.C.: Urban Land Institute and International Downtown Association.

———. 2010. "Amenity-Driven Economic Growth: Is It Worth Betting On?" *IEDC Economic Development Journal* 9 (1): 19–23.

Hovde, Sarah, and John Krinsky. 1996. *Manos a La Obra: Manual de Asociaciones de Vivienda Mutua y Cooperativas de Terreno para Residentes y Organizadores.* New York: Community Service Society of New York.

Howell, Kathryn Leigh. 2013. "Transforming Neighborhoods, Changing Communities: Collective Agency and Rights in a New Era of Urban Redevelopment in Washington, D.C." PhD diss., University of Texas at Austin. https://repositories .lib.utexas.edu/bitstream/handle/2152/23193/HOWELL-DISSERTATION-2013 .pdf?sequence=1.

Hoyt, Lorlene. 2005. "Planning through Compulsory Commercial Clubs: Business Improvement Districts." *Economic Affairs* 24 (4): 24–27.

———. 2008. "From North America to Africa: The Business Improvement District Model and the Role of Policy Entrepreneurs." In *Business Improvement Districts: Research, Theories, and Controversies,* edited by Göktu☒ Morçöl and Ulf Zimmermann, 111–39. Boca Raton, Fla.: CRC Press/Taylor & Francis.

HUD (U.S. Department of Housing and Urban Development), Office of Community Planning and Development. 1984. "Consolidated Annual Report to Congress on Community Development Programs." https://archives.hud.gov /offices/cpd/communitydevelopment/congress/1984.pdf.

Hughes, Sarah Anne. 2103. "Get to Know a Mayoral Candidate: Jack Evans." *DCist*, December 31. http://dcist.com/2013/12/get_to_know_mayoral_candidate_jack _evans.php.

Hunan Chinatown Restaurant. 1995. Testimony by Linda L. Lee, vice president, Hunan Chinatown Restaurant, in Support of Bill 11–464, "Business Improvement Districts Act of 1995." Committee Report, Council of the District of Columbia. kwiktag ~ 062 318 257 DC Council. http://dcclims1.dccouncil.us /images/00001/CP11/062318257_1.pdf.

Hurley, Amanda Kolson. 2016. "DIY Urban Planning Is Happening All Over the Country. Is It Only for White People?" *Washington Post*, October 27. https:// www.washingtonpost.com/posteverything/wp/2016/10/27/diy-urban -planning-is-happening-all-over-the-country-is-it-only-for-white-people /?utm_term=.7e3ab35d792f.

Huron, Amanda. 2014. "Creating a Commons in the Capital: The Emergence of Limited-Equity Housing Cooperatives in Washington, D.C." *Washington History* 26 (2): 57–67.

Huyssen, Andreas. 2003. *Present Pasts: Urban Palimpsests and the Politics of Memory.* Cultural Memory in the Present series. Stanford, Calif: Stanford University Press.

Hyra, Derek S. 2015. "The Back-to-the-City Movement: Neighbourhood Redevelopment and Processes of Political and Cultural Displacement." *Urban Studies* 52 (10): 1753–73. https://doi.org/10.1177/0042098014539403.

———. 2012. "Conceptualizing the New Urban Renewal: Comparing the Past to the Present." *Urban Affairs Review* 48 (4): 498–527. https://doi.org/10.1177 /1078087411434905.

———. 2016. "Commentary: Causes and Consequences of Gentrification and the

Future of Equitable Development Policy." *Cityscape: A Journal of Policy Development and Research* 18 (3): 169–77.

———. 2017. *Race, Class, and Politics in the Cappuccino City*. Chicago: University of Chicago Press.

Hyra, Derek S., and Sabiyha Prince, eds. 2015. *Capital Dilemma: Growth and Inequality in Washington, D.C.* New York: Routledge.

Iken, Matthias. 2015. "Luxusmeile Neuer Wall: Zwischen Weltmarken und Heimischen Individualisten." *Hamburger Abendblatt*, March 3.

International Downtown Association. 1995. Testimony by Richard Bradley, President, International Downtown Association, Bill in Support of 11–464, the Business Improvement Districts Act of 1995. Committee Report, Council of the District of Columbia. kwiktag ~ 062 318 257 DC Council. http://dcclims1 .dccouncil.us/images/00001/CP11/062318257_1.pdf.

Irazábal, Clara. 2014a. "Introduction: What Do We Mean by 'Transbordering Latin Americas?'" In *Transbordering Latin Americas: Liminal Places, Cultures, and Powers (T)Here*, edited by Clara Irazábal, 1–20. Routledge Research in Transnationalism, no. 28. New York: Routledge.

———, ed. 2014b. *Transbordering Latin Americas: Liminal Places, Cultures, and Powers (T)Here*. Routledge Research in Transnationalism, no. 28. New York: Routledge.

Isenberg, Alison. 2004. *Downtown America: A History of the Place and the People Who Made It*. Historical Studies of Urban America series. Chicago: University of Chicago Press.

Izadi, Elahe. 2012. "Meridian Hill Park or Malcolm X Park?" D.C. *Centric: Race, Class, the District*. WAMU 88.5 American University Radio.

Jackson, Kenneth T. 1987. *Crabgrass Frontier: The Suburbanization of the United States*. New York: Oxford University Press.

Jacob, Kathryn Allamong. 2003. "Like Moths to a Candle: The Nouveaux Riches Flock to Washington, 1870–1900." In *Washington Odyssey: A Multicultural History of the Nation's Capital*, edited by Francine Curro Cary, 79–96. Washington, D.C.: Smithsonian Books.

Jacobs, Jane. [1961] 1992. *The Death and Life of Great American Cities*. New York: Vintage Books.

Jaffe, Harry, and Tom Sherwood. 2014. *Dream City: Race, Power, and the Decline of Washington, D.C.* Anniversary ed. [Jackson, Tenn.]: Argo-Navis.

Janofsky, Michael. 1995. "Congress Creates Board to Oversee Washington, D.C." *New York Times*, April 8.

Jarvis, Charlene Drew. 1995. "Report on Bill 11–464: The Business Improvement Districts Act of 1995." Committee Report. Economic Development Committee, Council of the District of Columbia. http://dcclims1.dccouncil.us/images/00001/CP11/062318257_1.pdf.

———. 1997a. Opening Statement for Public Roundtable to Consider: 1997 Amendments to Business Improvement District Act of 1996. District of Columbia.

———. 1997b. Transcript Pages: Subcommittee on the District of Columbia of the

Committee on Government Reform and Oversight, House of Representatives, 105th Congress, May 22. Washington, D.C.

Jarvis, Charlene Drew, and Jack Evans. 1991. "District of Columbia Business Improvement Districts Act of 1991, B9–039." Council of the District of Columbia. http://lims.dccouncil.us/Legislation/B9-0392?FromSearchResults=true.

Jenkins, Mark. 2005. "Where Does This Bus Go? The D.C. Circulator Struggles to Get out of the Red." *Washington City Paper*, October 7. http://www.washingtoncitypaper.com/news/article/13031856/where-does-this-bus-go.

Johnson, Goldie Cornelius. 1993. Statement of Goldie Cornelius Johnson, Submitted to Be Included in the Record on Bill No. 10–86, "Business Improvement Districts Act of 1993." Council of the District of Columbia.

Joint Hearing: Oversight Hearing on D.C. Finances. 1995. Subcommittee on the District of Columbia of the Committee on Government Reform and Oversight and of the Committee on Appropriations of the House of Representatives, 104th Cong., 1st sess. Washington, D.C.: U.S. Government Printing Office.

Judkis, Maura. 2014a. "D.C. Diners Going Off-Menu with a Selection of Unique Supper Clubs and Dinner Locales." *Washington Post*, December 4, Going Out Guide. https://www.washingtonpost.com/goingoutguide/dc-diners -going-off-menu-with-a-selection-of-unique-supper-clubs-and-dinner -locales/2014/12/04/da4e5c7c-48d9-11e4-891d-713f052086a0_story.html?utm _term=.9cf80f8dca9c.

———. 2014b. "Diner en Blanc in D.C.: 'Where Diversity Meets Opulence Meets Instagram.'" *Washington Post*, September 5, 2014, Going Out Guide. https:// www.washingtonpost.com/news/going-out-guide/wp/2014/09/05/diner -en-blanc-in-d-c-where-diversity-meets-opulence-meets-instagram/?utm _term=.53cf22459573.

———. 2014c. "Dining 'En Blanc'? Don't Forget the Food." *Washington Post*, August 5, Going Out Guide. https://www.washingtonpost.com/news/going-out -guide/wp/2014/08/05/dining-en-blanc-dont-forget-the-food/?utm_term= .8777a35a75b7.

Kageyama, Peter. 2011. *For the Love of Cities: The Love Affair between People and Their Places*. St. Petersburg, Fla.: Creative Cities Productions.

Kamel, Nabil. 2014. "Learning from the Margin: Placemaking Tactics." In *The Informal American City beyond Taco Trucks and Day Labor*, edited by Vinit Mukhija and Anastasia Loukaitou-Sideris, 119–36. Cambridge, Mass.: MIT Press.

Kantola, Anu, and Hannele Seeck. 2011. "Dissemination of Management into Politics: Michael Porter and the Political Uses of Management Consulting." *Management Learning* 42 (1): 25–47. https://doi.org/10.1177/1350507610382489.

Kearns, Gerard, and Chris Philo, eds. 1993. *Selling Places: The City as Cultural Capital, Past and Present*. Policy, Planning, and Critical Theory series. Oxford: Pergamon Press.

Kelly, Casey R., and Kristen Hoerl. 2012. "Selective Amnesia and Racial Transcendence in News Coverage of President Obama's Inauguration." *Scholarship and Professional Work—Communication* 88 (May): 1–25.

Kennedy, Liam. 2006. *Race and Urban Space in Contemporary American Culture*. Tendencies: Identities, Texts, Cultures series. Edinburgh: Edinburgh University Press.

Knight, Jerry. 1981. "Preserving D.C. Architecture's Snail Darters." *Washington Post*, August 24.

———. 1982. "Panel's Plan for Downtown Is Blueprint of Vibrant City." *Washington Post*, July 19.

Kornberger, Martin. 2012. "Governing the City: From Planning to Urban Strategy." *Theory, Culture & Society* 29 (2): 84–106. https://doi.org/10.1177 /0263276411426158.

Kowinski, William Severini. 1981. "A Mall Covers the Waterfront." *New York Times*, December 13.

Kramer, Kirk. 2018a. "Heaven or Hell? Infernal Goings-on Roil Adams Morgan Business Community." *Dupont Current*, April 4. https://currentnewspapers .com/wp-content/uploads/2018/04/DP-Current-4.4.18.pdf.

———. 2018b. "Line Hotel Tax Assessment Lowered by \$33 Million." *Dupont Current*, April 4. https://currentnewspapers.com/wp-content/uploads/2018/04 /DP-Current-4.4.18.pdf.

Krinsky, John, and Maud Simonet. 2017. *Who Cleans the Park? Public Work and Urban Governance in New York City*. Chicago: University of Chicago Press.

Krumholz, Norman. 2011. *Making Equity Planning Work: Leadership in the Public Sector*. Philadelphia: Temple University Press. http://grail.eblib.com.au /patron/FullRecord.aspx?p=669500.

LaFraniere, Sharon. 1990. "Barry Arrested on Cocaine Charges in Undercover FBI, Police Operation." *Washington Post*, January 19, section A.

Landry, Charles. 2008. *The Creative City: A Toolkit for Urban Innovators*. 2nd ed. New Stroud, U.K.: Comedia.

Lardner, James. 1978. "Bad City Reputation Hampers Search for Aides, Barry Says." *Washington Post*, December 18.

Latino Economic Development Corporation. 1999. The "I Love Mount Pleasant" business directory. Washington, D.C.: LEDC and Mount Pleasant Business Association.

———. 2000. "Neighborhood Visioning: Final Report." Washington, D.C.: LEDC.

Lauber, Daniel. 2012. "District of Columbia Analysis of Impediments to Fair Housing Choice, 2006–2011." Washington, D.C.: District of Columbia Department of Housing and Community Development. http://www.prrac.org/pdf/DC-AI.pdf.

Lauria, Mickey. 1999. "Reconstructing Urban Regime Theory: Regulation Theory and Institutional Arrangements." In *The Urban Growth Machine: Critical Perspectives Two Decades Later*, edited by Andrew E. G. Jonas and David Wilson, 125–39. SUNY series in Urban Public Policy. Albany: State University of New York Press.

Lee, Barrett A., Daphne Spain, and Debra J. Umberson. 1985. "Neighborhood Revitalization and Racial Change: The Case of Washington, D.C." *Demography* 22 (4): 581–602.

Lee, Wonhyung. 2016. "Struggles to Form Business Improvement Districts (BIDs) in Los Angeles." *Urban Studies* 53 (16): 3423–38.

Lefebvre, Henri. 1996. *Writings on Cities*. Translated and edited by Eleonore Kofman and Elizabeth Lebas. Cambridge, Mass.: Blackwell.

———. 2011. *The Production of Space*. Translated by Donald Nicholson-Smith. Malden, Mass.: Blackwell.

Leitner, Helga, Jamie Peck, and Eric S. Sheppard, eds. 2007. *Contesting Neoliberalism: Urban Frontiers*. New York: Guilford Press.

Lenz, Mary. 1978. "Concern in Washington's 'Latin Quarter': How Much Longer Can the Melting Pot Survive?" *Washington Post*, September 7, Special section.

Lesko, Kathleen M., Valerie Melissa Babb, and Carroll R. Gibbs, eds. 2016. *Black Georgetown Remembered: A History of Its Black Community from the Founding of "The Town of George" in 1751 to the Present Day*. Washington, D.C.: Georgetown University Press.

Levy, Paul. 2001. "Paying for the Public Life." *Economic Development Quarterly* 15 (2): 124–31. https://doi.org/10.1177/089124240101500202.

———. 2010. "Business Improvements in Philadelphia: A Practitioner's Perspective." *Drexel Law Review* 3 (1): 71–87.

Lieberman, Mark. 2016. "ANC Seeks Statue Upgrade as Part of Unity Park Work: Adams Morgan Project Covers Broader Beautification." *Dupont Current*, December 21.

Lippman, Thomas W. 1974. "Adams-Morgan: Community Divided: Residents Are Split on Whether Renovation Trend Is Desirable." ProQuest Historical Newspapers: *Washington Post*, p. C1, March 25.

Lipsitz, George. 1995. "The Possessive Investment in Whiteness: Racialized Social Democracy and the 'White' Problem in American Studies." *American Quarterly* 47 (3): 369–87.

Lloyd, James M. 2015. "Fighting Redlining and Gentrification in Washington, D.C.: The Adams-Morgan Organization and Tenant Right to Purchase." *Journal of Urban History*, January. https://doi.org/10.1177/0096144214566975.

Loeb, Vernon. 1997. "D.C.'s Mild-Mannered Mayor." *Washington Post*, October 24, section B1.

Logan, John R., and Harvey Luskin Molotch. 1987. *Urban Fortunes: The Political Economy of Place*. 20th anniversary ed. Berkeley: University of California Press.

Losada Romero, César. 2016. "A New Babylon: Bottom Up Urban Planning and the Situationist Utopia." *Joelho: Revista de Cultura Arquitectonica*, no. 7: 104–15. https://doi.org/10.14195/1647-8681_7_8.

Lou, Jackie Jia. 2013. "Representing and Reconstructing Chinatown: A Social Semiotic Analysis of Place-Names in Urban Planning Policies of Washington, D.C." In *Social Inequality & the Politics of Representation: A Global Landscape*, edited by Celine-Marie Pascale, 110–25. Los Angeles: SAGE.

Lowry, Kathy. 1997. "The Purple Passion of Sandra Cisneros: Did San Antonio's Leading Latina Writer Repaint Her Historic Home to Honor Her Heritage—

Or Was It Just a Color Scheme?" *Texas Monthly*, October 1997. http://www
.texasmonthly.com/articles/the-purple-passion-of-sandra-cisneros/.

Lundegaard, Karen M. 1996. "Philadelphia Story: Parallels to Washington Abound."
Washington Business Journal, December 30. http://www.bizjournals.com
/washington/stories/1996/12/30/story9.html.

Lyall, Katharine C. 1986. "Public-Private Partnerships in the Carter Years." *Proceedings of the Academy of Political Science* 36 (2): 4–13.

Lydon, Mike, and Anthony Garcia. 2015. *Tactical Urbanism: Short-Term Action for Long-Term Change*. Washington, D.C.: Island Press.

Lynch, Kevin. [1960] 2005. *The Image of the City*. Joint Center for Urban Studies.
Cambridge, Mass.: MIT Press.

MacDonald, Heather. 1996a. "BIDs Really Work." *City Journal*, Spring. https://www
.city-journal.org/html/bids-really-work-11853.html.

———. 1996b. "Why Business Improvement Districts Work." Issue brief, Manhattan
Institute, May 1. https://www.manhattan-institute.org/html/why-business
-improvement-districts-work-5613.html.

Mackinnon, Timothy David. 2017. "Capitol Navy Yard: A 21st Century Transition."
PhD diss. Rutgers University.

MacLean, Nancy. 2017. *Democracy in Chains: The Deep History of the Radical Right's Stealth Plan for America*. New York: Viking.

Mallett, William J. 1994. "Managing the Post-Industrial City: Business Improvement
Districts in the United States." *Area* 26 (3): 276–87.

Manning, Robert D. 1998. "Multicultural Washington, D.C.: The Changing Social
and Economic Landscape of a Post-Industrial Metropolis." *Ethnic and Racial Studies* 21 (2): 328–55. https://doi.org/10.1080/014198798330043.

Manzi, Tony, and Bill Smith-Bowers. 2005. "Gated Communities as Club Goods:
Segregation or Social Cohesion?" *Housing Studies* 20 (2): 345–59. https://doi.org
/10.1080/0267303042000331817.

Marcus, Lawrence. 1999. "The Micropolitics of Planning." *Review of Higher Education* 23 (1): 45–64.

Markusen, Ann. 2013. "Fuzzy Concepts, Proxy Data: Why Indicators Would Not
Track Creative Placemaking Success." *International Journal of Urban Sciences* 17
(3): 291–303. https://doi.org/10.1080/12265934.2013.836291.

Marquez, Benjamin. 1993. "Mexican-American Community Development Corporations and the Limits of Directed Capitalism." *Economic Development Quarterly* 7 (3): 287–95. https://doi.org/10.1177/089124249300700307.

Marshall Heights Economic Development Corporation. 1995. Testimony by
Michael Morton, Business Development Manager, in Support of Bill 11–464,
Business Improvement Districts Act of 1995. Council of the District of Columbia. http://dcclims1.dccouncil.us/images/00001/CP11/062318257_1.PDF.

Martin, Deborah G. 2004. "Nonprofit Foundations and Grassroots Organizing:
Reshaping Urban Governance." *Professional Geographer* 56 (3): 394–405.

Massey, Doreen. 1994. *Space, Place and Gender*. Cambridge: Polity Press.

Masur, Kate. 2010. *An Example for All the Land: Emancipation and the Struggle over Equality in Washington, D.C.* Chapel Hill: University of North Carolina Press.

Maszak, Peter, Nathan W. Gross, and Stephen W. Porter. 1996. "Stirrings of Hope for Downtown D.C. Business Initiatives, Tax Breaks, and Regulatory Reform Bring Promise of New Development." *Legal Times*, October 20, 1996.

Matthews, Paulette, Greta Fuller, C.A.R.E., et al. v. District of Columbia Zoning Commission, D.C. Housing Authority, D.C. Office of Planning, Office of the Deputy Mayor for Planning and Economic Development, D.C. Department of Housing and Community Development, et al. 2018. Class Action Civil Rights Complaint, Civil Action No. 1:18-cv872. United States District Court for the District of Columbia. https://files.acrobat.com/a/preview/3c4af2ec-cd10-47a8-844a-0abobabdob9b.

Mayer, Caroline E. 1984. "Rouse Co. Gambles on Downtown D.C. with National Place." *Washington Post*, May 14. https://www.washingtonpost.com/archive/business/1984/05/14/rouse-co-gambles-on-downtown-dc-with-national-place/7db77cb5-e6eb-4906-8b00-625f4be9de12/?utm_term=.19088e1f05f8.

McCabe, Brian J. 2016. *No Place like Home: Wealth, Community, and the Politics of Homeownership.* New York: Oxford University Press.

McCalla, John. 2003. "Coffee Cultured." *Washington Business Journal*, March 3. https://www.bizjournals.com/washington/stories/2003/03/03/story6.html.

McCarthy, Ellen. 2008. "Creating a Living, Lively Downtown: Lessons Learned from Gallery Place, Washington, D.C." *Real Estate Review* 37 (4): 71–88.

McFarlane, Audrey. 2003. "Preserving Community in the City: Special Improvement Districts and the Privatization of Urban Racialized Space." *Stanford Agora: An Online Journal of Legal Perspectives* 4.

———. 2007. "Putting the 'Public' Back into Public-Private Partnerships for Economic Development." *Western New England Law Review* 30: 22.

———. 2009. "Operatively White? Exploring the Significance of Race and Class through the Paradox of Black Middle-Classness." *Law and Contemporary Problems* 72: 163–96.

McGovern, Stephen J. 1998. *The Politics of Downtown Development: Dynamic Political Cultures in San Francisco and Washington, D.C.* Lexington: University Press of Kentucky.

McKenzie, Evan. 2011. *Beyond Privatopia: Rethinking Residential Private Government.* Washington, D.C.: Urban Institute Press.

Mele, Christopher. 2000. *Selling the Lower East Side: Culture, Real Estate, and Resistance in New York City.* Minneapolis: University of Minnesota Press.

Melton, R. H. 1995. "A Neighbor Knocks on Home Rule: Fairfax's Rep. Tom Davis Steps into D.C's Fiscal Mess." *Washington Post*, February 22.

Meriwether, C. 1897. "Washington City Government." *Political Science Quarterly* 12 (3): 407–19.

Metropolitan Police Department. N.d. "Metropolitan Police Department: ABC Establishment Reimbursable Program Agreement." Patrol Services & School Se-

curity Bureau, Washington, D.C. Accessed March 13, 2018. https://abra.dc.gov
/publication/abc-establishment-reimbursable-program-agreement-mpd.

Metzger, John T. 2000. "Planned Abandonment: The Neighborhood Life-Cycle
Theory and National Urban Policy." *Housing Policy Debate* 11 (1): 7–40.

Michel, Boris, and Christian Stein. 2015. "Reclaiming the European City and Lobbying for Privilege: Business Improvement Districts in Germany." *Urban Affairs
Review* 51 (1): 74–98. https://doi.org/10.1177/1078087414522391.

Milloy, Courtland. 2014. "Marion Barry's Eulogy to Pay Homage to a Different Side."
Washington Post, December 2.

Miraftab, Faranak. 2004. "Public-Private Partnerships: The Trojan Horse of Neoliberal Development?" *Journal of Planning Education and Research* 24 (1): 89–101.
https://doi.org/10.1177/0739456X04267173.

———. 2005. "Globalization of Neoliberal Policies and Privatization." Paper prepared for presentation at "Navigating Globalization: Stability, Fluidity, and Fric-
ation," Norwegian University of Science and Technology, Trondheim, Norway,
August 4–5.

Mitchell, Bruce, and Juan Franco. 2018. "HOLC 'Redlining' Maps: The Persistent
Structure of Segregation and Economic Inequality." National Community Reinvestment Coalition (NCRC). https://ncrc.org/wp-content/uploads/dlm
_uploads/2018/02/NCRC-Research-HOLC-10.pdf.

Mitchell, Don. 2003. *The Right to the City: Social Justice and the Fight for Public
Space*. New York: Guilford Press.

Mitchell, Jerry. 2001. "Business Improvement Districts and the 'New' Revitalization
of Downtown." *Economic Development Quarterly* 15 (2): 115–23. https://doi.org
/10.1177/089124240101500201.

———. 2008. *Business Improvement Districts and the Shape of American Cities*.
Albany: State University of New York Press.

Modan, Gabriella Gahlia. 2007. *Turf Wars: Discourse, Diversity, and the Politics of
Place*. New Directions in Ethnography no. 1. Malden, Mass.: Blackwell.

———. 2008. "Mango Fufu Kimchi Yucca: The Depoliticization of 'Diversity' in
Washington, D.C. Discourse." *City & Society* 20 (2): 188–221. https://doi.org
/10.1111/j.1548-744X.2008.00017.x.

Modan, Gabriella Gahlia, and Katie Wells. 2015. "Representations of Change: Gentrification in the Media." In Hyra and Prince, *Capital Dilemma*, 315–29.

Molotch, Harvey. 1976. "The City as a Growth Machine: Toward a Political Economy of Place." *American Journal of Sociology* 82 (2): 309–32. https://doi.org
/10.1086/226311.

———. 1993. "The Political Economy of Growth Machines." *Journal of Urban Affairs*
15 (1): 29–53. https://doi.org/10.1111/j.1467-9906.1993.tb00301.x.

Monteilh, Richard, and Marc Weiss, eds. 1998. "The Economic Resurgence of
Washington, D.C.: Citizens Plan for Prosperity in the 21st Century." District of
Columbia Department of Housing and Community Development. http://www
.globalurban.org/The_Economic_Resurgence_of_Washington,_DC.pdf.

Monti, Daniel J. 1999. *The American City: A Social and Cultural History*. Malden, Mass: Blackwell.

Morçöl, Göktuğ, Lorlene Hoyt, Jack W. Meek, and Ulf Zimmermann, eds. 2008. *Business Improvement Districts: Research, Theories, and Controversies*. Public Administration and Public Policy no. 145. Boca Raton, Fla.: CRC Press/Taylor & Francis.

Moss, Jeremiah. 2017. *Vanishing New York: How a Great City Lost Its Soul*. New York: Dey Street/William Morrow.

Mount Pleasant Main Street Program. 2005. "Mount Pleasant Public Space Design Mini-Charrette." Final report. Funded by reStore DC / DC Main Street.

Mukhija, Vinit, and Anastasia Loukaitou-Sideris, eds. 2014. *The Informal American City: Beyond Taco Trucks and Day Labor*. Urban and Industrial Environments series. Cambridge, Mass.: MIT Press.

Müller, Hannes. 2015. *Baugemeinschaften als städtebauliches Entwicklungsinstrument: Ein möglicher Beitrag nachhaltiger Quartiersentwicklung*. Research report. Wiesbaden: Springer VS.

Muller, John. 2011. "The Legacy of D.C.'s 1968 Riots." *Greater, Greater Washington* (blog). April 8.

Myers, Dowell. 2016. "Peak Millennials: Three Reinforcing Cycles That Amplify the Rise and Fall of Urban Concentration by Millennials." *Housing Policy Debate* 26 (6): 928–47. https://doi.org/10.1080/10511482.2016.1165722.

Nadeau, Brianne. 2017. "DC's Newest Main Street Organization Brings New Resources to Help Columbia Heights and Mount Pleasant Thrive." *Brianne K. Nadeau, Councilmember, Ward 1* (blog). January 11, 2017. http://www .brianneknadeau.com/dc_s_newest_main_street_organization_brings_new _resources_to_help_columbia_heights_and_mount_pleasant_thrive (not a working link).

National Performance Review. 1995. "Managing Results: Initiatives in Select American Cities." http://govinfo.library.unt.edu/npr/library/fedstat/24e6 .html.

Naveed, Minahil. 2017. "Income Inequality in DC Highest in the Country." *DC Fiscal Policy Institute Blog*, December 15.

Neighborhood Development Assistance Program, Peoples Involvement Corporation. 1995. Testimony presented by Ron Wilson, director, on behalf of Bill 11-464, Business Improvement Districts Act of 1995. Council of the District of Columbia. http://dcclims1.dccouncil.us/images/00001/CP11/062318257_1.PDF.

Newsom, Michael deHaven. 1971. "Blacks and Historic Preservation." *Law and Contemporary Problems* 36: 423–31.

New York City Economic Development Corporation (NYCEDC). 2018a. "Inwood NYC Planning Initiative Environmental Review." 17DME007M.

———. 2018b. "Manhattan Community Board 12 Business Development Committee Meeting." Report presented at the Manhattan Community Board 12 Business Development Committee Meeting, February 6.

New York Times. 1985. "Thousands of Ethiopians Form a Diverse Community." July 5. https://www.nytimes.com/1985/07/05/us/thousands-of-ethiopians-form-a -diverse-community.html.

Nicodemus, Anne Gadwa. 2013. "Fuzzy Vibrancy: Creative Placemaking as Ascendant US Cultural Policy." *Cultural Trends* 22 (3–4): 213–22. https://doi.org/10 .1080/09548963.2013.817653.

NION, Brand Hamburg (Initiative Not in Our Name, Marke Hamburg). 2010. "Not in Our Name! Jamming the Gentrification Machine: A Manifesto." *City* 14 (3): 323–25. https://doi.org/10.1080/13604813.2010.482344.

Nisbet, Elizabeth. 2018. "Local-Level Philanthropic Partnerships in Public Education: Dilemmas for Equity and Public Responsibility." *Journal of Urban Affairs*, February, 1–19. https://doi.org/10.1080/07352166.2017.1421432.

Nnamdi, Kojo. 2011. "Mount Pleasant: 20 Years after the Riots." *Kojo Nnamdi Show*, NPR, May 5. http://thekojonnamdishow.org/shows/2011-05-05/mt-pleasant -20-years-after-riot.

Noyes, Crosby. 1895. "Editorial." *Evening Star*, March 16. http://chroniclingamerica .loc.gov/lccn/sn83045462/1895-03-16/ed-1/seq-4/.

Nussbaum, Martha. 2003. "Capabilities as Fundamental Entitlements: Sen and Social Justice." *Feminist Economics* 9 (2–3): 33–59. https://doi.org/10.1080 /1354570022000077926.

Oates, Wallace E. 2006. "The Many Faces of the Tiebout Model." In *The Tiebout Model at Fifty: Essays in Public Economics in Honor of Wallace Oates*, edited by William A. Fischel and Wallace E. Oates, 21–45. Cambridge, Mass: Lincoln Institute of Land Policy.

Ocejo, Richard E. 2014. *Upscaling Downtown: From Bowery Saloons to Cocktail Bars in New York City*. Princeton, N.J.: Princeton University Press. http://dx.doi .org/10.23943/princeton/9780691155166.001.0001.

O'Cleireacain, Carol. 1997. "The Orphaned Capital: Adopting the Right Revenues for the District of Columbia." Washington, D.C.: Brookings Institution Press.

O'Cleireacain, Carol, and Alice M. Rivlin. 2001. "Envisioning a Future Washington: Research Brief." Brookings Greater Washington Research Program. Washington, D.C.: Brookings Institution.

O'Connell, Jonathan. 2013a. "Tysons Corner Tries to Create Neighborhood Feel." *Washington Post*, October 21.

———. 2013b. "With Farmers Markets, Street Festivals Tysons Corner Tries to Become a Real Neighborhood." *Washington Post*, October 17.

———. 2016. "Can a New Park Help Bridge the Gulf between Two Communities?" *Washington Post*, January 24, Magazine section.

O'Connor, Alice. 1996. "Community Action, Urban Reform, and the Fight against Poverty: The Ford Foundation's Gray Areas Program." *Journal of Urban History* 22 (5): 586–625.

Office of Planning, District of Columbia. 2004. "A Vision for Growing an Inclusive City: A Framework for the Washington, D.C. Comprehensive Plan Update." Washington, D.C.: District of Columbia Office of Planning.

———. 2010. "Creative Capital: The Creative DC Action Agenda." Washington, D.C.: District of Columbia Office of Planning.

———. 2012. "D.C. Retail Action Strategy: Adams Morgan." Washington, D.C.: District of Columbia Office of Planning.

———. 2015a. "I AM: Ideas for Adams Morgan: Neighborhood Profile 2015." http://www.anc1c.org/index.php/pse/category/133-envision-adams-morgan.

———. 2015b. "I AM: Ideas for Adams Morgan: Vision Framework 2015." http://www.anc1c.org/index.php/pse/category/133-envision-adams-morgan.

———. 2016. "Office of Planning Launches Creative Placemaking Initiative." https://planning.dc.gov/release/office-planning-launches-creative-placemaking-initiative.

———. 2017. "Crossing the Street: Building DC's Inclusive Future through Creative Placemaking." https://planning.dc.gov/sites/default/files/dc/sites/op/page_content/attachments/Crossing%20the%20Street%20Zine_Spread_2017.12.27%20%28NXPowerLite%20Copy%29.pdf.

———. 2018. "DC Cultural Plan." Working Draft for Public Review, January 18. https://d3n8a8pro7vhmx.cloudfront.net/dcculturalplan/mailings/1006/attachments/original/Draft_DC_Cultural_Plan_January_2018_.pdf?1516381667.

Office of the Chief Financial Officer, District of Columbia. 2006. "District Ends FY 2005 with $1.6 Billion Fund Balance." February 1. https://cfo.dc.gov.

Office of the Deputy Mayor for Planning and Development, District of Columbia. 2007. "District Launches Creative Economy Initiative: D.C.'s Focus on Idea People Can Transform Neighborhoods." https://dmped.dc.gov/release/district-launches-creative-economy-initiative-dcs-focus-idea-people-can-transform.

———. 2012. "The Creative Economy Strategy for the District of Columbia." Washington, D.C.: Office of the Deputy Mayor for Planning and Development.

Oldenburg, Ray. 1999. *The Great Good Place: Cafés, Coffee Shops, Bookstores, Bars, Hair Salons, and Other Hangouts at the Heart of a Community.* New York: Marlowe.

———, ed. 2001. *Celebrating the Third Place: Inspiring Stories about the "Great Good Places" at the Heart of Our Communities.* New York: Marlowe.

Orloff, Patricia. 1993. *Racial and Ethnic Tensions in American Communities: Poverty, Inequality, and Discrimination.* Vol. 1 of *The Mount Pleasant Report.* Washington, D.C.: United State Commission on Civil Rights.

Osborne, David, and Ted Gaebler. 1992. *Reinventing Government: How the Entrepreneurial Spirit Is Transforming the Public Sector.* New York: Plume.

Oswalt, Philipp, Klaus Overmeyer, and Phillip Misselwitz. 2009. "Pattern of the Unplanned." In *Pop Up City*, edited by Terry Schwarz and Steve Rugare. Cleveland, Ohio: Cleveland Urban Design Collaborative, College of Architecture and Environmental Design, Kent State University.

———, eds. 2013. *Urban Catalyst: The Power of Temporary Use.* Berlin: DOM.

Padua, Pat. 2015. "Former Music Venues of Washington: d.c. space." *DCist* (blog). May 12. http://dcist.com/2015/05/former_music_venues_of_washington_d.php#photo-1.

Pate, Travis. 2016. "DC—Who Is Moving In and Who Is Moving Out: A Snapshot from the 2014 American Community Survey." *District of Columbia State Data Center Monthly Brief*, April. Government of the District of Columbia, Office of Planning, State Data Center. https://planning.dc.gov/sites/default/files/dc /sites/op/page_content/attachments/DC-Who%20Is%20Moving%20Out %20and%20Who%20Is%20Moving%20In%20Snapshot_1.pdf.

Paton, Kristeen. 2016. *Gentrification: A Working-Class Perspective*. New York: Routledge.

Perl, Peter. 1999. "Race Riot of 1919 Gave Glimpse of Future Struggles." *Washington Post*, March 1.

Peyroux, Elisabeth, Robert Pütz, and Georg Glasze. 2012. "Business Improvement Districts (BIDs): The Internationalization and Contextualization of a 'Travelling Concept.'" *European Urban and Regional Studies* 19 (2): 111–20.

PICA (Pennsylvania Intergovernmental Cooperation Authority). 2016. "About Us." PICA. http://www.picapa.org.

Pichardo, Carolina. 2017. "City Invests $1.2 Million to Boost Small Business, Beautification Projects." *DNAinfo New York*, June 28, 2017.

Pierre, Jon, ed. 1998. *Partnerships in Urban Governance: European and American Experiences*. New York: St. Martin's Press, 1998.

Plotz, David. 1995. "The Laboratory of Dr. Gingrich: You Thought the Control Board Was a Big Deal? Just Listen to the GOP's Latest Plans for the District." *Washington City Paper*, June 2. http://www.washingtoncitypaper.com/news/article /13007434/the-laboratory-of-dr-gingrich.

Popkin, Susan J., Diane K. Levy, Laura E. Harris, Jennifer Comey, and Mary K. Cunningham. 2004. "The Hope VI Program: What about the Residents?" *Housing Policy Debate* 15 (2): 385–414.

Porter, Michael E. 1995. "The Competitive Advantage of the Inner City." *Harvard Business Review*, May-June: 55–71.

Pratt Center for Community Development. 2018. "New Report Reveals Sleight of Hand behind Displacement Measurement and How It Fails Communities of Color." September 17. New York City: Pratt Center. https://prattcenter.net/new -report-reveals-sleight-hand-behind-displacement-measurement-and-how-it -fails-communities-color.

Pratt, Sharon. 2011. "Lessons from a D.C. Riot." *Washington Post*, August 12, Opinions section. https://www.washingtonpost.com/opinions/lessons-from-a-dc -riot/2011/08/12/gIQAQO2kBJ_story.html.

Price, Eric. 2001. Testimony of Eric Price, Deputy Mayor for Planning and Economic Development, before the House Appropriations Subcommittee for the District of Columbia, on the Subject of Economic Development in the District of Columbia. 107th Congress, session 1. http://www.dcwatch.com/govern /econo10426.htm.

Prince, Sabiyha. 2014. *African Americans and Gentrification in Washington D.C.: Race, Class, and Social Justice in the Nation's Capital*. Burlington, Vt.: Ashgate.

Prince of Petworth. 2014. "Dear PoPville—'Why Is Meridian Hill Park Sometimes Called Malcolm X Park?'" *PopVille* (blog), July 21. https://www.popville.com /2014/07/meridian-hill-malcolm-x-park-dc/.

Pritchett, Wendell E. 2003. "The 'Public Menace' of Blight: Urban Renewal and the Private Uses of Eminent Domain." Cornell University Faculty Scholarship Paper 1199. http://digitalcommons.law.yale.edu/cgi/viewcontent.cgi?article=1451& context=ylpr.

———. 2008. "Which Urban Crisis?: Regionalism, Race, and Urban Policy, 1960–1974." *Journal of Urban History* 34 (2): 266–86. https://doi.org/10.1177 /0096144207308678.

PUMA (Progressive Urban Management Associates). 2002. "Adams Morgan Business Improvement District: Observations and Recommendations." Denver. Internal unpublished draft report.

Purcell, Mark. 2014. "Possible Worlds: Henri Lefebvre and the Right to the City." *Journal of Urban Affairs* 36 (1): 141–54. https://doi.org/10.1111/juaf.12034.

Pyatt, Rudolph A. 1985. "Aiding Small Retailers," *Washington Post*, August 27.

———. 1992. "Losing a BID for Downtown Development." *Washington Post*, December 14.

———. 1995. "Backing D.C. Council's Current Bid to Revitalize Commercial Districts." *Washington Post*, December 25.

———. 1996. "Jarvis's Idea May Be D.C.'s Missing Inc." *Washington Post*, October 7.

Reardon, Ken, and John Forrester, eds. 2016. *Rebuilding Community after Katrina: Transformative Education in the New Orleans Planning Initiative*. Philadelphia: Temple University Press.

Reed, Adolph L. 1999. *Stirrings in the Jug: Black Politics in the Post-Segregation Era*. Minneapolis: University of Minnesota Press.

Reeves, Richard V. 2017. *Dream Hoarders: How the American Upper Middle Class Is Leaving Everyone Else in the Dust, Why That Is a Problem, and What to Do about It*. Washington, D.C.: Brookings Institution Press.

Regan, Tim. 2016. "Mayor Bowser Awards 'Emerging BID' Grant to H Street Main Street." *Hill Now* (blog), April 19. https://www.hillnow.com/2016/04/19/mayor -bowser-awards-emerging-bid-grant-to-h-street-main-street/.

Relph, Edward. [1976] 2008. *Place and Placelessness*. Research in Planning and Design, no. 1. London: Pion.

Richards, Greg, Lénia Marques, and Karen Mein, eds. 2015. *Event Design: Social Perspectives and Practices*. Routledge Advances in Event Research series. Milton Park, Abingdon, U.K.: Routledge.

Rickenbacker, Shawn L., John Krinsky, and Susanna Schaller. 2018. "Inwood Rezoning Proposal: Review and Report." New York: City College of New York, City University of New York.

Rivlin, Alice M. 2003. "Revitalizing Washington's Neighborhoods: A Vision Takes Shape." Discussion paper. Washington, D.C.: Brookings Institution. https:// www.brookings.edu/wp-content/uploads/2016/06/rivlinrevitalizing.pdf.

Rodriguez, June Naylor. 1997. "Purple House." *Chicago Tribune,* October 11. http://articles.chicagotribune.com/1997-10-11/news/9710110138_1_purple-house-south-alamo-street-humble-houses.

Rodriguez, Ydanis. 2018. "NYC Council Member Ydanis Rodriguez: Small Business Breakfast Forum: Special Guest Gregg Bishop, Commissioner of NYC Department of Small Businesses." Presentation on economic sustainability and mobility for small businesses, Business Forum Breakfast, New York, June 15.

Rothstein, Richard. 2017. *The Color of Law: A Forgotten History of How Our Government Segregated America.* New York: Liveright, W. W. Norton.

Rouse, James W., and Nathaniel S. Keith. 1955. "No Slums in Ten Years: A Workable Program for Urban Renewal." Report to the Commissioners of the District of Columbia.

Rubin, Mark. 2003. "100,000 New Taxpayers Does *Not* Have to Mean 100,000 New Residents for the District of Columbia: Expanding the District of Columbia's Tax Base through Sustainable Neighborhood Revitalization Requires an Integrated Strategy That Meets the Community, Housing and Employment Needs of New and Existing Residents." DC Agenda Neighborhood Information Service research paper. Washington, D.C.: DC Agenda. http://www.neighborhoodinfodc.org/pdfs/NIS100K.pdf.

Rusk, David. 2017. "Once upon a Time in NoMA: D.C. History, Demographics and Urban Development." D.C. Policy Center, June 5. https://www.dcpolicycenter.org/publications/once-upon-time-noma/.

Russello Ammon, Francesca. 2004. "Southwest Washington, D.C., Urban Renewal Area." In Historic American Buildings Survey. Washington, D.C.: National Park Service, U.S. Department of the Interior. http://cdn.loc.gov/master/pnp/habshaer/dc/dc1000/dc1017/data/dc1017data.pdf.

Rydell, Robert W. 1987. *All the World's a Fair: Visions of Empire at the American International Expositions, 1876–1916.* Chicago: University of Chicago Press.

Sadik-Khan, Janette, and Seth Solomonow. 2016. *Streetfight: Handbook for an Urban Revolution.* New York: Viking.

Saff, Grant. 1994. "The Changing Face of the South African City: From Urban Apartheid to the Deracialization of Space." *International Journal of Urban and Regional Research* 18 (3): 377–91. https://doi.org/10.1111/j.1468-2427.1994.tb00274.x.

Sagalyn, Lynne B. 2007. "Public/Private Development: Lessons from History, Research, and Practice." *Journal of the American Planning Association* 73 (1): 7–22. https://doi.org/10.1080/01944360708976133.

SBS, New York City Department of Small Business Services. 2015. "Business Improvement Districts Trends Report." New York: SBS.

Schaller, Susanna. 2007. "BIDding on Urbanity with Business Improvement Districts: Re-Making Urban Places in Washington, D.C." PhD diss., Cornell University.

———. 2018. "Public-Private Synergies: Reconceiving Urban Redevelopment in Tübingen, Germany." *Journal of Urban Affairs,* May, 1–20. https://doi.org/10.1080/07352166.2018.1465345.

Schaller, Susanna, and Sandra Guinand. 2017. "Pop-Up Landscapes: A New Trigger to Push Up Land Value?" *Urban Geography* 39 (1): 54–74. https://doi.org/10.1080/02723638.2016.1276719.

Schaller, Susanna, and Gabriella Gahlia Modan. 2005. "Contesting Public Space and Citizenship: Implications for Neighborhood Business Improvement Districts." *Journal of Planning Education and Research* 24 (4): 394–407. https://doi.org/10.1177/0739456X04270124.

———. 2011. "'Safe and Clean': Community Reactions to Neighborhood Business Improvement District (NBID) Marketing in a Multi-Ethnic Neighborhood." Paper presented at the RC21 Research Committee 21: Sociology of Urban and Regional Development of the International Sociological Association Conference, Amsterdam, July 7.

Schneider, Howard, and David A Vise. 1995a. "Barry Says Home Rule Government Unworkable, Urges U.S. Takeover of District." *Washington Post*, February 3.

———. 1995b. "Barry's Fiscal Plan Includes Deep Cuts in Social Services." *Washington Post*, February 18.

———. 1995c. "Barry's Plea for Bailout Rejected on Hill." *Washington Post*, February 23.

———. 1995d. "House Panel Approves Strict Control Board for District." *Washington Post*, March 30.

Schrag, Zachary M. 2014. *The Great Society Subway: A History of the Washington Metro.* Creating the North American Landscape series. Baltimore: Johns Hopkins University Press.

Schwartz, Carol. 2006. "Report on Bill 16-634, the 'District Department of Transportation D.C. Circulator Amendment Act of 2006.'" Legislative report. Committee on Public Works and the Environment, Council of the District of Columbia. http://lims.dccouncil.us/Download/1211/B16-0634-COMMITTEEREPORT.pdf.

Schwartzman, Paul. 2018. "Lawsuit: D.C. Policies to Attract Affluent Millennials Discriminated against Blacks." *Washington Post*, May 25, 2018, D.C. Politics ed. https://www.washingtonpost.com/local/dc-politics/lawsuit-dc-policies-to-attract-affluent-millennials-discriminated-against-blacks/2018/05/24/3549f7fe-5a1e-11e8-858f-12becb4d6067_story.html?utm_term=.630ca1506465.

Scotchmer, Suzanne. 2002. "Local Public Goods and Clubs." In *Handbook of Public Economics*, vol. 4, edited by Alan J. Auerbach and Martin Feldstein, 1998–2036. Amsterdam: North Holland.

Sedgwick, Eve. 1988. "Privilege of Unknowing." *Genders*, March, 102–24. https://doi:10.5555/gen.1988.1.102.

Seigel, Saul. 1974. "Letter from IDEA President Saul Seigel to President Richard Nixon with Enclosures." January 7. White House Central Files (WHCF): Subject Files: LG (Local Governments): Box 7. Nixon Presidential Library, Yorba Linda, Calif.

Shapiro, John, and Ken Bowers. 2003. "Washington, D.C.: Economic Policy Papers." Phillips, Preiss Shapiro Associates. Prepared for the District of Columbia Office of Planning.

Shipp, Sigmund. 1996. "The Road Not Taken: Alternative Strategies for Black Economic Development in the United States." *Journal of Economic Issues* 30 (1): 79–95.

Shoenfeld, Sarah, and Mara Cherkasky. 2017. "A Strictly White Residential Section: The Rise and Demise of Racially Restrictive Covenants in Bloomingdale." *Washington History* 29 (1): 24–41.

Shook, Jill Suzanne, and Susan P. Ortmeyer. 2012. In *Making Housing Happen: Faith-Based Affordable Housing Models*, edited by Jill Suzanne Shook, 68–80. 2nd ed. Eugene, Ore.: Cascade Books.

Siegel, Frederick F. 1997. *The Future Once Happened Here: New York, D.C., L.A., and the Fate of America's Big Cities.* San Francisco: Encounter Books.

Slacum, Marcia A. 1984a. "D.C. Council Approves Parts Of 20-Year Plan." *Washington Post*, January 18. https://www.washingtonpost.com/archive/politics/1984 /01/18/dc-council-approves-parts-of-20-year-plan/b749cf57-9499-4715-87b6 -58392db04d72/?utm_term=.1386e6f8fa66.

———. 1984b. "D.C. Protects 200 Buildings in Downtown Historic Areas." *Washington Post*, March 25. https://www.washingtonpost.com/archive/local/1984/03 /25/dc-protects-200-buildings-in-downtown-historic-areas/858c9907-4690 -4825-8263-6bf133d8646a/?utm_term=.3391e3d33b98.

Smith, Neil. 1996. *The New Urban Frontier: Gentrification and the Revanchist City.* New York: Routledge.

———. 2002. "New Globalism, New Urbanism: Gentrification as Global Urban Strategy." *Antipode* 34 (3): 427–50. https://doi.org/10.1111/1467-8330.00249.

Smith, Rend. 2010. "MPD's Private Security Branch: How the District Can Force Bars to Hire D.C. Cops as Guards." *Washington City Paper*, August 6, 2010. http://www.washingtoncitypaper.com/news/article/13039342/mpds-private -security-branch-how-the-district-can-force-bars.

Smith, Sam. [2006] 2016. "The Birth of DC's Neighborhood Commissions: Remarks at a Conference in 2006." *Sam Smith's Essays* (blog), September 21. https:// samsmitharchives.wordpress.com/2016/09/21/the-birth-of-dcs-neighborhood -commissions/.

Smith, Will. 2011. "Opportunity to Buy at a Discount in Capitol Riverfront." *Urban Turf: DC Real Estate in Real Time*, March 16. http://dc.urbanturf.com/articles /blog/opportunity_to_buy_at_a_discount_in_capitol_riverfront/3179.

Sorkin, Michael. 1992. "See You in Disneyland." In *Variations on a Theme Park: The New American City and the End of Public Space*, edited by Michael Sorkin, 205–33. New York: Hill and Wang.

Spence, Lester K. 2015. *Knocking the Hustle: Against the Neoliberal Turn in Black Politics.* Brooklyn, N.Y.: Punctum Books.

Squires, Gregory D., and Charis Elizabeth Kubrin. 2006. *Privileged Places: Race, Residence, and the Structure of Opportunity.* Boulder, Colo: Lynne Rienner.

Stein, Perry. 2015. "Which D.C. Neighborhood Can Boast the Biggest Millennial Growth?" *Washington Post*, March 20, Local section. https://www.washington

post.com/news/local/wp/2015/03/20/which-d-c-neighborhood-can-boast
-the-biggest-millennial-growth/?utm_term=.a89oaooo4597.

Stein, Samuel. 2018. "Progress for Whom, toward What? Progressive Politics and
New York City's Mandatory Inclusionary Housing." *Journal of Urban Affairs* 40
(6): 770–81. https://doi.org/10.1080/07352166.2017.1403854.

Steinberg, Stephen. 2010. "The Myth of Concentrated Poverty." In *The Integration
Debate: Competing Futures For American Cities*, edited by Chester Hartman and
Gregory Squires, 213–29. New York: Routledge.

Stevens, Michael. 2016. "Capitol Riverfront: CSG Policy Academy TOD & Building
Communities: Capitol Riverfront Case Study." May 20. http://knowledgecenter
.csg.org/kc/system/files/Stevens%20-%20CSG%20Policy%20Academy
%20Presentation%202016%20(5-20-16).pdf.

Stevens, Michael, David Suls, and Natalie Avery. 2016. "The Impact of Business
Improvement Districts in D.C." Panel presentation, Tuesdays at APA, American
Planning Association), Washington, D.C., June 7. Audio file and PowerPoint
presentation. https://www.planning.org/tuesdaysatapa/2016/dc/jun/.

Stone, Clarence N. 1993. "Urban Regimes and the Capacity to Govern: A Political
Economy Approach." *Journal of Urban Affairs* 15 (1): 1–28. https://doi.org
/10.1111/j.1467-9906.1993.tb00300.x.

Stuart, Guy. 2003. *Discriminating Risk: The U.S. Mortgage Lending Industry in the
Twentieth Century*. Ithaca, N.Y.: Cornell University Press.

Summers, Brandi Thompson. 2015. "H Street, Main Street, and the Neoliberal Aesthetics of Cool." In Hyra and Prince, *Capital Dilemma*, 299–314.

Suntikul, Wantanee, and Timothy Jachna. 2016. "The Co-Creation/Place Attachment Nexus." *Tourism Management* 52 (February): 276–86. https://doi.org
/10.1016/j.tourman.2015.06.026.

Swisher, Kara. 1993. "Downtown Coalition Mourned: Partnership's Demise Seen as
Lost Opportunity." *Washington Post*, January 11.

Talen, Emily. 2015. "Do-It-Yourself Urbanism: A History." *Journal of Planning History* 14 (2): 135–48. https://doi.org/10.1177/1538513214549325.

Tarrow, Sidney G. 2011. *Power in Movement: Social Movements and Contentious
Politics*. Rev. and updated 3rd ed. Cambridge Studies in Comparative Politics
series. Cambridge: Cambridge University Press.

Tattersall, Jane, and Richard Cooper. 2014. "Creating the Eventscape." In *Strategic
Event Creation*, edited by Liz Sharples, Philip Crowther, Daryl May, and Chiara
Orefice, 141–44. [Oxford]: Goodfellow.

Thomas, June Manning. 1989. "Detroit: The Centrifugal City." In *Unequal Partnerships: The Political Economy of Urban Redevelopment in Postwar America*,
edited by Gregory D. Squires. New Brunswick, N.J.: Rutgers University
Press.

Throgmorton, James A. 2003. "Planning as Persuasive Storytelling in a Global-
Scale Web of Relationships." *Planning Theory* 2 (2): 125–51. https://doi.org
/10.1177/14730952030022003.

Tiebout, Charles M. 1956. "A Pure Theory of Local Expenditures." *Journal of Political Economy* 65 (5): 416–24.

Till, Karen E. 2012. "Wounded Cities: Memory-Work and a Place-Based Ethics of Care." *Political Geography* 31 (1): 3–14. https://doi.org/10.1016/j.polgeo.2011 .10.008.

Toner, Robin. 1986. "A 'Rainbow Ward' with Clouds." *New York Times*, February 2.

Travis, Dempsey J. 1979. "The Black Ghetto: New White Frontier." *Counselors of Real Estate: Real Estate Issues* 4 (1): 1–16.

Trieschmann, Laura. 2005. "Intensive-Level Survey of the Washington Heights Area of Washington." Report prepared for D.C. State Historic Preservation Office by EHT Traceries. http://www.kaloramacitizens.org/calendar/files /WH_Survey_Report.pdf (nonworking link).

———. 2008. "Intensive-Level Survey of Lanier Heights, Washington, D.C." Report prepared for D.C. State Historic Preservation Office by EHT Traceries. http:// docplayer.net/24479868-Intensive-level-survey-of-lanier-heights-washington -d-c.html.

Trudeau, Dan. 2018. "Tracing New Urbanism's Suburban Intervention in Minneapolis–St. Paul." *Journal of Planning Education and Research* 38 (1): 25–38. https:// doi.org/10.1177/0739456X16671996.

Urban Turf Staff. 2015. "The DC Neighborhoods with the Best Price Appreciation in 2015." *Real Estate, DC Urban Turf* (blog). http://dc.urbanturf.com/articles/blog /the_dc_neighborhoods_with_the_best_price_appreciation_in_2015i/10691.

U.S. Census. 2000. "Census 2000 Summary File 3 (SF 3)—Sample Data: Per Capita Income in 1999 (Dollars)." https://www.census.gov/census2000/sumfile3.html.

U.S. Commission on Civil Rights. 1962. "Housing in Washington, D.C." Washington, D.C.: U.S. Commission on Civil Rights.

U.S. National Crime Prevention Council. 1974. Downtown Urban Renewal Area, 1st–3rd Action Years: Environmental Impact Statement. Northwestern University, digitized, February 26, 2013.

Vanberg, Viktor J. 2005. "Competitive Federalism, Government's Dual Role, and the Power to Tax." Research 15/05. Freiburg Discussion Papers on Constitutional Economics. Albert-Ludwigs-Universität Freiburg: Instituts für allgemeine Wirtschaftsforschung Abteilung Wirtschaftspolitik und Ordnungsökonomik. http://www.eucken.de/fileadmin/bilder/Dokumente/DP2015/Discussion paper_1505.pdf.

———. 2016. "Competitive Federalism, Government's Dual Role and the Power to Tax." *Journal of Institutional Economics* 12 (4): 825–45. https://doi.org/10.1017 /S1744137416000011.

Vidal, Avis C. 1996. "CDCs as Agents of Neighborhood Change: The State of the Art." In *Revitalizing Urban Neighborhoods*, edited by W. Dennis Keating, Norman Krumholz, and Philip Star. Studies in Government and Public Policy series. Lawrence: University Press of Kansas.

Vise, David A., and Howard Schneider. 1995. "Who's in Charge? Marion Barry and

Newt Gingrich Promised a Revolution. They've Delivered a City That Still Can't Pay Its Bills. The Reasons Are as Old as Washington." *Washington Post*, December 17, 1995. https://www.washingtonpost.com/archive/lifestyle/magazine /1995/12/17/whos-in-charge-marion-barry-and-newt-gingrich-promised-a -revolution-theyve-delivered-a-city-that-still-cant-pay-its-bills-the-reasons -are-as-old-as-washington/3949331c-8162-4d7e-b0c3-c7dc6da7f505/?utm _term=.25865dfc5b79.

Voelker, Jessica. 2012. "Constantine Stavropoulos on His New Spot, the Coupe, Opening This Week." *Washingtonian* (blog). October 1. https://www.washing tonian.com/2012/10/01/constantine-stavropoulos-on-his-new-spot-the-coupe -opening-this-week/.

Vollmer, Annette. 2011. *Business Improvement Districts: Erfolgreicher Politikimport aus den USA?* Bern: Peter Lang.

Walsh, Sharon W., and John Burgess. 1989. "D.C.'s Image a Source of Worry to $2 Billion Tourism Industry." *Washington Post*, March 17.

Ward, Kevin. 2006. "'Policies in Motion,' Urban Management and State Restructuring: The Trans-Local Expansion of Business Improvement Districts." *International Journal of Urban and Regional Research* 30 (1): 54–75. https://doi.org /10.1111/j.1468-2427.2006.00643.x.

———. 2012. "Entrepreneurial Urbanism, Policy Tourism, and the Making Mobile of Policies." In *The New Blackwell Companion to the City*, edited by Gary Bridge and Sophie Watson, 726–37. Oxford: Wiley-Blackwell. http://doi.wiley.com /10.1002/9781444395105.ch63.

Warner, Mildred E. 2011. "Club Goods and Local Government: Questions for Planners." *Journal of the American Planning Association* 77 (2): 155–66. https://doi .org/10.1080/01944363.2011.567898.

Washington Heights BID. 2018. "Inwood Art Works Culture Hub." Last accessed October 15, 2018. https://www.whbid181.org.

WDCEP (Washington DC Economic Partnership). 2006. "DC News: Rising Creativity Spurs the District's Economy." Washington DC Economic Partnership.

———. 2013. "DC Neighborhood Profiles." Washington, D.C.: Washington DC Economic Partnership. http://wdcep.com.

———. 2015. "DC Neighborhood Profiles." Washington, D.C.: Washington DC Economic Partnership. http://wdcep.com.

———. 2018. "DC Neighborhood Profiles." Washington, D.C.: Washington DC Economic Partnership. http://wdcep.com.

Weaver, Timothy P. R. 2016. "'America's Mayor' Comes to Power in Philadelphia, 1951–1991." In *Blazing the Neoliberal Trail: Urban Political Development in the United States and the United Kingdom*, 199–242. Philadelphia: University of Pennsylvania Press. http://www.jstor.org/stable/j.ctt18z4gk7.8.

Webster, Christopher J., and Lawrence Wai-Chung Lai. 2003. *Property Rights, Planning and Markets: Managing Spontaneous Cities*. Cheltenham, U.K.: Edward Elgar.

Weiss, Marc A. 2002. "The Economic Resurgence of Washington, D.C.: Citizens Plan for Prosperity in the 21st Century." Washington, D.C.: Global Urban Development. http://www.globalurban.org/Lessons_of_WDC_Economic_Strategy .pdf.

Whyte, William H. 1980. *The Social Life of Small Urban Spaces*. Washington, D.C.: Conservation Foundation.

———. 1988. *City: Rediscovering the Center*. Philadelphia: University of Philadelphia Press.

Widdicombe, Gerry. 2010. "The Fall and Rise of Downtown D.C.: The Revitalization of Downtown, Greater Downtown and Center City." *Urbanist*, January 10.

Wiener, Aaron. 2013. "With $50 Million in Hand, NoMa Looks to Close 'Parks Deficit.'" *Washington City Paper*, May 29, 2013. https://www.washingtoncitypaper .com/news/housing-complex/blog/13123386/with-50-million-in-hand-noma -looks-to-close-parks-deficit.

———. 2015. "Opportunity Cost: How a New Loophole Could Give Landlords a Bigger Edge on D.C. Tenants." *Washington City Paper*, February 15, Midnight ed. http://www.washingtoncitypaper.com/news/article/13046583/opportunity -cost-how-a-new-loophole-could-give-landlords-a.

Wilgoren, Debbi. 2005. "D.C. Planner Takes Command of Anacostia Waterfront Project: Land-Use Proposal for Stadium District among Top Priorities." *Washington Post*, January 3.

Williams, Anthony. 2017. "What Data-Driven Mayors Don't Get." *City Lab*, March 19. https://www.citylab.com/equity/2017/03/what-data-driven-mayors-dont -get/520092/.

Williams, Brett. 1988. *Upscaling Downtown: Stalled Gentrification in Washington, D.C.* Anthropology of Contemporary Issues series. Ithaca, N.Y: Cornell University Press.

Williams, Kim Prothro. 2015. "Ward 1 Heritage Guide: D.C. Historic Preservation." D.C. Historic Preservation Office. https://vdocuments.mx/documents/ward-1 -heritage-guide.html.

Wilson, John A., Charlene Drew Jarvis, and Jack Evans. 1993. "Business Improvement Districts Act of 1993, B10–0186." Council of the District of Columbia. http://lims.dccouncil.us/Download/2709/B10-0186-INTRODUCTION.pdf.

Wolf, James F. 2006. "Urban Governance and Business Improvement Districts: The Washington, D.C. BIDs." *International Journal of Public Administration* 29 (1–3): 53–75. https://doi.org/10.1080/01900690500408981.

Wyman, Stephen H. 1989. "Tourism Official Tries to Sell the World on D.C." *Washington Post*, June 5. ProQuest.

Yates, Clinton. 2014. "Diner en Blanc Proves Slightly Harried, but Fun for Its First Time in the District." *Washington Post*, September 5.

Yellin, Eric Steven. 2016. *Racism in the Nation's Service: Government Workers and the Color Line in Woodrow Wilson's America*. Chapel Hill: University of North Carolina Press.

Young, Iris Marion. 2011. *Justice and the Politics of Difference*. Princeton, N.J: Princeton University Press.

Zapata, Celestino, and Josh Gibson. 2006. *Adams Morgan*. Then & Now series. Charleston, S.C: Arcadia.

Zippel, Claire. 2016. "A Broken Foundation: Affordable Housing Crisis Threatens D.C.'s Lowest-Income Residents." DC *Fiscal Policy Institute* (blog), December 8. https://www.dcfpi.org/all/a-broken-foundation-affordable-housing-crisis -threatens-dcs-lowest-income-residents/.

Zukin, Sharon. 1995. *The Cultures of Cities*. Malden, Mass.: Blackwell.

———. 2009. "New Retail Capital and Neighborhood Change: Boutiques and Gentrification in New York City." *City & Community* 8 (1): 47–67.

———. 2011. *Naked City: The Death and Life of Authentic Urban Places*. Oxford: Oxford University Press.

INDEX

Index entries in italics indicate an image or table.

CPSIA information can be obtained
at www.ICGtesting.com
Printed in the USA
BVHW031707080223
658145BV00014B/859